Teaching and Learning Chinese as a Foreign Language

Hong Kong University Press thanks Xu Bing for writing the Press's name in his Square Word Calligraphy for the covers of its books. For further information, see p. iv.

For Tom, Jenny and Julie

Teaching and Learning Chinese as a Foreign Language
A Pedagogical Grammar

Janet Zhiqun Xing

香港大學出版社
HONG KONG UNIVERSITY PRESS

Hong Kong University Press
14/F Hing Wai Centre
7 Tin Wan Praya Road
Aberdeen
Hong Kong

© Hong Kong University Press 2006

ISBN 962 209 762 6 (Hardback)
ISBN 962 209 763 4 (Paperback)

Secure On-line Ordering
http://www.hkupress.org

British Library Cataloguing-in-Publication Data
A catalogue record for this book is available from the British Library.

Printed and bound by Pre-Press Ltd., in Hong Kong, China

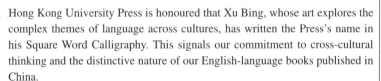

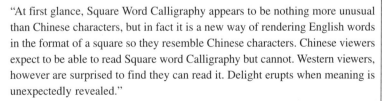

Hong Kong University Press is honoured that Xu Bing, whose art explores the
complex themes of language across cultures, has written the Press's name in
his Square Word Calligraphy. This signals our commitment to cross-cultural
thinking and the distinctive nature of our English-language books published in
China.

"At first glance, Square Word Calligraphy appears to be nothing more unusual
than Chinese characters, but in fact it is a new way of rendering English words
in the format of a square so they resemble Chinese characters. Chinese viewers
expect to be able to read Square word Calligraphy but cannot. Western viewers,
however are surprised to find they can read it. Delight erupts when meaning is
unexpectedly revealed."

— Britta Erickson, *The Art of Xu Bing*

Contents

Appendices

Preface

Teaching and learning Chinese as a foreign language (FL) has recently drawn much attention from both the Eastern and Western hemispheres. Due to the unique linguistic characteristics of the Chinese language, its acquisition exerts difficulty on some occasions as well as excitement on others. In this book, I have attempted to focus on content and methodology that may not only help to ease the difficulty in understanding the Chinese language and reduce the pain in both teaching and learning Chinese, but at the same time generate some excitement in pursuing the language. I have tried to keep in mind both language practitioners and applied linguists; I can only hope that both groups will be able to benefit somewhat from this book.

In 1992 when I was still a graduate student at the University of Michigan (UM), I was offered a summer job teaching Chinese at the prestigious Chinese Summer School, Middlebury College. Out of sheer excitement, I gave up a UM paid opportunity to present my research paper at the First International Conference on Chinese Linguistics held in Singapore in August that year and threw my full energy into Middlebury. Yet, the nine-week summer teaching drained me. I became a lost and totally exhausted instructor with no energy for "fun" in my lesson. I felt I was lost among so many experienced teachers at Middlebury even though I worked so hard day and night, trying to be a good teacher. Then I realized that diligence and intelligence did not necessarily make a good teacher; one also has to know functional grammar well and know how to handle different classroom situations. Simply put, one must know *how* to teach in addition to knowing what to teach. Ever since then, I promised myself that I would gain that experience and this book may be considered a report of my learning experience.

On the other hand, this book may serve as a synopsis of my teaching Chinese and research on teaching Chinese as a foreign language in the last ten years, during which time I have benefited a great deal from numerous mentors, friends, colleagues, and students — too many to list here. Nevertheless, I would like to thank Dr Scott McGinnis and Dr Shou-hsin Teng who not only inspired me to write this book but also supported me at various stages in creating it. My special thanks go to those colleagues in Europe and Australia whom I have never met, but have provided various data for this book via email messages.

I am very grateful to Dr Jianhua Bai (Kenyon College), Dr Cheng-zhi Chu (University of California at Davis), Dr Song-ren Cui (Bowdoin College), Dr Shengli Feng (Harvard University), Dr Lening Liu (Columbia University), Dr Ruyu Song (National Taiwan Normal University), and Dr Hongyin Tao (University of California at Los Angeles) for reading and giving me valuable comments on various chapters of the book. My special gratitude goes to the three anonymous reviewers who reviewed the proposal and two anonymous reviewers who read the complete manuscript and gave me so many constructive suggestions and comments. Last, but definitely not least, I am indebted to Randi Hacker for her numerous insightful comments and for proofreading the first draft of the manuscript. Needless to say, all errors or shortcomings rest entirely with the author.

I was touched and still am when I think about how Clara Ho, editor of Hong Kong University Press, first contacted me for a possible book proposal on the pedagogical grammar of Chinese. Without her enthusiasm and support, I might not have been able to give this book its current shape. For that, I thank her from the bottom of my heart.

The bulk part of the book was written during the 2003–2004 academic year when I was granted a three-quarter sabbatical leave. I would like to thank the Faculty Research Bureau of Western Washington University for providing partial support and thus enabling me to prepare the manuscript.

1 Preliminaries

1.1 Aims of This Book

This book is designed to help teachers and students of the Chinese language learn the most recent developments in teaching and learning Mandarin Chinese as a foreign language (henceforth FL). More specifically, it discusses the theoretical models developed for Chinese language pedagogy and acquisition,[1] provides theoretical grounds for selecting teaching materials, and proposes applicable methodology for teaching and learning Chinese. For classroom activities, it demonstrates procedures for teaching and acquiring the five identified content areas: pronunciation, characters and words, sentences, discourse, and culture. These five areas are selected because of their unique characteristics and functions in Chinese and the complexity inherent in their teaching and acquisition.

Teaching and learning Chinese as a FL,[2] as with any other discipline, requires theoretical guidelines. These guidelines, however, may differ from those in other fields in that they are not pure theories; rather they are derived from the practice of teaching and learning Chinese as a FL as well as from research of language pedagogy and foreign language acquisition (FLA). In the process of the implementation of these guidelines, problems and difficulties may occur. However, by solving the problems and overcoming the difficulties, these guidelines are further improved and eventually the field of teaching Chinese as a FL is further developed. In this book, I propose a number of guidelines regarding curriculum design, teaching materials and teaching methodology, based on my own teaching and research experience, as well as incorporating the experiences of many students, teachers and specialists in the fields of teaching and learning Chinese as FL that I have become acquainted with over the last twenty years.

Tones, along with initials and finals, are the foundation of Chinese pronunciation, speaking and listening skills. First, I explain the results of theoretical and empirical studies of acquisition of the tones, initials and finals of the Chinese sound system. Then, I show procedures and strategies for teaching and learning the sound system. Since the majority of students who learn Chinese as FL have a non-tonal native language, the acquisition of tones is the main difficulty and/or problem that manifests itself in different ways for different students. Although the acquisition of some Chinese initials and finals which do not exist in students' native languages may also be problematic, the scope of difficulty seems much smaller than that of tone acquisition because every Chinese character has a tone, including the neutral tone, but not every character has an initial or final that does not exist in students' native languages.

Characters (zi 字) are considered the most difficult component in the acquisition of the Chinese language by students whose native languages have an alphabetical writing system. Because of their shapes, characters are often referred to as logographic writing or pictographic writing, which leads many people to believe that if they are good at drawing, they should be able to learn Chinese characters better. It has also been suggested that the difficulty in learning Chinese lies in the lack of association between characters and sounds. English, for instance, has an alphabet of twenty-six letters, each of which represents a sound or two. So when students have learned those sounds, it becomes easier for them to sound out a word (regardless of whether they have learned the International Phonetic Alphabet) and then write the word. This phonetic ease is even more apparent in a language like Spanish in which each letter has one and only one phonetic pronunciation.

Chinese characters, however, were created differently. The majority of characters have two parts — phonetic and semantic — neither of which is categorized and learned in the "alphabetic" way, so it is difficult for students to decode this "unsystematic" Chinese writing system. This book also aims to guide students in learning the logical aspects of Chinese characters and recognizing a variety of methods for building up a vocabulary pool, an essential component in the development of students' reading and writing competence.

A sentence is the minimum unit needed to express a complete idea and is likely to be the minimum goal for any student learning Chinese. Based on research into both first and foreign language acquisition, I will reveal the most recent trends in teaching and learning sentences and demonstrate the principles and procedures of acquiring Chinese sentences. The emphasis will be on the acquisition of unique Chinese sentence structures, such as topic-comment construction and constructions with various types of complements. Unlike traditional lectures on Chinese grammar, I will provide detailed guidelines for students to follow in the development of their discourse competence. The objective in discussing sentences is not to help students analyze the structure of Chinese sentences but rather to enable them to use different sentences to construct paragraphs to use in authentic communicative situations.

Until recently, the teaching of discourse did not attract significant attention. In the history of teaching Chinese as FL, as well as that of Chinese linguistics, characters and sentences have been the mainstream areas of interest and research. When applied linguists and pedagogical specialists realized that students could not compose coherent paragraphs even after learning many sentence structures, they began to investigate the role of discourse devices used for the connection of sentences/ideas and paragraphs/multiple ideas, and the effect of different genres used for different communicative purposes. The result of this type of investigation has led to the awareness of the importance of discourse and pragmatic factors in foreign language acquisition. Slowly, various discourse devices and pragmatic factors in communication have been included in curriculum design and classroom teaching. I will discuss methods of teaching and learning various levels of discourse devices and offer discourse activities of various types in speaking, reading and writing Chinese.

Many researchers claim culture and language are two closely related components of society (Sapir 1949[1921], Hymes 1964, Byram 1989, Kramsch 1993, Hinkel 1999). I support this view only to the extent that understanding Chinese culture enhances the learning of the Chinese language, but the former is not an absolute condition for the latter. For example, if a student knows nothing about Chinese tradition, customs, history, people's eating habits, etc., this student can still learn to produce a perfect Beijing accent and talk with people on the streets of China about where s/he wants to go and what s/he wants to do. It is true, though, that if students know Chinese tradition and customs, their conversation with native speakers may be more interesting and effective and the sentences they use might be pragmatically more appropriate than otherwise, to say nothing of giving them an enhanced ability to understand at least some of the metalinguistics of any utterance. The challenge that teachers now face is one of format; they must identify the broad and far ranging elements of Chinese culture, then classify them into layers according to the degree of their difficulty of acquisition, in the same way as grammatical elements have been treated. This is the goal of Chapter 8: I will develop a framework for categorization of cultural elements in teaching Chinese as FL and use illustrative examples to demonstrate the procedure of application of cultural elements in teaching Chinese.

In general, this book may serve as a manual for teaching and learning Chinese as FL at all levels, training potential Chinese language teachers, or designing a Chinese language curriculum. For the convenience of readers with different backgrounds, linguistic jargon is purposely avoided in all topics of discussion and illustration. When a technical term has to be used, explanation always follows. References are provided on occasions when a given subject is a target of early research, so that teachers, students, pedagogy specialists, and applied linguists interested in the subject may consult them for further study.

1.2   Chinese Grammar and Pedagogical Grammar of Chinese

The study of Chinese grammar has a long history, although it may be said that the modern study of Chinese grammar began with Mǎ Jiànzhōng's （马建忠）*Mǎ Shì Wén Tōng*《马氏文通》Chinese Grammar (1898[1983]). Focused mainly on the words *zì* (字) and *cí* (词), Mr Ma used more than seven thousand illustrative sentences to explain various functions of different types of words in Chinese. Ma's nineteenth-century book has been studied extensively since its publication and is widely considered a work of art in the area of Chinese grammar. Ma's work has not only helped students of Chinese learn Chinese grammar, but has also set the course for future studies of Chinese grammar. Here in the twentieth century, we have seen that words and their functions in sentences constitute the bulk of Chinese grammar. It is probably for this reason that researchers studying Chinese grammar are referred to as grammarians instead of linguists like their counterparts in the West.

More recently, Lǚ Shūxiāng, together with his research team, shared with us his understanding of contemporary Chinese grammar through *Xiàndài Hànyǔ Bābǎi Cí* (现代汉语八百词, Eight Hundred Chinese Words, 1980). According to his preface, Lǚ prepared this work for non-native Mandarin and non-native Chinese speakers, as well as language teachers and researchers. The content of this work is primarily focused on function words (虚词 *xūcí*), unlike *Mǎ Shì Wén Tōng* which includes both function and content words(实词 *shící*). Based on the part of speech (e.g. noun, verb, adjective, adverb, etc.) and syntactic function (e.g. subject, object, predicate, etc.) of each word, Lǚ categorizes the function of every word and illustrates its usage. Presumably, Lǚ's focus on function words lies in the difficulty of teaching and learning these words in Chinese. This leads to the following questions: Is straight Chinese grammar the same as pedagogical Chinese? If so, can we use *Xiàndài Hànyǔ Bābǎi Cí,* or similar types of grammar books as teaching aids in Chinese classes? If not, why not?

My answer to the first question is "no"; the two types of grammar are different. Chinese grammar should comprise all rules, both prescriptive (i.e. how language should be used) and descriptive (i.e. how people actually use the language), relevant to pronunciation, meaning (i.e. semantic), sentence structure (i.e. syntax), discourse and pragmatics. This grammar is practiced by native speakers and studied by grammarians, linguists and other interested researchers. Pedagogical grammars of Chinese, on the other hand, may consist of two parts: (1) grammar that teachers teach students who learn Chinese as FL and (2) the methodology of teaching this grammar. In other words, pedagogical grammar concerns issues of what grammar to teach and how to teach it to students of Chinese as FL. This overlaps with the definition given by Odlin (1994: 1) "the term pedagogical grammar usually denotes the types of grammatical analysis and instruction designed for the need of second language students." With the specification of the content of pedagogical grammar, it becomes easy to answer the two questions raised at the end of the preceding paragraph. That is, we cannot completely rely on grammar books, such as *Xiàndài Hànyǔ Bābǎi Cí*, to teach because they only provide grammar that teachers may teach students, and not the methodology of how to teach grammar. However, as many teachers have already put this into practice, we can consult with these types of grammar books when we teach certain grammatical functions. In addition to Lǚ's work, Chinese teachers often consult a few other grammar books: Chao's *A Spoken Chinese* (1968), Li and Thompson's *Mandarin Chinese* (1981), and Liu's *Modern Chinese Grammar* (实用现代汉语语法 *Shíyòng Xiàndài Hànyǔ Yǔfǎ* 2002[1983]). In comparison, there is no single handbook of the pedagogical grammar of Chinese. Many Chinese teachers have to search publications by the *Chinese Language Teachers Association* (CLTA) for guidance and enlightenment. I hope this book will broaden the choices for teachers who need pedagogical assistance when teaching Chinese as FL.

1.3   Prior and Current Work on Language Pedagogy and Acquisition

To discuss research into teaching Chinese as a FL, I have to start with the study of language pedagogy and foreign language acquisition (FLA) including second language acquisition (SLA), which is, to some researchers, elucidated or illuminated by studies of theoretical linguistics (cf. Brumfit and Johnson 1979, Ellis 1985, Schachter 1988, Gass and Schachter 1989, Eckman et al. 1995, Gass and Selinker 2001). As far as the scope of FLA is concerned, researchers vary in their opinions. Some researchers distinguish pedagogy from foreign language acquisition; others consider pedagogy a part of foreign language acquisition (e.g. Cook 2001, Ellis 1999, Bachman and Cohen 1998, Romírez 1995, Krashen 1982). Newmyer and Weiberger (1988: 41–42) point out that "the struggle of the field (SLA) to free itself from its ties to pedagogy has been slow and arduous, and is still a long way from being totally achieved … Nevertheless, the field of second language learning research shows every sign of shedding its legacy of direct involvement in pedagogical questions." Gass and Schachter (1995: 17) further argue that if teachers and researchers understand the goals and needs of the other's field, they will succeed in making both pedagogy and FLA/SLA theory better all around. The works of both Newmyer and Weiberger and Gass seem to suggest that language pedagogy and FLA should be distinct fields of research; however, in practice, it is difficult to separate one from the other.

1.3.1   *Pedagogy*

As early as the 1960s, Newmark and Reibel (1968: 232) pointed out that language teaching has shifted the emphasis away from "mastery of language use to mastery of language structure." This shift refers to the movement of structuralism in linguistic and applied linguistic research. "Mastery of language use" emphasizes the *meaning* of language, whereas "mastery of language structures" emphasizes the *form* of language. Hymes (1979: 1[1971]) further explains this shift as follows:

> We have come to see the task of syllabus design, for example, as very much one of selecting structural items and grading them in suitable order for teaching. Our syllabuses have often been little more than ordered lists of structures, which we have then proceeded to teach by means of a strategy that has become all but universal. The strategy works like

> this: we present a structure, drill it, practice it in context ... then move to the next structure. In this way, we gradually synthetically build up the inventory of structural items our students can handle. We reward structural correctness and chastise structural inaccuracy. Success or failure in language learning, as interpreted both through examination results and through student or teacher judgment, has generally come to be assessed in terms of ability to manipulate the structure of the language.

This description provides a vivid picture of how language teaching is affected by the direction of linguistic research — structuralism in this case. Specifically, linguists first provide an answer to 'What is language?' Then, language teachers derive an answer from the linguist's answer to "What knowledge and skills are involved in language proficiency?" (Hymes 1971)

When Chomsky's transformational generative grammar came into being in the late 1950s, the concept of *competence* and *performance* became the center of discussion among not only linguists but also applied linguists and pedagogy specialists. According to Chomsky (1965: 5), competence refers to "the speaker-listener's knowledge of his language," while performance is defined as "the actual use of language in concrete situations." Following Chomsky's explanation of the relationship between language and humans, Hymes (1971) introduced the concept of *communicative competence* — focusing on language in use, the social dimension of language and the concern with language as a form of communication — into language pedagogy and research. Since then, the communicative-based approach in teaching FL has attracted generations of researchers and teachers. This is partly because the communicative approach covers a wide range of topics for research and discussion but more importantly because this approach is more stimulating than the earlier structure-based approach. In other words, the communicative approach involves not only language components, but also their relationship with the people who use the language and the society in which the language is used (cf. Wertsch 1994). As a result, communicative-based syllabi, curricula, teaching materials and teaching and learning guidelines have spread throughout the world and been made known to every language teacher who is interested in the current developments in language pedagogy in the twentieth century (e.g. Lǚ 1981, Rivers 1983, Richards and Nunan 1990, Liu 2002).

1.3.2   Foreign language acquisition

Apart from language pedagogy, the study of foreign language acquisition (FLA) deals with three major areas: (1) the theoretical model of foreign language acquisition, (2) learning content and methodology, and (3) classroom behavior studies. To be more specific, these three areas raise questions relevant to the relationship between theoretical linguistics and FLA, the way of processing learning materials and transferring knowledge of the target language — i.e., learnability, and the procedure of classroom activities.

It has been debated in the last several decades whether the research and practice of FLA has been guided by studies of theoretical linguistics. Some argue that an adequate model of FLA is quite impossible without a coherent theory of language (e.g. Dulay et al. 1982, Schachter 1988, Gregg 1989, Flynn and Martohardjono 1996). Some take the opposite position, i.e., that FLA has established its own system of study based on empirical data from learning FL, and therefore, it is autonomous, independent from the theory of natural language (e.g. Gass 1979, Bley-Vroman 1989, Eckman et al. 1995). Others position themselves between the two views just mentioned: a coherent theory of language (e.g. universal grammar) would be enhanced by evidence from foreign language data, and vice versa. In other words, linguistic theories derived from first language acquisition and FLA theories derived from foreign language teaching and learning can benefit from each other (cf. Gass and Schachter 1989).

In addition to the debate of the role of theoretical linguistics in FLA, one central issue that has concerned researchers of FLA has been learnability, i.e. what and how a non-native speaker can learn in a foreign language classroom. Questions often raised are: How do students learn a sound system to achieve speaking and listening competence? How do they build up their vocabulary pool for reading and writing competence? How do they learn sentences, discourse and pragmatic devices well enough to compose cohesive, coherent paragraphs? Moreover, how do students acquire other socially related knowledge so that they can use the language effectively in communication? Among these questions associated with learnability, researchers have prioritized syntax (i.e. sentence structure) and phonology (i.e. a pronunciation system) as central to linguistic theory and more critical to language pedagogy, and vocabulary or orthography, discourse and culture as important elements, but less critical than syntax and phonology (cf. Odlin 1994, Coady and Huckin 1997, Doughty and Williams 1998, Hinkel 1999, Rose and Kasper 2001).

Research on grammar and vocabulary/orthography acquisition can be traced back to the early nineteenth century when the translation method became common in second/foreign language acquisition. The translation method was primarily used for studying literary texts. It encouraged students to learn etymology, develop dictionary skills and master critical sentence structures. After nearly a century of popularity, the translation method was criticized and challenged for its lack of attention to a newly identified practical and realistic function, namely, oral proficiency (cf. Zimmerman 1997). This led to a series of discussions and debates on the need for reform in language pedagogy both in Europe and in the United States. As a result, two new methods were introduced into the teaching of foreign language: the natural method and the situation teaching method. With the natural method, sentences were learned through natural conversation and vocabulary was explained with labeled pictures, demonstration and the association of ideas (Rivers 1983, and Richards and Rodgers 1986). In other words, this method encourages students to use sentences and vocabulary in utterances. The situation teaching method, on the other hand, aimed to develop students' reading skills. For the first time, vocabulary was considered one of the most important aspects of foreign language learning and priority was placed on developing a scientific and rational basis for selecting the vocabulary content of language courses (Richards and Rogers 1990, Zimmerman 1997). When the audio-lingual method was implemented in foreign language learning during the Second World War, pronunciation and grammar became the center of language learning. Students were taught sound systems through listening to recordings and taught grammatical points through examples and drills rather than through analysis and memorization of rules. This method quickly attracted numerous language students, teachers and researchers alike because a foreign language was, for the first time in history, not approached in an unspoken way anymore. During this period, when one concern within language teaching was the acquisition of structure patterns, vocabulary items were selected according to their simplicity and familiarity. New words were introduced through drills but only enough new words to make the drills possible (Fries 1945, Rivers 1968, Larsen-Freeman 1986).

The most recent method developed in teaching and learning a foreign language is the communicative teaching method. This method is applied to the acquisition of every component of a language: sound system, orthography, sentence structure, discourse and culture. It promotes fluency over accuracy and emphasizes the communicative function of words and sentences, namely, their appropriateness in discourse and communication (cf. Van Ek 1976, Widdowson 1978, Rivers 1983, Zimmerman 1997, Nation 2001). The fluency-over-accuracy theory seems to have generated a lot of discussion in the last two decades; however, the appropriateness approach closely related to discourse, pragmatic, and cultural factors appears to have held its position steadily during the same period.

These acquisition methods and this research in FLA have mostly been developed and practiced in the acquisition of European languages. In the following section, let us see how they can also relate to and influence the pedagogy and acquisition of Chinese as FL.

1.3.3   *Chinese as a foreign language*

Teachers and researchers committed to teaching Chinese as a foreign language (FL) generally do not consider Chinese pedagogy and Chinese acquisition two distinct areas of inquiry, as do some European and American applied linguists of foreign language acquisition (see discussion in previous sections). The majority of research papers (e.g. those published by the *Journal of the Chinese Language Teachers Association* [JCLTA] or the *Chinese Teaching in the World*), and books on Chinese as FL mix both teaching and learning Chinese in discussion, but distinguish elements (tones, grammar, discourse, etc.) to be taught and learned. Another characteristic of Chinese language pedagogy research and acquisition is that Chinese teachers and pedagogy specialists have long been influenced by the research of European and American applied linguists. This is probably not only because European and American teachers and researchers have a longer and richer history of teaching European languages to foreign students than Chinese teachers have teaching Chinese to foreigners, but also because many Chinese teachers and researchers have learned English as FL and have been trained to teach Chinese as FL in Europe and the United States.

Although in China the practice of teaching Chinese to foreigners can be traced back to the Tang dynasty (seventh–ninth century), it was not until the twentieth century that academia started to pay attention to teaching Chinese as FL. With an increasing demand for Chinese teaching both in and outside China, teachers and researchers of the Chinese language came to realize the importance of selecting teaching materials and teaching methodology to maximize students' learning potential. This, consequently, led to the birth of research on the teaching and learning of Chinese as FL. By the twentieth century, the traditional Chinese teaching approach was memorization. It was believed that once a student memorized a good number of characters, phrases and grammatical sentences, this student should be able to speak, read, and write the language. Prior to this period, some Western scholars attempted to detect a grammatical system for the Chinese language, but concluded with disappointment that Chinese was "illogical" and had "no grammatical system" (Ramsey 1987: 49). The only recommendation they could offer to students of Chinese as FL was to use the traditional Chinese method — i.e., the memorization and/or translation approach then popular also in Europe and the United States.

When the Second World War broke out in 1941, more students in Europe and North America became interested in learning Chinese in their own countries. Chinese teachers residing in these regions were either native Chinese speakers using, most likely, traditional Chinese teaching methods for teaching Chinese as FL or Western non-native Chinese teachers using the grammar-translation and/or the newly introduced audio-lingual method. During the Second World War and for approximately three decades afterward, research on teaching and learning Chinese as FL was generally neglected both in and outside China.

In the 1970s, when China finally opened its door to foreign countries, learning Chinese as FL began to gather momentum and research on teaching Chinese was also taken more seriously than ever before: not only by Chinese language teachers but also by Chinese linguists. In 1966, the *Journal of Chinese Language Teachers Association* (JCLTA), the first professional journal designated for research of teaching Chinese as FL, was established in the United States. Since then, teachers, pedagogy specialists and linguists have used it as a forum in which to share their understanding of, ideas about and suggestions on how to teach and learn Chinese as FL. Among the numerous articles published in the JCLTA, have been many that have influenced the direction the field of Chinese language teaching and learning has taken. Ronald Walton can be considered a pioneer scholar in the field: He published several articles (1989, 1992, and 1996) in JCLTA introducing the emerging field of Chinese pedagogy, and reflecting on his vision for Chinese language instruction in the United States.

Richard Chi (1989, 1996) has been known for his dedication to proficiency-based instruction, teaching materials and testing. Many teachers and researchers (Walker 1996; Kubler 1997a, 1997b; Ross 1997; Wong 1996; Gallagher 1999; Chen 1998, 2003) have contributed a great deal to the development of Chinese curricula. Some (Teng 1997, 1998; Xing 1998, 2003; McDonald 1999) have made an effort to establish a working model for a pedagogical grammar of Chinese, while others have been detailing the process of teaching different skills in Chinese. For listening and speaking skills, teachers and researchers have discussed issues related either to teaching and learning tones (McGinnis 1996, 1997; Lundelius 1992; and Chen 1997, Feng 2004) or to comprehension and conversation strategies (Kubler 1993, Yang 1993, Yeh 1997). Everson (1988, 1998) and Everson and Ke (1997) have paid special attention to reading skills. Many other teachers (e.g. Packard 1990, Ke 1998, Lü 1999b, Yang 2000, Yin 2002) have focused on teaching and learning Chinese characters, however, few issues have discussed writing skills (Feng 2003a, 2003b), unless research (Norment 1994, Xing 1998, Chu 2002, Cui 2003) on both spoken and written discourse is counted. In addition to the four skills, there have appeared a good number of discussions on computers and technology in relation to teaching and learning Chinese (Yao 1996, Alber 1996, Zhang 1998, Xie 1999, Bai 2003, Chan 2002, 2003). Cultural and psychological factors involved in the process of pedagogy and acquisition have also attracted many teachers and researchers (Packard 1989, Lan 1994, Myer 1997, 2000, Wen 1999, Li 1999, Hong 1997, 2002).

It is indeed the case that JCLTA has been the only major resource on Chinese language pedagogy and acquisition for the last thirty years in the English speaking world. In China, other than two Chinese journals (《世界汉语教学》, Shìjiè Hànyǔ Jiāoxué, "Chinese Teaching in the World" and 《语言教学研究》, Yǔyán Jiāoxué Yánjiū, "Language Pedagogy and Research"), designated to research articles on Chinese language pedagogy, there have not been many books systematically addressing various issues relevant to teaching and learning Chinese as FL in the last twenty years. Lü (1999a), Liu (2002), Zhao (2004) are among the few that provide some urgently needed information for Chinese language teachers. This situation, nonetheless, may change in the next thirty years. With an increasing number of students rushing to China to learn Chinese, the China National Office for Teaching Chinese as a Foreign Language (*Hànbàn,* 汉办) and the Graduate Institute of Chinese as a Second Language (*Huáyánsuǒ,* 华研所), Taiwan, began to realize the importance of research in the field. In 2002, *Hànbàn* launched, for the first time in history, a large-scale research project on teaching Chinese as FL. Sixty-five projects (see the list at http://www.hanban.edu.cn) were allocated to pedagogy specialists and linguists for exploration of various aspects of teaching Chinese to non-native speakers. The outcome of some of these projects has already been published. Since the establishment of *Huáyánsuǒ* in 1995, its faculty members have carried on numerous research projects on teaching and learning Chinese as FL and have trained a large number of graduate students in the field. All this is a clear indication that the field of Chinese as FL has advanced rapidly in China in recent years.

Examining the literature of Chinese pedagogy and acquisition makes it clear that the guiding principle of teaching and learning Chinese as FL has gradually changed in the last century from grammar-translation-based to function-based (still a dominant approach used by many Chinese programs in the US) and then to proficiency or communicative-based. More and more factors (e.g. discourse, pragmatic, cultural, psychological, etc.) have been identified to relate to the process of teaching and acquisition. Yet, up to the present time, no system or framework that can connect these factors together has been developed. This current work aims to establish such a system.

1.4   Where and Who?

At the beginning of the twenty-first century, it is not difficult to find a university or college, a secondary school or a weekend school that teaches Chinese, no matter which continent one goes to. No one doubts that the rise and fall of Chinese language programs is directly related to the status of the economy and political situation in China. When China has either political or economical problems, Chinese programs shrink; conversely, when the Chinese economy booms, Chinese programs throughout the world thrive. In the following, I will provide an overview of the types of Chinese language programs in the world and a few of the characteristics of students who learn Chinese as FL.

1.4.1   Chinese language programs

In the last two decades, many universities, colleges and secondary schools instituted new Chinese language programs in response to students' popular demand for this language (cf. Walton 1989, Chou 1999, Teng and Yeh 2001, Fitzgerald et al. 2002, Walker and Li 2003). In addition to that, new summer Chinese intensive programs, study abroad programs (in China), weekend or Sunday schools have been established every year. In general, Chinese language programs may be classified into five types:

- Four-year college/university Chinese programs
- K-12 Chinese programs
- Weekend/Sunday schools
- Intensive programs (both in China and outside China)
- Other Chinese courses (including short-term training classes)

According to the Center for Advanced Research on Language Acquisition affiliated with the National Language Research Center, 506 public higher institutions in North America have a Chinese language program (over 95 percent of them are in the United States); 15 higher institutions have intensive summer programs; and 21 higher institutions sponsor a study abroad program in China. It should be noted that these statistics might not be accurate; however, they give us a general idea of the prevalence of Chinese programs in North America. According to a news report from *Xīnhuá News Agency*, January 17, 2003, the United States alone has about 1,000 universities and colleges that offer courses in Chinese as FL. Presumably, the discrepancy between the statistics given by the two sources lies in the exclusion of private colleges and universities. Surfing through the list of institutions with a Chinese program in North America maintained by the Center for Advanced Research on Language Acquisition, it can be seen that every single state in the United States, as well as every province in Canada, has at least one college level Chinese program. The majority of these programs offer at least two or three years of Chinese courses along with some elective courses related to Chinese history, culture or society.

In Europe, Chinese language programs have also grown in the last two decades. In France, 152 universities and colleges offer Chinese courses as FL to nearly 10,000 students, according to Professor Joël Bellassen, the president of the French Chinese Language Teachers Association (FCLTA). Among them, 14 institutions offer a Chinese major and 102 institutions offer non-major Chinese courses. In Great Britain, the situation is somewhat different; not as many universities and colleges offer Chinese courses. Most of the programs are in public schools, namely government sponsored institutions. My sources (see Table 1.1) show that in Great Britain only 20 universities and colleges have Chinese language programs for full-time undergraduates and postgraduate students. However, 127 colleges offer part-time or evening Chinese classes, including Mandarin, Cantonese and related cultural courses primarily for immigrants from Hong Kong. In German-speaking countries — Germany, Austria, Switzerland, etc. — Chinese language programs can be found at major universities that also have a China-related course of study, such as Sinology or Modern China Studies. Among the 135 higher institutions offering Chinese courses, only 40 of them are regular four-year colleges and universities; the rest are college extended programs.

Some Asian countries, such as Japan, Korea and Singapore, have a long history of Chinese language programs because of their geographic location and social, economical, and political ties with China. A survey conducted by Teng and Yeh (2001) shows that South Korea has the largest student body of Chinese as FL among all Asian countries. Other countries, such as Thailand, Vietnam and Indonesia, do not have a long history of teaching Chinese as FL; however, in recent years, there have been a growing number of higher institutions interested in establishing a Chinese language program to meet the demand of students. The China National Office for Teaching Chinese as a foreign Language (NOCFL), or *Hànbàn* reports that majority of foreign students who study Chinese at Chinese colleges and universities come from Korea, Japan and a few other South East Asian countries.

In Australia, Mandarin Chinese was available at 29 colleges/universities in 2001 with an enrollment of 1,338 students (see report by Fitzgerald, the Asian Studies Association of Australia 2002). Fitzgerald's report also showed that the study of Mandarin Chinese grew steadily in Australia in the 1990s.

K-12 Chinese programs, on the other hand, are not as popular as those at universities and colleges in most parts of the world, except for some Asian countries. Statistics from the National Language Research Center, the same source from which college level Chinese program statistics are cited, show that in North America 86 public schools offer Chinese courses to approximately 38,000 students. Compared with the number of other major foreign language programs at K-12 public schools in North America, this number is rather small. However, compared with the number of Chinese programs in North America a few decades ago, we do see an increase. In the state of Washington, Chinese programs have emerged at several reputable middle schools and high schools (both public and private) in the last several years. Lakeside School, known as the best private secondary school in the Seattle area, started its Chinese program in the year 2000. Three years later, this school offers four levels of Chinese courses. It is worth noting that a significant number of French K-12 schools (total 136 schools with approximately 20,000 students, including students from weekend/Sunday schools) offer Chinese courses (cf. Bellassen 2004). This number is twice more than the number of colleges and universities offering Chinese language programs in France, and comparable to the number of public schools providing Chinese courses in the United States. In German-speaking countries, there is also a reasonable number (57 according to FASK, School of Applied Linguistics and Cultural Studies) of K-12 schools with Chinese language programs, considering Chinese is offered there as a third language after English.

In Asia, South Korea topped all other countries in the number of Chinese programs offered (1,138 public high schools and 18 private high schools) and in student enrollment in Chinese courses (82,520 public school students and 20,300 private school students), according to a report by Teng and Yeh (2001). These numbers coincide with the report from *Hànbàn* showing that North Korea sent the largest number of students to China to study Chinese in 2001–2003.

The number of Chinese weekend or Sunday schools has also boomed in recent years because many children of Chinese immigrants are sent to Chinese schools by their parents. In addition, the number of adopted Chinese girls has also affected enrollment numbers in Chinese schools because adoptive parents who promised to educate their adopted daughters in Chinese culture are registering them in Chinese schools across the US to learn Chinese language and culture. In the United States, more than 270 Chinese schools were registered as non-profit organizations in 2004, with an enrollment of more than 36,000 students nationwide, according to statistics provided by the Chinese School Association at the United States. Other countries, such as France, Great Britain, and Japan, have similar weekend and Sunday Chinese schools, but the number of schools and students in these countries is substantially lower. Other relevant statistics from these countries are not available (see Table 1.1).

Table 1.1   Statistics of Chinese language programs and student enrollment (Mandarin and Cantonese)*

	Univ./College (Students)	K-12 (Students)	S. School (Students)	Others** (Students)
N. America[1]	506 34,153[2]	86 (38,000)	270*** (36,000+)	53 (n/a)
Japan[3]	84 (n/a)	303 (15,390)	n/a	186 (36,314)
S. Korea[3]	215 (34,727)	1154 (102,820)	n/a	n/a
Australia[4]	29 (1338)	300+ (80,000+)	38 (8,000+)	n/a
France[5]	152 (9,400+)	136 (20,000+)	n/a	n/a
UK[6]	19 (n/a)	n/a	n/a	127 (n/a)
German-speaking countries[7]	135 (approx. 4,000)	57 (n/a)	n/a	n/a
China[8]	300+ (60,000)	n/a	n/a	n/a
Total	2027 (25 million)[8]	n/a	n/a	n/a

*   The numbers in the cells refer to schools having Chinese as a foreign language and those in parentheses represent student enrollment.

**   There might be some overlap between the numbers under "Other" and "China," primarily because both categories include "Study Chinese in China" programs.

*** It should be noted that these numbers only include the enrollment for those heritage schools with primarily mainland Chinese immigrant connections, and not the ones with mainly Taiwan connections.

1.   Statistics at the university/college level are quoted from the website maintained by the Center for Advanced Research on Language Acquisition, National Language Research Center (http://carla.acad.umn.edu/lctl/access.html). The number for Sunday Schools (or Chinese Schools) is from the website of the Chinese School Association in the United States (see http://www.csaus.org). "Other" includes summer intensive programs both in the US and in China (see http://www.studyabroad.com).

2.   This only includes the number of US students taking Chinese in the fall of 2002 from the report of the Modern Language Association of America, January 2004.

3.   Data from a survey conducted by Teng and Yeh (2001), Institute of Teaching Chinese as a Second Language, National Taiwan Normal University.

4.   University/College data are cited from *Maximizing Australia's Asian Knowledge* by John Fitzgerald et al. (2002). Other data were provided by James Wu, the president of the Chinese Language Teacher's Federation of Australia.

5. Data provided by Professor Joël Bellassen, president of the French Chinese Language Teachers Association.

6. This figure only reflects government-sponsored Chinese programs at colleges and universities (see http://www.hotcourses.com).

7. Dr Andreas Guder, a professor at Johannes Gutenberg Universität Mainz, provided some data   for Chinese programs in Germany. Other data was provided by FASK (http://www.fask.uni-mainz/de/inst/chinesisch/shindeutsch.htm)

8. The data is reported by *Xīnhuá News Agency*, January 17, 2003 and provided by the China National Office for Teaching Chinese as a Foreign Language (NOCFL).

1.4.2   Chinese language practitioners

Throughout this book, the term "Chinese language practitioners" is used to refer to teachers and students of Chinese as FL. Although the members of these two categories of language practice vary in terms of status/position, attitudes and personality, they engage in activities that are very dependent on goals: to teach or learn communicative skills in the target language. These two members function as if they are a married couple practicing the Chinese language. Both of them have to work hard, learn from each other and cooperate with each other to create a harmonious environment so that teachers become skillful in teaching and students become knowledgeable and competent in communication in Chinese. Without this harmony, the two groups will struggle through the course of teaching and learning with teachers becoming frustrated and students failing to learn communicative skills in the end. To avoid this situation, it is important for teachers and students to understand and respect the responsibilities and characteristics of each other in the process of teaching and learning Chinese.

1.4.2.1   Teachers and teacher training

Chinese language teachers can be classified into three types based on their background and experience with the Chinese language: (1) native speakers with non-Western education and teacher training, (2) native speakers with Western education and teacher training, and (3) non-native speakers with Western education and teacher training. Each of these types may be further divided into two sub-types: (1) those with training in Chinese linguistics or related fields, and (2) those with training in Chinese literature or related fields. All of these types and sub-types of teachers have certain teaching tactics in common, but each type can also develop its own teaching characteristics influenced by training and/or personality.

The term "Native Chinese teachers with non-Western education and training" refers herein to those whose native language is Chinese and who teach Chinese as FL in China, Taiwan, or other East Asian countries. These teachers, seen in decreasing numbers in recent years, are notably influenced by the Chinese traditional teaching method, namely, the teacher-centered method. They are strict in the classroom, and friendly and hospitable outside the classroom, especially with their students. Most of these teachers have at least a college degree in social sciences or humanities. In comparison, non-native Chinese teachers who receive Western education and teacher training are more inclined to use the student-centered method. Most of them are skillful, even meticulous, in the design of different class activities and games to sustain students' interest in learning Chinese. It is relatively easy for them and their students to gain mutual understanding because they share the same or similar cultural roots. However, it might be difficult for some teachers in this group to gain students' confidence in their Chinese competence because they are not native speakers. This is, obviously, not an issue for native Chinese teachers regardless of whether or not they received Western education and training. Native Chinese teachers who have received education and teacher training in the West seem to fall between the two types of teachers just discussed. They are trained in both traditional Chinese methods and newer Western methods. In addition, they are familiar with Western culture and students' learning habits. They can be as creative as any other language teacher. This is probably why the majority of Chinese teachers at all institutions belong to this type. Their goal is to "stimulate student interest in language, to develop the learner's confidence in their own abilities, to discover truth about the structure of language under study, and to help raise learners' consciousness not only about what is systematic about the language they are learning but also about learners' own linguistic strength and weakness" (Riggenbach 1999: 25).

Not surprisingly, Chinese teachers with different educational backgrounds teach Chinese with different strategies. Teachers with a linguistic degree, for instance, may prefer to explain how to pronounce a certain sound by using linguistic jargon (e.g. place and manner of articulation — labial, fricative, retroflex, etc.), when teaching the Chinese sound system, whereas teachers with a literature background may briefly go over the sound and leave time for interesting stories about their experience in learning the sound. Each type of teaching has its own merits and each can achieve excellence through cumulative experience and a variety of training.

In the twenty-first century, Chinese teachers and potential Chinese teachers have more training opportunities than ever before. Workshops with various themes, such as the Workshop for Business Chinese, the Workshop for Teaching Chinese via Internet, and a workshop for assessment of student performance, can be found almost every year. Chinese language teacher associations have been established on almost every continent including but not limited to:

- the French Chinese Teachers Association (FCLTA)
- the Association of Chinese Language Teaching in German-speaking Countries
- the Chinese Language Teachers Federation of Australia (CLTFA)
- the Association of Chinese Language (中国语学会, *Zhōngguó yǔ xuéhuì*, Japan)

- the Chinese Language Teachers Association (CLTA)
- the International Society for Chinese Language Teaching
- the National Council of Association of Chinese Language Schools
- the Chinese School Association in the United States
- the Chinese Language Association of Secondary-Elementary School (CLASS)

These associations for Chinese language teachers aim to advance the teaching and learning of the Chinese language and to encourage and disseminate studies and research in Chinese language pedagogy, as noted in the by-laws of the CLTA. Most of these associations hold an annual meeting so that teachers can gather and exchange or share new ideas relevant to the teaching and research of Chinese as FL.

However, the fundamental training of Chinese teachers lies in graduate schools for teachers of foreign languages. In the 1990s, several universities started programs to specifically train Chinese teachers, among them the Institute of Teaching Chinese as a Second Language at the National Taiwan Normal University, master's or equivalent programs in Teaching Chinese as a Foreign Language at the University of Iowa, University of Colorado, Beijing Language University, Ohio State University, and National Office for Teaching Chinese as a Foreign Language. Graduates from these programs become Chinese teachers positioned at many competitive universities and colleges in many different countries around the world. With the continued demand for Chinese language teachers, teacher-training programs will undoubtedly continue to grow in the future.

1.4.2.2   Students

It was noted earlier that the number of students choosing Chinese as FL at all academic levels has steadily increased in the last two decades worldwide. We may group students according to their geographical locations and the linguistic similarity of their native language to that of Chinese: in other words, Asian students and Western students. Within these two groups, we may further subdivide them into adult learners and younger learners. What follows is a discussion of the characteristics of each of these groups.

Asian students, with a large number from Japan and South Korea, have certain advantages in learning Chinese. Since Japanese students have already learned how to write Kanji — Japanese words derived from and similar to Chinese characters — when they start learning Chinese, their initial writing skill is clearly better than students whose native language is not Japanese. Many of them, however, have difficulty in pronouncing palatal sounds (e.g. j, q, x) and retroflex sounds (i.e. *zh, ch, sh*) and have difficulty in distinguishing [n] from [l]. Most Korean students also start to learn Chinese characters at an early age. Due to the influence of Chinese characters and pronunciation in the Korean language, students can associate the pronunciation of Chinese words with the sounds, pronunciation and characters of Korean words. Similarly, Vietnamese and Burmese students can learn Chinese tones without much difficulty because their native languages are tonal too. By comparison, Western students have none of the advantages that Asian students have. In North America and Europe, students generally find that tones and logographic characters are the two most difficult components of the Chinese language because their native languages are neither tonal, nor logographic. They are alphabetical languages whose pitch of accents is rarely linked to semantics. Consequently, it has become almost conventional wisdom in Western countries that if a student is good at learning Chinese tones and characters, this student can learn Chinese.

Younger students of Chinese as FL adopt a different learning pattern in comparison to adult students. In North America, younger learners are either extremely competitive (otherwise they would not choose to learn Chinese) or have some kind of background in or connection to Chinese (e.g. their family members are native Chinese speakers). In other words, they have either a will or a way to learn Chinese well. Those who have the will can learn Chinese faster than adult learners because they can memorize words faster and imitate sounds better than adults do and their affective filter is less opaque making it less embarrassing to imitate such foreign sounds. For those young learners who have a background or for heritage speakers, a certain level of listening, or even speaking, competence has been attained before formal learning begins, so they can easily surpass adults in listening and speaking. For adult learners who do not have any of these advantages, the acquisition of all four skills — listening, speaking, reading and writing — is much more difficult. Due to the lack of data and analysis of younger students, I will not do any parallel comparison between younger students in Asian and Western countries.

1.5   Standards and Assessment

Pedagogy specialists and applied linguists have long been developing standards in addition to guidelines, for teaching and learning a foreign language, as well as assessment tools to measure students' communicative competence and performance. Many language practitioners also know that teaching and learning guidelines and assessment methods often change with the development of new theories and frameworks in foreign language acquisition. During the first half of the twentieth century, structuralism — emphasizing sentence structures — dominated all linguistic related fields. As a result, teaching and learning a foreign language, including Chinese, was guided by grammar/structure-based standards. Be they curricular, textbooks, or tests, all centered on grammatical structures of the target language (cf. Bachman 1990).

During the second half of the twentieth century, functionalism — emphasizing language function in communication with an emphasis on communication skills/function — gradually gained popularity in linguistic research (Hymes 1971, Johnson and Johnson 1979, Berns 1990) and, applied linguistics and foreign language acquisition and pedagogy soon followed the trend. Foreign language teaching then switched from the grammar/structure-based approach to function-based, then to performance or proficiency-based. This switch was evidenced by the publication of function- and proficiency-oriented textbooks, revision of curricula to pave the road for achieving new teaching and learning goals, and most notably by the development of proficiency guidelines for teaching and learning and proficiency-based assessment, which I will discuss in further detail in the next three sections.

According to the American Council on the Teaching of Foreign Languages (ACTFL), proficiency guidelines "identify stage of proficiency, as opposed to achievement, thus they are not intended to measure what an individual has achieved through specific classroom instruction, but rather to allow assessment of what an individual can and cannot do, regardless of where, when, or how the language has been learned or acquired." (ACTFL Proficiency Guidelines 1986) This makes it clear that "guideline" and "assessment" are two different yet closely related concepts. In other words, guidelines are a means for assessment of students' proficiency level. It should be noted that in reality, proficiency guidelines have been incorporated into teaching and learning a foreign language far beyond what was originally intended. Many language programs and teachers use the proficiency guidelines to guide their curriculum design, instruction preparation, program evaluation, evaluation, and student achievement assessment (Chi 1996, Higgs 1984, Omaggio 1986).

I agree with the ACTFL's original proposal that guidelines should only be used to assess students' proficiency level. One may argue that students' proficiency level is an indication of the effectiveness of the teachers' instruction, which is, in turn, an indication of the effectiveness of a program's curricular goals and therefore, the proficiency guidelines should not only be used to assess student proficiency level, but also to assess teacher performance and program effectiveness. The problem with this argument is that there are many other means of measurement and factors that affect teacher performance and program effectiveness, such as student-teacher ratio, student retention, program goals, program type, etc. If the proficiency guidelines are considered the only means to evaluate teachers and programs, it can be very difficult to substantiate the purpose of evaluation or assessment.

The most recent standards developed by ACTFL are the *Standards for Foreign Language Learning: Preparing for the 21st Century* (1996). Breaking the tradition of developing standards for teaching and assessment, these new standards aim to lay out goals and content range of language learning for students. I will discuss and comment on these standards in 1.5.3.

1.5.1 ACTFL Proficiency Guidelines and OPI

The American Council on the Teaching of Foreign Language (ACTFL), founded in 1967 by the Modern Language Association of America, is the only US national organization representing teachers of all languages at all education levels. Its mission statement lays emphasis on promoting and fostering the study of languages and cultures as an integral component of American education and society. Similar organizations also exist in Europe (e.g. The European Center for Modern Languages) and other parts of the world; however, no organization has ventured to develop guidelines for the teaching and acquisition of foreign languages the way ACTFL has in the United States.

In the early 1980s, when performance and proficiency became the center of discussion in foreign language acquisition, ACTFL took the initiative to develop a series of national guidelines and standards for teaching and learning foreign languages other than English. In 1986, it published the *Proficiency Guidelines* and language-specific guidelines for Chinese, Classical Languages (Latin and Greek), French, German, Italian, Japanese, Portuguese, Russian, Spanish. In 1996, ACTFL published the *Standards for Foreign Language Learning: Preparing for the 21st Century*. Two years later, based on the generic standards, seven language-specific standards, including Chinese, were developed. Besides ACTFL, some other organizations, such as the National Foreign Language Center and the China National Office for Teaching Chinese as a Foreign Language (*Hànbàn*), also developed guidelines and standards for teaching, learning and assessment. In the following sections, I will discuss some of the most influential guidelines and standards used by Chinese language practitioners.

CHINESE PROFICIENCY GUIDELINES

With an increasing demand for Chinese language programs in the United States and other parts of the world, the American Council on the Teaching of Foreign Language (ACTFL) published the Chinese Proficiency Guidelines in 1986.[3] These Guidelines provide a detailed description of four proficiency levels: Novice, Intermediate, Advanced, and Superior. Novice and Intermediate Levels are further divided into three sub-levels: Low, Mid, and High; while Advanced has two sub-levels: Advanced and Advanced-Plus. Superior does not have any sub-levels. All (sub-) levels are described in terms of the four skills: speaking, listening, reading, and writing. Following is a brief summary of each level:

Speaking:

> *Novice-Low*: No functional ability to speak Chinese. Oral production is limited to a few common loan words in English and perhaps a few high frequency phrases (谢谢 *xièxiè*, 你好 *nǐhǎo*.)

Novice-Mid: No functional ability to speak Chinese. Oral production is limited to basic courtesy formulae. Can count from one to ten, name basic colors, common nouns, and food items.

Novice-High: Emerging ability to make short statements utilizing simple formulaic utterance and ask simple questions.

Intermediate-Low: Can ask and answer simple questions and initiate and respond to simple statements in the present time.

Intermediate-Mid: Can ask and answer questions involving areas of immediate need, leisure time activities, and make simple transactions.

Intermediate-High: Can describe daily activities, likes and dislikes in detail and express agreement and disagreement.

Advanced: Can make rather complicated factual comparisons and handle arrangements with Chinese administrators.

Advanced-Plus: Emerging ability to support opinions, explain in detail, and hypothesize.

Superior: Can support opinions and hypothesize on a broad range of concrete and abstract topics.

Listening:

Novice-Low: No practical understanding of spoken Chinese.

Novice-Mid: Sufficient comprehension to understand some memorized words within predictable areas of need.

Novice-High: Comprehend some sentence-length utterances in situations where the context aids understanding.

Intermediate-Low: Comprehension areas include such basic needs as: meals, lodging, transportation, time, simple instructions.

Intermediate-Mid: Limited understanding of topics beyond a variety of survival needs, such as personal history and leisure time activities.

Intermediate-High: Able to understand major syntactic constructions.

Advanced: Able to understand face-to-face, non-technical speech in standard Chinese spoken by a native speaker in controlled context.

Advanced-Plus: Often shows remarkable ability and ease of understanding, but comprehension may break down under tension or pressure.

Superior: Sufficient comprehension to understand the essentials of all speech in standard Chinese, including hypothesis, supported opinion, and technical discussion.

Reading:

Novice-Low: No functional ability in reading Chinese.

Novice-Mid: Able to identify/recognize a small set of graphic elements and characters.

Novice-High: Can identify a limited number of characters components and characters common to high-frequency sets of listable categories encountered in areas of immediate need.

Intermediate-Low: Can read, for basic survival and social needs, simple connected, specially prepared material and can puzzle out pieces of some authentic materials with considerable difficulty.

Intermediate-Mid: Sufficient comprehension to understand specially prepared discourse for informative purposes and to understand with use of a dictionary main ideas and some facts in authentic materials paralleling oral language.

Intermediate-High: Able to understand simple discourse of paragraph length in specially prepared materials relying on low-level, high-frequency sentence patterns.

Advanced: Sufficient comprehension to read edited materials within narrow topic range, particularly in areas of specialization or high interest, characterized by structure which increasingly mirrors that of authentic materials.

Advanced-Plus: Can comprehend materials of a more general nature where structure, though simple and constrained, truly mirrors the essential features of authentic expository prose.

Superior: Able to read a narrow range of authentic, expository materials, including areas of professional interest, without the use of a dictionary.

Writing:

Novice-Low: Can copy isolated characters with simple stroke configuration.

Novice-Mid: Able to copy characters with more complex stroke of configuration.

Novice-High: Can write frequently used memorized materials.

Intermediate-Low: Can write in highly colloquial, conversational style, some forms of personal communication.

Intermediate-Mid: Writing style is still reflective or the grammar and lexicon of speech, but quantity is increased and quality is improved.

Intermediate-High: Able to meet most practical writing needs and limited social demands.

Advanced: Writing is obviously reflective of speech but a limited ability in authentic Chinese writing style is present.

Advanced-Plus: Writing is characterized by the emerging use of patterns, lexicon, and structural devices typical of authentic Chinese written style.

Superior: Writing is characterized by predominance of authentic Chinese rhetorical style, with many limitations, over colloquial, speech-influenced writing.

These guidelines identify the stages of proficiency in the Chinese language. They provide a common measurement for assessment of what an individual can and cannot do in the areas of listening, speaking, reading and writing (Kotenbeutel 1999). Even though these guidelines have been received and reviewed positively by many teachers and researchers, many Chinese teachers remain skeptical of their practical function in teaching and learning Chinese. The most appealing argument against the use of the guidelines seems to be that the guidelines do not help teachers and students in actual teaching and learning.

ORAL PROFICIENCY INTERVIEW

Following the Proficiency Guidelines, ACTFL developed the Oral Proficiency Interview (OPI) in 1989. OPI is a standardized procedure for the global assessment of functional speaking ability. Similar to the rating system of the Proficiency Guidelines, the OPI rates students as Novice, Intermediate, Advanced, and Superior with Low, Mid, and High as their sublevels. The OPI takes the form of a 10–30-minute tape-recorded conversation between a trained interviewer and the interviewee whose speaking proficiency is being assessed. All potential interviewers have to be trained at an OPI workshop to receive a certificate for official oral proficiency interviews. Since the content of each interview can be unique to the interviewee and his or her responses, the interviewer is expected to have the ability to respond and adjust the line of questioning and task posing. An experienced interviewer formulates questions based on a continuous assessment of the interviewee's proficiency and on the topics that emerge in the conversation (ACTFL 1989).

Since the publication of OPI, ACTFL organizes OPI workshops every year. Many Chinese teachers have participated in the training and become certified OPI interviewers. Nonetheless, some Chinese teachers view OPI the same as the ACFTL Proficiency Guidelines i.e. they feel that both endeavors lack practical function in the process of teaching and learning Chinese as FL.

1.5.2 *Hànyǔ Shuǐpíng Kǎoshì*

The Chinese Proficiency Test or *Hànyǔ Shuǐpíng Kǎoshì* (汉语水平考试, HSK) was created at Beijing Language University in 1988 for students whose native language is not Chinese. The purpose of this test, similar to OPI, is to assess students' Chinese proficiency level. If students pass the test, they receive a certificate, which may be used for job applications or college applications. HSK is classified into three   proficiency categories and eleven   levels: (1) Basic Chinese Test 基础汉语水平考试 *Jīchǔ Hànyǔ Shuǐpíng Kǎoshì* (Low, mid and high); (2) Elementary-Intermediate Chinese Test 初、中等汉语水平考试 *Chū Zhōngděng Hànyǔ Shuǐpíng Kǎoshì* (elementary low, mid, high and Intermediate low, mid, high); and (3) Advanced Chinese Test 高等汉语水平考试 *Gāoděng Hànyǔ Shuǐpíng Kǎoshì* (advanced and superior). The Center of HSK at Beijing Language University suggests that students who have completed 100 to 800 hours of study may take the Basic Chinese Test, those who have completed 400 to 2,000 study hours may take the Elementary-Intermediate Chinese Test, and those who have completed 3,000 hours or more may take the Advanced Chinese Test. For students who learn Chinese in a regular Chinese program at an American university or college, this means they must take Chinese for at least two years in order to take the Basic Chinese Test, assuming that they take one hour of Chinese a day, five days a week, and thirty weeks a year. At this rate of progress, students may not be ready for the Intermediate Chinese test before graduation from college, unless they participate in an intensive Chinese program or study abroad program in China. For the Advanced Test, students are expected to reach native or near native proficiency.

HSK is quite similar to OPI in terms of categorization and specification of proficiency levels. The only major difference is that OPI is designed to evaluate students' oral proficiency, whereas HSK is a written test with multiple choice questions so it is likely to reflect students' reading skill rather than listening, speaking or writing skills.

Since the establishment of HSK in 1988, there have been an increasing number of students interested in the tests. To date, 44 centers have been founded to administer the tests in China and 55 centers exist in Asian, European, North American, and Pacific island countries. By the year 2004, it was projected that approximately 380,000 students will have taken the tests. These numbers, as predicted by *Hànbàn,* the central administration of HSK, will continue to rise. Readers interested in specific locations or levels of the tests may consult the websites: http://www.hsk.org.cn or http://www.hanban.edu.cn.

1.5.3   Teaching and learning standards

Due to concerns that national guidelines are mainly applicable at the college level, and not at the secondary level, the National Foreign Language Center gathered teachers of the Chinese Language Association for Secondary Schools (CLASS) and compiled the *Guidelines for Chinese Language Teaching in Secondary Schools* in 1990. These guidelines were intended to guide teachers in curriculum development, instruction preparation, choice of instructional materials, and assessment of student performance. Seven content areas were suggested comprising two levels of learning:

1. Function
2. Topic
3. Level
4. Patterns
5. Vocabulary List
6. Character List
7. Culture Topic

Function refers to a student's Chinese competence in socializing, providing information, expressing information and feeling, getting others to adopt a course of action, etc. *Topic* includes personal identification, family life, shopping, education, leisure, etc. *Level* specifies two proficiency levels in listening, speaking, reading, writing and culture. *Pattern* lists 34 grammatical points suggested for students to master in the course of completing two levels of study. *Vocabulary List* provides a list of words that students are expected to produce and understand, while *Character List* identifies characters that students are expected to read and write in context. *Culture Topic* covers 28 subjects ranging from Chinese names to color terms and body language, from Chinese festivals to Chinese ideology.

Compared with the Chinese Proficiency Guidelines, the guidelines for Chinese teaching at secondary schools provide detailed information of what should be taught to K-12 students. They are straightforward and easy to follow for teachers even if they do not have any training in the application of the guidelines.

In 1996, ACTFL published its first set of learning standards: *Standards for Foreign Language Learning: Preparing for the 21st Century*. Broadening the content range of language learning by venturing well beyond the traditional four skills of listening, speaking, reading and writing and the occasional study of culture, the new standards dramatically changed the paradigms under which teachers have taught in the past (Phillips 1999). Five content areas were targeted in the standards: Communication, Cultures, Connections, Comparisons, and Communities, also known as the Five Cs. The Communication standard was designed to help students to gain communicative competence in a foreign language. The Culture standard aimed to help students gain knowledge and understanding of the culture in which the foreign language is used. The Connection standard encouraged students to use a foreign language to explore interdisciplinary content. The Comparison standard was meant to develop students' insight into the nature of and relationship between language and culture. And, lastly, the Community standard provided students with guidance in using a foreign language in communities where the language is spoken as a native language (L1). Over the last several decades, the first two Cs have been discussed much more often in the literature of foreign language acquisition and emphasized in the design and development of traditional foreign language curriculum than the last three Cs. Notice that the understanding of culture appears to be a major element in all five standards.

Building upon these five national standards, the Chinese standards were derived in 1998, expanding and tailoring the progress indicators and learning scenarios with Chinese language specific examples, as outlined below.

COMMUNICATION (沟通): Students engage in conversations, provide and obtain information, express feelings and emotions, and exchange opinions in Chinese. Students understand and interpret written and spoken language on a variety of topics in Chinese. Students present information, concepts, and ideas to an audience of listeners or readers on a variety of topics.

CULTURES (文化): Gain knowledge and understanding of the cultures of the Chinese-speaking world. Students demonstrate an understanding of the relationship between the practices and perspectives of the cultures of the Chinese-speaking world. Students demonstrate an understanding of the relationship between the projects and perspectives of the cultures of the Chinese-speaking world.

CONNECTIONS (贯连): Connect with other disciplines and acquire information. Students reinforce and further their knowledge of other disciplines through the study of Chinese. Students acquire information and recognize the distinctive viewpoints that are only available through Chinese language and culture.

COMPARISON (比较): Develop insight into the nature of language and culture. Students demonstrate understanding of the nature and concept of language and culture through comparisons of the Chinese language and culture with their own.

COMMUNITIES (社区): Participate in multilingual communities at home and around the world. Students use the Chinese language both within and beyond the school setting. Students show evidence of becoming lifelong learners by using Chinese for personal enjoyment and enrichment.

Since these are guidelines for learning Chinese, both teachers and students should understand and practice accordingly. The biggest challenge for teachers is probably the addition of cultural elements to traditional curriculum areas and instructional approaches. Questions, such as what cultural elements should be included in the curriculum and how to implement the inclusion of these cultural elements in language instruction, have to be addressed first. Chapter 8 of this book takes a look at these questions.

1.6   Mandarin vs. Other Dialects

Chinese is generally considered to have seven mutually unintelligible dialects: Mandarin, Wú, Xiāng, Gàn, Kèjiā (Hakka), Yuè (Cantonese), and Mǐn, among which Mandarin has the largest population of speakers — 70 percent of China's Hàn ethnic group (Norman 1988). In addition, Mandarin is the standard language of China and as such is recognized as one of the five languages used by the United Nations. This is why most universities and colleges in the world offer courses in Mandarin instead of other Chinese dialects. Cantonese is also taught at some universities in North America and Great Britain due to the demand of new immigrants from Hong Kong and Guǎngdōng areas. However, in comparison to Mandarin, Cantonese has a much smaller student body.

For the reasons stated above, Mandarin is chosen to be the target dialect for discussion throughout this book. When other dialects, such as Cantonese, become a subject of discussion, it will be clearly noted and explained. For instance, when discussing skill-oriented Chinese classes in Chapter 2, I examine factors involved in curriculum design. In this case, students of native Cantonese are mentioned because they can read and write already. The only skills they intend to acquire are listening and speaking. For Chinese teachers of non-Mandarin dialects, this book may not be as useful as for Mandarin teachers because non-Mandarin dialects and Mandarin have different phonological systems (tones, initials and finals — discussed in Chapter 4) and somewhat different grammar (sentence structure — discussed in Chapter 6) even though they have the same writing system (orthography — discussed in Chapter 5).

1.7   Summary and Outline of the Book

In this chapter, I have outlined the approaches and guidelines of Chinese pedagogy and acquisition. The basic idea is that the communicative approach is the guiding principle and that we need to develop a system that will integrate all major factors relevant to teaching and learning Chinese into everyday practice so that teachers and students will benefit from such work. While much remains to be understood about this kind of a working pedagogical model, my previous work on pedagogical grammar and teaching experience gives me reason to believe that a pedagogical system of Chinese must be built on two foundation elements: content (what to teach and learn) and process (how to teach and learn).

Chapter 2 discusses the content of a pedagogical grammar of Chinese. Questions such as what constitutes a pedagogical grammar of Chinese, how to choose teaching materials and design various types of curricula, will be addressed. Chapter 3 focuses on teaching methodology. First, I review factors that have been identified in the field that have affected teaching and learning methods both in and outside China. Then I introduce two working models in teaching and learning Chinese as FL. Toward the end of this chapter, I discuss the relationship between methodology and accuracy, class size, and program type and provide teachers and students with suggestions for practice. In Chapters 4 to 8, I turn to teaching and learning different elements of Chinese, from pronunciation, characters, sentences, and discourse to culture. Each chapter reviews earlier and current approaches to teaching and learning the subject of the current chapter, explains limitations, and suggests a working model.

It should be clear that Chapter 1 is an overview of the field of teaching and learning Chinese as FL, Chapters 2 and 3 cover two major content areas affecting all phases of teaching and learning Chinese, and Chapters 4 to 8 concentrate on teaching and learning individual element of the Chinese language. It is my hope that by breaking the approach down into these three layers of discussion and illustration, I can present a clearer picture of the system for teaching and learning Chinese as FL.

2

Pedagogical Grammar of Chinese: Content

2.1　Introduction

It was discussed in Chapter 1 that Chinese grammar differs from pedagogical grammar in that the former focuses on all rules of a language, whereas the latter refers to what and how teachers might teach students of Chinese as a foreign language (FL). Even though traditional understanding of Chinese grammar is limited to rules relevant to words and sentence structures, it does not mean that pedagogical grammar should follow that tradition. We propose that the scope of pedagogical grammar of Chinese include, but not be limited to, the rules of teaching and learning the five major areas: pronunciation, characters and words, sentences, discourse-pragmatic and culture. The first two areas are set for foundational skills; without learning them, students cannot speak, understand, read or write. The last three areas are instrumental for students to be successful in communication with the language.

Traditional understanding of the content of a pedagogical grammar of Chinese (PGC) entails explanation of sentence structures, which most likely arose from grammar books derived from linguistic research. Grammar books such as these in Chinese include *Xiàndài Hànyǔ Bābǎi Cí* (现代汉语八百词, "Eight Hundred Chinese Words") by Lǚ Shū-xiāng (1980) and *Shíyóng Xiàndài Hànyǔ Yǔfǎ* (实用现代汉语语法, "Modern Chinese Grammar") by Liú Yuè-huá et al. (2002[1983]). There are also two Chinese grammar books in English often used for pedagogical purposes: *Mandarin Chinese: A Functional Grammar* by Li and Thompson (1980) and *A Spoken Chinese* by Chao (1968). Even though these reference books are all useful, there are some differences between the Chinese pedagogical grammar and their English counterparts. Chinese teachers find those written in Chinese more convenient to use than those written in English because of the large selection of illustrative examples; those in English usually contain a chapter on the sound system of Chinese, but those in Chinese do not. Operating within the framework of the above definition of PGC, this chapter will discuss two major areas relevant to the content of PGC: curricula and teaching materials. Technically, curriculum may not be considered a component of PGC. Practically, however, it is so closely related to teaching materials that it is difficult to touch on one subject without mentioning the other. For this reason, this chapter will first discuss curricula for students of various types, and then focus on selecting and evaluating teaching materials.

2.2   Curriculum

To implement successful use of materials of foreign language acquisition, pedagogical specialists have to design and develop curricula adequate for various types of learners. Learners may be divided into roughly two groups: adult learners and young learners. These two groups may be further subdivided thusly: college students, professionals, grade school students, and weekend school students. Each of these groups has different patterns of learning and moves at a different pace; hence, each requires a different curriculum to meet its goals of learning and to optimize its learning potential. In addition to a core curriculum, many Chinese language programs at universities and colleges have also designed various kinds of extra-curricular activities to strengthen the skills acquired in regular classroom settings.

Before discussing the content of different types of curricula, it should be noted that there have been a number of questions relevant to curriculum design repeatedly debated over the last century regarding the course of teaching Chinese as FL. First, there is the procedure of acquiring the four skills (i.e. listening, speaking, reading, and writing). Some teachers prefer teaching pronunciation (i.e. Chinese initials, finals and tones) first and then reading and writing second; others suggest teaching all four skills at the same time. Naturally with this difference, curricula for elementary Chinese at different institutions vary. Teachers who prefer teaching pronunciation first often design their first-year curriculum in such a way that they spend the first two to four weeks solely on the Romanized alphabet. During this period, no Chinese character is introduced to students. After two to four weeks, when they master all Chinese sounds, students start to learn characters with the help of the Romanized alphabet. The advantage of this approach is that beginning students can focus on Chinese pronunciation at the outset and learn it well. The disadvantage is that students are later inclined to separate the sound of a character from its form and meaning. Hence, it takes more time for them to unite the three elements (i.e. sound, form, and meaning) of a word and memorize it. Also, it is more difficult to retain characters using this method as association of character and sound is interrupted by the dependence on phonetic spelling rather than graphic recognition. In comparison, teachers who prefer teaching all four skills simultaneously, introduce the Romanized alphabet along with characters. So, in the first week of classes, students learn not only tones and some initials and finals, but also a few characters, such as *nǐ hǎo* 你好 ! By the end of the first week, students are expected to be able to understand, say, read and write this most frequently used greeting in Chinese. The drawback of this approach, however, is that it may take up to six weeks for students to learn all initials and finals in Chinese as opposed to the two to four weeks required using the former method. Another possible shortcoming of this approach is that students may focus more on learning characters, leaving little time for accurate pronunciation of initials, finals, and tones. As a result, they may not master the sound system as well as those who devoted their first two to four weeks just to the sound system.

The second question often discussed at the annual meeting of Chinese language teachers associations (e.g., the CLTA and FCLTA) and considered by curriculum designers is which version of characters, (or *hànzì*), (traditional/complicated versus simplified) should be taught. In recent years, it appears that an increasing number of teachers and students are inclined to adopt simplified characters due to practical concerns from students about job opportunities and the continuing development of the economic and political status of the People's Republic of China in the world. Not since the Chinese government introduced more than 500 simplified characters in 1956 and another 853 characters in 1977, have there been more institutions outside China teaching simplified characters (cf. 语言文字规范手册, *Yǔyán Wénzì Guīfàn Shǒucè,* 1993). Statistics (Moore et al. 1992) show that in the 1960s and 1970s, almost all universities and colleges in the US, offering Chinese courses, taught traditional/complicated characters. However, by the end of the 1990s this had changed: approximately half of institutions continued to teach traditional/complicated characters while the other half taught simplified characters. The most recent survey shows that the number of institutions in the United States teaching simplified characters continues to rise and "a great majority of institutions in France teach simplified characters" (according to the president, Dr Bellassen, of French Chinese Language Teachers Association [FCLTA] 2003). A certain number of institutions continue to teach traditional/complicated characters to beginners. Their reasons for this approach can be summarized in this way: (1) traditional/complicated characters retain their original semantic and phonetic components; (2) Graduate students need learn them to read classical Chinese; and (3) traditional/complicated characters look prettier than their simplified counterparts. Out of the same concerns, institutions teaching either simplified or traditional/complicated characters often require their second- and/or third-year students to at least learn to read the version they did not learn at the elementary level. This way, even if students can write only one version of the characters, they can recognize and even read both versions.[1]

The third frequently asked question among Chinese teachers involves the Chinese Romanization system — a method of using the Roman alphabet to pronounce Chinese characters. In the history of teaching Chinese as FL, a number of Romanization systems have been developed for students whose native language uses the Roman alphabet to learn Chinese. The best-known Romanization system for quite a long time was Wade-Giles, first published in English in 1859 by Thomas Francis Wade. Similar systems were also developed for French (e.g., École français d'Extrême-Orient, or EFEO system) and for

German (e.g., the Lessing-Othmer system). However, since *pīnyīn* was developed and introduced in 1958, it has not only become the only system used in learning Chinese in Mainland China, but has also gradually taken a lead among all competing systems outside China. In 2000, the Library of Congress adopted it for indexation replacing the veteran system of Wade-Giles due to *pīnyīn*'s widespread use by the United States government for more than two decades and by the United Nations and most of the world's media. Similar to the increasing use of simplified characters in teaching Chinese outside China, *pīnyīn* has won over more and more students and teachers. Dr C. P. Chou from Princeton University argued at the annual meeting of CLTA, 2002, that to choose *pīnyīn* over other systems in the twenty-first century was as simple as it was to choose the complicated version of characters a half century ago.

As indicated above, three essential elements in Chinese language curriculum design are: (1) to choose a Romanization system, (2) to decide upon a version of characters and (3) to select a procedure in the acquisition of sounds and characters. It appears that these decisions have become easier to make in the twenty-first century than ever before. In the following three sections, I will discuss different types of curricula used by the majority of Chinese learners around the world.

2.2.1   *Curriculum for adult learners*

The term "adult learners" refers to college students or those who are 18 years or older. My experience in teaching adult learners suggests that to design and develop an adequate Chinese curriculum for this student population requires not only the understanding of why they are taking Chinese, but more importantly, how teachers can assist them in reaching their learning goals. Students have their learning goals; teachers have their teaching goals and curriculum is the means by which both students and teachers can achieve these goals. Since teachers design curriculum, they, then, become solely responsible for creating the method by which both their own goal of teaching and students' learning goal can be successfully met. In the following, I discuss two types of curricula: the Integrated Curriculum for regular college level Chinese classes and the Subject/Skill Specified Curriculum for other adult learners.

2.2.1.1   Integrated curriculum

At four-year universities and colleges outside China, most Chinese curricula have been designed to enable students to acquire four skills: listening, speaking, reading and writing (cf. McGinnis 1999, Kubler 1997a, Ross 1997 Walker 1996). In the past two decades, some pedagogy specialists (e.g. Chi 1996) have come to prefer the term "proficiency-based" to describe the nature of their curricula, some (e.g. Ning 1993) have developed what is called a performance-based curriculum, while others (e.g. Chu 1999) have suggested a learner-centered curriculum. Regardless of the terminology used to describe the curriculum, the type that focuses on these four skills in Chinese language competence is referred to as an *integrated curriculum* throughout this book. It is probably not a coincidence that the goal set by a majority of integrated curricula proponents at four-year colleges seems analogous to the proficiency levels described in ACTFL's Chinese guidelines (1986) discussed in Chapter 1.

Many institutions with a strong Chinese language program (e.g., Harvard University, Princeton University, Cambridge University, University of Paris, University of Columbia, Middlebury College, etc.) offer four-year Chinese courses: Elementary Chinese, Intermediate Chinese, Advanced Chinese, and Classical/Modern Chinese. In comparison, many state/provincial universities and small colleges are more often found to offer two to three levels of Chinese: elementary, intermediate and advanced. Although the number of levels that four-year universities and colleges offer varies, the primary goal of their curriculum stays the same, namely, to train adult students in the acquisition of the four skills of the language.

A typical integrated curriculum places an equal emphasis on listening, speaking, reading and writing. Teachers are expected to design activities and exercises for both in and out of class to enhance students' learning of these components. In this computer age, learning activities can be as creative as any work of art. Following is a generic description of some common practices in the teaching and learning of the four skills:

- Listening:
    - Teacher: help students make the distinction between Chinese sounds and/or clusters of sounds and gain comprehension of same.
    - Student: at the early stage of learning, listen to audio tapes and take advantage of CALL (Computer-Assisted Language Learning resources) by using some of the many programs available on CD; later listen to native speakers, watch and listen to TV programs.
- Speaking:
    - Teacher: speak mostly or only Chinese to students; create opportunities for students to speak Chinese.
    - Student: speak Chinese with teachers and anyone else with whom they can practice Chinese.
- Reading:
    - Teacher: provide students with sufficient materials to read, in addition to reading exercises in textbooks; help them identify discourse cues and to develop their reading tactics.
    - Student : read all genres in Chinese — letters, notes, signs, Internet text, newspaper, literature, etc.

- Writing:
  — Teacher: help students learn to write individual characters, then clusters of characters; guide them in learning the flow of Chinese sentences and various discourse cohesion/coherence strategies.
  — Student: think Chinese word structure, sentence structure and discourse structure while they write.

To illustrate this type of curriculum, sample syllabi for Levels 1–3 Chinese are provided in Appendices I to III. Compared with other types of curricula, the integrated curriculum is relatively easy to design and develop because most students start learning Chinese at the same or similar proficiency level and the teachers' goal is to develop students' four proficiency skills (see Chi 1996 and Chu 1999). Occasionally, we hear reports that students set their goals to acquire aural/oral skills at lower levels of Chinese classes and then reading and writing at higher levels (see McGinnis 1999), however, this discrepancy between the teachers' goal and students' goal does not seem to have influenced the mainstream curricula of Chinese language programs. In comparison, other types of curricula, such as those to be discussed below, are more complicated and difficult to develop, and consequently are less likely to be simulated than the integrated curriculum.

2.2.1.2   Subject/Skill-oriented curriculum

An emerging challenge to curriculum specialists of the Chinese language in recent years has been to design courses for students who seek to learn certain specific skills and/or subjects. Courses such as Business Chinese, Medical Chinese, and Legal Chinese, are *subject-specific*, and those such as Chinese Reading and Writing, Chinese for False Beginners, Survival Chinese, etc., are *skill-specific*. Whether it is subject- or skill-specific, a feasible and successful curriculum requires constant research and an understanding of the background and needs of students, as pointed out by Chen (2003).

For subject-specific students, teachers must identify at least two factors in order to develop an adequate curriculum for them: (1) students' Chinese proficiency level and (2) students' motivation for taking the course. Using Business Chinese as an example, we can expect it to attract two types of students: professional (e.g., lawyers, doctors, engineers, etc.) who take the course to enhance their career and/or professional growth, and regular college students, including both graduate and undergraduate, who are either majoring or minoring in Business and who are making an effort to increase their future job potential (cf. Wen 1999). As far as these students' Chinese competence is concerned, the difference among them is no less than that of their backgrounds and motivations. Some students have native or near-native competence in speaking because of their family background, some have lived in Chinese-speaking countries, some have taken many Chinese courses, and others have no Chinese training at all. In this case, Chen (2003) suggests three types of courses based on students' proficiency needs: Survival competence for beginners, functional competence for students at the intermediate level, and professional competence for native or near-native students. Chen (2003) also reports that though the majority of students, regardless of their background and Chinese proficiency levels, take at least one Business Chinese course in hopes of developing or improving their oral proficiency, only students at the professional competence level seek a more integrated curriculum. Once students' background and needs are identified, it is time to focus on activities related to Business Chinese. Hong (1996: 34) suggests the following list:

- Listening to radio and TV broadcasts on any business topic, including commercials, advertisements, interviews, and business news;
- Reading newspaper articles, reports, commentaries, dedicated business publications which cover international and Chinese economic development;
- Writing advertisements, business letters, memoranda, invitations, product descriptions and user's instructions;
- Speaking about business presentations, discussing real world reports, job interviews and telephone conversations, and role playing scenarios such as chairing business meetings, conducting negotiations, placing orders and planning social gatherings;
- Practicing appropriate social manners according to Chinese customs to avoid unnecessary conflict or embarrassment that might arise due to etiquette differences between the two cultures;
- Becoming familiar with the Chinese political and economics systems through reading and other media, researching topics such as finance, insurance, foreign trade and economics within the Chinese business and management environment in order to identify the most appropriate and efficient approach to accomplishing business missions.

This might be perceived as a well-thought out wish list for many teachers who have taught Business Chinese, yet no one can deny the fact that it incorporates almost all possible major activities involving the need for and use of Business Chinese. Teachers of courses at different competency levels may select and modify their list of activities (to be carried out both in and outside classrooms) based on student needs.

To reiterate the factors in the preparation for teaching Business Chinese, three areas have been identified: students' backgrounds, their needs, and course activities. The first two areas fall outside the parameters of the integrated curriculum discussed earlier. However, all three areas are essential to the design of Business Chinese courses, or more accurately, any subject-specific courses. Whether it is Business Chinese or Medical Chinese or Academic Chinese or

Chinese for Special Purposes, the difference between them is merely the subject area and the activities designed for the course. Since students' backgrounds and needs within any subject-specific course should be similar, curriculum specialists need only modify the modular curriculum of one subject-specific course by designing different activities to tailor it to another.

In comparison, the curriculum for skill-specific courses serves quite a different purpose. In courses such as Reading and Writing Chinese, students' backgrounds and needs seem similar, namely, they can understand and speak Chinese and their purpose in taking this course is to learn to read and write Chinese. In this case, class activities have to focus on honing students' reading and writing competence, (this is sometimes mistakenly considered a short version of the integrated curriculum by some teachers.) Since training students in reading and writing when they already possess listening and speaking skills is different from training students simultaneously in the four skills — listening, speaking, reading and writing — class activities should vary accordingly. Based on an empirical study of reading Chinese conducted by psychologists (e.g., Tzeng, Huang and Wang 1977; Perfetti and Zhang 1991; Inhoff and Liu 1998; Perfetti and Tan 1998; Wang, Inhoff, and Chen 1999) and by pedagogy specialists (e.g., Mickel 1991, McGinnis 1992, Emerson and Ke 1997, Lu 1997, Shen 2000), the following activities are suggested for a course in reading Chinese:

- Match the written Chinese character with illustrative pictures or drawings
- Read aloud to hear the sound of the corresponding character
- Read letters and cards to families and friends
- Read online Chinese with notations or a dictionary at the elementary level, and then read online materials without notations or a dictionary at the higher level.
- Read signs, billboards, community regulations and all other forms of public communication
- Read intensively in class (students are required to understand every part of the target material).
- Read extensively outside class (students are only required to understand the general meaning of the target material).
- Read newspaper articles and advertisements (from simple to complicated coverage).

One crucial component of reading class, as well as the closely related writing class, is developing in students an inventory of effective reading strategies. Different genres of texts may require different tactics to read and comprehend. For instance, advertisements do not use cohesive devices; professional articles often have a topic sentence for each paragraph and discourse connectors, but fewer subjective expressions than narrative stories; dialogues often omit subject, yet contain more discourse particles and repetition of expressions than other forms of texts. All these suggest that to reach the goal of a reading class, students need to learn discourse devices to enable them to read fluently and comprehend the reading materials well.

Another commonly seen skill-specific course is called *Survival Chinese*. In this class, students' backgrounds may vary but their reason for taking the course is the same: to acquire some basic survival skills in Chinese that will enable them to function on a day-to-day basis. Normally, the duration of this type of class is relatively short: one quarter/semester or a couple of months, and it primarily emphasizes speaking. Topics covered by this course may include the following:

- Greeting and parting
- Shopping
- Dining
- Traveling
- Weather and time
- Reading labels and caring for clothing and filling out enquiry forms
- Entertaining and holidays

Students taking this course are often professionals or spouses or temporary residents or new arrivals who need to learn survival skills in order to function in China. Classes of this type attract students if they are fun, practical and involve many lively activities, characteristics they share with classes designed for young learners to be discussed in the following section.

2.2.2   *Curricula for young learners*

Outside China, the second largest group of Chinese students is comprised of young people, students in Kindergarten through 12th grade (i.e. K-12) who take Chinese in regular public and weekend schools, as mentioned in Chapter 1. To help these young students learn Chinese efficiently and effectively, curriculum specialists need to design a curriculum tailored to young learners' psychological learning patterns. Unlike adults, young learners can memorize concepts quickly and apply them well in natural communication, but they lack the endurance, sustained interest, and analytical skills of adult learners (see Krashen, Scarcella and Long 1982; McLaughlin 1984; Johns 1988). These physical and psychological limitations and advantages create a challenge for curriculum designers and teachers. Although in the last decade, we have seen the rise of organizations such as the *Chinese Language Association for Secondary-Elementary Schools* (CLASS), which encourages specialists and teachers to endeavor to design innovative curricula and to implement them into classroom teaching and learning (cf. Wang 1999, Moore 1996, Wong 1996, Gallagher 1999), Chinese curricula for young learners still appear to be in the early stages of development.

According to the *Guideline for Chinese Language Teaching in Secondary Schools* published in 1990 by the National Foreign Language Center, high school students should be exposed to functions, topics, vocabulary, characters, patterns, and cultural topics. In 1998 based on the national standards for foreign languages, the ACTFL published the "five communicative goals" of Chinese Standards that define what K-12 students should know and be able to do. (See discussion in Chapter 1, section 1.5.3.) These goals emphasize the development of students' communicative competence and understanding of the Chinese culture. In other words, speaking, listening and understanding Chinese are considered top priority in the K-12 curriculum. In recent years, more and more schools and teachers have made the effort to interpret, follow and implement national standards into daily classes. Nonetheless, it is still a challenge for many K-12 and other types of Chinese teachers to create an appropriate curriculum with concomitant activities to reach those goals.

Take the Chinese classes offered at Lakeside Schools (both middle and high school) in Seattle, for example. Adam Ross, a respected teacher in the field who teaches first through third-year Chinese at Lakeside High School sets the following goals for his third-year Chinese students:

> ... to complete our work with the Chinese II curriculum in *Integrated Chinese Level I Part 2*. We will then move to more advanced materials with a focus on life and cultural values in China using *Crossing Paths* and *Shifting Tides*. In these units, students will give additional presentations on aspects of Chinese Culture. (Ross 2003)

From this description, it is clear that "culture" is the ultimate or final focus of this class. However, when discussing those goals with Adam, I found that he has been frustrated by the difficulty of getting his students to achieve higher scores on Chinese achievement tests, such as the HSK or SAT II Chinese Test, because of the discrepancy between Chinese proficiency/achievement tests emphasizing reading and writing skills and national standards they follow in the classroom emphasizing skills in speaking and understanding culture.

When comparing the Chinese classes at Lakeside School with the Northwest Chinese School (a weekend school) in the Seattle area, I find a different pattern. The Northwest Chinese School was established in the early 1990s. Since then, the school has grown rapidly. In the autumn of 2004, it offered 12 levels of Chinese classes and had over six hundred students enrolled. Among the students, more than ninety percent are heritage students; namely, their parents are native Chinese speakers but they were born in the United States, and may be able to understand simple Chinese, but cannot read or write Chinese. In recent years, the credits students earn at the Northwest Chinese School are recognized by most high schools in the local regions and more than 3,000 universities and colleges in North America and around the world. According to the principal of this school, their success has been built on the high standard and quality of their teachers and the support from students' parents. On examining their curricula, I find that teachers lay a heavy emphasis on pronunciation, characters, drill exercises, reading, and writing; in other words, the structure is similar to a traditional college curriculum. While cultural elements are also explained and practiced from time to time, it is certainly not the focus of this school's curriculum. Unlike the students from Lakeside schools, when students of Northwest school take standard proficiency tests, such as the SAT II Chinese Test, many of them receive a perfect score.

It is probably not fair or adequate to compare the curriculum and Chinese proficiency level of students from middle/high schools with the curriculum and proficiency level of heritage students from Chinese Sunday schools but looking at both their curricula, we can get a glimpse of the causal relationship between the goals set by teachers and the performance of students.

2.2.3   *Extra-curricular activities*

Most strong Chinese programs have developed some informal extra-curricular activities for students in order to reinforce and expand upon what they cover in the classroom. Such activities include, but are not limited to, individual conferences, email groups, chat rooms, Chinese tables/corners, calligraphy clubs, painting clubs, cooking clubs, movie clubs, and so on. These informal activities not only help students strengthen their speaking, listening, reading and writing skills, but also stimulate their interest in Chinese language and culture.

The simplest and easiest activity is the individual conference, which allows teachers and students to meet one-on-one to discuss students' problems and progress outside scheduled class. In the earlier stages of students' learning, this kind of conference gives students individual private tutorial time with their teacher to practice pronunciation. A student may either record his/her voice when reading a text or a dialogue prior to the meeting. During the meeting, a teacher can go over the recording with the student and help the student recognize and understand his/her mistakes so that s/he will pay extra attention to them in the future. At the intermediate and advanced level of learning, an individual conference may focus on assessing and improving student performance in skill areas such as reading and writing. Teachers interested in the purpose, content and procedures of individual conference may consult with Liang (2004) and Zhang (1984).

Email groups and chat rooms are probably the most convenient activity for students, especially adult students, because of the flexibility and accessibility afforded by the easy access to the computer and Internet. Reading and writing Chinese on the Internet used to be unthinkable in the Western world because computer and keyboard were not designed for input of logographic characters but now, thanks to the development of a variety of computer software and operating systems, it has become as accessible and convenient as reading and writing English. Students can use an email group/list and chat room to practice their use of *pīnyīn* or other Romanized Chinese alphabets, and reading and writing Chinese characters (cf. Xie's website: http://www.csulb.edu/~txie/online.htm).

Chinese tables are often found in the cafeterias or dining halls of universities and colleges. The term refers to a group of students who occupy a special table where they speak/practice Chinese while they eat. Students, either native Chinese or not, may participate. Discussions are freewheeling: they can discuss topics related to their daily life or current issues of social, economic, or political concerns. The purpose of this activity is simply to encourage natural conversation in Chinese and to give students the practice they need to increase their learning and speaking competence.

Clubs for students with special interests are another means of enhancing Chinese competence. Calligraphy clubs help students practice writing characters; painting clubs attract students interested in Chinese art; cooking clubs draw students from different backgrounds and of different interests together to prepare and eat Chinese cuisine; and movie clubs help students further their listening comprehension and understanding of Chinese history, people and culture. These clubs, meeting weekly or monthly, can directly or indirectly enhance students' interest in and ease with the Chinese language.

Clearly, all extra-curricular activities are helpful, but not all Chinese language programs can offer all of those discussed above. In many schools, these activities are considered, after all, "extra," and they are not part of the "core" curriculum. Despite the truth of this, we encourage all Chinese programs to make the effort to institute and incorporate as many extra-curricular activities as possible into their curriculum.

2.3   Teaching Materials

Teaching materials are an indispensable component in the development of an adequate curriculum. Chinese teaching materials designed expressly for non-native learners can be traced back to the fourteenth century. *Lǎo Qǐdà* and *Piáo Tóngshì* are believed to be the earliest Chinese instructional materials produced during the fourteenth century for Korean students (Wadley 1987). The format of these teaching materials is simple: Chinese texts with notation of Korean pronunciation and translation, but effective for Korean students in learning Chinese. Both textbooks were used for nearly five centuries in Korea. When European missionaries of different religions arrived in China during the sixteenth to nineteenth centuries, there arose an urgent need to learn the language of this unknown land. Missionaries composed numerous Chinese textbooks and dictionaries (e.g. Matteo Ricci 1580, João Rodriguez 1604, Francisco Varo 1703, Joseph de Prémare 1831) that were a reflection of their perception and interpretation of the Chinese language and culture filtered through their linguistic knowledge of Latin (see Breitenbach 2003). Most of these teaching materials used the Latin grammatical system to illustrate types of words and structures in Chinese. These works took the form of dictionaries with word-by-word glossaries and textbooks with vocabulary, conversational texts and translations into French, English, German, Spanish, Portuguese, Russian, and other Western languages (cf. Matteo Ricci 1580, João Rodriguez 1604, Francisco Varo 1703, Joseph de Prémare 1831, Giles 1872, Wade and Hillier 1886, Gibson 1887). According to the current standards for Chinese language acquisition, these instructional materials were not effective in either teaching or learning. However, back then, they were certainly useful for students who were seriously committed to learning Chinese. After the turn of the century and with the onset of the New Cultural Movement (May Fourth Movement in 1919), teaching materials for both native and non-native Chinese students began to focus primarily on colloquial Chinese (白话, *báihuà*, cf. Baller 1912; Ratay 1927; Wang 1930; Ware 1939a, 1939b; CCCF 1943, Chao 1948a and 1948b), a significant change from, and some might say improvement over, the works of the missionaries. These earlier colloquial teaching materials laid a solid foundation for the future pedagogy of the Chinese language.

In the last several decades, numerous new Chinese textbooks and accompanying materials in various languages have been published both inside and outside China. Some of these materials have been used by generations of students, whereas others have not endured the test of time. The most popular textbooks in the United States, during the second half of the twentieth century, were the *Chinese Reader* series by John DeFrancis (1963, 1964, 1968). Europe and other parts of the world, by comparison, preferred *Practical Chinese Reader* (PCR) by Liú Xún et al. (1981). published in Beijing, China. PCR was recently revised to remain competitive in today's greatly enlarged field.

Here at the onset of the twenty-first century, a few more textbooks have emerged and gained regional popularity: *Integrated Chinese* by Ted Yao et al. (2005 [1997]) published in the United States, and *Methode d'Intiation à la langue et à l'ecriture chinoises*, also known as *Zì*, by Joël Bellassen (1997) published both in France and China, to name just two. In addition to the traditional format of textbooks, more and more audio, video, Internet materials and computer learning tools have become available to teachers and students in recent years. With new teaching materials added to the inventory every day, it becomes a challenge for most teachers to determine and choose what materials to use and when to use them. This situation concurs with the observation and remarks of Dr Timothy Light, former president of the Chinese Language Teachers Association, who said: "I think there are sufficient good teaching materials available to Chinese teachers. The problem is that not all teachers know how to choose and use them."

To meet this challenge, pedagogy specialists have initiated an open forum for the discussion of criteria used in evaluating Chinese teaching materials. Some (e.g. Dew 1997) call teachers' attention to the frequency factor of grammatical elements; some (e.g. Teng 1997, 1998) suggest that pedagogical grammar be autonomous and accessible; some (e.g. Xing 1998, 2000) stress discourse and pragmatic factors in teaching and learning Chinese. Based on these studies, the following two sections present a working model to define and identify teaching materials, or rather grammatical elements, for teachers of Chinese as FL.

2.3.1   Primary elements

Among Chinese teaching materials, some elements may be considered primary, while others may be considered secondary.[2] This book defines a primary grammatical element as:

> One that must be taught by teachers and learned by students for communication purposes, and without which certain ideas or situations cannot be expressed successfully. Conversely, a secondary grammatical element is defined thusly: one that does not have to be the focus of teaching either because students' language competence will not be affected by not learning these elements or because students can learn these elements by themselves based on knowledge of their native language or other languages.

These definitions of primary and secondary elements of PGC imply that the frequency or communicative need of a given grammatical element helps determine its status.

Using the definition given above, we may consider the following categories as primary elements of PGC:

- Contextual sentential markers (e.g., 了 *le,* 吗 *ma,* 吧 *ba,* 呀 *ya*, etc.)
- Special constructions (e.g., the 把 *bǎ* construction, the causative construction, the 被 *bèi* construction, etc.)
- Complements (e.g., resultative, potential, etc.)
- Discourse connectors (e.g., 就 *jiù,* 才 *cái*, etc.)
- Discourse devices (e.g., emphasis, contrast, etc.)
- Word order alternatives

Notice that contextual sentential markers are first on the list. This is because we need them in all means of communication: speaking, reading, writing and listening. One should realize that as soon as we open our mouths or listen to people chatting, we use or hear those markers. Also, whether you read a dialogue in a textbook or sit in a classroom, you will see or hear those markers. Without contextual sentential markers, it can be difficult to express, for instance, the idea of change in situation, which is simply expressed by 了 (*le*) as illustrated in (2.1), or the various types of opinions or attitudes expressed by 吗 (*ma*), 呢 (*ne*), 吧 (*ba*), as illustrated in (2.2)–(2.4).

(2.1)   我们已经都吃了饭了。
       wǒmen yǐjīng dōu chīle fàn le.
       "We have already had our meal."
       (Implication: We are not hungry right now.)

(2.2) 别这样做嗎。
    bié zhèi yàng zuò ma.
    "Please don't do that."
    (Implication: The speaker tries to soften his/her critical opinion of the listener's action.)

(2.3) 你怎么会这样做呢?
    nǐ zeme huì zhè yàng zuò ne?
    "How could you do that?"
    (Implication: The speaker expresses his/her disbelief or consternation at what the listener has done.)

(2.4) 我们去吃饭吧。
    wǒmen qù chīfàn ba.
    "Let's go to eat."
    (Implication: The speaker expresses his/her opinion as a suggestion, not as an order.)

Similarly, if one wants to express a "disposal" action as exemplified in (2.5), s/he has to use the 把 *bǎ* construction. Or if one wants to place more emphasis on the recipient of an action than on the doer of the action, a topic comment construction or a 被 *bèi* construction should be used, as shown in (2.6)–(2.7).

(2.5) 他把书都放在桌子上了。
    tā bǎ shū dōu fàng zài zhuōzi shàng le.
    "He has put all of the books on the table."

(2.6) 这件事儿已经讨论过了。
    zhèi jiàn shìr yǐjīng tǎolùn guò le
    "This issue has already been discussed."

(2.7) 云南大学被评为全国的重点院校之一。
    Yúnnán dàxué bèi píng wéi quánguó de zhòngdiǎn yuànxiào zhīyī.
    "Yunnan University has been accredited as one of the key institutions in China."

Because of the importance and unique function of these special constructions in communication (please note that every single Chinese grammar book and numerous journal articles have discussed these constructions), they should be considered primary elements and be systematically explained in PGC.

It is well known that complements in Chinese grammar do not exist in English, German, French, or Spanish. When a student wants to describe a situation, such as "Someone had walked (for a long time), and (as a result) s/he became tired," one should use the construction in (2.8) or in (2.9).

(2.8) 他　走　路　走　累　了。
Tā　zǒu　lù　zǒu　lèi　le
(lit.) he walk road walk tired [aspect]

(2.9) 他　走　路　走　得　很　累。
Tā　zǒu　lù　zǒu　de　hěn　lèi
(lit.) he walk road walk [result] very |tired

English does not have counterparts to the constructions in (2.8)–(2.9). In fact, English may not have any of the various types of Chinese complements: resultative complements as in (2.8)–(2.9), directional complements as in (2.10)–(2.11), potential complements as in (2.12)–(2.13), descriptive complements as in (2.14)–(2.15), and countable complements as in (12.6)–(2.17) (cf. Liu 2002).

(2.10) 老师从教室走出来。
lǎoshī cóng jiàoshī zǒu chūlái.
"The teacher walked out of the classroom."

(2.11) 下课以后，学生们都走下楼来。
xiàkè yǐhòu, xuéshēngmen dōu zǒu xià lóu lái.
"After class, students walked downstairs."

(2.12) 老师的话他听不懂。
lǎoshī de huà tā tīng bù dǒng.
"He cannot understand what the teacher said."

(2.13) 今年夏天这篇文章写不完了。
jīnnián xiàtiān zhèi piān wénzhāng xiě bù wán le.
"This article cannot be finished this summer."

(2.14) 那个孩子长得像他父亲。
nà ge háizi zhǎng de xiàng tā fùqin.
"That child has grown to look like his father."

(2.15) 他说汉语说得很流利。
tā shuō hànyǔ shuō de hěn liúlì.
"He speaks Chinese fluently."

(2.16) 他吃药吃了三年了。
tā chī yào chī le sān nián le.
"He has been taking the medication for three years."

(2.17) 老师点<u>了一下头</u>。

　　　　lǎoshī diǎn <u>le yíxià tóu.</u>

　　　　"The teacher nodded his head a little bit."

Notice that the English translations of sentences (2.8)–(2.17) either have quite different structures from their Chinese counterparts, or that some parts of these English sentences play different grammatical roles than their Chinese counterparts. What makes Chinese complements more significant in PGC is that they are frequently used in both spoken and written texts whereas in English a complement is not considered salient by teachers, grammarians, or linguists alike.[3] The combination of the absence of complements in the students' native language and the common use of complements in Chinese communication makes them primary elements in PGC. It is this same combination that makes complements one of the most difficult yet most crucial Chinese grammatical elements to learn (cf. Liu 1998); without mastering this grammatical element, students' Chinese competence cannot progress beyond a low level.

Discourse connectors constitute another major part of PGC. This category includes such words as conjunctions (e.g. *hé* 和 "and", *dànshì* 但是 "but", *yě* 也 "also") and discourse adverbs (e.g. *nàme* 那么 "in that case", *zhèiyàng* 这样 "in this case", *yīncǐ* 因此 "therefore"). The importance of their role in communication can be seen from the descriptive term "discourse connector." Without connectors, it can be difficult to compose a coherent paragraph or even speak coherently. If students do not know them, they will become mired at the sentence level and most likely be unable to move beyond simple sentence constructions. Some of the conjunctions (e.g. *búdàn* 不但 … *érqiě* 而且　"not only … but also", *zhǐshì* 只是 "only because") are easy for students to learn because they are equivalent to discourse connectors in their native language (e.g. "*not only … but also*" in English, "*nicht nur …, aber auch*" in German and "*non seulement …, mais également*" in French), but, not surprisingly, many of them are not. Take *jiù* (就, "just, only"), one of the connectors most frequently used by native Chinese speakers, for example. Unless this grammatical element is explicitly implemented in the curriculum, non-native speakers find it unnatural and avoid using it. Furthermore, *jiù* has many different functions in discourse as illustrated in (2.18), and, in Chinese, many situations can be expressed only by using *jiù*. Thus, we have to consider this kind of discourse connector as a primary element in PGC.

(2.18) [夫妻的一段对话 "A dialogue between a husband and a wife]

　　太太：　　天快亮了。我起床**就**给你做早点。

　　　　　　*tiān kuài liàng le. wǒ qǐchuáng **jiù** gěi nǐ zuò zǎo diǎn.*

　　Wife:　　"It's almost daybreak. As soon as I get up, I will prepare breakfast for you."

先生：　嗯，今天我得早点上班，所以随便吃点**就**走。

　　　　*en, jīntiān wǒ de zǎodiǎn shàng bān, suǒyǐ suíbiàn chī diǎn **jiù** zǒu.*

Husband: "Okay, I have to go to work early today, so I will quickly eat something and go."

太太：　你**就**这么对待一天最重要的一顿饭吗？

　　　　*nǐ **jiù** zheme duìdài yi tiān zuì zhòngyào de yídùn fàn ma?*

Wife:　"How can you be so casual about the most important meal of a day?"

先生：　我**就**是不想吃，你**就**别啰嗦了。

　　　　*wǒ **jiù**shi bù xiǎng chī, nǐ **jiù** bié luōsuō le.*

Husband: "I just don't want to eat. Please stop wagging your tongue."

太太：　你这人怎么说不吃**就**不吃了呢？

　　　　*nǐ zhèi rén zěnme shuō bù chī **jiù** bù chī le ne?*

Wife:　"How can you be so stubborn about not eating?"

先生：　不吃**就**是不吃，你怎么没完没了？

　　　　*bù chī **jiù**shì bù chī, nǐ zěnme méiwán méiliǎo?*

Husband: "'Do not want to eat' simply means 'not eat'. Can't you stop?"

太太：　我好心好意，你**就**这样对待我？

　　　　*wǒ hǎoxīnhǎoyì, nǐ **jiù** zhèiyàng duìdài wǒ?*

Wife:　"I have all the good intentions. How can you treat me like that?"

先生：　好好，**就**算我不好，行了吧? **就**这么点事，　何必呢？

　　　　*hǎohǎo, **jiù** suàn wǒ bùhǎo, xíng le ba? **jiù** zhème diǎn shì, hébì ne?*

Husband: "Okay, Okay. It's my fault, okay? Why are you making a fuss over such a trifling matter?"

太太：　你们男人，**就**是没有一个好东西！

　　　　*nǐmen nánrén, **jiù**shì méiyǒu yíge hǎo dōngxi!*

Wife:　"You men are all alike. There's not a single decent one among you!"

先生：　哎？！**就**事论**就**走了。]

　　　　*ai?! **jiù**shì lùnshì, bié xiāchě! [shuō wán jiù zǒu le.]*

Husband: "Oh?! Let's stick to the matter at hand, don't get off the subject! [After saying this, he leaves.]"

太太：　你**就**别再回来！

　　　　*nǐ **jiù** bié zài huílai!*

Wife:　"Don't come back again!"

Although to some native speakers, some of the 就 (*jiù*) usages may not be as natural as others in the dialogue given above, they are all possible in the given discourse. Astute readers may realize that the English translations of those 就 (*jiù*) in (2.18) do not necessarily completely reflect their original Chinese meanings. Since the functions of 就 are so varied, it is difficult even for native speakers to clearly categorize them (Lü 1980), not to mention foreign language learners. Yet native speakers do not seem to have problems using them in all forms of communication. This situation will undoubtedly cause problems for PGC.

It should be pointed out that *jiù* represents only one type of discourse connector in Chinese. Many other types should also be considered primary elements in a PGC. Discourse connectors, such as *suīrán* 虽然 "although" ... *dànshì* 但是 "but", *yī* 一 ... *jiù* 就 ... "as soon as", *yīnwèi* 因为 "because" ..., *suǒyǐ* 所以 "therefore" ..., etc., have one thing in common: they all come in pairs to make up complex sentences expressing a logical and coherent situation or idea. This kind of grammatical structure is not as common in English as in Chinese. Among Chinese discourse connectors, 73 percent of them can be used in pairs (cf. Liu 1983: 184–5), whereas in English, only a few of them can be paired up and most English connectors are used individually in discourse (cf. Quirk et al. 1985, Zhang 1983, Leech and Svartvik 1994). Due to this difference and the importance of discourse connectors in communication, we must consider them primary elements in pedagogical grammar.

Discourse devices are similar to discourse connectors in that both are used to build a frame of discourse that describes a complicated yet coherent idea or situation. They differ, however, in that discourse devices may not require the use of a specific word; instead, they may employ different sentence patterns, stress or word order to express a certain situation or idea. For instance, when someone wants to emphasize something, s/he has a choice of a number of discourse devices to achieve this: (1) using different intonation as in (2.19); (2) placing an emphasized element at the beginning of the sentence as in (2.20); and (3) using emphatic particles (e.g. *lián* 连 "even" ... *dōu* 都 "all", *shènzhì* 甚至 "even") as in (2.21).

(2.19) 他就喜欢这个人。 (With high pitch on "this person")
   tā jiù xǐhuān zhèige rén.
   "He just likes **this person**."
   (Implication: he does not like anybody else.)

(2.20) 这个人，他就喜欢。
   zhèige rén, tā jiù xǐhuān.
   "He **just likes** this person."
   (Implication: he does not care what people say about the person.)

(2.20) 他连这个人都喜欢。
   tā lián zhèige rén dōu xǐhuān.
   "He even likes this person."
   (Implication: he is not choosy about whom he likes.)

In all three of the sentences above, 这个人 *zhèi ge rén* "this person" is emphasized, but each sentence uses a different discourse device to convey a different implication. Language students should learn these devices and the differences between them in order to communicate effectively. In some ways, this is not that dissimilar to English where word order and stress can change, subtly or not so subtly, the meaning of a sentence.

The last category in the list of primary elements of PGC is word order alternatives. This category may be considered a type of discourse device. It is listed as a separate category here because I believe it to be one of the most important grammatical elements in PGC. I suggest that students learn the basic word order of Chinese (i.e. Subject + Verb + Object) and its major discourse function on the first day of their language class and gradually develop and expand their knowledge and understanding of the many other alternative orders, the use of which separates the non-native from the native or native-like speaker. Since approximately 90 percent of Chinese sentences in modern written texts use the basic word order and the remaining 10 percent (including the OSV construction, the topic comment construction, the so-called passive construction, etc) use other word orders (Xing 1993: 15–16), students must learn how to use constructions such as those in (2.22)–(2.24) to express complicated coherent discourse ideas as their proficiency level rises. Most importantly, they should know when to use the basic word order and when to use those alternative orders.

(2.22) <u>饭</u>都吃完了。
      <u>fàn</u> dōu chīwán le.
      "The food is all eaten."

(2.23) 他<u>什么人</u>都喜欢。
      tā <u>shénme rén</u> dōu xǐhuān.
      "He likes everybody."

(2.24) <u>这种人</u>就得给他一点颜色看看。
      <u>zhèizhǒng rén</u> jiù de gěi tā yìdiǎn yánsè kànkan.
      "This kind of person should be taught some lessons."

Notice that the patients or receivers of the action of the verb in (2.22)–(2.24) are all located in the preverbal position, not in the post-verbal position as in the basic word order of Chinese. This is because in these sentences the receivers, i.e. the food, everybody, this kind of person, of the action are stressed elements. Since these types of constructions are commonly used in communication and are uniquely structured in Chinese, they must be included in PGC.

It has become apparent that all primary elements in pedagogical grammar discussed so far share the following properties: they are (1) commonly used in communication; (2) uniquely structured in Chinese and/or non-existent in the students' native language; and (3) functionally important in communication. These characteristics may be further summarized into three words: commonality, uniqueness, and importance. We may conclude that if a grammatical element has all three of these properties, it can be considered a primary element of PGC. Since the list of primary elements at the beginning of this section is not intended to be exhaustive, teachers may use these three properties as criteria in evaluating other grammatical elements and determining whether they should be considered primary in teaching/learning and curriculum design.

2.3.2 *Secondary elements*

Based on our understanding of primary elements of PGC, we can use the following more explicit definition for secondary elements:

> If a grammatical element does not have all three of the properties of primary elements of pedagogical grammar (i.e. commonality, uniqueness, and importance) then it is a secondary or non-primary element of Chinese pedagogical grammar.

Using this definition, we may consider the following list of grammatical elements secondary or non-primary:

Secondary Elements:
- Parts of speech (e.g., noun, verb, adjective, adverb, etc.)
- Meaning of words
- Fixed expressions (e.g., idioms, proverbs, etc.)
- Sentence structures (e.g., subject + verb + object)

Many teachers like to assign "parts of speech" to words when explaining their meaning, especially teachers in China. They do not only talk about parts of speech, but also ask students questions such as 这是什么词? (*Zhèi shì shénme cí?* "What is the part of speech of this word?"). Unless a student asks specifically for this clarification, it is, in my view, a waste of students' time; students do not need to know the part of speech to be able to use the word in context or communication. Evidence supporting this point of view can be found not only in first language acquisition, but also in foreign/second language acquisition (Dulay and Burt 1974, Eckman and Hastings 1977, Wells 1985, Rutherford 1987, Bialystok 1991, Beck 1998). As a matter of fact, we all know this from our own experience with learning our first language: When children first acquire the use of a word, they do not learn its part of speech. Since part of speech is not commonly mentioned or used in communication, it is not an important or *primary* element of pedagogical grammar or communicative competence. Furthermore, since parts of speech are used to describe the grammatical property of words and are used in all grammar books and dictionaries of all languages, it is not unique to Chinese either. All these properties lead to the conclusion that the status of parts of speech is secondary in pedagogical grammar of Chinese and possibly across the language continuum.

Another example of a secondary element of PGC is of semantics: the meaning of words. We often hear teachers asking students this question: "这个词 (or 字) 是什么意思? *Zhèi ge cí/zì shì shénme yìsi?*" ("What does this word mean?" or "What is the meaning of this word?"). Upon hearing this question, one can envision a few scenarios: (1) Students know the answer and respond to the question in Chinese. (2) Students know the answer and respond to the question in English. (3) Students do not know the answer so the teacher has to explain the meaning of the word in question. Let us examine the three scenarios in more detail. Among these three scenarios, the first one probably pleases the teacher most and the third one the least. However, none of the scenarios indicates that the given question is useful in helping students' learning. If students know the meaning of the word, then there is no need to spend classroom time explaining it. If students, especially intermediate and advanced students, do not know the meaning, the teacher's explanation may not help them remember the meaning of the word faster or better than if they figure it out themselves, because the definition can "go in one ear and out the other." Even if the teacher's explanation turns out to be helpful to some students, it may not be wise for teachers to spend a lot of classroom time on it. Therefore, neither the question nor the explanation has significant pedagogical implications. Certainly, this does not mean that students should not learn the meaning of words. There is no doubt that students should learn the meaning of words, because words are the basic units of the language. The issue is how words can be learned most efficiently and whether the meaning of words should be considered a primary element of pedagogical grammar. I suggest that students gradually acquire the habit of learning word meanings on their own (e.g., by looking them up in dictionaries or textbooks, or figuring them out based on context) and teachers only check to see whether students know how to use those words in context or communication and not by isolated, non-contextual definition. If students cannot use words correctly, teachers should then demonstrate their functions in discourse. Since the meanings of words in Chinese, especially those of concrete words (e.g., those expressing time, place, person, etc.) can be straightforward, the need to explain them either in grammar books or in classrooms becomes less than primary.

Fixed expressions, such as idiomatic or habitual expressions, should also be considered secondary in pedagogical grammar. The major reason for this classification is that the use of these expressions is not fundamental in communication; rather it is the icing on the cake (i.e., 锦上添花 *jǐnshàng tiān huā*). For example, one does not have to use the idiomatic expression 锦上添花 to express the idea of "make things even better by adding something extra." One can simply say "好上加好 *hǎo shàng jiā hǎo*" or "已经很好了, 还可以更好 *yǐjīng hěn hǎo le, hái kěyǐ gèng hǎo*." As a result, we rarely see or hear students using idiomatic or fixed expressions, no matter how many they have learned from class or their textbooks. Furthermore, since most fixed expressions have a unique structure and discourse meaning, students normally have to memorize each expression as a new vocabulary item. Naturally, if students know how to express an idea in simple and plain Chinese, they are unlikely to make the extra effort to dig into their memory for a complicated idiomatic expression unless their Chinese has reached a level that permits them to use idiomatic expressions in a native-like way. We know from our teaching experience that even when students' Chinese competence reaches the advanced level, they often make funny mistakes (such as those in [2.25)] when using idiomatic expressions).[4]

(2.25)a. 老师，您真不简单，您的学生<u>无孔不入</u>。[比较： "桃李满天下"]

lǎoshī, nín zhēn bù jiǎndān, nín de xuésheng wúkǒngbúrù. [cf. *táolǐ mǎn tiānxià*]

"Teacher, you are really something! You have students all over the world."

(Note: Both 无孔不入 *wúkǒngbúrù* and 桃李满天下 *táolǐ mǎn tiānxià* can mean "students are found everywhere." However, the first one has negative connotation and the second one does not.)

b. 我们班的同学都是<u>郎才女貌</u>。[比较： "长得都不错"]

wǒmen bān de tóngxué dōu shì lángcáinǚmào. [cf. *zhǎng de dōu búcuò*]

"The guys in our class are all talented and the girls are all beautiful." (Note: "郎才女貌" is normally used to describe an ideal couple: the husband has talent and the wife has beauty.)

c. 老师每天都<u>数一数二</u>。 [比较： "点名"]

lǎoshī měitiān dōu shǔyīshuér. [cf. *diǎnmíng*]

"Our teacher calls students' names every day."

(Note: "数一数二" is often used to convey the idea of "top number X" as in "The University of Michigan is often ranked topic 5 among the state universities in the United States."

Most grammar books discuss types of sentence structures that exist in Chinese and many Chinese teachers patiently explain various types of constructions by using such terminology as subject, predicate, object, complement, etc., in classroom teaching. I suggest that the explanation of sentence structure, like the categorization of words by part of speech, should be kept to a minimum. This is partly because the explanation of Chinese sentence structure itself does not help students improve their communicative competence, and partly because the functions of different constructions are more important than the structures of sentences themselves. From the study of both first and foreign/second language acquisition (Schmidt and McCreary 1977, Bley-Vroman 1988, Bialystok 1991), we know that students do not need to know which part is the subject and which is the object when they communicate, nor do they need to know the name of the element after *bèi* in the so-called passive construction or after *lián* in the emphatic construction introduced by "*lián ... dōu/yě*" (e.g. 他连星期天都上班. *Tā lián xīngqī tiān dōu shàngbān. Even on Sunday he has to go to work.*). What they need to know, though, is the context and rationale of using the passive construction and the emphatic construction. In the following chapters, discussion will turn to the methodology of teaching various types of primary grammatical elements of PGC. Since different grammatical elements have different functions in communication or discourse, PGC should emphasize function, not structure. If students only learn how to change an active construction into the passive mood (e.g., by moving the object into the subject position and moving the subject after *bèi* before the verb) without knowing when and why passive constructions are used, the learning becomes useless and, in teaching any language, usefulness is a key to achieving communicative competency.

So far, I have discussed both primary and secondary elements of PGC. The distinction between primary and secondary elements is extremely important in teaching Chinese as FL and even more important in defining the role in pedagogical grammar for Chinese. It has been suggested that language practitioners and pedagogy specialists should all make such a distinction to avoid unnecessary work in teaching and learning. It should also be pointed out that the lists of both primary and secondary elements given earlier are not meant to be exhaustive. Using the suggested definitions of those two types of elements, one should be able to evaluate all grammatical elements and determine their primary or secondary importance in PGC and, in turn, use this information to shape, focus and streamline lesson plans.

2.4   Stratification of Pedagogical Grammar of Chinese

With the guidelines explicitly explained in the preceding sections, teachers are expected to teach most, if not all, of the primary elements of PGC within a three-year or four-year Chinese language program. To many teachers and textbook compilers, what becomes a challenge, then, is to determine what elements should be covered during first-year Chinese courses and what should be covered in subsequent years. Furthermore, teachers and curriculum designers are often uncertain about how much of a given element should be taught at each level.

One way to identify pedagogical grammar to be learned by students of different levels is to classify grammatical elements into three levels: elementary, intermediate and advanced, based on the frequency of their occurrence in communication and on their degree of difficulty of acquisition. As far as frequency of grammatical elements is concerned, one can simply consult with the frequency count of words (see 现代汉语常用字频度统计, *Xiàndài hànyǔ chángyòng zì píndù tǒngjì,* by GYWGWH 1989). To judge the difficulty of grammatical elements in acquisition, however, teachers have to rely on their teaching experience, textbooks or guidelines (e.g. the ACTFL profiency guidelines 1996).

2.4.1   Elementary materials

Most current Chinese textbooks for elementary Chinese include the following grammatical elements:

- Tones and tone change (e.g. tone sandhi)
- Initials and finals

- Stroke order for characters
- Character structure (e.g. semantic vs. phonetic components)
- Numerical expressions
- Time expressions
- Interrogative constructions (e.g., V-not-V, wh-questions)
- Basic word order
- Simple topic-comment construction
- Noun phrases (e.g., measure words and the possessive marker)
- Modal auxiliaries
- Compounding and reduplication
- Simple complements
- Simple comparative constructions
- Basic usage of aspect markers (e.g., *le* 了, *zhe* 着, *guo* 过)
- Simple adverbs and conjunctions
- Some sentential particles (e.g., *ba* 吧, *ne* 呢, *ma* 吗)

All these grammatical elements have a very high frequency rate on account of their common occurrence in natural communication and their discourse pragmatic functions are straightforward. Students should be able to learn them conceptually without much difficulty, although to be able to use them spontaneously may still take some time. There are also grammatical elements which are high on frequency account, but have complicated discourse pragmatic functions, such as the *bǎ* construction. One question often asked in the past is whether the *bǎ* (把) construction should be taught to first-year students. If the answer is "no," as in the case of the *Practical Chinese Reader*, students very soon find themselves "speechless" or wrong when they need to express situations involving the action of "disposal" — how a person is handled, manipulated, or dealt with; how something is disposed of; or how an affair is conducted (see Li and Thompson 1981: 468). If the answer is "yes," teachers, then, have to take at least an hour or two to explain how, when and why the *bǎ* (把) construction is used in discourse, not to mention the time that students need to digest and practice the construction. Most students at the elementary level do not seem to enjoy any grammar lectures. They do better practicing how to use certain grammatical elements and simple patterns. The solution to this dilemma is in personal choice: some teachers and textbooks choose to include the *bǎ* (把) construction in their first-year Chinese curriculum; others leave it until second-year Chinese. A third group of teachers prefers to include the *bǎ* (把) construction in first-year lessons, but keeps its explanation to a minimum, so that students only learn the one function of the construction illustrated in their textbook. Then, when they are introduced to the other *bǎ* (把) functions later on in their studies, they are at least familiar with it.

Just as grammatical elements should not be taught in isolation, so content areas have to be specified so students learn how to use grammatical elements in real communicative situations; real communicative situations should be used whenever possible. In elementary Chinese textbooks, the following conversation topics are often included (cf. Yao et al. 1997):

- Greetings
- Family
- Dates and time
- Hobbies
- Visiting friends
- Making appointments
- Studying Chinese
- School life
- Shopping
- Talking about the weather
- Transportation
- Dining
- At the library
- Asking directions
- Birthday party
- Seeing a doctor
- Dating
- Renting an apartment
- Post office
- Sports
- Travel
- Hometown
- At the airport

These topics cover a wide range of daily survival conversations likely to be necessary for successful communication among students and non-professionals and given adequate learning opportunities, they are, in my view, sufficient to enable students to learn the grammatical elements listed earlier. Sometimes, students appear so overwhelmed with the sheer amount of content material that they cannot fully digest or master the use of one grammatical element in real communicative situations before the class moves on to another.

2.4.2 *Intermediate materials*

At the intermediate level, many of the elements identified and taught as elementary Chinese grammar should be reviewed and taught again with some variation so that newly introduced elements can build upon the previously learned ones. One major difference between the elementary and secondary level of grammar lies in the complexity of a given grammatical element. Since most of the grammatical elements have more than one function in discourse, it is easier for both teachers to teach and students to learn simpler functions at the elementary level and incrementally more complicated functions at the higher levels. This is why the word "simple" has been taken out of the list of intermediate grammar points below:

- Word order (e.g., basic vs. alternative)
- Topic-comment construction
- Complex sentences
- Modal auxiliaries
- Various types of complements
- Comparative constructions
- Aspect markers (e.g., *le* 了)
- Discourse connectors (e.g., *cái* 才, *jiù* 就, *yàobùrán* 要不然)
- Sentential particles (e.g., *ba* 吧, *ne* 呢, *ma* 吗)
- Special constructions (e.g., the *bǎ* 把 construction, the *bèi* 被 construction)
- Discourse devices (e.g., contrast, emphasis, cohesion)

Second-year Chinese grammar inevitably focuses on sentences and their usage in paragraph discourse: a logical progression from first-year grammar's emphasis on words and their functions. Each of the grammatical elements listed above should be learned in a cumulative manner, as suggested by Teng (1997), Liu (1998) and Xing (2003); i.e. grammatical elements should be explained and practiced in order from simple brief functions to increasingly more complicated functions concomitant with the progression of students' proficiency level.

Along with intermediate grammatical elements, content material in intermediate Chinese textbooks ranges from discussing how to choose a major to a variety of topics beyond survival needs. Chou et al. *Intermediate Reader of Modern Chinese* (1992) include the following lessons for second-year Chinese students:

- A Letter to Parents (i.e. Beginning of a new semester)
- Father's Response
- Telephone
- Job application
- Letter I: Rape and Robbery
- Letter II: Live Together
- Letter III: Abortion and Drug
- Letter IV: Love and Marriage
- Letter V: Generation Gap and Women's Right
- Discussion of the Five Letters
- Go to China
- Concerns of Chinese Youth
- China's Population
- Beijing, Shanghai, and Taipei

- Confucius
- Great Wall and Great Canal
- Hú Shìh
- Lǔ Xùn
- Student Movements and the Cultural Revolution
- How to Translate Foreign Names into Chinese
- War in Middle East

Professor Chou's *Intermediate Reader* is probably among the first group of textbooks emphasizing subject matters described in the lessons. In comparison, traditional textbooks, such as DeFrancis' *Intermediate Reader* or *Intermediate Chinese*, emphasizes more the use of vocabulary (e.g. frequency) and grammar than interesting topics when compiling the textbooks. Evidently, students have to learn vocabulary and grammar in order to advance their communicative competence. However, without interesting subjects or topics to talk about, language class may become boring and monotonous. Unfortunately, there are not many Chinese textbooks that satisfy both needs.

2.4.3   *Advanced materials*

At the advanced level, grammatical study most likely centers on discourse structures, production of coherent paragraphs and different styles of speech/writing, even though grammatical elements continue to be learned in a cumulative way. In other words, all grammatical elements listed for the intermediate level should be reiterated in textbook lessons for advanced Chinese. Feng (2003a) has advocated for years the importance of teaching written grammar at the advanced/superior level, warning language practitioners that without it, students will never be able to write formal Chinese. Due to my limited knowledge and experience with teaching Chinese at the superior level, this book will not discuss materials or methodology relevant to that level. Nonetheless, my teaching experience from the elementary to the advanced level suggests that continued review of lower levels of grammatical elements enhances the learning of advanced grammar because the latter is built on the former. Following are some of the most important elements commonly seen in advanced teaching materials:

- Discourse connectors
- Discourse devices
- Formal vs. informal speeches
- Speech acts
- Pragmatic factors
- Idiomatic usage
- Literary, prosodically bound, and technical/specialized expressions

Students at this stage have a good understanding of Chinese grammar in general. What they need most is to digest what they have learned and make the effort to use grammatical functions and expressions in various contexts and communicative situations. Bai et al. (1996) include the following topics in their third-year textbook, *Beyond the Basic: Communicative Chinese for Intermediate/Advanced Learners*:

- Childhood
- Describing a Person
- Master Salesperson
- Every Field of Work
- Problem-solving
- Lunch
- Music
- Crime
- Love
- Poverty
- Culture
- Happiness
- Elections
- Movies
- Extemporaneous Speech

The purpose of choosing these topics for advanced Chinese is to stimulate student interest in conversing about subjects that they are familiar with and to develop their description, narration and reasoning competence in Chinese. National and international current affairs are also very good topics for advanced class discussion because of their topical, timely nature, but they fail the test of time and are, therefore, often excluded from textbooks of advanced Chinese. Nonetheless, a careful selection of an appropriate amount of non-textbook teaching materials about current affairs can not only pique students' interest in learning, but also reinforce what they have learned about commonly used grammatical elements in colloquial Chinese speech and writing.

So far, I have discussed three levels of Chinese teaching materials. One may find that beyond third-year Chinese there are fewer textbooks and other teaching materials available. This is probably because there are fewer users and therefore it becomes less profitable for publishers to produce such materials. Jin et al. (2000) compiled a multi-media courseware for advanced (third- or fourth-year) Chinese, including textbooks, workbook, CD ROM, audio and video cassettes. Topics in this set of teaching materials range from single-parent households, film and theatre personalities, to baby adoptions, peasants and private entrepreneurs, and market economy. In addition, students at the fourth-year level and above can be given authentic literature and media by teachers so the need for texts is less critical and the need for teacher creativity and resourcefulness is proportionately more critical.

2.5   Authenticity

The authenticity of teaching materials is a subject of consideration when compiling teaching materials for students of different proficiency levels. In the field of teaching Chinese as FL, two major camps have been formed: those who believe in traditional controlled teaching materials, and those who believe in pure authentic materials. Traditional teaching materials are most likely composed and filtered by teachers and textbook compilers so that the number of characters and sentence structures used in lessons fall within the limit of the students' ability, whereas pure authentic materials are selected from various publication genres without editing and rewriting and, therefore, contain structure and vocabulary not always covered in class. Influenced by the performance and proficiency approach to foreign language acquisition, some teachers prefer using authentic language materials, such as street signs, restaurant menus, train schedules, newspaper articles etc. as teaching materials while others ignore these types of materials completely especially at the earlier stages of acquisition. In recent years, more and more teachers see the benefit of using both types of materials in teaching. This leads to the following questions: What constitutes authentic material? What is the significance, if any, of using one type of material over another? There is no question that newspaper articles, advertisements, street signs, television news and shows, radio broadcasts, etc. provide authentic Chinese. The question that has long been debated among Chinese language teachers at the annual meeting of the CLTA is whether a dialogue or essay written by Chinese teachers with a controlled number of characters, sentences, and discourse devices is also considered authentic Chinese. It is an interesting question and, not surprisingly; there is no agreement on its answer. Some say yes, some are less certain, and others say no. Interestingly, if we put the question aside and limit our examination to the existing teaching materials, we find that the amount of commonly recognized authentic material included in textbooks increases along with student proficiency levels. In other words, students with higher Chinese proficiency use more authentic materials than those with lower proficiency. Courses, such as Newspaper Reading and Chinese Film, are usually offered at the intermediate high or advanced low level using the ACTFL scale. This is because students with intermediate or higher level Chinese proficiency are able to comprehend and digest authentic materials better than those with lower proficiency. Imagine teaching elementary Chinese with only authentic materials, such as a recorded conversation among family members at dinner table or at a birthday party without editing any part; teachers would have to explain many different concepts before students could understand the speech at all, not to mention how long it would take students to communicate in the same manner. This would result in a low success rate among students and a classroom atmosphere not conducive to learning. Hence, I suggest that at the elementary level at least, teaching materials must be controlled to the extent that students can feel successful at acquiring some rudimentary communicative skills, such as how to greet people, how to order at a restaurant, how to talk about student daily activities, etc. Intermediate Chinese, on the other hand, may mix controlled materials with less controlled materials. When students reach the Advanced level, fewer controlled or no controlled materials at all can be most beneficial to increasing their language proficiency. We know that the language in highly controlled materials may not often be heard or used naturally by native Chinese speakers, but certainly native speakers can understand it. As far as whether this kind of controlled material is authentic, this may not be the most salient consideration at elementary levels so I will leave it to the reader to decide.

I conclude this section with a note that I once left to my eight-year-old daughter who studied Chinese at a local Chinese weekend school for three weeks. I took special care to limit the characters used in the note to those she had learned. She was very proud that she understood the meaning. Is the note authentic?

(2.26) 雁君： 妈妈去学校了。你在家，关门。我二点看你。— 妈妈

Yànjūn: *māma qù xuéxiáo le. nǐ zài jiā, guān mén. wǒ liǎng diǎn kàn nǐ. — māma*

[Yànjūn, Mom went school. You stay at home and lock the door. I will see you at 2 o'clock. – Mom]

2.6   Conclusion

Chinese language teachers might not have to determine the content of PGC because the textbooks they choose may have predetermined it for them. The questions are, then, how, to choose a textbook? Is there such a thing as a "good" textbook or a "bad" textbook? This chapter has discussed many factors relevant to teaching materials. It is suggested that teachers follow the guidelines in selecting their teaching materials. Although textbook compilers and pedagogical specialists may determine the content of PGC, it is teachers themselves who shape and mold it to fit their teaching method and style. The following chapter will discuss in detail another major component of pedagogical grammar — teaching methodology.

3 Methodology

3.1 Introduction

The methodology[1] of teaching and learning has been referred to as the pedagogical process (cf. Little 1994: 99), separate from pedagogical content as discussed in Chapter 2. Because of the importance of the pedagogical process, a number of approaches have been generated over the last several decades, among them grammar-translation, audio-lingual, communicative, functional-notional, and proficiency (e.g. Bloomfield 1942; Leech and Svartvik 1975; Krashen 1982; Ellis 1985, 1997, 1999; Prabhu 1987; Cui 1993; Lantolf 2000; Kumaravadivelu 2003). Each of these approaches was proclaimed at one time or another to be the best for language teaching. Of them, the communicative approach, since its inception has received perhaps the most criticism because its mechanism for teaching and learning opposes all traditional approaches, yet interestingly enough it has become perhaps the most popular approach used in foreign language teaching today. Little (1994: 101–3) points out that the communicative approach — at one time considered useless for pedagogical purposes because of its lack of focus on grammar and correctness — has gained in popularity in recent years due to a strong consensus that has emerged in favor of a communicative version of pedagogical grammar. This consensus seems to have been reinforced by more research and case studies on the acquisition of various foreign languages (e.g. Widdowson 1978, Lü 1981, Brumfit 1984, Phillipson et al. 1991, Tomlin 1994, Lapkin 1998, Kanno 1999, Ellis and Hooper 2001).

One major issue pertaining to the pedagogical process of Chinese is how teachers can best help students acquire Chinese language competence. Earlier literature on this subject suggests that a number of factors should be taken into consideration in the process of teaching and learning Chinese:

1. Sequencing Factor (cf. Dew 1997, Teng 1998)
   STATEMENT: It is derived from the frequency count of occurrence of grammatical elements in speaking and writing.

PEDAGOGICAL RATIONALE: The most frequently used grammatical elements should be taught and learned first, whereas the least frequently used elements should be taught last.

2. Autonomy and Simplification Factor (cf. Teng 1997 and 2002)
    STATEMENT: It encourages teachers and pedagogy specialists to develop a system for Pedagogical Grammar of Chinese (PGC).
    PEDAGOGICAL RATIONALE: Language practitioners must be able to easily comprehend grammatical elements.

3. Accumulation Factor (cf. Teng 1997, Liu 1998)
    STATEMENT: Grammatical elements are explained and practiced from simple brief functions to increasingly more complicated functions in consonance with the progression of students' proficiency level.
    PEDAGOGICAL RATIONALE: Students build a solid and systematic foundation of PGC.

4. Discourse and Pragmatic Factor (cf. Xing 1998, 2000, 2003)
    STATEMENT: Any grammatical element should be taught in terms of when and why it is used in communication.
    PEDAGOGICAL RATIONALE: Students learn how to use grammatical elements in communication.

5. Cultural Factor (cf. McGinnis 1994, Hinkel 1999, Myers 2000, Christensen and Warnick 2004)
    STATEMENT: The most complex part of learning to participate in a truly Chinese society lies with the combination of linguistic/grammatical elements and cultural elements, such as gestures, proximity and other aspects of behavior.
    PEDAGOGICAL RATIONALE: Without cultural elements, students cannot communicate successfully.

6. Psychological Factor (cf. Titone and Danesi 1985, Gass et al. 1989, Healy and Bourne 1998, Arnold 1999)
    STATEMENT: Psychological factors, such as circumstances under which students perform best, should be taken into consideration to enhance learning.
    PEDAGOGICAL RATIONALE: Different students have different learning abilities. Ignorance of, and ignoring, this fact can lead to pedagogical failure.

7. Motivational Factor (cf. Gardner and Lambert 1972, Samimy and Lee 1997, Wen 1999, Dörnyei and Schmidt 2001)

STATEMENT: Highly motivated students should be taught with a different, yet equally encouraging method than less motivated students.
PEDAGOGICAL RATIONAL: Students with different motivations can all learn Chinese effectively and efficiently.

8.   Learning Environment (cf. Bar-Lev 1995, Chao 1997)
STATEMENT: A total immersion language environment requires a different teaching method from an hourly learning environment.
PEDAGOGICAL RATIONALE: Students can take advantage of their learning environment.

All eight factors are relevant to the methodology of teaching PGC. Some pedagogy specialists emphasize the sequence of grammatical elements, some prefer an autonomous and simple system in teaching PGC, some propose a cumulative teaching method, some suggest that the teaching of PGC should be centered on discourse pragmatic factors, some believe that the teaching method should vary according to students' motivation and the learning environment, whereas others focus on cultural and psychological factors in teaching and learning Chinese. The theoretical background and practice preference of these pedagogical specialists determine which factor they will argue for. Clearly, each of these eight factors plays an important role in one or more phase(s) of teaching and learning Chinese. The question that arises is how to integrate these factors into the curriculum design of Chinese language programs and balance them in teaching without overemphasizing one while ignoring the other(s). In the following sections, teaching and learning methods used in both the East (in China) and the West (outside China) will be introduced first, then suggested models will be discussed.

3.2   Chinese Methods (in China)

As noted in Chapter 1, in China, teaching Chinese as a foreign language (FL) was not considered a serious subject of study until recent years. Accordingly, there have been a few comprehensive studies of teaching methodology, even though the practice of teaching and learning Chinese as FL can be traced back centuries.

From the sixteenth to the nineteenth centuries, numerous Chinese textbooks and dictionaries were composed by Western missionaries and scholars and published in China (e.g. Matteo Ricci 1580, João Rodriguez 1604, Francisco Varo 1703, Joseph de Prémare 1831, Giles 1872, Hiller 1886, Gibson 1887). It is clear from these publications that early Chinese teaching used the Latin grammar system to explain the types of words and structures in Chinese. Incidentally, these materials provide us with a glimpse of the method of teaching and learning Chinese during that period: Word-by-word glossaries seem to have been a common practice, whereas explanation of so-called particles, such as *le* (了), was rare and, when occurring, non-systematic. Self-teaching and learning was common; classroom setting was not. When Western missionaries and scholars gradually learned the language, many of them became teachers and compilers of teaching material. Consequently, their teaching methods were constrained by their learning experiences.

With the abolition of imperialism and the establishment of the Republic of China at the beginning of the twentieth century, teaching and learning Chinese entered a new era. Students, native and non-native, set as their goals learning to speak or write colloquial/spoken Chinese (白话, *báihuà*) in order to communicate with ordinary Chinese people (cf. Baller 1912; Ratay 1927; Wang 1930; Ware 1939a, 1939b; CCCF 1943; Chao 1948b). For non-native students, every native speaker, not just the educated people, was a potential teacher. This new motivation for learning Chinese along with the relative availability of teachers opened the door to creative teaching and learning methods. An American teacher described the teaching philosophy of teachers who taught Chinese to Western students in Beijing for three decades during the first half of the twentieth century as follows:

> Effective study of a language should begin with the use of the ear, then the vocal organs, to be followed by the use of the eye and the hand. In other words, we should hear, speak, then write, and finally read. To master a language, memorizing is essential. The student is advised to memorize one or more sentences from each of the lessons. In order to write Chinese, it is essential that the characters be formed using the same order of strokes as that followed by Chinese teachers. (CCCF 1943: Introduction)

In addition to being informative, this philosophy also sheds light on the preferred order of teaching the four skills — listening, speaking, writing and reading — in the early twentieth century, which is surprisingly similar to the Western educators' understanding of the four skills that came about a century later. Furthermore, the emphasis on memorization seems influenced by the Chinese tradition of learning. There is an old Chinese saying suggesting that memorization of three hundred Tang poems will ensure the ability to speak about them. In this case, we may say that the method of teaching and learning Chinese employed during the early twentieth century reflects the influence of both Western and Chinese traditions of teaching and learning.

In the 1940s , when both research and pedagogy of the Chinese language reached new heights, the civil war in China broke out and interrupted the advancement of teaching and learning Chinese in that country. During the following three decades, Western students who wished to learn Chinese in a total immersion environment could only go to Taiwan or Singapore to accomplish their goal. When China opened up again in the early 1980s, thousands of foreign students rushed there to learn the language and explore career opportunities. After the turn of the twenty-first century, millions of Western students travel to China every year to "conquer" Chinese, a language that was dubbed the most difficult by the National Council of Less Commonly Taught Languages (NCOLCTL). When commenting on the teaching method used by their Chinese teachers in China after returning to their home country, students often reveal that they have learned a great deal from their teachers and summarize their method as teacher-centered, rather than the student-centered method they were used to in their home institutions. This seems to suggest that during this particular period, the influence of the Chinese traditional teaching method, also known as "the duck-feeding" method, remained strong in teaching Chinese as FL. However, this traditional teaching method in China can be seen to be changing before our eyes. With the increasing number of Chinese programs established and sponsored by both Chinese and Western colleges and universities in China, Western teaching methods, such as the student-centered approach, have been introduced — and are gaining a foothold — as well. In December 2004, *Hànbàn* (China National Office for Teaching Chinese as a Foreign Language) invited 15 Chinese professors from the United States to give lectures on teaching various aspects of Chinese as FL at the Beijing Language University. As a result, Chinese teachers in China have adopted many of the popular Western teaching strategies — among them diversifying class activities and engaging students in active and positive learning — which Western students are used to and enjoy in foreign language learning environments.

3.3   Non-Chinese Methods (outside China)

The earliest practice of teaching Chinese as a foreign language (FL) outside China can be traced back to the seventeenth to nineteenth centuries. We may categorize the styles of teaching during this period two ways: traditional Chinese style and Western style. The Chinese style was influenced by traditional Chinese teaching and learning methods used in China and practiced by Chinese immigrants residing outside China. This style emphasizes memorization and is characterized as a teacher-centered method, as described in the preceding section. The Western style of teaching Chinese influenced by the way Indo-European languages as foreign languages had been taught for years.

During the last several centuries, many methods of teaching Indo-European languages as foreign languages have been developed. However, the most influential ones have been those that developed along with the invention and utilization of electronic devices, such as the radio, tape recorder, television, and computer. These devices made it possible to use the audio-lingual method to learn a foreign language both in and outside classrooms and with or without an actual human teacher. This represented a significant advance from the traditional grammar-translation method that had been in common use for centuries. After this, function-oriented approaches, such as the communicative, functional-notional, and proficiency methods, became popular. These methods, although different in name and emphasis, share the same or similar goal: to facilitate students' acquisition of communicative skills and proficiency in a foreign language.

When Western teaching methods of various types were developed for teachers of Indo-European languages, Chinese teachers who had been educated and offered lectureships in Europe and North America made an effort to apply those methods in their Chinese classes. It appeared that each time a new teaching approach was introduced for teaching an Indo-European language, this same approach would then be put into experimental use and/or practice by Chinese teachers who wished to stay on the cutting edge of methodology. Consequently, Chinese teachers in the West may be classified into three types: (1) Those who follow suit in the teaching styles of other languages; (2) those who combine Western styles with traditional Chinese methods; and (3) those who simply use traditional Chinese teaching methods. The first two types are more commonly seen at American colleges and universities than the third type. Nonetheless, teaching methods used in college and K-12 in the West in the twenty-first century are sufficiently different to merit separate discussion.

3.3.1   *Four-year College Chinese*

During the twentieth century, many Chinese teachers at four-year colleges in the West (i.e. Europe and North America) were Chinese graduate students who pursued their study of other disciplines at the institution where they taught Chinese. These teachers, often under the supervision of a professor in (East) Asian Studies, did not have any formal training in teaching Chinese as FL. Despite this, the arrangement satisfied both sides: the college could hire graduate students at a fraction of what it would cost to hire trained teachers and the graduate students definitely needed the financial support no matter how paltry. As a result, their teaching methods (such as they were) reflected their understanding and experience of their own language acquisition as native speakers.

Due to the increasing number of Chinese college students leaving China for North America or Europe to pursue further education towards the end of the twentieth century, the pool of potential Chinese teachers grew and that pool of potential employers could afford to be more selective. Thus, the field became more competitive. Those who had some kind of experience or training in teaching Chinese or linguistics had the advantage in finding and procuring positions as Chinese lecturers at four-year universities and colleges in the West. Once hired, they taught their Chinese classes with enthusiasm and a variety of activities. Their pedagogical and/or linguistic knowledge of the Chinese language enriched their classroom instruction.

The most recent trend in teaching Chinese as FL is communicative-oriented. That is, all teaching methods have to serve the purpose of developing students' communicative competence. The underlying requirements of this approach for effective Chinese teachers (and, indeed, for effective teachers of any foreign language) is a thorough knowledge of pedagogical theories and the capability of creating a lively and positive learning environment for students. Graduates who receive their master's or higher degree in Teaching Chinese as a Foreign Language or related fields should be equipped with the knowledge of pedagogical theories. On the other hand, lecturers who have taught at one or more of the internationally recognized Chinese programs, such as Middlebury Summer School and Princeton in Beijing, should gain valuable experience in how to create a challenging, yet productive and positive environment in which students can learn Chinese effectively. This leads to the question: What constitutes a model teaching method? Liu (2002: 137–8) proposes a four-step model (i.e. perception period, comprehension period, reinforcement period, and implementation periods). While agreeing with Liu on the general direction, Xing (2003) suggests that a good teaching model should comprise three qualities: (1) developmentally appropriate, (2) practically executable, and (3) functionally applicable. These three qualities are illustrated in Figure 3.1.

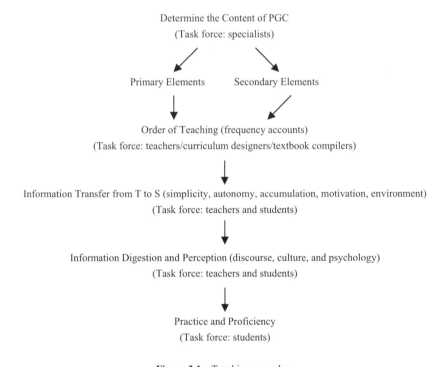

Figure 3.1   Teaching procedure

To be "developmentally appropriate," teaching methods have to coincide with the order in which materials are taught (i.e. frequency accounts of grammatical elements). "Practically executable" refers to the process of information transfer from teachers to students. A successful transfer should take into consideration the factors of simplicity of linguistic jargon, autonomy and accumulation in presenting grammatical elements to students, and motivation and environment of learning. Finally, teachers should always explain a grammatical element in such a way that it is immediately "functionally applicable." Take the so-called passive construction or the *bèi* 被 construction as an example: traditional lectures on this construction often start with structural analysis, namely, how to change an active construction into a *bèi* construction by moving the object to the subject position, placing the subject after *bèi* and before the verb, and leaving the verb at the end if there are no other elements in the sentence, as diagrammed in (3.1):

(3.1)   "That child took away three green apples."

	那个孩子	拿走了	那三个绿苹果。
	nà ge háizi	*ná zǒu le*	*nà sānge lǜ píngguǒ*
Active construction:	Subject	Verb	Object

⇩

Passive construction:	Object	***bèi***	Subject	Verb
	那三个绿苹果	被	那个孩子	拿走了。
	nà sānge lǜ píngguǒ	***bèi***	*nà ge háizi*	*ná zǒu le*
	"Three green apples were taken away by that child."			

Students traditionally do many exercises switching sentences from active to passive. I believe that this kind of teaching and practice is useless and misleading because students will not learn to really use the *bèi* construction, no matter how good they are at the switching exercises. What will help students acquire communicative competence in using the *bèi* construction, however, is to tell them why and when this construction is used in communication and then give them situations in which they can create and produce original sentences using the *bèi* construction in conversation. Furthermore, students should be aware that the *bèi* construction is not equivalent to the English passive construction (e.g. Chinese *bèi* constructions are likely to express the meaning of adversity; English passives are not. The verb in the *bèi* construction has to convey the meaning of "disposal" whereas the verb in English passive does not. See Chapter 6 for detailed discussion of the acquisition of construction.) This is why one often cannot find a corresponding *bèi* construction for a given active construction. Since the *bèi* construction has a number of semantic and discourse-pragmatic functions such as adversity, emphasis on patient, concealing the agent, it is necessary to first determine which function or functions should be taught at the earlier stage of acquisition and which function(s) later. Then, an appropriate method needs to be used to explain those functions to students so that they can understand them easily and apply them in communication comfortably. This is the time when discourse-pragmatic, cultural, psychological, motivational factors and learning environment play highly interconnected roles in teaching and learning. Xing (2003) summarizes the proposed teaching procedures as follows:

(a) Determine when a given grammatical element should be introduced to students;

(b) Determine and categorize the functions of a given grammatical element and schedule times for each function to be introduced;

(c) Explain different layers of functions respectively with simple descriptive language;

(d) Give examples illustrating the different functions;

(e) Provide *dos* and *don'ts*;

(f) Provide opportunities for students to go through various stages of practice: initial attempt, error making, receiving guidance and encouragement, making corrections, producing correct examples, and finally, becoming proficient;

(g) Guide students to smoothly move forward from one stage to another with awareness of students' psychological biases and of the cultural characteristics of the Chinese language.

Under (f) list students' responsibilities and, in all the remaining categories, list teachers' responsibilities and the process of teaching the language. Liu Xun (2002: 141–3) also discusses teachers' responsibility in classroom and categories them into five sections: organizing class, reviewing and assessing old materials, introducing new materials, reinforcing new information, assigning homework. Comparing Liu (2002) with Xing (2003), we find Liu's work emphasizes more pedagogical procedures, whereas Xing intends to figure out the most adequate procedures. Nonetheless, both provide a range of guidance for Chinese teachers to follow. Two types of suggested models will be provided in detail in Section 3.4. In the following sections, I will discuss the characteristics of teaching methods used in K-12 Chinese classes.

3.3.2 K-12 Chinese

Traditionally, two traits distinguish K-12 Chinese from college Chinese in the West: students' goals and teachers' means. The learning goals of K-12 students are often not as clearly and uniformly defined or stated as those of college students. On the other hand, due to young learners' mental and psychological characteristics, teachers of Chinese have to rely more on psychological and motivational factors and the creation of a fertile learning environment than on the other factors described at the beginning of this chapter.

Most high schools in the West require students to take one foreign language course. For students in non-English speaking countries, the first choice of a foreign language will most likely be English because of its international popularity and status as the lingua franca of the world business community. For native English students, on the other hand, the choice usually falls within the family of Indo-European languages, languages such as Spanish, French and German, which are linguistically similar to English and, hence, practically easier to learn than non-Indo-European languages, such as Chinese. Who, then, would choose to learn Chinese in a K-12 school environment? Statistics (see Watzke 2003) show that among students who take a foreign language in US public high schools (total number of students: close to 6 million), only 3 percent take Chinese. Some surveys (see Chu 1999), though, report a steady increase in the number of students taking Chinese in recent years. Most of these students belong to one of two types: (1) students of Chinese heritage, or (2) highly capable students seeking greater academic challenge and interested in Chinese culture and society. The term "students of Chinese heritage" refers to those whose parents or grandparents are native Chinese speakers. This group of students study Chinese because their parents want them to, or because it is easier for them to learn Chinese than another foreign language, or because they hear and speak the language at home. In comparison, the second type of student chooses Chinese either because they want to learn a difficult language or because they recognize and are intrigued by some of the unique characteristics of the language or the culture spoken and practiced by one-fifth of the world population. The characteristics of these two groups determine how they will learn Chinese: that is, the student of Chinese descent/heritage, who may already have achieved a certain level of listening and speaking skill in Chinese, is likely to learn the language somewhat passively because their parents want them to learn the language, whereas the students without any Chinese background will learn the language enthusiastically and actively because the undertaking has been their own choice. Teachers, thus, have to develop teaching methods that work with these students' motivations and psychological attitude towards learning Chinese.

For students of Chinese heritage at the K-12 level (including those in public, private and weekend schools), teachers seem to have to strive to sustain students' interest in classroom learning, while placing an emphasis on reading and writing skills for those — especially heritage speakers — who already have some spoken Chinese but have not been schooled in either reading or writing. For students who do not have any Chinese at all, teachers can use the same method they use in teaching other young students; that is, focusing on speaking and listening at the beginning and then gradually advancing to reading and writing. This is a bit different from the approach used for college students, but coincides with the national standards for Chinese language teaching in secondary schools (see discussion in Chapter 2, Section 2.2.2) established by the American Council on the Teaching of Foreign Languages (ACTFL).

The difference in teaching focus adopted by teachers of heritage students as compared to that of teachers of non-heritage students at the K-12 level is clearly seen at Chinese schools and secondary schools in the state of Washington (Table 3.1).[2] Compare the exercises that the two types of schools use during a typical fifty-minute class of elementary-intermediate Chinese:

Table 3.1   Activity duration of Chinese class at K-12 schools

	Heritage School	**Regular School**
Pronunciation exercises	3	2
Character exercises	5	3
Grammar-patterns	4	4
Speaking exercises	3	3
Listening exercises	2	4
Reading exercises	4	3
Writing exercises	4	2
Cultural knowledge	2	4
Games	2	4

Notes: On a scale of 1–5, number 1 is considered the least important activity and number 5 the most important.

The data in Table 3.1 show that Chinese teachers in heritage schools spend more time on characters, reading and writing exercises than those in regular middle schools and high schools. On the other hand, teachers at regular schools put more emphasis on listening, cultural knowledge and games than those at heritage schools. Both groups of teachers appear to view grammar-patterns as very important (i.e. 4) and speaking as important (i.e. 3). These results seem to suggest that teachers at both types of schools have made some effort to incorporate students' background and needs into their curriculum and teaching activities.

3.4   Suggested Model

Two teaching models will be recommended in this section: the layering method and the stratification method. The layering method discusses how teachers can categorize and teach various functions of a certain grammatical element. The stratification method, on the other hand, focuses on how to teach grammatical functions at different grade levels. These two methods should be used together to achieve the highest effectiveness in teaching both college and K-12 students.

3.4.1   Layering method

In teaching Chinese as FL, the layering method suggests that the functions or usage of any grammatical elements should be divided into three categories: basic function, commonly used function, and special function. The purpose of this categorization is to meet the requirement of developmental appropriateness in teaching PGC as discussed earlier in this chapter. The categorization should progress coincidentally with the students' language competence. We may define the three functions of a grammatical element in the following way (Table 3.2):

Table 3.2   Definitions of the three functions of grammatical elements:

FUNCTION	DEFINITION
The basic function	This function is closely related to the original meaning or function of a grammatical element.
The commonly used function	This function is the most commonly used function of a grammatical element in discourse.
The special function	This function is often used in special situations or phrases, such as idioms or fixed expressions.

Taking the *bèi* construction as an example, we may illustrate the three functions in the following ways:

(I)   THE BASIC FUNCTION:

This function is used when something undesirable happens to somebody who is the focus of conversation or communication. For instance:

i.   说谎话的人常被人看不起。
      shuō huǎnghuà de rén cháng bèi rén kàn bù qǐ.
      "Liars are often looked down upon by others."

ii.   下面的人不是要被压坏了吗?   ("Integrated Chinese," p. 141)
      xiàmiàn de rén bú shì yào bèi yāhuài le ma?
      "Wouldn't those people underneath be crushed?"

Notes: "Look down upon" and "crush" are used to describe something undesirable. Students should also know that only a certain type of action (e.g. projecting a certain effect on somebody or something) can be expressed by the *bèi* construction).

(II)   THE COMMONLY USED FUNCTION:

This function is used when the performer/perpetrator of an action is unknown or is not meant to be mentioned in discourse, or the receiver of an action is more important than the performer/perpetrator in discourse. For instance:

我的学生证被人拿走了。 ("Integrated Chinese," p. 148)
wǒ de xuéshēng zhèng bèi rén ná zǒu le.
"My student ID was taken away by someone."

Notes: The performer ("somebody") of the action "to take" is less important than the receiver ("my student ID") of the same action. In addition, the receiver, not the performer, is the focus of the discourse. This is close to the passive construction in English both syntactically and semantically wherein the object rather than the subject is the focus of the sentence.

(III) THE SPECIAL FUNCTION:

This function is used in idiomatic or fixed expressions, as shown below:

这话被你打了折扣了吧?   (Lǚ, p. 56)
zhèi huà bèi nǐ dǎ le zhékòu le ba?
"These words have been adjusted by you, haven't they?"

Notes: This is not a typical *bèi* construction, so students should learn this usage or memorize the whole sentence at the advanced level.

It should be pointed out when explaining the three layers of function of the *bèi* construction, that simple descriptive language, not linguistic jargon (cf. Teng 1997, 2002), should be used to make sure that students fully understand when and why the *bèi* construction is used in discourse. As soon as students comprehend the function, they should make an effort to use the *bèi* construction in communication. They will go through various stages of practice: effort making, error making, receiving guidance and encouragement, making corrections, producing correct examples, and finally, becoming proficient. Teachers should be able to provide appropriate guidance for students to move forward from the low levels to the more advanced stages of practice. When students complete the whole practice process, that is, when they can apply the *bèi* construction successfully in communication, one ultimate goal of PGC has been achieved.

Let us now examine another grammatical element and its pedagogical process: spatial and temporal expressions. Based on their communicative function and the criteria suggested in Chapter 2 for evaluating grammatical elements, namely importance, commonality, and uniqueness, spatial and temporal expressions should be considered primary elements of PGC. If one looks at their frequency account (GYWGWH 1989), *shàng* (上) is listed as the ninth most frequently used word and *xià* (下) as the thirty-first most frequently used. This means they should be introduced to students early. In the following, I will use *shàng* (上) and *xià* (下), one pair of temporal and spatial expressions in Chinese, as examples to illustrate the layering method in teaching (also see Xing 2000).

(I)   THE BASIC FUNCTIONS:

(A) Temporal meaning: *shàng* 上 expresses a point of time already passed; while *xià* 下 expresses a time concept in the future.

上个月我没有去学校, 但是下个月我得去了。
shàng ge yuè wǒ méiyǒu qù xuéxiào, dànshì xià ge yuè wǒ děi qù le.
"Last month I did not go to school, but next month I have to go."

Note: The temporal meaning of *shàng/xià* cannot be applied across the board. One cannot say 上天/年 *shàng tiān/nián* or 下天/年 *xiàtiān/nián*. Instead, one has to say 昨天/去年/上一年 *zuótiān/qùnián/shàng yi nián* "yesterday/last year/the year before last" or 明天/明年/下一年 *míngtiān/míngnián/xià yi nián* "tomorrow/next year/the year after next."

(B) Spatial meaning: *shàng* 上 expresses a point or surface above the reference point in space; *xià* 下 expresses a point/surface below/under the reference point.

i.   桌子上没有什么书, 但是桌子下却放满了书。
zhuōzi shàng méiyǒu shénme shū, dànshì zhuōzi xià què fàngmǎn le shū.
"There are no books on the table, but there are many under the table."

ii. 上山容易, 下山难。
shàng shān róngyì, xià shān nán
"It is easier to climb a mountain than to walk down a mountain."

(II) THE COMMONLY USED FUNCTIONS:

(A) *Shàng* 上 is used to express higher status or more favorable situation, while *xià* 下 expresses lower status or less favorable situation. For instance:

i.   这个人十七岁就考上了北京大学, 毕业后当上了公司的老板, 不久爱上了一个漂亮的女孩子, 很快又抱上了一个大胖小子, 每天都能吃上大鱼大肉。人们都说这人算是过上好日子了。
zhèi ge rén shíqī suì jiù kǎoshàng le Běijīng dàxué, bìyuè hòu dāngshàng le gōngsī de lǎobǎn, bùjiù àishàng le yige piàoliàng de nǚháizi, hěn kuài yòu bàoshàng le yige dà pàng xiǎozi, měitiān dōu néng chīshàng dà yú dà ròu. rénmen dōu shuō zhèi rén suàn shì guò shàng hǎo rìzi le.
"This guy was admitted to Peking University when he was only seventeen. After graduation, he became the boss of a company. Not long after, he fell in love with a beautiful girl. Soon after that, he had a boy. Now every day he can

eat good food like fish and meat. People say that this guy is really living a great life."

ii. 这个人三十出头才娶下个老婆，两年后生下个小丫头，不久老婆生了病，吃不下饭，说是生孩子时落下的病根子。后来日子就过不下去了。有人说：他这样的下场是命中注定的。

zhèi ge rén sānshí chūtóu cái qǔxià ge lǎopo, liǎng nián hòu shēngxià ge xiǎo yātou, bùjiǔ lǎopo shēng le bìng, chī bú xià fàn, shuōshì shēng háizi shí luò xià de bìnggēnzi. hòulái rìzi jiù guò bú xiàqù le. yǒurén shuō: tā zhèiyàng de xiàchǎng shì mìng zhōng zhùdìng de.

"This guy did not get married until he was thirty-something. Two years later, he had a little girl. Not long after that his wife became sick and could not keep food down. It was said that she became ill from the birth of their child. Soon she was unable to go on living. People say that he was fated to have this kind of life."

(B) *Shàng* 上 is associated with the meaning of "more," *xià* 下 is associated with "less."

十人以上的班有两个老师教，十人以下的班只有一个老师。

shí rén yǐshàng de bān yǒu liǎngge lǎoshī jiāo, shí rén yǐxià de bān zhǐ yǒu yíge lǎoshī.

"If a class has more than ten people, there will be two teachers teaching it ; If there are fewer than ten people, only one teacher."

(C) *Shàng* 上 is associated with the meaning of "beginning," while *xià* 下 is associated with the meaning of "ending."[3]

i. 听说这个人现在很不好，不但染上了性病，而且还吸上了白面儿。

tīngshuō zhèi ge rén xiànzài hěn bùhǎo, búdàn rǎnshàng le xìngbìng, érqiě hái xīshàng le báimiànr.

"It is said that this person's current situation is not very good. He has not only contracted a sexually transmitted disease, but also started snorting cocaine."

ii. 警察在后面闪红灯，他只好把车停下了。

jǐngchá zài hòumiàn shǎn hóngdēng, tā zhǐhǎo bǎ chē tíng xià le.

"The police officer was flashing red lights behind her, so she had to bring her car to a stop."

(III) SPECIAL FUNCTIONS：

Shàng (上) has extended its function to include the abstract meaning of a point/surface as it relates to space, but *xià* (下) has no such function.

i. 他在给父母的信上说，美国各大报纸上的文章都说用民航飞机撞炸世贸中心的
    恐怖分子来自中东国家。

    tā zài gěi fùmù de xìn shàng shuō, Měiguó gè dà bàozhǐ shàng de wénzhāng dōu
    shuō yòng mínháng fēijī zhuàngzhà Shìmào Zhōngxīn de kǒngbù fènzǐ dōu láizì
    Zhōngdōng guójiā.

    "In the letter to his parents, he said that many major US newspapers all agreed that
    the terrorists who used civilian airplanes to crash into the World Trade Center came
    from Middle East countries."

ii. 为什么党员在思想上和作风上得起带头作用？

    wèi shénme dǎngyuán zài sīxiǎng shàng hé zuòfēng shàng děi qǐ dàitóu zuòyòng?

    "Why do Party members have to play a leadership role both intellectually and
    morally?"

From the illustrations given above, we see that *shàng* (上) and *xià* (下) have
a number of functions in discourse and communication, both literal and figurative.
Clearly, language students cannot absorb all functions at one time or even in a
short time. They have to start from the most basic functions, then move on to
more commonly used functions, and finally reach the most complicated abstract
functions. Teachers may even divide one category of functions, for instance, the
commonly used functions, into several phases of teaching and learning to make
sure that students understand those functions and can use them successfully in
communication before moving on. In addition to classifying these functions,
teachers may also explain *do*s and *don't*s using simple descriptive language. As
far as cultural and psychological factors relevant to students' success in
acquisition are concerned, they may vary from one grammatical element to
another. In learning *shàng* (上) and *xià* (下), students should be informed of an
interesting and revealing Chinese cultural bias connected with these two words:
giving birth to a boy is *shàng* (上) whereas giving birth to a girl is *xià* (下), as
illustrated above under the commonly used function. Once students understand
the reason behind the contrast or grammatical usage, it should be easier for them
to learn, retain, and eventually use those functions in communication.
Psychological factors may be hard to pin down in this case. However, if teachers
can artfully use *shàng* (上) and *xià* (下) in natural language within the context of
students' every day activities, they may raise students' spirits and thus motivate
them to study hard and make good progress which brings to mind an idiomatic
expression: 好好学习, 天天向上 *hǎo hǎo xuéxí, tiāntiān xiàngshàng* ("A good
student studies hard and makes progress day by day").

From the two cases illustrated above, it should be clear that any grammatical
element, be it a sentence or a word, can be categorized into three functions of
progressively complicated and more abstract usage and taught in a pedagogically
layered manner. In the following, I will introduce another method that may be
used hand in hand with the layering method in teaching different levels of
Chinese.

3.4.2 Stratification method

The stratification method refers to the method of teaching Chinese that is based on students' proficiency level. I will use the term Elementary Method to refer to the method recommended for teachers who teach beginning Chinese, Intermediate Method for second year Chinese and Advanced Method for third year Chinese or higher. It will be suggested that each of these three levels of methods utilize a different teaching strategy to optimize students learning potential and progress.

3.4.2.1 Elementary Chinese

As mentioned in Chapter 2, elementary Chinese focuses on the pronunciation and function of words. This is to say that the teaching method used for Elementary Chinese primarily processes the components of the Chinese pronunciation system, and Chinese characters and their usage. Traditionally, students of Chinese as FL learn the pronunciation system through three components: initials, finals and tones. Chinese characters are often acquired by learning stroke type, stroke order, and components of characters — the radical and phonetic parts, and the meaning of characters. Since teaching and learning tones and words will be discussed in detail in Chapters 4 and 5, this section will focus on the general teaching approach recommended for teaching Level 1 Chinese.

There have been a number of studies on learning characters (e.g. Xing 2001a; Lin 2000; Yin 1997; Everson 1998; Ke 1998; Sergent and Everson 1992; Hayes 1987, 1990; Pachard 1990). Most of these studies discuss issues relevant to the recognition and production of characters by students. Few studies raise questions about teaching strategies for learning the sound system and characters in the classroom. This book advocates a teaching approach for Level 1 Chinese that is creative, innovative, and humorous; one that students will find enjoyable and conducive to learning Chinese. The rationale behind this approach can be explained in at least two ways: (1) Humor, innovation and creativity in teaching are ways of mitigating to some extent the difficulty of learning Chinese, a substantially different language from students' native language in both sound and form, and (2) they help sustain students' interest in learning the language especially at the elementary level. This approach is somewhat different from the "perception" period (感知阶段, *gǎnzhī jiēduàn*) proposed by Liu Xun (2002: 137) which emphasizes on perception of Chinese through viewing, listening and reading. Once students manage to learn the sound system and approximately 400 basic characters necessary to function at the lowest communicative level, it becomes relatively easy, less threatening and more attractive for them to continue the course of learning the language.

So, how can we teach Elementary Chinese creatively, innovatively, and with humor? These characteristics can be incorporated into teaching Chinese sounds in many different ways including the addition of a computer/audio/video component in classroom teaching to create a multi-function environment for students to acquire Elementary Chinese. Following is a suggested lesson progression teachers and students may follow in the process of teaching and learning the Chinese sound system:

- A general introduction to the sound system in Chinese;
- Explanation and demonstration of unique Chinese sounds (e.g. retroflex, palatal, tone) in a creative and humorous manner;
- Asking students to listen to audio/video/computer programs to imitate the sounds they are not familiar with;
- Interacting with students to identify their areas of difficulty in learning certain sounds;
- Helping students associate Chinese sounds with more familiar non-Chinese sounds so that they can remember them;
- Guiding students in the use of those sounds in a meaningful conversational context;
- Praising and rewarding those who can pronounce difficult sounds well;
- Encouraging those who have difficulty learning some of the sounds;
- Correcting students in a sincere, encouraging and acceptable manner;
- Testing and recording students' progress and problems;
- Continuously practicing difficult sounds until students master them.

In the list given above, all actions, such as introduce, explain, demonstrate, interact, help, guide, praise, encourage, correct, test, and exercise, can be conducted in a creative, innovative, and humorous manner. To be creative, innovative and humorous in teaching Elementary Chinese, three areas are most important: teaching material, teaching method and learning method. Teachers should be creative in choosing teaching materials. By not limiting teaching materials to a textbook, teachers may use materials provided by the Internet, CD ROM, audio/video tapes, and cartoon pictures, whatever may draw students' interest in Chinese and learn the basic skill of communication. Teaching method, similar to teaching material, can be innovative and interesting. Although it is true that teachers' personalities may influence their teaching method, any teacher can be creative and innovative in their own special ways. Quiet teachers may draw or use cartoon pictures to demonstrate how to pronounce a certain initial; active teachers may interact with students directly in a friendly and pleasant way to make sure they can pronounce a certain difficult tone; teachers who know a number of foreign languages may use similar sounds in other languages to demonstrate the way to pronounce Chinese sounds; teachers who are good at telling anecdotes may tell students a relevant story (sometimes embarrassing, sometimes funny stories) to help students memorize a certain concept or learn a way to pronounce a certain sound, and so on. The most important issue here is that teachers be open-minded in their ways of teaching and keep looking for the most interesting and effective ways of teaching students the basic skills of communication in Chinese. While teachers work hard on their teaching method, students should be creative and innovative in figuring out a fun and effective way to learn the basic skill of communication in Chinese. Other than the ways recommended by teachers, students may try various ways to master a certain area of skill. Taking learning characters as an example, students may try to write a certain character many times either on paper or on a computer. If this does not help to memorize the character, they may listen to the pronunciation of the character, repeat it, and then try to write it. Another way to learn characters is to listen to a story in which new characters are used, to guess the meaning of those new characters, to sound out the characters, to match them with their written forms and then write them out. Students may also make up a story about a certain character. For instance, the character (家, *jiā*, "home/family"), students may deconstruct the character first: roof radical with a pig underneath the roof, then make a story about the character: Having a roof (namely a house) and domestic animal (namely pigs) means one has a home or family. Through various methods, students should be able to identify some method(s) that are most suitable to them and ultimately enjoy learning the language. When students find their Chinese class enjoyable, they will show interest in learning the materials seriously. When they have the interest, they will be able to learn it well. Interest, therefore, is the most critical milestone that students should reach at the level of Elementary Chinese. And, it is a teachers' responsibility to help students to reach that milestone. It is suggested in this section that teachers can best fulfill their responsibility with a creative, innovative, and humorous style of teaching Elementary Chinese.

3.4.2.2   Intermediate Chinese

Intermediate Chinese is different from Elementary Chinese in that it is designed to instruct students in the learning of Chinese sentences and paragraphs and their discourse and communicative functions, regardless of the theoretical approach one may prefer. The traditional method of teaching Intermediate Chinese focuses on sentence structure. The problem inherent in this model is that students often find themselves able to explain the whys and wherefores of Chinese sentences without the concomitant and more important ability to use them in real communication. To prevent this outcome, I suggest a different approach for teaching Intermediate Chinese; to teach the grammatical elements at this level in such a way that students will learn when, why and how to use them through natural discourse and communication. If a student can use the *bǎ* (把) or the *bèi* (被) construction in conversation correctly, it does not matter if s/he can explain the structures of these constructions. Some recent studies (e.g. Xing 1996, 1998, 2003; McDonald 1999) also share this view of teaching. Romirez (1995) and

McDonald (2000) suggest that grammar be taught through text and Xing has for years advocated teaching grammatical elements based on their discourse and communicative functions. Following are a list of activities that teachers and students may carry out in teaching and learning Intermediate Chinese:

- Identify a grammatical element in discourse;
- Explain why it is used in a particular discourse (the reason can be pragmatic, semantic, cultural, psychological, etc.);
- Demonstrate other situations under which the same grammatical element can be used;
- Ask students to come up with some situations in which they think a given grammatical element might be used;
- Guide students in understanding the various discourse and pragmatic functions of the given grammatical element;
- Guide students in the use of the given grammatical element in various contexts (e.g. in conversation and essays) until they can use it freely and correctly in communication.

All the activities given above are relevant to when, where and why a grammatical element is used in communication. A teacher may also start teaching a grammatical element by providing students with various types of texts and dialogues and asking them to identify the grammatical element(s) and to summarize when and where, if not why, the given grammar is used. This way, students learn how to use the given grammar from the very beginning. When the teacher explains the reasons why the grammar is used in a given discourse, it is extremely important to demonstrate with everyday language, not linguistic jargon, so that students can understand it easily and digest it completely. Furthermore, when students try to use a newly acquired grammatical element in conversation or written discourse, teachers should encourage them; the application of simple forms of the targeted grammatical elements or the basic function and/or commonly used function (see discussion in 3.4.1) to their discourse helps secure correct usage. After students have built their confidence by using the basic functions of the grammar successfully, they may move on to a higher level of learning and usage.

3.4.2.3   Advanced Chinese

By the time students finish two levels of Chinese, they should have learned approximately 800 to 1,000 Chinese characters and many major grammatical structures in Chinese, and should be able to understand, speak, read and write relatively simple narratives and dialogues related to daily-life activities (cf. ACTFL guidelines 1986). If they begin studying Advanced Chinese, they should be ready to listen, speak, read and write Chinese as much as they possibly can. This semi-immersion approach is plausible and effective according to studies of both first and second/foreign language acquisition (cf. Harley et al. 1990, Connor 1996, Ur 1996, Doughty and Williams 1998, Riggenbach 1999), because students learn more and faster when exposed to more Chinese discourse. A teacher's task at this level, then, is to provide students with as many opportunities and as much assistance as possible in listening, speaking, reading, and writing Chinese and provide extensive exposure to different genres and content, as illustrated below.

- Ask students to listen to a dialogue/story or read a representative article, then ask them to explain how different ideas, paragraphs and themes are connected to one another, thus encouraging the aural recognition of discourse connectors; then ask students to complete a writing assignment in which they use these discourse connectors and coherent devices they have just learnt;
- Ask students to watch television programs and movies of different genres,(current affairs, documents, action, drama, art, etc.), then narrate the stories and/or discuss the themes of those movies and television programs for the class, and, finally, write a report on their reflections;
- Ask students to read newspaper articles, prose or excerpts from novels, or expository essays about Chinese culture, history, politics, economy, etc., discuss or even debate the topics in those writings in class, then write a report in one of the styles they've just read stating their own point of view;
- Encourage students to make friends with and talk to native Chinese speakers to learn about Chinese culture and customs and then compare and write about the differences and similarities between Chinese and students' native culture and customs;
- Take students or encourage them to visit, study in and live in Chinese environments (such as China towns or China) so they can totally immerse themselves in the language.

It should not be difficult to see that the focus of Advanced Chinese is cohesive paragraphs and language usage styles. To teach how to speak and write a coherent paragraph, teachers have to demonstrate comprehensively and students have to listen and read extensively a wide variety of discourse types across a wide range of authentic literary genres composed of coherent paragraphs. (cf. Yang 1993, Norment 1994, Myer 1997, Li 1999, Spring 1999). For language style, including formal versus informal speeches, speech acts and genre variations, students learn better through constant comparisons and cumulative exposure to those styles (cf. Kubler 1993, 1997; Tang 1996; Kirkpatrick 1996).

To summarize the stratification method, it is suggested that teaching Elementary Chinese should focus on how to present materials to students in a creative, innovative, and humorous way to engage students' interest in learning Chinese. For Intermediate Chinese, it is recommended that every grammatical element, whether sentence or particle, be taught in terms of when, where, and why it is used in discourse and communication. Finally, at the Advanced level, it is suggested that a teacher's foremost responsibility is to immerse students in listening, speaking, reading, and writing Chinese as much as possible so that they can hear, see and produce the discourse structures found in coherent paragraphs and discourse devices from different styles of the language.

When comparing the layering method with the stratification method, we see that the former explains how to layer teaching materials (i.e. the basic function, the commonly used function, and the special function of grammatical elements) whereas the latter shows how to use these materials to best teach different levels of Chinese classes. These two methods should not be separated in classroom teaching; rather they should be integrated to form a more comprehensive curriculum.

3.5   Characteristics of Classes

In addition to the layering and stratification methods, two other factors should be taken into consideration in teaching Chinese as FL: class size and class type. Class size is often determined by class type and program type. The size of intensive classes offered by prestigious universities is normally smaller than regular classes offered by average state universities. Class type, on the other hand, is designed based on need of students. That is whether students need intensive or extensive classes.

3.5.1   Class size

Many teachers find it easier to teach small classes (i.e. those with fewer than 20 students) than large classes (i.e. those with 20 students or more), regardless of the teaching method they use. My experience suggests that the most effective and efficient way to teach large classes is to make students the center of class by giving them sufficient time to ask questions about the materials covered in class and to give each student at least one meaningful, if not challenging, question or task to fulfill every day based on their competence. After all, students should not only be the center of learning, but also the center of teaching as well.

3.5.2   Class Types

Two types of Chinese classes are commonly seen: intensive and extensive. Intensive Chinese classes are most likely offered through summer programs at colleges and universities outside China and through year-round programs in China. Students enrolled in this type of class have three or more contact hours of Chinese every day. On the other hand, the term extensive refers to those Chinese classes that meet one hour a day, four or five times a week. Another difference between intensive and extensive classes is that students who take intensive Chinese are not likely to take any other subjects or classes at the same time, whereas for students of extensive classes, Chinese is only one of the perhaps three to five courses they take as a full-time student. The differences between the two types of classes determine the way and the speed in which students in these classes learn Chinese and, indeed, call upon teachers to use different teaching techniques to coordinate with students' learning patterns and enhance their learning progress.

Traditional intensive Chinese classes favor the "duck-feeding," or, rather, teacher-centered method. That is, in this class, teachers give lectures on how to speak, listen, read, and write Chinese and students digest the content after class. In the last several decades, intensive classes, such as those offered at the Chinese Summer School at Middlebury College and many American university-sponsored study abroad programs, are divided into four segments: (1) the full-size class (大班, *dà bān*) with 20 to 25 students; (2) the medium-size class (中班, *zhōng bān*) with approximately 10 students; (3) the small-size class (小班, *xiǎo bān*) with approximately 5 students; and (4) the individual session (个别谈话, *gèbié tánhuà*). Each of these four segments has its own function: the full-size class is designated for lectures and some practice; the medium-size class for further explanation, practice and comprehension of key language components of that day; the small-size class for practice speaking and grammatical elements, and the individual session for helping students with their own questions and problems in learning the materials covered on that day. This model has been used successfully for years at Middlebury language schools. It seems that the key factor in the success of this model is that teachers there use a student-centered method in all segments of the class. Needless to say, the particular setting of the Middlebury intensive classes, the adoption of a total immersion policy and teacher training, as well as division of classes into four segments have also contributed to the success.

Other than using a student-centered approach, providing challenging content and enrichment opportunities are two other characteristics necessary to successful teaching and learning within the intensive Chinese class environment. Students who choose to take intensive Chinese are often those who have both the desire and determination to acquire a high degree of language competence in a relatively short period of time. In other words, these are highly motivated students and the degree of motivation is directly proportional to the level of challenge a teacher can introduce into the lesson. Because of this, teachers in this environment can challenge students at every level of learning by providing diverse and exciting learning opportunities and giving them new tasks daily so that by the end of each day, each week, each month, students will experience a sense of achievement (cf. Walker 1989 and Kubler 1997).

Students enrolled in Chinese classes of the extensive type make up a majority of the total population of those students studying Chinese as FL. This student population varies substantially from that of intensive classes in terms of motivation, background and purpose in learning the language. It is, therefore, to a certain extent, more challenging to teach extensive classes than intensive classes.

Even though the student-centered method may still be the most favored in extensive classes, the challenging approach may not work here because it may scare potential good students away from the class by piling too much on too quickly. Hence, at the beginning of extensive classes, the teacher needs to determine the motivation, background and purpose of each student who has signed up for the class, and then plan lessons and choose teaching techniques accordingly. For highly motivated students, the challenging approach may be useful. Students with a Chinese background may require more reading and writing lessons. Students taking Chinese because their parents want them to or only to fulfill a certain requirement will present the biggest challenge because, teachers have to find ways to engage students' own interest in learning the language. Finally, students who want to learn the language, but are not good at it challenge teachers to be patient and work continuously to build their confidence in this foreign language-learning environment.

3.6   Accuracy

For more than twenty years, teachers and researchers have been divided into two camps over the issue of accuracy in teaching and learning Chinese as FL. The main issue concerned here is with accuracy of students' competence in using and communicating in Chinese. Although this is not an issue that arose exclusively within the field of teaching Chinese as FL (see Van Ek 1976, Widdowson 1978, Rivers 1983, Zimmerman 1997, Nation 2001), it has certainly engendered numerous exciting debates, sometimes emotional and personal, among Chinese teachers. One camp may be classified as "the accuracy-oriented" group and the other as "the proficiency-oriented" group. The accuracy-oriented group asserts the importance of teaching students to use correct tones, grammar and discourse connectors in conversation and accuses the proficiency-oriented group of only paying attention to reaching a certain communicative goal without accurate use of grammar. The proficiency-oriented group, on the other hand, argues that since the purpose of acquiring a foreign language is to develop students' communicative competence in Chinese, it is most important to teach students how to reach a certain communication goal. For example, when teaching students how to order in a Chinese restaurant, the proficiency camp emphasizes teaching students how to be understood when ordering their dish without worrying about achieving perfect tones or syntax, whereas those in the accuracy camp insist that accurate grammar and tones be used with accuracy translating into communicative competence. Observant teachers soon realize that the disagreement between the two camps is not substantial and can be modified relatively easily so that both camps' points of view can be integrated and incorporated, i.e. proficiency with accuracy. Using this approach, students may have to learn the topic-comment structure to effectively and accurately order a dish at a restaurant, as demonstrated below:

(3.2) 服务员： 你们想吃点什么？

    fúwúúyun: *nīmen xiǎng chī diǎn shénme?*

    [Waiter： What do you want to eat?]

    学生： 有没有什么特别的中国菜？

    xuéshēng: *yǒu méiyǒu shénme tèbié de zhōngguó cài?*

    [Student: Do you have any special Chinese dish?]

    服务员： 有、有、有。比如：红烧茄子、糖醋鱼、酸辣汤什么的。

    fúwúúyun: *yǒu, yǒu, yǒu. bǐrú: hóngshāo qiézi, tángcù yú, suānlà tāng shénme de.*

    [Waiter: Certainly. For instance, (we have) eggplant sautéed in soy sauce, sweet-and-sour fish, hot-and-sour soup, etc.]

    学生： 红烧茄子有什么好吃的？

    xuéshēng: *hóngshāo qiézi yǒu shénme hǎochī de?*

    [Student: Eggplant sautéed in soy sauce? How good is that?]

    服务员： 那你要个糖醋鱼吧？！

    fúwúúyun: *nà nǐ yào ge tángcù yú ba!*

    [Waiter: Then, how about sweet-and-sour fish?!]

    学生： 糖醋鱼是不是有很多糖？

    xuéshēng: *tángcù yú shì bú shì yǒu hěnduō táng?*

    [Student: Is there a lot of sugar in sweet-and-sour fish?]

    服务员： 有一些糖，有一些醋。甜甜的，酸酸的，好吃极了。

    fúwúúyun: *yǒu yixiē táng, yǒu yixiē cù. tiétié de, suānsuān de, hǎochī jíle.*

    [Waiter: There is some sugar and some vinegar. It is a bit of sweet and a bit of sour. It tastes really good.]

    学生： 可是，我是学生，没有很多钱。糖醋鱼是不是很贵？

    xuéshēng: *kěshì, wǒ shì xuéshēng, méiyǒu hěnduō qián. tángcù yú shì bú shì hěn guì?*

    [Student: But, I am a student and do not have a lot of money. Is sweet-and-sour fish very expensive?]

    服务员： 不太贵。九块钱一个。

    fúwúúyun: *bú tài guì. jiǔ kuài qián yigè.*

    [Waiter: Not really. It is $9 each.]

    学生： 好吧。不过吃了糖醋鱼，晚上就没钱再买饭了。

    xuéshēng: *hǎo ba. buguò chī le tángcù yú, wǎnshàng jiù méiyǒu qián zài mǎi fàn le.*

    [Student: Okay. But if I have sweet-and-sour fish, I won't have money to buy anymore food later.]

In this dialogue, when the student seeks information from the waiter, it is natural to use the topic-comment construction (i.e. 红烧茄子有什么好吃的？ *hóngshāo qiézi yǒu shénme hǎochī de?* 糖醋鱼是不是有很多糖？ *tángcù yú shì bú shì yǒu hěn duō táng?*) This is also true of the waiter's direct answer. Although the topic-comment construction may not be the only construction suitable for this situation, it appears if students learn some typical patterns that work in a certain situation, it will increase the proficiency as well as the accuracy of communication.

3.7   Conclusion

This chapter has introduced and discussed a number of approaches, models, and factors relevant to the methodology of teaching Chinese as FL. Now, can we draw a definite conclusion regarding which method is the best? Probably not. Every comparison is relative and based on when, where, why and how of the teaching and learning, how these are conducted over time and who is involved in the process. One method may turn out disastrous when employed by one teacher, but may be successfully implemented by another and vice versa. Similarly, an effective method used in one program does not necessarily guarantee its effectiveness in another. All these variables oblige teachers to assess students and curriculum anew in each class situation before determining which teaching method should be used in class. It is certainly true that some methods are, in general, better than others, but no method is always better than another. Experienced teachers change their teaching strategies when they teach different classes, or when the learning environment and schedules change; flexibility, sensitivity to students' need and adaptability are three of the most important tools in any teacher's pedagogical toolbox.

4 *Pronunciation*

4.1 Introduction

Tone (声调, *shēngdiào*) is one of the two most distinctive features separating Chinese from Indo-European and many other languages in the world (the other feature is the writing system to be discussed in Chapter 5). Every Chinese character has a tone and every tone is built in lexicon, which means tone affects the meaning of words. Because of this property, Chinese tones have attracted not only numerous linguists and Chinese philologists to investigate their characteristics and functions, but also specialists on Chinese language acquisition who try to discover an effective way for students of Chinese as FL to acquire tonal competence. Although studies show that the modern dialects of Chinese present a wide variety of tonal systems ranging from three to ten different tones (Chen 2000: 13–19), this chapter only discusses the tonal system and tonal acquisition of Mandarin Chinese. Among the many modern Chinese linguists, Chào Yuán-rèn (赵元任) is considered one of the most versatile scholars who not only helped to shape the field of modern Chinese linguistics, but also made an immeasurable contribution to the field of Chinese pedagogy. He developed a method to measure the four tones in Mandarin Chinese on a pitch scale of 5 (Chao 1930), as illustrated below. This tool helped unravel the mystery of Chinese tones.

Tone 1: high level	55	as in *mā* 妈 "mother"	or in *wēn* 温 "warm"
Tone 2: middle rising	35	as in *má* 麻 "hemp"	or in *wén* 闻 "hear"
Tone 3: low falling rising	214	as in *mǎ* 马 "horse"	or in *wěn* 吻 "kiss"
Tone 4: high falling	51	as in *mà* 骂 "curse"	or in *wèn* 问 "ask"

The four different diacritics over the vowels illustrated above represent the four tones in Mandarin Chinese. They are so simple and easy to understand that they, in the years since their first publication, have become the most commonly used teaching and research method describing the four tones. Notice that each tone has at least two numbers to describe pitch range: the first number stands for the starting pitch value and the last number for its ending pitch value. The middle number, shown for the third tone, stands for the point of changing pitch contour.

The duration of each pitch range stays approximately the same as that of a syllable final accompanying the tone (e.g. *ā, én, iǎo, ìng*). In addition to the four distinctive tones, Mandarin also has a neutral tone most likely attached to function words (e.g. *le* "aspect marker", *ma* "interrogative marker", *de* "possessive marker"), second character of compound words (e.g. 漂亮 *piàoliang* "beautiful" and 认识 *rènshi* "to recognize"), or reduplicated words as in *bàba* 爸爸 "dad", *māma* 妈妈 "mom", *jiějie* 姐姐 "older sister", etc. Unlike the four tones discussed above, the neutral tone is normally unmarked. Occasionally, one may see a little circle above to mark the neutral tone (e.g. *å*), but most teachers and researchers simply do not mark it.

After Chao's introduction of marking tones with numeral numbers, many researchers began to pay attention to issues relevant to the perception and production of these four tones by both native Chinese children, students of Chinese as FL, and researchers (Chao 1948b, Kiriloff 1969, Cheng 1973, Li and Thompson 1977, Yue-Hashimoto 1980, Shen 1985, Miracle 1989, Repp and Lin 1990, Fox and Qi 1990, Blicher et al. 1990, Chen 1997, McGinnis 1997). The results of these studies have benefited Chinese teachers by improving their understanding of the characteristics of tones and their behaviors in acquisition. However, it is not clear how many teachers are willing to incorporate those research results into teaching Chinese as FL, either because of their limited knowledge of the physiology involved in tone production or because of the complex concept involved in perception, which will be addressed in Section 4.3.

Another issue that has attracted many researchers' and teachers' attention is tone sandhi, which refers to the situation in which certain tones adjacent to one another in natural oral discourse, change in consequence of this juxtaposition. Mandarin has a number of instances of tone sandhi; however, I will focus only on the three cases that students have to learn in order to achieve communicative tonal competence. The first and the most important tone sandhi in Mandarin involves the third tone. When two third-tones are next to each other, the first third tone usually transforms into the second tone. Also, when the third tone is followed by any other tone, it transforms into a half third tone, namely the first half marked "21" on the pitch scale (i.e. 214 => 21) (see Duanmu 2000: 237–54 for detailed discussion on tone 3 sandhi). The other two well-known cases of tone sandhi in Mandarin are related to the character 一 *yī* "one" and the character 不 *bù* "not". Both of the characters change their original tones (一 *yī* first tone and 不 *bù* fourth tone) when they are followed by the fourth tone; they either change to the second tone (e.g. 一个 *yī gè* => *yí gè* 不是 *bù shì* => *bú shì*) or change to the neutral tone (e.g. 一个 *yī gè* => *yi gè* ; 不是 *bù shì* => *bu shì*) depending upon speakers or discourse styles. If they are pronounced as the second tone, the words are likely emphasized in discourse. If they are pronounced as the neutral tone, however, they are likely unstressed (as used most in natural oral discourse).

When discussing tones, I must also mention *pīnyīn* (拼音). *Pīnyīn*, which is "spelling and sound" in Chinese, is a Roman alphabet, diacritical mark notation system that indicates how a given character is pronounced. *Pīnyīn* consists of two components: initials (声母, *shēngmǔ*) and finals (韵母, *yùnmǔ*). Mandarin Chinese has 23 initials and 34 finals, as shown in Tables 4.1 and 4.2 (cf. Chao 1948b, Li and Thompson 1981, Norman 1988).

Table 4.1   Initials in Mandarin Chinese

Labial	*b(u)o*	*p(u)o*	*m(u)o*	*f(u)o*	*wo*
Alveolar	*de*	*te*	*ne*	*le*	
Velar	*ge*	*ke*	*he*		
Palatal	*ji*	*qi*	*xi*	*yi*	
Dental sibilant	*zi*	*ci*	*si*		
Retroflex	*zhi*	*chi*	*shi*	*ri*	

For pronunciation reasons, a vowel is added to each of the initials listed in Table 4.1. The Table also uses the traditional order in which those initials are learned by native Chinese schoolchildren. Some teachers may introduce the contents of the Table as a sort of Chinese alphabet at the beginning levels, while others prefer to use more technical terms, such as initial, labial (唇音, *chūn yīn*), and retroflex (圈舌音, *juǎnshé yīn*). Among these 23 initials, the four retroflexes and three palatals (腭音 *é yīn*) have generated the most discussion among researchers and received the most attention from teachers and students due to the difficulty and complexity involved in the place and manner of articulation of those initials, which I will explain in more detail in Section 4.3.

Table 4.2   Finals in Mandarin Chinese

a	*ai*	*ao*	*an*	*ang*				
e	*ei*	*en*	*eng*	*er*				
i	*ia*	*iao*	*ian*	*iang*	*ie*	*iong*	*iu in*	*ing*
u	*ua*	*uai*	*uan*	*uang*	*ui*	*uo*	*un*	
	ou	*ong*						
ü	*üe*	*üan*	*ün*					

Most of the finals in Table 4.2 can define characters by themselves without an initial (e.g. 爱 *ài* "love", 安 *ān* "peace"). A few others need an initial to complete them, such as *lěng* 冷 "cold" or *lóng* 龙 "dragon"; Mandarin does not have a character pronounced *eng* or *ong* with or without a tone. When using Table 4.2, one should be aware that if a final begins with an *i* or *u* and is used without an initial, it is realized in *pīnyīn* orthography as *y* or *w*, as in *ian=>yan* and *uan=>wan*. If the final starts with *ü* and stands alone, *y* should be added to the *pīnyīn* representation, as *üe=>yüe*.

In the acquisition of Mandarin finals, those with the *e* and *ü* sound are most challenging to English students than the rest of the finals because English does not have either vowel. (For French students whose native language has the *ü* sound, however, only *e* is relatively difficult to acquire.) These facts suggest that whatever sounds (vowel or consonants) do not exist in students' native language pose potential acquisition problems. It is essential for teachers to be fully aware of students' background and difficulty, and more importantly, find suitable ways to tackle students' difficulty and help them acquire pronunciation competence. This is the goal of this chapter. In the following section, I discuss the common teaching and learning models used by most universities and colleges in North America. Then Section 4.3 offers some explanation of the common problems encountered during the pursuit of pronunciation competence. Finally, Section 4.4 recommends some activities that can help students learn tones and *pīnyīn* effectively.

4.2   Common Teaching and Learning Models

Since its invention during the Second World War, the audio-lingual method has become a primary means of teaching and learning foreign languages. The reasons for its popularity are simple: it is easy to use and it is more effective for learning pronunciation than the old translation method that does not involve listening or speaking competence. Students of Chinese as FL benefit even more from the audio-lingual method because of the property of tones. With audio tapes, students are trained to listen to standard pronunciation, identify and distinguish tones and *pīnyīn* notation, and then imitate and produce them correctly. Different teachers and students use different ways to execute the process.

Chinese teachers whose goal is to train students in the four skills: listening, speaking, reading, and writing, all teach the Mandarin sound system (i.e. tones, initials, and finals) at the beginning of students' first-year Chinese (e.g. Chinese 101 or Chinese 001). Teachers differ on the length of time spent and method of instruction. Some teachers spend the first two weeks on the sound system exclusively; some spend the first four weeks on it adding more exercises; while others spend six weeks or even longer completing the instruction on tones, initials and finals, and introducing some Chinese characters and their discourse functions along the way. This is the only group of teachers that teaches the sound system along with Chinese characters. Influenced by the traditional audio-lingual method, most teachers present tones or initials and finals as minimal pairs (e.g. *mā* vs. *mà*, *zī* vs. *cī*), triplets (e.g. *jī, qī, xī*) or minimal quadruplets (e.g. *lān, lán, lǎn, làn*) (cf. Ma 1999, Ma and Smitheram 1996), then ask students to listen to tape recordings and practice instructed tones, initials and finals. In recent years, due to the rapid development of computer technology, more and more teachers are making the effort to develop their own computer courseware to enhance students' acquisition of the sound system in Chinese. Even without creating their own courseware, teachers can find a wide variety of courseware available on the market.

Pronunciation Module developed by Ma and Smitheram (1996) is an example of one type of courseware. Students may use it to listen to minimal pairs or quadruplets, record and then listen and compare their own voice with the standard one, do identification and differentiation exercises, or test themselves on tones, initials and finals. Notice that even though all these activities are carried out on computer, they are similar to the traditional audio-lingual method in that both use an instrument (tape recorder vs. computer) to acquire the skill of pronunciation competence. Teachers may also print out the exercises and ask students to do them in the classroom. The advantage of using such computer software, however, lies in its ability to interact with users and the versatility of its exercises, which traditional tape recorders cannot offer. In addition, tape recorders are considered out of date and are rapidly being replaced by computers and CD ROM.

As far as classroom instruction and acquisition are concerned, there are two competing camps among Chinese teachers: (1) those who correct students' pronunciation errors whenever they hear them and (2) those who emphasize perception and production leaving students to develop the ability of self-correction. Each group is extremely passionate about its view and it is difficult, if not impossible, for either camp to convince the other of the merits of its approach. Those (e.g. Professor Perry Link at Princeton University) who insist on correcting students' pronunciation errors as often as possible believe that only by doing so can students acquire the beautiful standard Mandarin pronunciation (e.g. the Beijing accent). The other camp of teachers (e.g. Bar-Ler 1991), on the other hand, argues that students have to build their confidence in pronouncing individual tones and words first before using them in discourse and constant error correction discourages students from developing such confidence. It appears that both camps have good reason to believe in what they consider the best way to teach students' Mandarin pronunciation, yet both appear to have developed their view based on their own observation and/or experience with their own students.

For Chinese programs that depend on enrollment, teachers prefer not to scare students away at the beginning stages of learning by coming down hard on them for pronunciation. Instead, they focus on building students' confidence in perceiving and producing tones and words first to secure students' interest in taking Chinese. Although many teachers are fully aware of the fact that once students develop the habit of producing certain sounds incorrectly, it is extremely difficult, if not impossible, to correct them later, they feel it is important to balance the quantity of student enrollment against the quality of spoken Chinese. Of course, it is ideal if teachers can manage to correct students' errors without causing them to lose their interest and confidence in learning Chinese; a difficult, but not impossible goal. Relevant discussion on this subject is given in Section 4.4.

4.3   Difficulties in Acquisition

Studies on both perception and production reveal that for students of Mandarin, confusion often arises between the second and third tone, and the first and fourth tone (Shen 1989, Miracle 1989, Repp and Lin 1990, Blicher et al. 1990, McGinnis 1996, Chen 1997). As far as the cause for this confusion is concerned, some (e.g. White 1981) believe Mandarin tones have a significantly wider pitch range than a non-tonal language such as English, and therefore, non-native Chinese students have difficulty identifying and producing the highest and lowest pitch points, as found in the first and the fourth tones. Others (e.g. Repp and Lin 1990) argue that the difficulty and confusion between the second and third tones are derived from the fact that both tones end with a rising pitch even though the second tone starts at the middle point on the pitch scale of tones and the third tone starts dips to the lowest pitch on the scale. Unfortunately, students who speak non-tonal languages, according to Rapp and Lin (1990), are less sensitive to such a minor tonal difference. Chen (1997) suggests that the difficulty and confusion that non-native students of Chinese have are caused by interlanguage interference. In other words, when students of non-tonal languages learn the tones and characters of Mandarin Chinese, they can run into difficulty and confusion because their native language does not require the ability to distinguish pitch variations in the way that Chinese does. Furthermore, students try to apply the intonation patterns of their own language (such as rising pitch at the end of an interrogative sentence, falling pitch at the end of a statement in English, or level pitch in a middle of sentence) to Chinese utterances which makes for non-existing tones in Chinese, humorously referred to as Chinglish (Chinese + English).

To enhance the teaching of Mandarin tones, some teachers (e.g. Li and Thompson 1977, Shen 1989) rank the four tones in terms of difficulty. Chen's (1997: 35–36) analysis suggests that the first and the fourth tones are more difficult to acquire than the second and the third tones, though pitch errors can occur in all four. His experiment on the pronunciation of the four tones by native American English speakers shows that students tend to pronounce the first tone (with the pitch value of 55) as a mid-level tone (33) (non-existent in Mandarin), and assign the fourth tone (51) with either non-existing level tone (with the pitch value of 22 or 33) or a non-existent contour tone (with the pitch value of 53). The second tone may be pronounced as either non-existent level tone 22 or 33, while the third tone may be pronounced either as a non-existent level tone 22 or as a non-existent contour tone 23/13 or 213. Notice that two types of errors emerge among students' pronunciation in Chen's study (1997): (1) creation of level tones, 22 and 33, non-existent in Mandarin; and (2) shortening the pitch range of all four tones (e.g. 55=>33, 51=22/33, 35=>22/33, and 214=>213/23/13). Based on these results, Chen concludes that the most comfortable pitch range for American students is in between 2 and 4. Since both ends of the pitch range of the first tone and the fourth tone fall outside the comfortable zone, they are more difficult for American students to pronounce, especially at the beginning stages.

Mandarin initials and finals pose difficulty for students in a somewhat different manner since they are not pertinent to pitch variation, but rather more relevant to place of articulation (i.e. position of the tongue) and manner of articulation (i.e. how air flows when a sound is produced.) Three groups of initials seem more difficult for non-native students of Chinese to learn than the remaining initials in Mandarin: (1) retroflex: *zhi, chi, shi*, (2) palatals: *ji, qi, xi*, and (3) sibilants: *zi, ci* and *si*. According to Norman (1988:141), the difficulty in identifying and pronouncing Mandarin retroflexes and palatal sounds appears to arise from the same reason that the difficulty in producing Mandarin tones with a wider pitch range does, namely, sounds (initials or tones) that do not exist in students' native languages are difficult to learn.[1] It should be noted that the three sibilants (*zi, ci* and *si*), which often confuse native Chinese speakers with retroflexes (*zhi chi* and *shi*), may sound difficult to students of native English at the beginning. However, soon students will realize that English actually has all three sibilants and they are not difficult to learn at all. The difference between Mandarin and English, though, is that Chinese uses them as initial consonants (as in *zài* 在 [dzài] "be located at", *cài* 菜 [tsài] "vegetable", and *sài* 賽 [sài] "competition"), whereas English uses the first two only in the syllable final position (as in *kids* [kɪdz] and *cats* [kæts]).[2]

The linguistic features and the difference between Chinese and English initial consonants seem to suggest that retroflex and palatal sounds in Mandarin Chinese are equally difficult for native English speakers to acquire. Mandarin sibilants, on the other hand, may require more explanation, but should be easier to learn than retroflexes and palatals because English has those sibilants. The remaining initials in Mandarin should not pose any problems for native English speakers because they all exist in English as well.

Among the 34 finals, most of them are straightforward and easy to learn. Only a few may take *some* students a bit more time to pronounce comfortably. The vowel *ü* and the other finals that contain the *ü* sound (e.g. *üe, üan, ün*), for example, may require much explanation for students whose native language does not have the vowel *ü*. Modeling of its tongue and lip positions will help. Another final sound that appears difficult for American students is the vowel *e* and its associate *uo*. My classroom experience suggests that students are capable of pronouncing these two finals well; only that they cannot remember them, which leads me to believe that the problem arises from the orthography of these finals. That is, when students see the orthography *e* or *uo*, their first reaction is to register them as the English vowels and then to pronounce them as English sounds. Teachers have to remind students of the Mandarin sounds when asking them to pronounce them.

Evidently, the two cases of difficulty in learning Mandarin finals are of different types. One is derived from the absence of the sound in students' native language and the other is derived from the interference of orthography. In either case, students need teacher's assistance to learn those finals well. In the following section, I will discuss how teachers can best use classroom activities to help students overcome the two areas of difficulty and learn the Mandarin sound system.

4.4   Suggested Model for Teaching and Learning

This study recommends that the Mandarin sound system, including tones, initials and finals, be taught and learned simultaneously with Chinese characters. In what follows, I explain why and how this recommendation should be executed.

During the first few weeks of first-year Chinese, teachers may introduce students to a variety of information about the Chinese language: the writing system, pronunciation system, distribution of Mandarin Chinese speakers, and interference with social-cultural norms, etc. They carry on a number of activities, such as practicing tones, initials, finals, and characters. This way, students have a general understanding of the Chinese language and its association with students' native languages. I believe that if students learn only the sound system during the first few weeks without characters, students will be able to pronounce and read *pīnyīn* well; however, when it comes to knowing characters, it may take students twice as much time, if not longer, to learn the same number of characters as those who learn characters simultaneously with the sound system. The reason is that once students become comfortable with reading and pronouncing *pīnyīn*, they tend to separate *pīnyīn* from learning characters. If this occurs, students may have to go through three or four extra steps to learn a character: (1) learn the pronunciation (*pīnyīn*), (2) learn how to write the character, (3) learn the meaning of the character, and (4) match the sound (*pīnyīn*) with the form (character) and meaning. More often than not, students who follow these steps are able to read Chinese correctly with *pīnyīn* but lose that ability when *pīnyīn* is not provided. This makes it problematic to read authentic material in Chinese, such as signs, maps, directions, advertisements, etc.

Each of those four steps requires time to accomplish. It appears that the fewer steps students need to take, the more efficiently students learn characters. An ideal situation would be for students to learn the sound, form and meaning of characters simultaneously so that when they see a character, they know how to pronounce it and when they say something, they know how to write it. Furthermore, since *pīnyīn* itself cannot function as a language because it is not a meaning-bearing system, students have to learn characters eventually. In this case, it is misleading to pamper students with only *pīnyīn* at the beginning and leave the core learning of characters to a later time.

A typical fifty-minute Chinese lesson during the first few weeks of students' first Chinese class may be prepared in the following way:

During the first half of class:
- Teacher:
    — Introduce a new group of initials, finals or tones;

    — Demonstrate how to pronounce these sounds;
- Students:
    — Imitate those sounds after a teacher or recording;
    — Practice those sounds with classmates (e.g. identification, distinguishing sounds);

During the second half of class:
- Teacher:
    — Introduce a group of characters, (especially those having the sounds that students worked on during the first half of the class);
    — Demonstrate how to pronounce those characters, how to write them and how to use them in communication;
- Students:
    — Listen to the teacher or recording how to pronounce those characters;
    — Practice those characters by articulating the sounds, writing the characters, and composing a mini-dialogue using the characters

By learning initials, finals, tones and characters at the same time, students will consciously and unconsciously associate these units; they will make it easier not to separate sound from form (i.e. character) or meaning.

As far as how to teach those confusing and difficult tones, initials and finals mentioned in 4.3 is concerned, teachers may try different methods with different sounds. Let us first discuss the acquisition of tones and then move on to initials and finals. Among the four Mandarin tones, two (first tone and fourth tone) are considered the most difficult because of their wide pitch range and the other two (second tone and third tone) are considered confusing because they both end with a rising pitch as discussed in 4.3. How, then, should teachers explain these tones to alleviate the difficulty and clarify the confusion? My teaching experience suggests that the best way to teach the first and fourth tones is to help students first *realize* (i.e. accept and understand) the pitch difference between Chinese and students' native language and then to ask students to imitate the tones and *feel* the difference. The first tone sustains the same pitch height, whereas the fourth tone falls to as low a pitch as students can possibly reach. As long as students realize and feel the difference, they should be able to pronounce the tones. It would also be beneficial for a teacher to help students realize their own pitch ranges (high, mid and low) before teaching different tone shapes, as suggested by Shen (1989). Once students become aware of their own idiosyncratic pitch range, they may be able to distinguish the high, mid, and low pitches of their own tones better. An anecdote expresses this well: When learning the character 谢谢 *xièxie* "thank you", a student once offered his impression of his teacher's pronunciation: "Professor, how come you sound angry when you say *xièxie*?" After confirming his correct impression on the falling pitch of the fourth tone, the teacher told him that if he could use an "angry" pitch and still a smiling face attitude when pronouncing *xièxie*, he would know how to express gratefulness in Mandarin!

The confusion between the second and the third tone, on the other hand, may be clarified by explaining the different pitch values of the two tones as they are realized in natural communication. Using the following mini-dialogue as an example, students can be informed of how tone sandhi applies and how the pitch value of the third tone changes.

> (4.1) a: 你好吗？
> *nǐ hǎo ma?*   "How are you?"
> Tone value: 214 +214+0=> 35+21+0
>
> b: 我很好。
> *wǒ hěn hǎo.*   "I am fine."
> Tone value: 214+214+214 => 21(4)+35+214

Notice that the lexical tone value of the third changes depending upon its context and its syntactic function. In (4.1a), two tone sandhi rules apply. The first rule applies to the first and the second character and the second rule applies to the second and the third character. As a result, the first character, originally having a third tone, is changed into a second tone (35) because it is followed by another third tone; the second character originally having a third tone changes into a half third tone because it is followed by a neutral tone. What makes the situation even more complicated is that when three third-tones are adjacent to one another; in this case, one has to figure out the syntactic function each of the three characters has, as shown in (4.1b). Since *wǒ* "I" is the subject and *hěn hǎo* "very good" is the predicate of the sentence, the tone 3 sandhi rule applies to *hěn hǎo* (which belong to the same syntactic category), not to *wǒ hěn* "I very" (which do not belong to the same syntactic category). This suggests that the tone 3 sandhi rule applies in accordance with the syntactic category of the characters involved. The only time that the third tone's pitch value is fully realized in natural communication utterance is when it is used at the end of a syntactic category or a sentence as *wǒ* "I" and *hǎo* "good" in (4.1b).

At this point, it is not clear whether students confuse the second tone with the third because the third tone changes into the second when applying to one of the tone 3 sandhi rules or because both tones end with the same raising pitch. Most of our students have no problem identifying or pronouncing individual words or phrases with the second and/or the third tone. However, when those words and phrases are used in sentences, a variety of errors occurs. This suggests that students are confused with the two tones at the sentence level, not at the lexical level. In other words, they know how to pronounce the two tones, but are not sure where to apply tone 3 sandhi and where not.[3]

One method that seems to be effective in teaching students to apply the tone 3 sandhi rules in natural conversation is to explain and demonstrate that the third tone in most cases reduces its pitch value by half. If a third tone is followed by another third tone, the second half of the tone is pronounced (pitch value 14); if followed by *any* other tones, however, the first half should be pronounced (pitch value 21). This is to say that the majority of third tones in natural conversation use a low-falling tone, and no rising pitch at all. When students understand this about the tone 3 sandhi, they can apply it with more confidence in natural conversation.

As far as the three groups of initials (retroflexes: *zh, ch, shi*, palatals: *j, q, x*, and sibilants: *z, c*) are concerned, confusion often arises between the retroflexes and sibilants and between retroflexes and palatals. By observing American students' errors in the last fifteen years, it appears that at least one reason for the confusion is threefold: (1) closeness of place and manner of articulation, (2) similarity in orthography and accompanying finals, and (3) interference of students' native language.

First, let us compare the retroflexes with the palatals. Both groups of sounds are articulated by placing a part of tongue (using the tip for retroflexes and the dorsal for palatals) against or near the palate of the vocal cord and both groups have a three-way comparison in terms of the manner of articulation: unaspirated (*zh* and *j*), aspirated (*ch* and *q*) and fricative (*shi* and *x*). For native English speakers whose native language does not have either group of sounds, it is indeed difficult to detect the minor difference. However, there is a major difference between the two groups. That is, the palatal sounds *only* occur before high front vowels, namely *i* and *ü*, as in *jī, jiàn, qiā, qiáo, xìn, xiŭ, xùn*, etc.,[4] whereas the retroflex sounds only occur before the remaining vowels (*a, e, u, ɪ*) in Mandarin, such as *zhè, zhá, chǎi, chàn, shū, shùn*, etc.[5] This situation is described as complementary distribution by linguists. If we explain this distribution difference clearly to students when introducing the two groups of sounds, along with demonstrations of how to pronounce the two types of sounds, students should be able to identify the difference first, and then practice producing them. Daily practice of these sounds can eliminate the interference from students' native language (such as confusing the English pronunciations of *j, ch*, and *sh* with their Chinese pronunciations because of orthography).

Interestingly, native speakers of Chinese rarely have problems distinguishing the palatal sounds from retroflexes. However, many native speakers either do not or cannot distinguish retroflexes from dental sibilants (*z, c, s*), such as in words 四 *sì* "four" vs. 试 *shì* "try", 春 *chūn* "spring" vs. 村 *cūn* "village," and 找 *zhǎo* "look for" vs. 早 *zǎo* "early." When students become aware of this situation, some may ask for the reason why they have to distinguish the two groups of sounds when even native speakers cannot do so. One answer that might convince students to continue to learn and master the two groups of sounds is to explain the difference between acquisition of Chinese sounds by native speakers and non-native Chinese speakers. For native Chinese speakers, they have numerous opportunities to hear the Chinese sounds long before they actually understand the meaning of those sounds. Hence, when they hear a sound, such as *sì*, they try to figure out the meaning by looking at its context. Taking the following sentence as an example,

(4.2) *tā *sì (shì) rén   wǒ yě *sì (shì) rén.*
       he **four/is** person, I also *four/is* person
       "He is a human being; I am a human being as well."

(4.3) *zhèi bú   *sì (shì) *sìsì (shìshì).*
       this not *four/is*   **?/fact**
       "This is not true."

In both (4.2) and (4.3), the *shì* syllable, which could mean "to be" or "thing", is mispronounced as *sì* with the possible meaning "four", yet native speakers do not have any problem identifying the correct meaning. No native speaker would interpret *sì* as "four", or "thing" because it does not make any sense in the given sentences. However, if the same sentences are heard by non-native students who know the distinction of the two syllables, but are not certain of their function in discourse, it is likely that they cannot understand the sentences. In other words, since native Chinese speakers acquire the sounds from natural discourse, so they are capable of distinguishing the two types of sounds and their meanings even if they are incorrectly pronounced. For non-native students, on the other hand, they learn the sounds in classroom, and hence, it is very difficult to develop the same discourse competence that native speakers have unless they live in a Chinese speaking community for a sustained period of time. Even if we do not mention the sheer fact that the distinction between retroflexes and sibilants is made in Standard Mandarin, students of non-native Chinese should learn and distinguish the two groups of sounds in order to understand the standard Chinese easily and to be understood by others correctly.

How can teachers help students distinguish retroflexes from sibilants and discriminate between the three contrastive sounds within each group? I suggest three acquisition procedures: (1) explanation, (2) discrimination, and (3) practice. The first step, explanation, should be given by teachers. When explaining retroflexes and sibilants, the emphasis should be on the different places of articulation and the different manners of articulation among the three retroflexes and the three sibilants. To help students discriminate between sounds, the following tongue-twister (4.4) works well.

(4.4) 四是四，十是十；
       sì shì sì, shí shì shí,
       "four is four, ten is ten"

       是四还是十，你来试一试。
       shì sì haishì shí, nǐ lái shì yí shì.
       "(Whether it) is four or ten, you give (it) a try."

Students can memorize and recite the sentences in (4.4) so that the distinction between retroflexes and sibilants stay in their minds and on their tongues, so to speak. At the early stages of learning Chinese, memorization of short passages containing key linguistic features of the Chinese language benefits students a great deal in their subsequent acquisition of the language. In addition to memorization, other practices, such as imitating or repeating a teacher or fellow students, also helps them identify and discriminate sounds in Chinese.

4.5   Conclusion

An effective way to help students acquire the Mandarin sound system is to explain the characteristics of tones and those sounds, demonstrate how to pronounce them, and practice those sounds with students through comparison, discrimination, and use in natural discourse. Since knowledge of the sound system is very useful to students learning the language, I suggest that students acquire the sounds system along with characters. This way, students learn the Chinese sounds and their meanings and character representations from the very beginning. The ultimate goal of teaching the sound system is to have students hear a Chinese syllable and know its meaning, and to have them see a character, and know how to pronounce it.

5 Characters and Words

5.1 Introduction

Chinese characters, also known as *hànzì* (汉字), is the writing form of the Chinese language. Lexicographers refer to Chinese characters as logographic writing, categorically different from alphabetical writing, in that Chinese characters are derived from graphs whereas alphabetical writing, such as Latin and Greek, are derived from syllables. Due to this difference, there has been much discussion in the past regarding the properties of Chinese characters and their acquisition. Some researchers (e.g. lexicographers) explore the origins of Chinese characters; some (e.g. anthropologists) link Chinese civilization or rather Chinese culture to the creation of Chinese characters; some (e.g. calligraphers) study and admire Chinese characters as art work; and others (e.g. applied linguists and Chinese teachers) seek a clearer understanding of the more practical aspects of Chinese characters, such as how to teach non-native students of Chinese to learn and use Chinese characters in communication. As a member of the "others" group, I devote this chapter to the discussion of current practices in teaching and learning Chinese characters in the field of teaching Chinese as FL and particularly to the discussion of an integrated model of teaching and learning Chinese characters.

5.1.1 Origins and evolution

To discuss character acquisition, we must inevitably mention the origin and development of Chinese characters. There are two widely spread stories about the origin of Chinese characters: (1) Characters were created by Cāng Jié (仓颉); and (2) characters originated from rope knotting. According to classical literature, such as *Lǚ Shì Chūn Qiū* (吕氏春秋, "Lǚ's Records"), *Xúnzǐ* (荀子, "Master Xun"), *Hánfēizǐ* (韩非子, "Master Hanfei"), and *Huáinánzǐ* (淮南子, "Master Huainan"), Cāng Jié is described as having an extraordinary appearance (e.g. four shining eyes and a long heavy beard) and the ability to write characters at birth approximately 4,600 years ago. The rope knotting method of creating characters was recorded in *Zhōu Yì* (周易, "The Change of the Zhou") and says that ancient people tied various kinds of knots in ropes to record events. Both stories have been told from generation to generation, but they have neither been proved nor disproved as regards the reality of the creation of characters.

Although most lexicographers and researchers disagree on the origin of characters,   they accept the six principles, *liù shū* (六书), of constructing or forming Chinese characters suggested by Xǔ Shèn (许慎) during the Han dynasty (206–220 AD): pictographic (象形, *xiàngxíng*), indicative (指事, *zhǐshì*), ideographic (会意, *huìyì*), picto-phonetic (形声, *xíngshēng*), mutually interpretive or notative (转注, *zhuǎnzhù*), and phonetic loan (假借, *jiǎjiè*). Since there has been so much discussion of the six principles in the past (Blakney 1935, DeFrancis 1984, Boltz 1994, Lù 2003), I will briefly describe them here. Pictographic characters might be the easiest for students to acquire because they are derived from drawings of objects even though the modern standard characters have lost many of the features of the original drawings. Indicative characters use symbols to express abstract meanings, such as using a point above a horizon line to indicate the concept of "over, above, on". The combination of pictographic and indicative principles produces ideographic or associative characters (e.g. 日 *rì* "sun" + 月 *yuè* "moon" = 明 *míng* "bright"). The most productive principle in constructing characters is the picto-phonetic method for it can take any existing pictographic form and combine it with any existing phonetic form to create a new character. This is why about ninety percent of Chinese characters belong to this category in modern Chinese (cf. DeFrancis 1984). The remaining two principles, mutually interpretive and phonetic loan, are minor in comparison with the four just discussed. In fact, they are not principles to develop new characters, but rather they are used to extend the meaning of existing characters. Moreover, they are not clearly defined by Xǔ Shèn. Later researchers sometimes use the mutually interpretative principle to refer to two characters that share the same ideograph (i.e. the radical — semantic component of a character) and same or similar phonetic component of characters, such as 考 *kǎo* and 老 *lǎo*. Both characters have the same radical and the same phonetic component *ǎo*, although 考 *kǎo* means "test" and 老 *lǎo* means "old"; they are mutually interpretative. Finally, the phonetic loan principle usually refers to a character that borrowed its form and sound from another existing pictograph to express abstract meaning (e.g. 來 *lái* originally a pictograph of "wheat" was later on borrowed to express the meaning of "come"). See Table 5.1 for more examples of characters developed using the six principles.

Table 5.1   Examples derived from the six principles of character construction

Six Principles	Examples
Pictographic	马、女、日、月、山、水、雨、鱼、目
Indicative	一、二、三、上、下、刃、本、甘、末
Ideographic	明、好、森、炎、旦、休、掰、卡、鸣
Picto-phonetic	请、情、晴、们、闷、样、洋、财、材
Notative	考、老；顶、颠
Phonetic-borrowing	都、来

A question closely related to the formation of Chinese characters concerns the style of the Chinese script. Researchers generally consider the oracle-bone scripture (甲骨文, *jiǎgǔwén*) from the earliest period of recorded Chinese history, the Shang dynasty (1750–1040 BC), the earliest known form of Chinese writing, although they are not certain if oracle-bone scripture is indeed the earliest Chinese writing or if some as-yet-undiscovered form exists (cf. Coulmas 2003, Yin 1997). As a starting point for the study of Chinese characters for both style and creation, the oracle-bone scripture (or *scapulamancy*) carved on ox scapulas and tortoise shells for divination, is characterized as pointed and angular. From that point on, at least six more styles of characters were developed at different periods: bronze (金文, *jīnwén*, the thirteenth to fourth century BC), seal (篆书, *zhuànshū*, the eighth to third century BC), clerical (隶书, *lìshū*, the second century BC), standard (楷书, *kǎishū*, the fourth century), cursive (草书, *cǎoshū*, based on the clerical script), and running (行书, *xíngshū*, based on the standard script). Each of these scripts has its own distinctive features: the bronze script was engraved on bronzeware, largely containing records of clan names; it is rounder, more symmetrical and has fewer strokes than oracle-bone characters. The seal script developed from the bronze script became the standard writing recognized by the Qin State of the late Zhou dynasty (770–221 BC). Seal characters have regulated forms and gently curved strokes and are often sub-grouped into greater seal (大篆, *dàzhuàn*) and lesser seal (小篆, *xiǎozhuàn*), with the latter being simplified from the former. After the seal script came the clerical script, which was adopted as the only writing for official and government documents by the Qin and Han dynasties (206 BCE–220 AD). The clerical characters break the tradition of the seal script by staying away from those difficult curved stokes and using primarily level and straight strokes for square and neat characters. Many lexicographers consider the clerical script a critical transition of Chinese characters from pictographic to logographic because it laid the foundation for the development of the later scripts, such as cursive. Also known as grass script, cursive script evidently refers to the style of fast writing of the clerical script, linking strokes together whenever possible. The standard script is also derived from the clerical script, distinctive from all its predecessors by its even more regulated strokes (straight and level lines) and square-formed structure, as shown in Table 5.2. The most recently developed script is the running script. It is the handwritten form of the standard script and is often characterized as falling between cursive and standard script. For the purpose of efficiency in writing and reading, many people prefer the running script to the cursive script (difficult to read) and standard script (time consuming to write).

In addition to this stylistic evolution, Chinese characters have also undergone several major reforms implemented by the Chinese government over time. The first and foremost important government figure to become involved in language policy was probably Qín Shǐ-huáng (秦始皇), the emperor of the Qin dynasty (221–206 BC), who declared the seal script the standard format of writing throughout the country. Since then, various styles of Chinese characters have been

Table 5.2   Nine styles of Chinese characters

	horse	cart	fish	dust	see	
Oracle bone script 甲骨文 (jiǎ gǔ wén)						The Oracle bone script was used during the Shang or Yin Dynasty (c. 1400-1200 BC)
Bronze script 金文 (jīn wén)						The Bronze script was used during the Zhou Dynasty (c. 1400-1200 BC).
Large Seal script 大篆 (dà zhuàn)						The Large Seal script was used during the Zhou Dynasty (c. 1400-1200 BC).
Small Seal script 小篆 (xiǎo zhuàn)						The Small Seal script was used during the Qin Dynasty (221-207 BC)
Clerical script 隸書 (lì shū)						The Clerial and Standard scripts first appeared during the Han Dynasty (207 BC - 220 AD). The Standard script is still used but is now normally called the "Traditional Chinese script".
Standard script 楷書 (kǎi shū)						
Running script 行書 (xíng shū)						The Running script has been used for handwritten Chinese since the Han Dynasty.
Grass script 草書 (cǎo shū)						The Grass script is the Chinese equivalent of shorthand and has been used since the Han Dynasty.
Simplified script 简体字 (jiǎntǐzì)						The Simplified script has been used in the P.R.C. since 1949. It is also used in Singapore.
hànyǔ pīnyīn 汉语拼音	mǎ	chē	yú	chén	jiàn	*Hanyu pinyin* has been used in the P.R.C. since 1958.
zhùyīn fúhào 注音符號	ㄇㄚˇ	ㄔㄜ	ㄩˊ	ㄔㄣ	ㄐㄧㄢˋ	*Zhuyin fuhao* was developed in China in 1913 and is still used in Taiwan.

(Courtesy of http://www.chinesesoftwareguide.com/chinese/characters/char02.htm.)

developed, among which the most noticeable was the development of the clerical script and the government's reinforcement by using it in all government and official functions. As mentioned above, the clerical script serves as a bridge between the seal script and the modern standard script so that it became easier for ordinary people to learn to read and write Chinese characters. In modern Chinese history, the most prominent language reform occurred during the New Cultural Movement (1911) which encouraged an open dialogue and debate about many culture-related issues, among which is the subject concerning the abolition of *wén yán* (文言, literary/classical Chinese) and its replacement with *bái huà* (白话, colloquial Chinese). This reform had indeed alleviated the difficulty of many native speakers reading and writing Chinese, not to mention foreign learners. The most recent reform in the writing of Chinese characters was carried out in three processes of simplification: (1) in 1956, the Chinese government promoted the use of 515 simplified Chinese characters to replace their traditional counterparts. This reform was received positively by the public because many of the simplified characters were developed and already commonly used by Chinese people and even those, which were not familiar to the public, were carefully analyzed and found to be linguistically feasible for simplification before they were promoted for use; (2) in 1964, the Chinese government issued additional documents regarding the simplification of 132 radicals; (3) in 1977, another 800 simplified characters were promulgated by the government. This introduction, however, was not as successful as the first one. The major resistance arose from the irregular use of simplified parts regardless of their semantic/phonetic interpretability. Consequently, some of the characters have never been accepted by the public; neither were they used by the media or schools. This was one of the reasons why in 1986 the government withdrew the simplified characters issued in 1977 (cf. 语言文字规范手册, *Yǔyán Wénzì Guīfàn Shǒucè,* "Handbook of Regulations for Chinese Characters" 1993).

The three processes of simplification reforms resulted in approximately 2,000 positively received simplified characters (including those with simplified radicals). Since these characters are commonly used in daily life, they are taught in public schools and used along with other Chinese characters in public communication. In mainland China, the traditional version of those simplified characters appears only in classical literature and documents. Graduate students may be required to learn them. However, in Taiwan and Singapore the traditional version of the characters is still used in schools and by the media. For programs in teaching and learning Chinese as FL outside China, the simplified version has gradually gained ground and become the first choice because of student demand as well as the linguistic advantages of the simplified version (see discussion in 2.2).

5.1.2 *Research on teaching and learning characters*

Teaching and learning Chinese characters might be two of the most challenging tasks in the acquisition of Chinese language proficiency (the others are teaching and learning tones discussed in Chapter 4). In the past, this challenge has generated numerous discussions and debates at conferences (e.g. the annual meeting of the CLTA), on the Internet (e.g. Chinese List) and in professional journals (e.g. the *JCLTA*, *Shìjiè Hànyǔ Jiāoxué,* 世界汉语教学, "Global Chinese Pedagogy") among pedagogy specialists and teachers. Many important questions have been raised during those discussions, for instance: (1) What is the most effective way to learn to write characters and recognize/read characters? (2) What are the similarities and differences between character learners of Chinese as FL and character learners of Chinese as L1? If there are any differences, how should teachers and curricular designers implement them into classroom teaching? (3) What is the relationship between character competence and other language skills, such as listening and speaking? The first question, dealing with the methodology of character learning and recognition, has been most frequently addressed in the pedagogical literature (DeFrancis 1984, Ke 1996, 1998; Everson 1998, Lü 1999b, Yang 2000, Zhang 2001, Huang 2003, Chu 2004). It appears that most teachers and specialists agree that character teaching and learning should start from the understanding of the structure of characters and its relationship to sound and meaning to reduce students' difficulty and fear of Chinese characters. However, they seem to have failed to develop a comprehensive model for teaching and learning the three components of characters (i.e. sound, meaning, and form) simultaneously to enable students to build a rich vocabulary pool for communication. This is partially due to the disagreement among pedagogy specialists on whether learning Chinese should start with learning to read and write characters along with learning pronunciation (i.e. tones and the Romanized pronunciation system such as *pīnyīn*) and partially due to the lack of research on this subject.

As to the second and the third questions mentioned above, there are reports (e.g. Yang 2000) showing the difference in character acquisition patterns among students of Chinese as FL, students of foreign-born Chinese and native students of Chinese. That is, students' Chinese background has a direct impact on their learning patterns, and therefore, teachers should teach them by using different strategies. Without a doubt, these kinds of studies help teachers understand better the nature of character learners. The follow-up step, which is missing in the pedagogical literature, is to work out specific means to teach students of different backgrounds and needs. To amend this shortage, I will investigate in detail the problems in acquisition of characters by students of different backgrounds and recommend some specific procedures for learning how to pronounce, and read characters for beginners of Chinese in Sections 5.4–5.5. In the section immediately following, I will first discuss the characteristics of Chinese characters, their structures and their usage in communication.

5.2   Structure of Characters

Character is commonly interpreted as *zì* (字) in Chinese. For non-native speakers of Chinese, this interpretation may not help at all for the obvious reason that it does not provide any linguistic property that non-native Chinese speakers are familiar with in their native languages. Some may refer *zì* (字) to word. Unfortunately, even linguists are not able to come up with an adequate definition or description for word. How, then, do we define Chinese *zì*, the very element that gives students of Chinese so much of a headache and such difficulty in acquisition? Linguists prefer using the term *morpheme* to refer to the smallest meaningful unit. Does *zì* refer to the smallest meaningful unit in Chinese? The answer is partially yes and partially no because radicals have meanings but they are not considered *zì*. However, the real question is, "Is it necessary to introduce the term "morpheme" to language students who are about to learn Chinese characters?" The answer is probably no, because language class is not a linguistic class and students should not spend too much time on linguistic terminology. Hence, the simplest way to explain *zì* might be as follows: *zì* is an independent logograph (i.e. symbol) composed of different strokes and having its own meaning. Although this explanation may not be applicable to every single Chinese character, it is generally true and gives beginning students of Chinese some ideas of the property of *zì*.

Aside from the definition of *zì*, it is crucial to explain the structure of characters to students regardless of whether they are serious about learning Chinese. This is because the structure of characters provides not only information about how characters are formed, but also knowledge of Chinese culture — history, people, philosophy, etc. (see relevant discussion in Chapter 8). I believe that adequate teaching of the structure of characters can attract students' interest in learning Chinese and free them from the fear of characters as well. Precisely for this purpose, the following two sections are devoted to two components of characters: semantic and phonetic.

5.2.1 *Radicals*

Radical (部首, *bùshǒu*) refers to the semantic component of characters. It is derived from pictographs that signal the meaning of a given character. It was noted in 5.1.1 that a great majority of modern Chinese characters are picto-phonetic, pictographic, indicative or associative. This means that the majority of Chinese characters have radicals and students of Chinese need to learn them if they want to learn how to read and write Chinese with any degree of proficiency. Generally speaking, Chinese language practitioners recognize the importance of radicals in the acquisition of Chinese characters (e.g. Carr 1981, DeFrancis 1984, Hayes 1987, Ke 1998, Lu 1999b, Chu 2004). The only debatable issue is how to teach characters in general and how to teach radicals in particular. They seem to agree that the acquisition of characters involves training in the ability to pronounce (including comprehension when hearing it), the ability to read, and the ability to write characters. These three abilities are, not surprisingly, associated with the three properties of characters: sound, meaning and form. The ability to pronounce and understand a character when hearing it relates primarily to the sound or phonetic component of the character. The ability to read a character involves not only an understanding of the phonetic component but also an understanding of the semantic component of the character. Lastly, the ability to write a character requires recognition and production of the form of a character. Clearly, the three properties of characters and the four skills (i.e. speaking, listening, reading, and writing) are interrelated and interactive. Failure to understand any one property among the three could lead to failure to acquire characters. Therefore, students of Chinese, especially beginning students, should be given enough sustained opportunities to learn and understand both the semantic and phonetic components of characters and to understand the principles behind the formation of characters.

Now the question is which radicals students should learn. Xŭ Shèn, who categorized the six principles in constructing Chinese characters, first identified 540 radicals in his dictionary *Shuō Wén Jiě Zì* (说文解字, "Explaining and Analyzing Characters"). Later, in the well-known dictionary, *Kāngxī Zìdiǎn* (康熙字典, "Kangxi Dictionary") published in 1717, 214 radicals were selected and used, based on their commonality among characters and distinction from other radicals. These 214 radicals have become the standard selections in modern dictionaries. Is it necessary for students to learn all 214 of these radicals? Not right away. I suggest that students learn the first 100 or so (the most productive radicals) during the first year of Chinese classes and leave the remaining radicals for later years. The method of selecting the first 100 radicals should be based on the frequency of the occurrence of a given radical. Teachers and students may also choose their favorite radicals to learn first and leave the rest for a time when they can appreciate their functions better. My Top 100 Radical Picks are listed in Table 5.3.[1]

There are a number of reasons that elementary students should learn the most commonly used radicals: most notably, these radicals may help them memorize the meaning of characters, use dictionaries, and learn Chinese tradition and ideology. Since the radical is the semantic component of a character, it provides clues to the meaning of the whole character as illustrated in Table 5.4.

When a character has two components and both can be used as semantic indicators, providing hints to the meaning of this character, it becomes easier for students to remember the meaning of the whole character, as illustrated by the characters in Table 5.4. However, the most commonly seen characters do not have two semantic components; instead they have one radical (i.e. the semantic component) and one phonetic component. I will discuss the phonetic component of characters in the following section. What makes radical recognition critical for students is that learning radicals such as those listed in Table 5.4, enables students to make educated guesses regarding the meaning of the characters in which the radicals are used. This kind of deductive reasoning activity not only helps students memorize characters but also makes learning interesting and enjoyable.

Another reason for students to learn radicals is to enable them to use dictionaries. It is well known that modern dictionaries (e.g. 现代汉语词典, *Xiàndài Hànyǔ Cídiǎn,* "Modern Chinese Dictionary"; 新华字典, *Xīnhuá Zìdiǎn,* "New Chinese Dictionary") sort characters or *hànzì* either by radical and stroke number or by alphabet. Students who are familiar with radicals can easily find new words in a dictionary. This is especially important for students who have studied Chinese for a year or so, because they need to expand their reading and listening beyond their textbooks and anything they read outside their textbooks is likely to contain new vocabulary that they might need to look up. A dictionary is the best tool to help students understand their reading and expand their vocabulary. For this reason, one or two dictionary lessons is recommended during the

Table 5.3   100 frequently used Chinese radicals

	Radical	Pīnyīn	Meaning	Examples
1.	丶	diǎn	"dot"	主、头、为、丹、义
2.	一	yī	"one"	七、三、天、下、才
3.	丨	gūn	"bow"	个、中、旧、非、串
4.	丿	piě	"slash"	久、千、么、午、乐
5.	乙	yǐ	"second"	九、也、乱、飞、书
6.	冫	bīng	"ice"	冰、冷、凉、寒、冻
7.	讠/言	yán	"words"	认、识、说、话、证
8.	八	bā	"eight"	只、兴、关、单、前
9.	亻/人	rén	"person"	从、会、和、们、位
10.	勹	bāo	"wrap"	句、包、匀、勾、勾
11.	丶	tóu	"head"	六、交、京、亭、享
12.	儿	ér	"son"	元、兄、先、光、允
13.	厶	sī	"private"	去、台、能、参、公
14.	又	yòu	"right hand"	友、双、对、欢、取
15.	阝/阜、邑	fù/yì	"hill/capital"	阳、际、都、那、邮
16.	刂/刀	dāo	"knife"	刚、刻、分、色、切
17.	力	lì	"power/strength"	办、功、加、务、男
18.	二	èr	"two"	于、开、元、云、些
19.	十	shí	"cross"	华、卖、南、真、毕
20.	厂	chǎng	"cliff"	厅、历、压、厕、厌
21.	饣/食	shí	"food"	饭、餐、饮、饿、馆
22.	幺	yào	"tiny/small"	乡、幼、幻、系、兹
23.	宀	bǎo	"roof"	它、安、字、完、室
24.	忄/心	xīn	"heart"	快、性、闷、忘、必
25.	氵/水	shuǐ	"water"	汉、江、汽、永、求
26.	广	guǎng	"shelter"	应、床、店、康、座
27.	门	mén	"door"	问、间、闻、闲、阅
28.	辶	zǒu	"walk/go"	过、边、这、远、运
29.	工	gōng	"work"	左、差、项、攻、巧
30.	土	tǔ	"earth"	在、地、场、坏、坐
31.	士	shì	"gentleman"	声、喜、壮、壶、志
32.	艹	cǎo	"grass"	茶、节、花、药、草
33.	大	dà	"big"	太、奇、央、奋、尖
34.	寸	cùn	"inch"	封、寻、耐、寺、导
35.	扌/手	shǒu	"hand"	打、找、把、拿、拜
36.	小	xiǎo	"small"	少、尘、当、堂、常
37.	口	kǒu	"mouth"	可、号、骂、叫、否
38.	囗	wéi	"enclosure"	国、因、回、园、图
39.	巾	jīn	"napkin"	帅、布、市、帮、带
40.	山	shān	"mountain"	岁、岛、岳、岗、岸
41.	夕	xī	"dusk"	岁、名、多、梦、够
42.	彳	chì	"pace"	很、行、往、待、得
43.	夂	suī	"peaceful place"	处、条、务、各、复
44.	犭/犬	quǎn	"dog"	狗、猪、猫、哭、臭
45.	弓	gōng	"bow"	张、引、弱、强、弹
46.	女	nǚ	"woman"	好、妈、奶、如、要
47.	纟/糸	sī/mǐ	"silk/thread"	红、约、练、经、绍
48.	子	zǐ	"child"	孩、孙、学、存、孝
49.	灬/火	huǒ	"fire"	灯、炎、照、热、炒
50.	户	hù	"household"	房、所、启、扇、雇

Table 5.3 (continued)   100 frequently used Chinese radicals

	Radical	Pīnyīn	Meaning	Examples
51.	礻/示	*shì*	"spirit"	礼、社、祖、祝、福
52.	玉/王	*yù/wáng*	"jade/king"	宝、玩、球、琴、班
53.	木	*mù*	"wood"	本、李、校、杯、林
54.	车	*chē*	"vehicle"	轻、较、输、篆、辆
55.	戈	*gē*	"weapon"	划、成、我、或、戒
56.	止	*zhǐ*	"stop"	此、步、肯、歧、耻
57.	日	*rì*	"sun"	旦、早、时、明、春
58.	见	*jiàn*	"see"	观、视、现、觉、览
59.	贝	*bèi*	"shell"	贵、赚、贺、财、赔
60.	父	*fù*	"father"	父、爸、爷、爹
61.	牛	*niú*	"cow"	告、物、靠、特、牺
62.	毛	*máo*	"hair"	毛、尾、笔、毫、毯
63.	气	*qì*	"air"	气、氛、氧、氮、氨
64.	攵	*pū/wén*	"touch/essay"	收、放、改、教、数
65.	片	*piàn*	"piece"	片、版、牌、牒
66.	斤	*jīn*	"axe"	新、斧、欣、断、斩
67.	爪	*zhuā*	"claw"	爪、受、采、爬、觅
68.	月/肉	*yuè/ròu*	"moon/flesh"	有、望、期、肚、肥
69.	欠	*qiàn*	"owe"	次、歌、欲、歉、歇
70.	穴	*xuè*	"cave"	空、穷、容、窗、穿
71.	立	*lì*	"stand"	立、产、亲、站、端
72.	疒	*bìng*	"illness"	病、症、疗、疼、瘦
73.	礻/衣	*yī*	"clothes"	衬、衫、被、表、袋
74.	石	*shí*	"rock"	硬、研、破、确、磊
75.	目	*mù*	"eye"	看、眼、睡、瞎、瞪
76.	田	*tián*	"field"	电、申、由、界、留
77.	皿	*mǐn*	"utensil"	盘、盆、益、盖、盒
78.	钅/金	*jīn*	"gold/metal"	钱、银、钞、钢、铁
79.	矢	*shǐ*	"arrow"	矢、知、矩、短、矮
80.	禾	*hé*	"plant"	禾、程、季、种、香
81.	白	*bái*	"white"	白、的、皓、皎、皂
82.	鸟	*niǎo*	"bird"	鸟、鸡、鸭、鸳、鸯
83.	母	*mǔ*	"mother"	母、每、毒、贯
84.	羊	*yáng*	"sheep"	羊、美、着、善、群
85.	米	*mǐ*	"rice"	米、类、粉、糕、糖
86.	耳	*ěr*	"ear"	闻、取、聋、聊、聪
87.	西	*xī*	"west"	西、要、票
88.	页	*xié*	"head"	顾、顶、颗、顺、预
89.	虫	*chóng*	"insect"	虫、虾、蛋、虽、蚂
90.	舌	*shé*	"tongue"	舌、乱、甜、辞、舔
91.	竹	*zhú*	"bamboo"	笔、笑、笨、第、等
92.	走	*zǒu*	"walk"	走、赵、赶、趁、越
93.	舟	*zhóu*	"boat"	船、航、般、舱、舰
94.	足	*zú*	"foot"	跑、踢、距、跳、路
95.	豖	*shǐ*	"pig"	豕、家、象
96.	身	*shēn*	"body"	身、躺、躲、躬、躯
97.	雨	*yǔ*	"rain"	雨、雪、雷、雾、需
98.	鱼	*yú*	"fish"	鱼、鲜、鲍、鲲、鲤
99.	隹	*zhuī*	"bird"	难、售、集、雀、雅
100.	虎	*hǔ*	"tiger"	虚、虏、虑、虐

Table 5.4 Illustration of the relationship between radical and meaning of characters

CHARACTER/MEANING	COMPONENTS	ANALYSIS
问 *wèn* "ask"	门+口	use mouth at someone's door
好 *hǎo* "good"	女+子	female next to a child
男 *nán* "man"	田+力	field and strength
看 *kàn* "look/watch/read"	手+目	hand is above an eye (to be able to see)
闷 *mēn* "stuffed"	门+心	heart is inside a door
苗 *miáo* "seedling"	艹+田	plant in the field
瘦 *shòu* "skinny"	疒+叟	sick old man
尘 *chén* "dust"	小+土	small particle of dirt
坐 *zuò* "sit"	人+人+土	two persons sit side by side on earth

elementary Chinese year to help students practice dictionary skills and strengthen their understanding of radical usage.

Some characters in Table 5.4 are associative or ideographs consisting of two radicals. These are fun characters to teach and learn. Students may learn what constitutes "good" 好 *hǎo* (女 *nǚ* "female" + 子 *zǐ* "child"), "man" 男 *nán* (田 *tián* "field" + 力 *lì* "strength"), and "skinny" 瘦 *shòu* (疒 *bìng* "sick" + 叟 *sōu* "old man") in traditional Chinese people's minds. Although teachers may not always come up with an interesting and true story about the formation of every character that students encounter during their first year of learning Chinese, it is certainly encouraging, if not motivating, for students to hear stories like the two mentioned above, which will instill in them interest in learning more characters. Although it is tempting to allow first-year students to create stories based on what they think the radical looks like to foster memorization, this is not encouraged or recommended because it can hamper acquisition and comprehension in later stages with other characters that use the same radicals.

5.2.2 *Phonetic components*

The most likely component to combine with a radical to form a character is the phonetic component. It is clear from the term itself that a phonetic component gives clues as to the pronunciation of a character in which the component is used. Once students have acquired both semantic components, namely radicals and phonetic components, they know the basic components of any given characters. However, unlike semantic components, there is a general lack of studies on phonetic components. Soothill (1942) is one of the few researchers who have made efforts in sorting out Chinese phonetic components. The only problem with Soothill's study is that he classifies 4,300 characters under 985 phonetic components; this classification seems too tedious and lacks a pedagogical system for students to learn the language efficiently during a short period of time. Apart from Soothill's dictionary of characters and phonetic components, there is no other systematic categorization of phonetic components by lexicographers or pedagogy specialists; consequently, it is not clear which phonetic components are the most commonly used and how many of them students of different levels should learn. This shortage of study on phonetic components may partially reflect the fact that phonetic components are often deemed not as critical as semantic components in the acquisition of Chinese characters. They may be perceived as more difficult to categorize than semantic components. Encouragingly, many semantic components can also be used as phonetic components, so once students learn the most commonly used semantic components, they know many phonetic components as well. However, the most commonly used semantic components are not necessarily the most commonly used phonetic components. Regardless of the difficulty involved, my experience indicates that failure to adequately teach phonetic components could seriously affect students' reading and speaking competence.

It should be noted that some Chinese researchers (Zhang 1990, Fu 1992, Fei 1996, Chu 2001, Huang 2003) have explored the most commonly used components, not phonetic components, among the most commonly used characters. Chu (2001) classifies the most commonly used components or *hànzì zuì chángyòng bùjiàn* (汉字最常用部件) into two types: those that can be used as a character independently (成字部件, *chéngzì bùjiàn*) and those that cannot (非成字部件, *fēi chéngzì bùjiàn*). Based on Chu's classification, we can see that all those components that cannot be used as independent characters are radicals or semantic components, as illustrated in Table 5.5a, but those that can be used as independent characters are not all radicals, as shown in Table 5.5b. Observant teachers may quickly realize that almost all the radicals given in Table 5.5a are also listed in Table 5.5b; the only difference is that those in 5.5a are reduced forms of radicals and those in 5.5b are regular forms. One may wonder why both forms of the same radicals are frequently used in modern Chinese characters. This can be explained by the fact that the reduced form of radicals is most often used as a semantic component of characters while the regular form is most often used as a phonetic component. Aside from those radicals with two forms, some components listed in Table 5.5b do not have a reduced form. In this case, some of the regular forms may be used as either a radical or a phonetic component, while others may only be used as a phonetic component. For instance, 马 (*mǎ,* "horse") can be used either as a radical in words, such as 驾 (*jià,* "ride"), 驴 (*lǘ,* "mule"), and 验 (*yàn* "examine"), or as a phonetic component in words such as 吗, (*ma,* "interrogative marker"), 骂 (*mà,* "scold"), and 妈 (*mā,* "mother"). 巴 (*bā,* "country"), on the other hand, is not a radical, therefore, can only be used as a phonetic component in words such as 吧 (*ba,* "sentence final particle"), 把 (*bǎ,* "object marker"), and (爸, *bà* "father").

Table 5.5a   Some most commonly used parts among 1,000 frequently used characters

PART	PINYIN	MEANING
亻	*rén*	"person"
讠	*yán*	"word"
冂	*jiǒng*	"border"
厶	*sī*	"private"
阝	*chén*	"city"
刂	*dāo*	"knife"
冫	*bīng*	"ice"
勹	*bāo*	"wrap"
宀	*bǎo*	"roof"
忄	*xīn*	"heart"
氵	*shuǐ*	"water"
幺	*yáo*	"little"
辶	*zǒu*	"walk/go"
艹	*cǎo*	"grass"
扌	*shǒu*	"hand"
犭	*quǎn*	"dog"
彳	*chì*	"pace"
夂	*suī*	"peaceful place"
纟	*sī/mī*	"silk/thread"
饣	*shí*	"food"
攵	*pū/wén*	"touch/essay"
灬	*huǒ*	"fire"
礻	*shì*	"spirit"
疒	*bìng*	"illness"
衤	*yī*	"clothes"
隹	*zhuī*	"bird"
钅	*jīn*	"gold/metal"
穴	*xuè*	"cave"

Table 5.5b   78 commonly used parts among 1,000 frequently used characters

PART	PINYIN	MEANING	PART	PINYIN	MEANING
八	*bā*	"eight"	目	*mù*	"eye"
巴	*bā*	"county"	牛	*niú*	"cow"
白	*bái*	"white"	女	*nǚ*	"woman"
贝	*bèi*	"shell"	皮	*pí*	"skin"
匕	*bì*	"dagger"	其	*qí*	"its"
不	*bù*	"not"	千	*qiān*	"thousand"
寸	*cùn*	"inch"	七	*qī*	"seven"
厂	*chǎng*	"shelter"	且	*qiè*	"this"
车	*chē*	"vehicle"	欠	*qiàn*	"owe"
虫	*chóng*	"insect"	人	*rén*	"man"
大	*dà*	"big"	日	*rì*	"sun"
刀	*dāo*	"knife"	山	*shān*	"mountain"
丁	*dīng*	"man"	生	*shēng*	"birth"
儿	*ér*	"son"	尸	*shī*	"corpse"
二	*èr*	"two"	十	*shí*	"ten"
耳	*ěr*	"ear"	石	*shí*	"stone"
方	*fāng*	"square"	矢	*shì*	"dart"
丰	*fēng*	"rich"	士	*shì*	"man"
戈	*gē*	"weapon"	土	*tǔ*	"earth"
艮	*gèn*	"hard"	田	*tián*	"field"
弓	*gōng*	"bow"	王	*wáng*	"king"
工	*gōng*	"work"	亡	*wáng*	"destroy"
广	*guǎng*	"cliff"	西	*xī*	"west"
禾	*hé*	"grain"	夕	*xī*	"dusk"
火	*huǒ*	"fire"	小	*xiǎo*	"small"
户	*hù*	"household"	心	*xīn*	"heart"
几	*jǐ*	"table"	已	*yǐ*	"stop"
己	*jǐ*	"self"	乙	*yǐ*	"second"
见	*jiàn*	"see"	羊	*yáng*	"sheep"
斤	*jīn*	"axe"	也	*yě*	"also"
巾	*jīn*	"napkin"	页	*yè*	"heading"
九	*jiǔ*	"nine"	又	*yòu*	"also"
口（囗）	*kǒu/wéi*	"mouth/enclosure	月	*yuè*	"moon"
力	*lì*	"power"	云	*yún*	"cloud"
立	*lì*	"stand"	止	*zhǐ*	"stop"
马	*mǎ*	"horse"	子	*zǐ*	"child"
门	*mén*	"door"	自	*zì*	"self"
米	*mǐ*	"rice"	中	*zhōng*	"middle"
木	*mù*	"wood"	乍	*zhà*	"beginning"

Although Chu's study is limited to the 128 most commonly used components among the 1,000 most frequently used characters, it is sufficient for students at the elementary level to acquire the basic knowledge of Chinese characters. Advanced students seeking more information on semantic and phonetic components may consult Huang (2003) and *Hànzì Shǔxìng Zidian* (汉字属性字典, "Chinese Character Property Dictionary") (1989). Since more than 80 percent of Chinese characters have the structure "semantic component + phonetic component" (形声字, *xíngshēng zì*), it is necessary for teachers and students not only to have a clear understanding of semantic components, but of phonetic components as well. Given a list of phonetic components such as the one in Table 5.5b, teachers may decide how they can best integrate those phonetic components into their character teaching curriculum. Adequate instruction in phonetic components along with semantic components accelerates students' character acquisition process. For instance, students may learn the groups of words in (5.1) together.

(5.1)

门 *mén*	们 *men*	闷 *mēn*			
"door"	"plural"	"stuff"			
白 *bái*	百 *bǎi*	柏 *bǎi*	伯 *bái*		
"white"	"hundred"	"pine"	"uncle"		
巴 *bā*	吧 *ba*	把 *bǎ*	爸 *bà*	叭 *bā*	
"scar"	particle	"hold"	"dad"	"trumpet"	
马 *mǎ*	吗 *ma*	妈 *mā*	骂 *mà*	蚂 *mǎ*	
"horse"	particle	"mom"	"scold"	"ant"	
方 *fāng*	房 *fáng*	放 *fàng*	仿 *fǎng*	纺 *fǎng*	访 *fǎng*
"square"	"house"	"place"	"imitate"	"textile"	"visit"
丁 *dīng*	盯 *dīng*	订 *dìng*	钉 *dīng*	町 *dīng*	叮 *dīng*
"man"	"stare"	"order"	"nail"	name	"sting"

Knowing the phonetic components, namely knowing the general sound those components impart to a character, students may pronounce and guess the meaning of those characters based on the meaning of the radicals with which those phonetic components are used to form those characters. This fact was actually recognized by scholars for decades (e.g. DeFrancis 1984), only that it has not been sufficiently incorporated into teaching characters. I suggest that first-year students learn all of the 78 phonetic components given in Table 5.5b and the 100 semantic components given in Table 5.3. Once they learn all these basic components, students should have a good foundation in the three elements of characters: form, sound, and meaning.

5.3   Characteristics of *ci*

Ci (词), which may be translated into English as "word," is a complicated term and difficult to define in the field of linguistics. Another character 辞 (*ci*) which has the same pronunciation as but a slightly different meaning from 词 (*ci*) is most likely used to refer to dictionary (see discussion below). It is interesting, though, that laypeople do not seem to have any problems using *ci* or *words* in their daily communication. For this reason, I will use Ding's (1961) simple definition concurred with by Norman (1988) to describe the usage of *ci* as a unit "which has a specific meaning and can be used freely." With this definition as a guiding tool, I devote this section to the description and discussion of the types and functions of *ci* in everyday Chinese. To ordinary Chinese people, *ci* is graphically different from *zi* in that a *ci* is likely to contain more than one *zi*. This difference is often seen in the title of dictionaries: some dictionaries are called 字典 (*zì diǎn,* "character dictionary"), some are called 词典 (*cí diǎn,* "word dictionary") , and others are called 辞典 (*cí diǎn,* "language dictionary"). Although these three types of dictionaries seem clearly defined as shown by their English translation, in reality this does not necessarily mean that if students want to find the meaning and usage of a character, they can look it up in a *zì diǎn* (字典). If the inquiry is into the meaning and usage of a character compounded with other characters, *cí diǎn* (词典) is the right source. However, if students wish to find a comprehensive explanation of a word, they should check a *cí diǎn* (辞典). The reason is that a *zì diǎn* often gives few examples of words for a given entry of a character while a *cí diǎn* often has some explanation of individual characters. More discussion of dictionary usage will be given in 5.6.2. In what follows, three major types of words in Chinese will be discussed: compound, reduplication, and loan words.

5.3.1   Compounds

The compound word in modern Chinese is harder to define than its counterpart in English. English compound words can be defined as a combination of two free morphemes (with the concept of free morpheme being equivalent to *ci* as described in the immediately preceding section), whereas Chinese compounds cannot be defined in the same way for two reasons: (1) some morphemes that were considered free morphemes in classical Chinese are not considered free in Modern Chinese and (2) the meaning of the compound is not always the same as or even similar to the combined meaning of the two free morphemes. Hence, Li and Thompson (1981: 46) characterize Chinese compounds as "polysyllabic units that have certain properties of single words and that can be analyzed into two or more meaningful morphemes even if some morphemes cannot occur independently in modern Chinese." Obviously, this is not an ideal description of compounds for students of Chinese as FL, but it at least gives teachers some idea of the linguistic description of the function of compounds in modern Chinese. For students, teachers may simply say that compounds are derived from combining two *zì* or *cí*, even though this is not technically an accurate linguistic description.

Because of the flexibility of compounding, it has become the most productive method of forming words in modern Chinese. Approximately 80 percent of Chinese words are compound words; this means that students of Chinese must learn both the method for forming compound words and the skills necessary to understand and use compound words in communication. There are a number of different ways to form a compound word, as illustrated below:

(1) Noun + noun	星期	名字	地方	孩子	汉语	电脑
	xīngqī	*míngzi*	*dìfāng*	*háizi*	*hànyǔ*	*diànnǎo*
	star-period	name-word	earth-square	child-son	Han-language	electricity-brain
	"week"	"name"	"place"	"child"	"Chinese"	"computer"

(2) Adj. + noun	老师	大家	高速	红叶	热心	好人
	lǎoshī	*dàjiā*	*gāosù*	*hóngyè*	*rèxīn*	*hǎorén*
	old-master	big-family	high-speed	red-leaf	hot-heart	good-person
	"teacher"	"everyone"	"high speed"	"maple leaf"	"enthusiastic"	"good person"

(3) Verb + noun	吃饭	学生	听话	演员	唱歌	回家
	chīfàn	*xuésheng*	*tīnghuà*	*yǎnyuán*	*chànggē*	*huíjiā*
	eat-food	learn-pupil	listen-words	perform-er	sing-song	return-home
	"eat"	"student"	"obedient"	"performer"	"sing"	"return home"

(4) Noun + verb	头疼	工作	日记	日落	公共	眼红
	tóuténg	*gōngzuò*	*rìjì*	*rìluò*	*gōnggòng*	*yǎnhóng*
	head-pain	work-do	day-record	sun-set	public-share	eye-red
	"headache"	"work"	"diary"	"sunset"	"public"	"jealous"

(5) Noun + Adj.	年轻	身高	口干	脸红	命苦	心酸
	niánqīng	*shēngāo*	*kǒugān*	*liǎnhóng*	*mìngkǔ*	*xīnsuān*
	year-young	body-high	mouth-dry	face-red	life-bitter	heart-sour
	"young"	"tall/height"	"thirsty"	"blushing"	"bad fate"	"sad"

(6) Verb + verb	观看	开关	进来	觉得	开始	请问
	guānkàn	*kāiguān*	*jìnlái*	*juéde*	*kāishǐ*	*qǐngwèn*
	watch-see	open-close	enter-come	feel-get	open-start	please-ask
	"observe"	"switch"	"enter"	"feel"	"start"	"may I ask"

(7) Verb + adj.	吃饱	分明	开满	漂亮	成熟	赶紧
	chībǎo	*fēnmíng*	*kāimǎn*	*piàoliang*	*chéngshú*	*gǎnjǐn*
	eat-full	divide-clear	open-full	flow-shine	become-ripe	hurry-tight
	"become full"	"distinctive"	"full of"	"pretty"	"mature"	"hurry up"

(8) Adj. + verb	好看	难吃	小产	近来	凉拌	直飞
	hǎokàn	*nánchī*	*xiǎochǎn*	*jìnlái*	*liángbàn*	*zhífēi*
	good-look	hard-eat	small-born	near-come	cool-mix	straight-fly
	"pretty"	"taste bad"	"abortion"	"recent"	"cold dish"	"fly direct"

(9) Adj. + adj.	干净	凉快	清楚	聪明	简单	酸辣
	gānjìng	*liángkuài*	*qīngchu*	*cōngming*	*jiǎndān*	*suānlà*
	dry-clean	cool-quick	clear-clear	clever-bright	simple-single	sour-hot
	"clean"	"cool"	"clear"	"clever"	"simple"	"hot & sour"

From the above examples, we see the following patterns:

Noun + noun	=>	noun phrase
Adj. + noun	=>	(most likely) noun phrase
Verb + noun	=>	either noun or verb phrase
Noun + verb	=>	(most likely) noun phrase
Noun + adj.	=>	(mostly) adjective phrase
Verb + verb	=>	verb phrase
Verb + adj.	=>	(stative) verb phrase
Adj. + verb	=>	(mostly) stative verb phrase
Adj. + adj.	=>	adj. phrase

It should be pointed out that when teaching compounding and compounds, grammatical terms, such as noun, verb, and adjective should only be used as tools assisting students' understanding of compounding and compounds. Any elaboration of these terms is not necessary because students should focus on the function not the structure of the compounds. For instance, when students learn the word 星期 (*xīngqī*, "week"), they may review or learn other compounds that contain one of the two characters: 星球 (*xīngqiú*, "star"), 火星 (*huǒxīng*, "Mars"), 明星 (*míngxīng*, "shining star"), 日期 (*rìqī*, "date"), 假期 (*jiàqī*, "vocation period"). When students learn the word 好吃 (*hǎochī*, "taste good"), they may expand their vocabulary to 好看 (*hǎokàn*, "good looking")，好听 (*hǎotīng*, "pleasant to hear"), 好热 (*hǎorè*, "very hot"), 好冷 (*hǎolěng*, "very cold"), 好帅 (*hǎoshuài*, "very handsome"), 好认 (*hǎorèn*, "easy to recognize"), 好说 (*hǎoshuō*, "easy to talk about"), etc. With sufficient examples, students should realize the function and structure of compounding without using those grammatical terms to explain them in class.

It should be clear that compounding is an effective way to expand students' vocabulary. There are a few other word-building methods in Chinese, but none of them is as productive and effective as the compounding method.

5.3.2   *Reduplication*

Many verbs and adjective can be reduplicated in Chinese, but not in English. Consider the following examples:

(5.2)	看看书	*kànkan shū*	"read a little bit of a book"
	聊聊天	*liáoliao tiān*	"chat a little bit"
	说说话	*shuōshuo huà*	"talk a little bit"
	跳跳舞	*tiàotiao wǔ*	"dance a little bit"
	唱唱歌	*chàngchang gē*	"sing a little bit"
(5.3)	介绍介绍	*jièshào jièshào*	"introduce a little bit"
	庆祝庆祝	*qìngzhù qìngzhù*	"celebrate a little bit"
	欢迎欢迎	*huānyíng huānyíng*	"welcome, welcome"
	讨论讨论	*tǎolùn tǎolùn*	"discuss a little bit"
(5.4)	红红的	*hónghóng de*	"very crimson"
	酸酸的	*suānsuān de*	"very sour"
	辣辣的	*làlà de*	"very spicy"
	大大的	*dàdà de*	"very big"
(5.5)	高高兴兴	*gāogāoxìngxing*	"be happy"
	舒舒服服	*shūshūfúfú*	"be comfortable"
	干干净净	*gāngānjìngjìng*	"be clean"
	清清楚楚	*qīngqīngchǔchǔ*	"be clear"

The words in (5.2) have their monosyllabic verb reduplication; those in (5.3) have their bi-syllabic verb reduplicated, those in (5.4) reduplicates their monosyllabic adjectives, and those in (5.5) reduplicates their bi-syllabic adjectives. Two issues are relevant to the acquisition of reduplication and deserve some discussion here: (1) the structure of bi-syllabic reduplication and (2) the communicative function of reduplication. Notice that the reduplicated words in (5.3) and (5.5) have different structures: "V1 + V2 + V1 + V2" and "adj1 + adj1 + adj2 + adj2". Most reduplication adheres to these patterns. However, with the increase in students' vocabulary, they may soon come to realize that not all verbs and adjectives use those structures to form reduplication. Some verbs may be reduplicated the way adjectives are (e.g. 粉红粉红的, *fěnhóng fěnhóng*, "very pink") and some adjectives may follow the pattern of verb reduplication (说说笑笑, *shuōshuō xiàoxiào,* "talk and laugh"). Furthermore, not all verbs and adjectives can be reduplicated. Since there seems to be no clear rules governing which verbs and adjectives can be reduplicated and which cannot (Li and Thompson 1981: 33), students should be cautious in forming reduplication with verbs and adjectives; memorization may work best in this case.

As far as the function of reduplication is concerned, it is reasonably straightforward. When verbs are reduplicated, they denote the meaning of briefly carried-on action of the verb. When adjectives are reduplicated, they either intensify the quality of what the adjective describes (e.g. 蓝天 *lán tiān* "blue sky" vs. 蓝蓝的天 *lánlán de tiān* "pretty blue sky") or make what the adjective describes more descriptive and vivid (e.g. 酸辣汤 *suānlà tāng* "hot-sour soup" vs. 酸酸的、辣辣的汤 *suānsuān de làlà de tāng* "very sour and very hot soup"). Students may find these kinds of functions interesting to learn and fun to use in communication, especially for students whose native language is English because English does not have many words that can be reduplicated as Chinese.

Apart from verbs and adjectives that are often reduplicated, kinship nouns and measure words can be reduplicated too. First-year students may find it challenging to pronounce reduplicated words because the second character in reduplicated words usually carries a neutral tone (e.g. 爸爸 *bàba* "father", 妈妈 *māma* "mother", 姐姐 *jiějie* "older sister", 弟弟 *dìdi* "younger brother", 妹妹 *mèimei* "younger sister", 哥哥 *gēge* "older brother"). Nevertheless, once they master these reduplicated kinship words, students have acquired the ability to produce the neutral tone.

What distinguishes reduplication from compounding is that reduplication is not a word building method; rather, it is a means of diversifying the style of discourse. It makes a conversation or discourse less formal and more interesting.

5.3.3   *Loan words*

Loan words (外来词, *wàilái cí*) refer to those words that are borrowed from other languages. There are many loan words in Chinese and undoubtedly, even more will be recruited into the vocabulary pool of the Chinese language in the future. With the rapid advancement of computing technology and global communication, it is inevitable that foreign words will continue to find their way into the Chinese lexicon. The issues relevant to the discussion of teaching and learning Chinese as FL is how to train students so that they can not only identify loan words in communication, but also become capable of introducing new loan words into Chinese so as to enhance their competence in Chinese communication.

Chinese has a long history of borrowing new words from foreign languages. Studies (e.g. Shi 2000) show that Chinese year names were probably borrowed from Babylonian during the Zhou dynasty (770 BC–221 BC). From loan word dictionaries (e.g. Cén 1990), we see that Chinese has not only borrowed words from the languages of neighboring countries, such as India (Hindu), Korea (Korean) and Japan (Japanese), but also from many European languages such as Latin, French, Russian, English and Spanish. Regardless of the source, these loan words may be roughly categorized into two types: (1) borrowed into Chinese based on their original pronunciation, as shown in (5.6), and (2) borrowed into Chinese based partially on their original pronunciation and partially on their original meaning as shown in (5.7). Words translated into Chinese from foreign languages, such as 电脑 (*diànnǎo,* "computer") and 下载 (*xiàzǎi,* "download"), are generally not considered loan words because those characters/words are Chinese words, not foreign words.

(5.6)	"sofa"	沙发	*shāfā*
	"jacket"	夹克	*jiákè*
	"pudding"	布丁	*bùdīng*
	"платы"	布拉吉	*bùlāji* (from Russian "skirt")
	"jeep"	吉普	*jípǔ*
	"modern"	摩登	*módēng*
	"salad"	萨拉	*sālā*
	"vitamin"	维他命	*vítāmíng*
	"coffee"	咖啡	*kāfēi*
	"Coca cola"	可口可乐	*kěkǒukělè*
	"Motorola"	摩托罗拉	*mótuōluólā*
	"McDonald"	麦当劳	*màidānglào*
	"bus"	巴士	*bāshì*
	"Benz"	奔驰	*bēnchí*
	"Bush"	布什	*bùshí*
	"Nixon"	尼克松	*níkèsōng*
	"Pennsylvania"	宾西法尼亚	*bīnxīfǎníyà*
(5.7)	motorcycle	摩托车	*mótuō chē*
	credit card	信用卡	*xìnyòngkǎ*
	apple pie	苹果派	*píngguǒ pài*
	Yuppie	雅皮士	*yǎpí shì*
	Hippie	嬉皮士	*xīpí shì*
	Thailand	泰国	*tàiguó*
	Chauvinism	沙文主义	*shāwénzhǔyì* (from French)
	ballet	芭蕾舞	*bāléi wǔ* (from French)
	bar	酒吧	*jiǔbā*
	champagne	香槟酒	*xiāngbīng jiǔ*
	AIDS	艾滋病	*àizī bìng*
	T-shirt	T恤衫	*tìxùshān*
	hamburger	汉堡包	*hànbǎo bāo*
	pizza	比萨饼	*bǐshà bǐng*
	Starbucks	星巴克	*xīngbākè*
	bowling	保龄球	*bǎolíng qiú*
	Internet	因特网	*yīntèwǎng*

From the examples in (5.6)–(5.7), it can be seen that those loan words that were borrowed into Chinese either because the concepts expressed by those words did not exist in Chinese life or because Chinese had not yet invented the words for those concepts at the time when they were borrowed. What makes the borrowing process complicated, though, is the rules that govern the conversion from foreign words and sounds into Chinese characters and sounds. Notice that none of the

Chinese words in (5.6)–(5.7) are phonetically identical to their counterparts in the language from which they are borrowed. Students might have to learn all the rules of conversions from foreign sounds to Chinese to be able to identify loan words. Advanced students might even be able to introduce some new loan words into Chinese. Table 5.6 lists some of the most commonly used Chinese characters that correspond to the 26 English letters combined with different vowels.

Table 5.6   Possible Chinese characters representing 26 English letters

Letter	Possible characters when converted into Chinese
a	阿 *ā*, 爱 *ài*, 奥 *ào*, 安 *ān*,
b	巴 *bā*, 白 *bái*, 贝 *bèi*, 伯 *bó*, 布 *bù*
c	卡 *kǎ*, 凯 *kǎi*, 塞 *cài*, 查 *chá*, 西 *xī*, 克 *kè*, 康 *kāng*, 库 *kù*
d	达 *dá*, 戴 *dài*, 多 *duō*, 丹 *dān*, 德 *dé*, 迪 *dí*, 杜 *dù*, 邓 *dèng*
e	伊 *yi*, 艾 *ài*, 埃 *āi*, 爱 *ài*
f	法 *fǎ*, 费 *fèi*, 芬 *fēng*, 弗 *fú*, 富 *fú*
g	加 *jiā*, 盖 *gài*, 高 *gāo*, 格 *gé*, 戈 *gé*, 吉 *jí*, 乔 *qiáo*, 治 *zhì*, 杰 *jié*
h	哈 *hā*, 海 *hǎi*, 瀚 *hàn*, 赫 *hè*, 亨 *hēng*, 希 *xī*, 霍 *huò*
i	伊 *yí*, 艾 *ài*, 英 *yīng*, 欧 *ōu*
j	吉 *jí*, 杰 *jié*, 朱 *zhū*, 约 *yuē*, 乔 *qiáo*, 夹 *jiā*
k	卡 *kǎ*, 凯 *kǎi*, 克 *kè*, 肯 *kěn*, 基 *jī*, 柯 *kē*, 库 *kù*
l	拉 *lā*, 莱 *lái*, 兰 *lán*, 劳 *láo*, 利 *lì*, 林 *lín*, 朗 *lǎng*, 路 *lù*, 罗 *luó*, 尔 *ěr*
m	马 *mǎ*, 麦 *mài*, 梅 *méi*, 莫 *mò*, 米 *mǐ*, 明 *míng*, 曼 *màn*, 蒙 *měng*
n	纳 *nà*, 男 *nán*, 尼 *ní*, 纽 *niǔ*, 诺 *nuò*, 恩 *ēn*
o	澳 *ào*, 奥 *ào*, 欧 *ōu*
p	波 *bō*, 博 *bó*, 佩 *pèi*, 皮 *pí*
q	昆 *kūn*, 奎 *kuí*
r	拉 *lā*, 兰 *lán*, 雷 *léi*, 洛 *luò*, 罗 *luó*, 利 *lì*, 鲁 *lǔ*
s	萨 *sà*, 塞 *sài*, 舒 *shū*, 施 *shī*, 西 *xī*, 谢 *xiè*, 雪 *xuě*, 辛 *xīn*, 斯 *xī*, 苏 *sū*
t	塔 *tǎ*, 泰 *tài*, 特 *tè*, 托 *tuō*, 顿 *dùn*
u	尤 *yōu*, 安 *ān*
v	范 *fàn*, 番 *fán*, 维 *wēi*, 弗 *fú*, 夫 *fū*
w	韦 *wěi*, 华 *huá*, 威 *wēi*, 文 *wén*, 惠 *huì*, 伍 *wǔ*
x	西 *xī*
y	约 *yuē*, 阳 *yáng*, 扬 *yáng*, 伊 *yí*
z	载 *zāi*, 赞 *zàn*, 曾 *céng*, 齐 *qí*, 其 *qí*

For English words such as "Clinton", the first step is to divide the word into Chinese monosyllabic segments: *c, lin, ton*. Since Chinese does not allow consonant cluster as "*cl*", "*c*" has to be converted into a character independent from "*lin*". Based on Table 5.6, the closest pronunciations and characters for the three segments are *kè* 克, *lin* 林, and *dùn* 顿. For place name like *Bellingham*, one may convert it into *běilínhàn* 北林瀚 (literally "north forest immeasurable") or *běilínhǎi* 北临海 (literally "north nearby sea"). However, since the meaning of *běilínhǎi* better fits the geographic feature of Bellingham in the state of Washington, US, it becomes the preferred choice.

It should be noted that the list of the possible Chinese characters representing the 26 English letters used with various vowels in Table 5.6 is not meant to be exclusive. Since Chinese is a language rich in homophones, any of the characters listed in the Table may be replaced by its homophone. In addition, Table 5.6 does not provide meaning for those characters exemplified. This is because for loan words, the key feature involved in borrowing from an original language to Chinese is retaining the sound of the original words, not meaning. As long as the meaning of a given character does not have any negative connotation, it can be used to represent the sound of a loan word. Certainly, it is ideal to find a perfect match between the sound and meaning of the original words and Chinese characters. It is said that one of the reasons why 可口可乐 (*kěkǒukělè*, "Coca cola", literal translation: "make one's mouth pleasant") has achieved immediate success and become one of the most popular soft drinks in China was due to its aptly translated brand name. However, while certainly something to strive for, such an ideal conversion as Coca Cola, which positively retains both its original phonetic and semantic properties is uncommon. Most loan words can only retain their phonetic property as those in (5.6) and some loan words may have a semantic feature added to the original phonetic form during conversion as those in (5.7). When not appropriately borrowed into Chinese due to the choice of meaningless homophonic characters, such as 起司 (*qǐsī,* "cheese"), loan words may soon be replaced by other more appropriately borrowed words or translated words (e.g. 奶酪 *nǎilào* "cheese").

Once students of Chinese as FL learn the possible characters representing the alphabet in Table 5.6, it becomes relatively easy for them to identify, read and learn purely phonetic-converted loan words, especially those borrowed from their native languages. If loan words are borrowed based partially on their sounds and partially on their meaning, students will have to have, in addition, knowledge of the Chinese words that best describe the meaning of the borrowed word in its original language along with the knowledge of characters that represent the sounds in the alphabet. For instance, when borrowing words denoting the meaning of some kind of food from English, Chinese words such as 饼 (*bǐng,* "cake"), 酒 (*jiǔ,* "wine"), and 包 (*bāo,* "bun") are added to the original words "pizza", "champagne", and "hamburger" to form the loan words 比萨饼 *bǐsà bǐng,* 香槟酒 *xiāngbīng jiǔ,* and 汉堡包 *hànbǎo bāo.* In these cases, without the additions, it would be difficult for Chinese people to understand the real meanings of the loan words.

Although loan words make up only a small percentage of all Chinese words, they are vital for students to learn in order to succeed in communication. This becomes even clearer when we look at the source language and the types of words that are often borrowed into Chinese. According to Shi (2000: 162–3), among 7704 loan words, 3,426 are from English, 882 from Japanese, 780 from Hindu,

401 from Russian and 400 from Mongolian with the remaining words coming from other languages. When classifying the loan words borrowed from English, Shi's statistics show that approximately two-thirds of them are related to technology, science, medicine, and industry with the remainder related to politics, economy, religion, entertainment, and daily activities. Since these areas are among the interests of students of Chinese, teaching loan words becomes a necessity.

Technically, words translated from other languages, such as those in (5.8) are not considered loan words: they are derived from other languages based on the meaning of the original words without regard to phonetic similarity; in fact, the Chinese characters used in translation are not pronounced similarly to the original words. The difference between translated words and loan words is so distinct yet so related that it is difficult to discuss and teach one type without mentioning the other.

(5.8)   "cream"   奶油   *nǎiyóu* (literal translation: milk oil)

"cheese"   奶酪   *nǎilào* (lit. milk junket)

"Windows 98"   视窗 98   *shìchuāng jiǔbā* (lit. viewing window 98)

"space shuttle"   航天飞机   *hángtiān fēijī* (lit. space airplane)

"mouse"   鼠器   *shǔqì* (lit. mouse instrument)

"broadband"   宽带   *kuāndài* (lit. wide band)

"browser"   浏览器   *liúlǎnqì* (lit. viewing instrument)

"motor"   电动机   *diàndàng jī* (lit. electric machine)

                  (cf. 马达   *mǎdá*)

"email"   电子邮件   *diànzǐ yóujiàn* (lit. electronic mail)

                  (cf. 伊妹儿   *yīmèir*)

When translating and introducing new foreign words into Chinese, some people prefer the literal translation method (e.g. "Test of English as a Foreign Language", 英语作为外语的考试, *yīngyǔ zuòwéi wàiyǔ de kǎoshì*) and some prefer metaphor or metonymy (e.g. "ice cream", 冰激淋, *bīngjīlín,* meaning something like "ice simulates the feeling of cool water" and "Sprite" 雪碧 *xuěbì* meaning that the soft drink is like snow and blue jade — cold and sparkling.) For students of Chinese as FL, words translated using the literal method may be relatively easy to understand, learn and use. Words derived from other methods may have to be learned as special new words because: (1) it is difficult to draw the connection between the original meaning and the metaphorical or metonymic meaning and (2) these words differ from other ordinary words in that they come from other languages. However, adequate and gradual introduction of the translated words along with loan words to students should make teaching and learning more interesting. With the increase of the number of loan words and translated words, students' communicative competence should also be improved.

5.4   Difficulties in Acquisition

In learning Chinese characters, the degree of difficulty for students may vary depending upon the writing system of students' native language. For native students of logographic writing, pronunciation of characters (e.g. initials, finals, and tones) may be more challenging than other areas. For native students of alphabetic writing, however, the most difficult task might be twofold: (1) writing and memorizing the form, meaning, and sound of characters, and (2) learning tones. Chapter 4 discussed the procedures in acquisition of tones and in the following section, I will recommend some specific procedures in learning to pronounce, read, and write characters.

5.5   Suggested Teaching and Learning Models

There are many different ways to help students learn Chinese characters. Following are a few that have been discussed in pedagogical literature or successfully used with students.

- Strokes and stroke order
- Storytelling
- Guessing based on semantic and phonetic components
- Compounding and sentencing
- Recognizing and using synonyms and antonyms
- Outrageous words (e.g. swear words)
- Word puzzles and word games
- Converting traditional to simplified characters and vice versa

To begin with, students should be introduced to the basic strokes of Chinese characters. There are eight types of strokes commonly used to compose characters: (1) *diǎn* "dot" as in 六， (2) *héng* "horizontal" as in 一， (3) *shù* "vertical" as in 十， (4) *piě* "downward left" as in 八, (5) *nà* "downward right" in as 入, (6) *tí* "upward right" as in 把, (7) *gōu* "hook" as in 小 and 字, and (8) *zhé* "cornering" as in 口 and 医. Each of these strokes may be considered to function as letters do in alphabetical languages (e.g. the Chinese character 人 *rén* "person" consists of two strokes: *piě* and *nà* while the English word "to" consists of two letters: "t" and "o"). One has to put them in a right order to form a character. Following is a list of rules for writing strokes of characters:

- From left to right   川，从
- From top to bottom   三，下
- From outside to inside   向，风，向
- From middle to sides   小，水，业
- Inside before closing   回，且，国

- Horizontal before other strokes   七，手，夫
- Main body before tying it all together   中，事
- Main body before the dot   我，发

Notice that, for the most part, two or more rules apply to one character (e.g. 想 *xiǎng* "think" applies five of the rules listed above: from top to bottom, from left to right, from outside to inside, inside before closing, horizontal before other strokes). Certainly, there are some exceptions to these rules. For instance, characters with the "walk and go" radical (辶) normally have whatever is inside the radical written before the radical (e.g. 文+辶 = 这). Another example is when the dot stroke is located squarely above other strokes, as in 文 and 字 or to the left as in 头 and 为; in cases like these the dot must be written first, *not* last. In general, the first two rules (from top to bottom and from left to right) apply to the majority of characters and they are the foundation of all the rules of stroke order (Cf. Yin 1997: 291–5).

When students have learnt how to put strokes into the right order, they may work on memorization strategies. Two strategies often used by students and said to be effective are: (1) the story telling method and (2) the guessing method. Both of these methods were briefly mentioned in the previous sections when discussing semantic and phonetic components of characters. Here I will provide more examples to illustrate the effectiveness of these two methods in learning and memorizing characters. The story telling method refers to the learning of characters through the telling of a story about them as shown in (5.9).

(5.9)	中 *zhōng* "middle"	When a vertical line (丨) pierces through a rectangular box (囗), it is in the middle.
	国 *guó* "country"	When a king (王) holds a seal (丶) and sits in the middle of a territory (囗), it is a country.
	明 *míng* "bright"	When a sun (日) is next to a moon (月), it is bright.
	家 *jiā* "home/family"	When there is a pig (豕) under a roof (宀), it is a household.
	姓 *xìng* "surname"	When a woman (女) gives birth (生) to a child, this child can carry on the last name of the family.

It appears that stories do not have to be true to the characters' historic back-stories from ancient times. As long as they help students memorize characters, they are good stories (except, as I mentioned earlier, if they will interfere with the meaning of the radicals in later more advanced study). The story telling method may be best used with characters created through the indicative and associative methods (see discussion in section 5.1). The guessing method, on the other hand, is effective for students memorizing picto-phonetic characters. When students have learned the basic radicals and phonetic components discussed in sections 5.2, they should be able to make intelligent guesses as to the meaning of given characters composed of those basic components, as illustrated in (5.10).

(5.10)	Radical		Phonetic		Character	English meaning
	讠	"word"	+ 青 =		请 *qǐng*	"polite words"
	氵	"water"	+ 青 =		清 *qīng*	"clear (water)"
	日	"sun"	+ 青 =		晴 *qíng*	"clear (sky)"
	忄	"heart"	+ 青 =		情 *qíng*	"feeling"
	鱼	"fish"	+ 青 =		鲭 *qīng*	"a type of fish"
	虫	"insect"	+ 青 =		蜻 *qīng*	"a type of insect"
	气	"air"	+ 青 =		氰 *qíng*	"a type of air"
	竹	"bamboo"	+ 青 =		箐 *qìng*	"a type of bamboo"

Although tones are unpredictable, meanings and spellings of the words listed above can be guessed based on the meaning of radicals and the pronunciation of the phonetic part 青 *qīng*. Clearly, both the story telling and guessing methods are based on the structure of characters and the psychological factors involved in teaching and learning characters. Without a clear understanding of character structure, there can be no basis for a story or for guessing anything about a given character. Similarly, without a clear understanding of the factors that motivate students to learn (e.g. fun, sense of achievement, intellectual challenge, and encouragement), it is difficult to attract students' interest in learning characters. The drawback of both the story telling and guessing methods, however, is that they cannot be used to explain all characters, as Chu (2004) pointed out. For instance, the simplified character 听 (*tīng,* "listen") has both a semantic component 口 (*kǒu,* "mouth") and phonetic component (斤, *jīn*), yet its meaning does not seem to have a direct relation with mouth (although one may argue that since words come from a mouth, "listen" does relate to "mouth"). The character 动 (*dòng,* meaning "move/motion") does not have the same or similar pronunciation as either of the two components: 云 (*yún,* "cloud") and 力 (*lì,* "power/strength"). Therefore, students should be cautious in pronouncing a new word that they have never heard before and guessing the meaning of this word out of context.

Other strategies for learning and memorizing characters may involve compounding, sentencing and playing word games using newly acquired words, finding their synonyms/antonyms, and even outrageous words (e.g. swear words). Compounding is a straightforward exercise. Students and teachers may spend 5–10 minutes on it every time students learn some new characters, as shown in (5.11). Similarly, students may also be encouraged to use newly acquired words in various communicative sentences, as illustrated in (5.12).

(5.11)	学	*xué*	"to learn, study"
	学生	*xuésheng*	"student"
	学习	*xuéxí*	"study"

学校	*xuéxiào*	"school"
学分	*xuéfēn*	"credit"
学费	*xuéfèi*	"tuition"
学问	*xuéwèn*	"knowledge"
同学	*tóngxué*	"classmate"
大学	*dàxué*	"university"
好学	*hàoxué*	"enjoy learning"
初学	*chūxué*	"start learning"
东亚学	*dōngyǎ xué*	"East Asian Studies"

(5.12) 学：学、学、学，每天都在学习有什么意思？

xué   *xué, xué, xué, měitiān dōu zài xuéxí yǒu shénme yìsi?*

"Study, study, study, why do we have to study everyday?"

你可以学好，也可以学坏，还可以学傻。

nǐ kěyǐ xuéhǎo, yě kěyǐ xuéhuì, hái kěyǐ xuéshǎ.

"You can learn to be a good person, a bad person, or even become an idiot."

店：我们先上书店，再去饭店，然后去商店。

diàn   *wǒmen xiān shàng shūdiàn, zài qù fàndiàn, ránhòu qù shāngdiàn.*

"First we'll go to the bookstore, then restaurant, then to the shops."

有钱逛店，没钱怎么办？

yǒu qián guàng diàn, méi qián zěnme bàn?

"Those who have money can shop everywhere, What about those who don't have money?"

期：每个学期的最后一个星期 "dead week" 中文怎么说？

qi   *měi ge xuéqī de zuìhòu yíge xīngqī zhōngwén zěnme shuō?*

"How to say 'dead week' the last week of a semester in Chinese?"

"死星期"？"死期"？还是"期末复习周"？

"sǐ xīngqī"? "sǐqī"? háishì "qīmò fùxí zhōu"?

"Dead week"? "dead period"? "final review week"?

Word games (e.g. Bingo), synonyms/antonyms, outrageous words/derogatory words (see *Wenlin* 2001, Xing 2001, Wang 1995) are fun for students to learn and work on. These activities do not take much time in class, yet they are excellent exercises for boosting students' interest in learning and giving them a sense of achievement that they have learned many characters and can use them in real conversations.

One last activity to be introduced in this section is converting traditional into simplified characters and vice versa. This activity does not enlarge students' vocabulary, but it does help students who learn one version of a character to acquaint themselves with the other version. The core concept of conversion that students need to be aware of is the eight principles used in simplification of characters and summarized by Times Books International (1985).

(1) Borrowing a simpler character which already has a meaning of its own with the same sound, though the tone may vary. For examples, 後=>后 *hòu* "after"; 裏=>里 *lǐ* "inside"；幹=>干 *gàn* "dry".

(2) Adopting existing common and simple variant forms. The only difference between the variants used to be the preference of style. For example, 個=>个 *gè* "measure word"; 萬=>万 *wàn* "ten thousand"; 甚=>什 *shèn* "very"; 頭=>头 *tóu* "head".

(3) Incorporating "grass style" characters used in cursive writing to eliminate total number of strokes. For example，馬=>马 *mǎ* "horse"; 樂=>乐 *lè* "happy"；興=> 兴 *xìng* "excited"；寫=>写 *xiě* "write".

(4) Revising the ideas conveyed by the character. For example, 寶=>宝 *bǎo* "precious" (under the "roof" the traditional version has three precious things, whereas the simplified only has one); 雙=>双 *shuāng* "pair" (the traditional form has two birds above a hand, while the simplified form only has two hands); 孫=>孙 *sūn* "grandchild" (beside the "child" radical, the traditional form contains the part meaning "offspring", while the simplified form has the part meaning "young" or "small"); 筆=>笔 *bǐ* "brush" (under the bamboo radical, the traditional form contains a part meaning "brush" while the simplified form has the character meaning "hair") .

(5) Replacing part of the character with a simpler phonetic element although tone may vary. For example, 嚇=>吓 *xià* "be scared"; 種=>种 *zhǒng* "plant"; 遠=>远 *yuǎn* "far"; 曆=>历 *lì* "undergo".

(6) Using only a part of the regular character. For example, 醫=>医 *yī* "medicine"; 飛 => 飞 *fēi* "fly"；聲=>声 *shēng* "sound"；氣=>气 *qì* "air"；電=>电 *diàn* "electricity"；號=>号 *hào* "number"；術=>术 *shù* "technique".

(7) Cutting down repeated elements or simplifying them. For example, 蟲=>虫 *chóng* "insect"; 齒=>齿 *chǐ* "tooth"; 競=>竞 *jìng* "compete".

(8) Replacing a number of different complex components with a simplified form common to all. For example, 歡=欢 *huān* "happy"; 觀=>观 *guān* "watch"; 漢=>汉 *hàn* "Han ethnicity"; 難=>难 *nán* "difficulty"; 對=>对 *duì* "correct"; 戲=>戏 *xì* "play"；雞=>鸡 *jī* "chicken".

I recommend that students be introduced to these principles of conversion either toward the end of elementary Chinese or at the beginning of intermediate Chinese. The rationale for this recommendation is that after students have learnt the 500 most frequently used characters and the 100 most frequently used radicals and phonetic components, they will have a good understanding of the structure of Chinese characters, which in turn will help them understand the principles of conversion better and apply them more easily in the recognition of new characters. Although the conversion principles were originally guidelines for conversion from traditional to simplified, they are equally instructive for conversion from simplified to traditional. Therefore, regardless of which version of characters students start with, the conversion principles can help them learn the other version.

So far, I have discussed several strategies in teaching and learning characters, among which the story telling and guessing methods are recommended for students, especially beginning students, to aid them in recognizing and memorizing the meaning, sound and form of characters. Then the method of association with other characters was briefly mentioned, which includes character usage in compounds and sentences, synonyms and antonyms, and word games. Lastly, the method of conversion between simplified and traditional characters was introduced so that students may be trained to recognize both versions of Chinese characters.

5.6   Words and References

As the basic unit in making up sentences, words, or rather *cí*, naturally become the focus of instruction and acquisition in elementary Chinese. This leads to the question of how many characters/*zì* and words/*cí* students should learn at each level. *Integrated Chinese,* Level 1/Part 1 by Yao et al. introduces 581 new *cí* (not *zì*), Level 1/Part II introduces another 602 new *cí Integrated Chinese* Level II compiles 1068 new *cí*. Since one *zì* can be compounded with another *zì* to form different *cí*, the number of *zì* included in these two textbooks is substantially fewer than *cí*. These numbers are comparable with textbooks of the same level. The *New Practical Chinese Reader 1–4* (which are suggested by the authors Liu et al. as elementary and intermediate textbooks) includes 326 new *cí* in Book 1 and 447 new *cí* in Book 2, 449 new *cí* in Book 3, and 514 new *cí* in Book 4. Another reading series was written by DeFrancis and has been used by many students for several decades: *Beginning Chinese Reader* introducing 400 characters/*zì* (1250 compounds/*cí*), *Intermediate Chinese Reader* containing 400 new characters/*zì* (2500 compounds/*cí*), *Advanced Chinese Reader* providing another 400 new characters (over 3,000 compounds/*cí*). Hence, the three levels of Chinese readers by DeFrancis present a total of 1200 new characters and some 7,000 compounds.

In comparison, native Chinese students learn approximately 2,500 characters at elementary school and another 1,000 characters at middle school and high school (cf. List of Frequently Used Characters in Modern Chinese, 现代汉语常用字表, *Xiàndài hànyǔ chángyòng zì biǎo,* 1988). With the acquisition of 3,500 characters, students can read 99.9 percent of newspaper articles. Most Chinese newspapers use approximately 2,500 Chinese characters. According to Yin's estimation (1997: 69–70), students of Chinese may understand more than 95 percent of newspaper articles after they learn 1800 characters, and students who know 1,000 characters may understand 90 percent of newspaper articles, and students who know 400 to 500 characters may understand 75 percent of newspaper articles. These estimations are based on the assumption that the characters in newspaper articles refer to general topics and that these characters fall on the list of most frequently used characters. If ordinary native literate Chinese know and use somewhere between 3,000 to 4,000 characters (cf. Norman 1988: 73), it is quite encouraging for students of Chinese as FL to be able to learn 1,000 to 2,000 characters and read over 90 percent of newspaper articles. A broad and quantitative reading would undoubtedly enhance students' reading ability and language competence.

To better understand and use new words, students have to own, and consult, at least one reference book, such as a dictionary. A good dictionary should have clearly printed characters (both traditional and simplified versions), phonetic notation, *pīnyīn* spelling with tones, part of speech, and examples illustrating usage. This dictionary should enable students to look up a word by radical and number of strokes or using *pīnyīn* spelling. Following is a short list of dictionaries that students may like to acquire:

- *Oxford Chinese-English Dictionary* by Oxford University Press
- *Far East Chinese-English Dictionary* by US International Publication
- *A Reverse Chinese-English Dictionary* (汉英逆引词典) by Shangwu Chubanshe
- *Modern Chinese Dictionary* (现代汉语词典) by Shangwu Chubanshe
- New Chinese Dictionary (新华字典) by Shangwu Chubanshe
- *Wenlin* (computer software)
- *Chinese Characters* – A Genealogy and Dictionary by Rick Harbaugh

The Oxford dictionary has a simple explanation for each entry and comes in pocket size; therefore, it has become the most popular dictionary among students of Chinese in the US. The dictionary published by Far East is an excellent reference book for students of Chinese as FL because it includes 8,000 entries, each of which is explained and exemplified in such a way that students can easily understand its use. The Reverse Dictionary may be most beneficial for students of intermediate and advanced levels. It sorts compound words based on the last character and illustrates their functions in both Chinese and English. Finally, the Modern Chinese Dictionary and New Chinese Dictionary are completely in Chinese and may be most useful for advanced students of Chinese or students with near-native Chinese competence. The last two references in the list are computer dictionaries. In recent years, it has become increasingly convenient for students to use online dictionaries when computer access is available and purchasing a new one online is affordable for almost every student. These dictionaries contain information about the development of characters, various writing styles and are a rich source of compound words. *Wenlin* allows students to create their own flash cards and compose sentences and essays, but Chinese Characters is limited to the meaning of characters.

5.7   Conclusion

Characters are challenging for students of Chinese as FL. This is a fact that cannot be denied. However, learning characters can be made enjoyable and rewarding as long as students are motivated to learn and teachers know how to teach and enjoy teaching. It has been demonstrated throughout this chapter that characters are logically structured and conceptualized. Once they understand the two basic components — semantic and phonetic — and their functions, students will have built a foundation for using characters in speaking, listening, reading, and writing. Certainly, this assumes that the purpose in learning characters is to use them in communication, not simply to identify and write individual characters in isolation. Following is a short paragraph illustrating the use of the two most frequently used characters: 你 *nǐ* "you" and 我 *wǒ* "I".

(5.13)   你 ni , 我 wo
你是你，我是我。
nǐ shì nǐ, wǒ shi wǒ.
"You are you; I am me."

你的东西不是我的东西，我的东西也不是你的东西。
nǐde dōngxi búshì wǒde dōngxi, wǒde dōngxi yě búshì nǐde dōngxi."
"Your stuff is not mine; my stuff is not yours."

我们不要把你和我，你的和我的混在一起，好不好？
wǒmen bú yào bǎ nǐ hé wǒ, nǐde hé wǒde hùn zài yiqǐ, hǎo bù hǎo?
"We should not mix you with me and yours with mine. Is that okay?"

In this short paragraph, the discourse functions of 你 *nǐ* and 我 *wǒ* and their plural forms (你们 *nǐmen* vs. 我们 *wǒmen*) used as pronouns, and possessive pronouns (你的 *nǐde* vs. 我的 *wǒde*) at both subject and object position are clearly demonstrated. These functions, I conclude, should be acquired by the beginning students when they learn the two characters 你 *nǐ* and 我 *wǒ*, along with their semantic (i.e. the radical) and the phonetic properties. In other words, the acquisition of characters should emphasize a character's form, sound and meaning. Neglecting any one of the three components may seriously hinder students' development of communicative competence in Chinese.

6 Sentences

6.1 Introduction

Western linguists and Chinese grammarians, regardless of their theoretical preference, generally agree that the sentence is the basic unit for studying a language. Sapir (1949a: 33) considers a sentence the "primary functional unit of speech and esthetically satisfying embodiment of a unified thought." Chao (2001[1968]: 41) points out that a sentence is the major language unit for grammatical analysis. Li and Thompson (1981: 85) specify a simple sentence as any sentence "that has just one verb in it." Norman (1988: 166) categorizes sentences into two types, major and minor, based on their grammatical constituents and frequency in discourse, including both oral and written. The major sentence, according to Norman, "contains both a subject and a predicate" while "a minor sentence contains only a predicate." Norman also asserts that "the frequent omission of pronominal subjects means that minor sentences are more common in Chinese than in English." All these definitions and explanations of sentence are instrumental for Chinese language teachers because they help teachers understand not only the nature of sentence, but also the importance of sentences in teaching Chinese. Comparing the assessments of sentence given by those great minds just mentioned, we see that Sapir's definition is function oriented, while Chao, Li and Thompson, and Norman definitions clearly lean towards grammatical, or rather syntactical, aspect of sentence. This difference may reflect the tendency of Chinese grammarians' tradition of emphasis on studying syntactic structure of the sentence rather than communicative functions of the sentence.

Students benefit little by learning only sentence structures; they must learn the function of sentences in order to communicate with them. That is, they have to learn when, where, why and how to use which sentences where natural in communication. It should be noted that this does not mean that students should not learn sentence structure at all, but rather that they learn sentence structure along with discourse and pragmatic functions, so that they can use them accurately in communicative discourse.

There are a number of different sentences in Mandarin Chinese. Based on their word order, function, and frequency in communication, we can divide them into two types: the basic sentence constructions and the unique sentence constructions. Basic constructions include the topic + comment and/or subject + verb + object (SVO) word order and constitute approximately ninety percent of written discourse in Chinese (cf. Xing 1993; Sun and Givón 1985), while the unique sentences include those special constructions such as the "disposal" construction, the passive construction, and the focus constructions. From a pedagogical point of view, students need to acquire the basic constructions first because of their commonality in both frequency and function. Unique sentence structures can be added as communicative competence grows. In what follows, I first discuss the acquisition of the basic constructions using three examples: the topic comment construction, the verb + complement construction, and the *le* (了) construction. Then I demonstrate the common practice in teaching and learning the unique constructions at American colleges and universities and provide recommended classroom activities which can help students learn those constructions. Considering the trouble students may have in learning subordinate clauses, I will briefly address the issue and then lay out the important facts that students should be aware of in composing and interpreting subordinate clauses in Chinese. The last section will conclude the chapter with a brief summary.

6.2   Acquisition of Basic Sentences

Since sentence is the minimal unit to express a complete idea as indicated by Sapir (1949a) and ninety percent of Chinese discourse is composed of the basic sentences, students have no choice but to learn the basic sentences in order to understand how native Chinese speakers express themselves and to be able to communicate with them. Among the basic constructions, students may find that some sentences are similar to those in other languages, such as English, and some are less similar and therefore harder to learn. For instance, when asked about summer, students may reply in Chinese using similar word order as they do in English, as shown in (6.1b).

(6.1)   a: 今年夏天你想做什么？
              jīnnián xiàtiān nǐ xiǎng zuò shénme?
              "What do you want to do this summer?"

         b: 我想去中国。
              wǒ xiǎng qù zhōngguó.
              "I want to go to China."

It takes little effort for native English speakers to learn to respond to the question in (6.1a). However, for Chinese sentences that do not have structurally similar English counterparts, the acquisition process can be quite different. Native English and other language speaking students have to learn the circumstances under which these constructions are used as well as whether they are functionally similar to certain constructions in students' native languages. For this reason, my discussion will be centered on three basic Chinese sentences: the topic-comment construction, the verb + complement construction, and the *le* construction. These three constructions are all basic common constructions in Chinese, yet they do not exist in English or many other languages. Hence, students of Chinese have to learn them.

6.2.1   *Topic-comment construction*

The topic-comment construction refers to any sentence that contains a topic and a sequence of words commenting on the topic, as demonstrated in (6.2)–(6.4). Although many researchers (Li and Thompson 1975; Tsao 1979, 1990; Shi 2000) consider Chinese a topic-prominent language, as opposed to a subject-prominent language such as English, they maintain that some of the basic Chinese sentences are the topic-comment constructions as those in (6.2)–(6.4), and some are the subject-predicate constructions as those in (6.5)–(6.6).

(6.2)   今天要下雨。
   jīntiān   yào xiàyǔ.
   TOPIC   COMMENT
   "Today (it) will rain."

(6.3)   功课做完了。
   gōngkè zuòwán le.
   TOPIC   COMMENT
   "(My) homework (is) finished."

(6.4)   苹果，我们都不吃皮。
   píngguǒ wǒmen dōu bù chī pí.
   TOPIC   COMMENT
   "Apple, we all do not eat (its) skin."

(6.5)   他常说笑话。
   Tā   cháng   shuō   xiàohua.
   SUBJECT   VERB   OBJECT
   "He often tells jokes."

(6.6)   他们昨天都在家。
   tāmen zuótiān dōu zài jiā
   SUBJECT   PREDICATE
   "They yesterday were all at home."

Notice that both topic and comment in the topic-comment construction consist of flexible elements. The topic in Chinese does not have to be the doer or agent of the action described by the verb in the sentence. Topic can be a concept of time as in (6.2) or a concrete thing as in (6.4). The comment may be a verb phrase or sentence and it may even contain a subject as *wŏmen* "we" in (6.4). This flexibility of constituents of the topic-comment construction is not available in English sentences, as illustrated by the English translations in (6.2)–(6.4). Without the elements in parentheses, the English sentences are not acceptable.

In teaching the topic-comment construction, the most important thing teachers can do is to explain the function of this construction: when to use this construction. By associating topics with something known or mentioned in previous discourse, students can be encouraged to comment on them using whatever structure they can think of. Whether the topic is "today's class" or "homework", students can freely comment on it as shown in (6.7)–(6.8).

(6.7) Q: 今天的课怎么样？

          jīntiān de kè zěnme yàng?

          "Today's lesson, how was it?"

      a: 今天的课太难了。

          jīntiān de kè tài nán le.

          "Today's lesson is too difficult."

      b: 今天的课我没有准备。

          jīntiān de kè wǒ méiyǒu zhǔnbèi.

          "Today's lesson, I did not prepare"

      c: 今天的课我学了很多东西。

          jīntiān de kè wǒ xuéle hěnduō dōngxi

          "(At) today's lesson, I learned a lot of things."

      d: 今天的课我觉得没意思。

          jīntiān de kè wǒ juéde méi yìsi.

          "Today's lesson, I think (it was) boring."

(6.8) Q: 你们的功课呢？

          nǐmen de gōngkè ne?

          "What about your homework?"

      a: 功课我忘了做了。

          gōngkè wǒ wàngle zuò le

          "Homework, I forgot to do (it)."

      b: 功课没带来。

          gōngkè méi dài lái.

          "Homework (I) did not bring (it)."

      c: 功课太多，没有时间做。

          gōngkè tài duō, méiyǒu shíjiān zuò.

          "Homework too much, (I) did not have time to do (it)."

d: 功课明天交，行不行？

gōngkè míngtiān jiāo, xíng bù xíng?

"Homework, (I'll) turn it in tomorrow, is that okay?"

f: 我的功课在这儿。

wǒde gōngkè zài zhèir.

"My homework is here." or "I have my homework."

The key task is to help students use sentence structures they have learned previously to comment on the topic. Any structures, from a predicate to a verb phrase to a statement to an interrogative sentence, can function as a comment. In addition, comparison between the topic-comment construction and its equivalent in students' native languages can also enable students to become conscious of the difference between Chinese and their native languages.

Due to the linguistic characteristics of the topic-comment construction discussed above, I suggest that it be taught at the elementary level after students have learned the basic structures of phrases and sentences (e.g. subject + verb + object, subject + predicate, and negative and interrogative constructions). Later, with the development of students' competence in expressing complicated ideas with complex sentences, teachers may reintroduce the topic-comment construction and ask students to comment on complicated topics with complicated comments, as shown in (6.9).

(6.9) Q: 你们对伊拉克战争有什么看法？

nǐmen duì yīlākè zhànzhēng yǒu shénme kànfǎ

"What do you think about the Iraqi war?"

a: 我觉得这次战争是一次正义的自由解放战争。

wǒ juéde zhèicì zhànzhēng shì yícì zhèngyì de zìyóu jiěfàng zhànzhēng .

"I think this war is for justice, freedom and liberation."

b: 得了吧，解放战争？解放谁？伊拉克人民？

dé le ba. jiěfàng zhànzhēng? jiěfàng shéi? yīlākè rénmín?

"Nonsense. Liberation war? Liberate who? Iraqis?

成千上万的伊拉克人没被解放，反而见了阎王爷。

chéngqiānshàngwàn de yīlākè rén *méi bèi jiěfàng, fǎnér jiànle yánwàngyé.*

"**Thousands of Iraqis** went to see the King of the Dead before being liberated."

c: 这次战争至少把萨达姆搞下台了。

zhèicì zhàngzhēng zhìshǎo bǎ Sàdámǔ gǎo xià tái le.

"**This war** at least got rid of Saddam."

d: 再说啊，这次战争花了美国多少钱？你知道吗？

zài shuō a, zhàicì zhànzhēng huāle měiguó duōshǎo qián? nǐ zhīdào ma?

"Besides, how much money does **this war** cost the US? Do you know?"

The topic (underlined) of the conversation given in (6.9) is about the Iraqi War started in 2003. Four people comment on this topic. Among them, three (6.9b, 6.9c and 6.9d) use the topic-comment construction to express their opinions. (6.9a) does not use a prototypical topic-comment construction; however, it is clear from the context "I" is not the topic of that sentence. Even though it is debatable whether grammatically "this war" is the topic of the sentence in (6.9a), no one disagrees that the focus of the sentence is on "this war", not "I" in the subject position. Clearly, both ideas and structures of comments in (6.9) are much more complicated than those in (6.7)–(6.8). The comments given by (6.9b), (6.9c) and (6.9d) use respectively the *bèi* construction, the *bǎ* construction and the rhetorical question, all structurally and functionally more advanced than the basic sentences used in (6.7) and (6.8).

We have seen that all the examples and facts discussed so far point to one conclusion: the topic-comment construction is a productive structure in Chinese. Any sentence structures that students have learned, simple or complicated, can be used as a comment in the topic-comment construction.

6.2.2 *Verb-complement construction*

Chinese does not have a grammatical system to express tense as many Indo-European languages; however, it has a complicated complement system to describe the status of the action expressed by the verb in a sentence. Compare the following example.

(6.10)   "I have finished (eating) dinner."

(6.11)   a.   我吃完晚饭了。
                wǒ chī-wán wǎnfàn le.
                "I have finished eating dinner."
          b.   *我完晚饭了。
                wǒ wán wǎnfàn le.

Notice that "finish dinner" in English implies "finish eating dinner" in (6.10); but *wán wǎnfàn* "finish dinner" in Chinese does not make sense to Chinese people so they have to say *chī wán wǎnfàn* "eat finish dinner" to indicate that the status of the action "eat" is completed, as shown in (6.11). Similarly, when asked about the status of any other action, such as 看 *kàn* "look/read" or 听 *tīng* "listen", one can use different words (underlined) to express status of the action (bold-faced), as illustrated in (6.12)–(6.13).

(6.12)   a.   你看，就是那个人！
                nǐ kàn, jiùshì nà ge rén.
                "(You) look, (it) is that person!"
          b.   我看见了。是他呀。
                wǒ kànjiàn le. shì tā ya.
                "I see (him). Oh, (it) is him."

(6.13)   a.   你们**听懂**我说的话吗？

nǐmen tīngdǒng wǒ shuōde huà ma?

"Did you hear and understand what I said?"

        b.   我听<u>不清楚</u>。

wǒ tīng bù qīngchu.

"I listen (but) not clear." (Or "I heard but not clearly.")

        c.   我听<u>不见</u>。

wǒ tīng bú jiàn.

"I listen (but) not perceive (it)." (Or "I heard but I did not get it.")

        d.   我听<u>懂</u>了。

wǒ tīng dǒng le.

"I understand."

In (6.12a), the central idea is to invite the listener to conduct the action "look" or "see". Not surprisingly, the listener responds with an appropriate complement in (6.12b) indicating the result (i.e. the status) of pursuing that action "look" with the word 见 *jiàn* "perceive something either visually or audibly". Thus, the verb + complement (*kàn* "see/look" + *jiàn* "perceive") expresses the meaning of "saw". Since any action expressed by a verb may hold different statuses, the same verb can carry different complements as shown in (6.13). When a teacher asks students if they "listened" and understood what s/he said as in (6.13a), one student (6.13b) says s/he "listened" but it was "not clear". Another student (6.13c) also said s/he "listened", but "could not hear". The third student (6.13d) gave a different answer — s/he "listened" and "understood" what the teacher said. Clearly, the "verb + complement" construction does not have an equivalent in English. We have to translate the verb-comment structure into either English sentences as (6.13a)–(6.13c) or one sentence that can combine the meaning of both the verb and complement in the original Chinese sentence as (6.13d).

Hence, the primary function of the verb + complement arises when an action expressed by the verb needs to be explained or commented on. Since different actions may be explained and commented on differently, one type of verb may only be used with a certain type of complement. For instance, action verbs may be complemented by another action verb as those given in (6.14) or stative verbs as those in (6.15). However, stative verbs can only be complemented by degree adverbs as those in (6.16).

(6.14)   打破   *dǎ-pò*   hit + break   "break"

            跑掉   *pǎo-diào*   run + away   "run away"

            找到   *zhǎo-dào*   look for + get   "find"

            出去   *chū-qù*   exit + go   "go out"

            进来   *jìn-lái*   enter + come   "enter (to the speaker)"

            进去   *jìn-qù*   enter + to   "enter (away from the speaker)"

(6.15) 哭累   *kū-lèi*   cry + tired   "cry until (you're) tired"
        睡多   *shuì-duō*   sleep + lot   "oversleep"
        写好   *xiě-hǎo*   write + good   "finish writing"
        拿下   *ná-xià*   take + down   "take down"
        看错   *kàn-cuò*   look + wrong   "incorrectly identify"

(6.16) 好多了   *hǎo-duōle*   good + lot + asp.   "very good"
        漂亮极了   *piàoliang- jile* beautiful + extreme + asp. "extremely beautiful"
        冷怕了   *lěng-pàle*   cold + afraid + asp.   "afraid of cold"
        吓坏了   *xià-huàile*   scare + bad + asp.   "badly scared"
        累死了   *lèi-sǐle*   tired + dead + asp.   "dead tired"

When teaching the verb-complement construction, the traditional method often categorizes complements into various types: resultative complements, directional complements, descriptive complements, potential complements, etc. Such a categorization may help students who have a good linguistic understanding of those terms learn complements. However, for most students learning Chinese as FL, it does not seem necessary to spend time learning the terms and distinguishing different types of complements. What they should concentrate on, instead, is the function of complements, that is, when they are used and what they are used for in discourse. Once students understand the fundamental reasons for using complements in Chinese and practice them accordingly, they should be able to acquire the construction.

Teachers may create various types of classroom activities to induce students to use the verb-complement constructions. For instance, students may be provided with different types of verbs and then be asked to come up with complements to further explain or comment on the verbs, as demonstrated in (6.17):

(6.17) a: 你们会说"听"什么？
            nǐmen huì shuō "tīng" shénme?
            "What would you use with 'listening'?"
        b: 我们可以说"听见"、"听到"，"听懂"…
            wǒmen kěyǐ shuō "tīng-jiàn", "tīng-dào", "tīng-dǒng" …
            "We may say 'listen-perceive', 'listen-receive', 'listen-understand' …"

            说 *shuō* "speak"   说完 *shuōwán* "finish speaking"
                                 说出 *shuōchū* "say something out"
                                 说到 *shuōdào* "talk about"
            读 *dú* "read"   读完 *dúwán* "finish reading"
                                 读到 *dúdào* "read to (a certain place)"
                                 读出 *dúchū* "read out"
            看 *kàn* "see"   看出 *kànchū* "see and realize"
                                 看见 *kànjiàn* "see and identify"
                                 看清楚 *kàn qīngchu* "see something clearly"

写 *xiě* "write"	写好 *xiěhǎo* "finish writing"
	写错 *xiěcuò* "write something wrong"
	写对 *xiěduì* "write something correctly"
用 *yòng* "use"	用过 *yòngguò* "have experience of using something"
	用光 *yòngguāng* "use up something"
	用惯 *yòngguàn* "use something and get used to it"
走 *zǒu* "walk"	走开 *zǒukāi* "walk away"
	走到 *zǒudào* "walk to"
	走出 *zǒuchū* "walk out"
跑 *pǎo* "run"	跑来 *pǎolái* "run out of (a place)"
	跑去 *pǎoqù* "run to (away from the speaker)"
	跑出 *pǎochū* "run out"
放 *fàng* "place"	放下 *fàngxià* "place something (at a place)"
	放到 *fàngdào* "place something in (a place)"
	放好 *fànghǎo* "place something in order"
想 *xiǎng* "think"	想得好 *xiǎngde hǎo* "think positively"
	想得美 *xiǎngde měi* "think beautiful things"
	想得开 *xiǎngde kāi* "think and open up one's mind"
跑 *pǎo* "run"	跑得快 *pǎode kuài* "run fast"
	跑得慢 *pǎode màn* "run slowly"
	跑得难受 *pǎode nánshòu* "run until (your feel) uncomfortable"
吃 *chī* "eat"	吃得好 *chīde hǎo* "eat well"
	吃得饱 *chīde bǎo* "eat and become full"
	吃得舒服 *chīde shūfu* "eat and feel good"
高兴 *gāoxìng* "happy"	高兴极了 *gāoxìng jíle* "extremely happy"
	高兴坏了 *gāoxìng huàile* "terribly happy"
	高兴死了 *gāoxìng sǐle* "extremely happy"
疼 *téng* "painful"	疼极了 *téng jíle* "extremely painful"
	疼坏了 *téng huàile* "very painful"
	疼死了 *téng sǐle* "dead painful"

Sufficient practice with verbs and their complements such as those given in (6.17) should enable students to understand the types of complements that can or cannot comment on or describe certain types of verbs and the difference between different types of complements. Teachers should also point out the restriction of certain types of complements (e.g. what kind of complements cannot be used with helping verbs) and ask students to compare those complements with 得 (*de* "complement marker") and 极了 (*jíle* "extremely") with those that do not have either 得 (*de*) and 极了 (*jíle*) and describe their functions in discourse. This way, it does not take long for students to realize the different function of the complements with or without 得 (*de*) and 极了 (*jíle*).

6.2.3   *The* le *construction*

The *le* (了) construction refers to sentences that have a *le* either after a verb (i.e. verb *le*) or at the end of a sentence (i.e. sentential *le*). Most linguists and Chinese grammarians consider these two different types of *le*. Due to their complicated syntactic, semantic and discourse pragmatic functions, the *le* constructions have attracted numerous linguists', grammarians', and pedagogical specialists' attention in the past (e.g. Chao 1968, Lǚ 1980, Li and Thompson 1981, Shi 1988, Sun 1996, Liu et al. 2001). Combining the findings of the previous studies with the experience of teaching *le* constructions in the classroom, most teachers do not seem to have any difficulty developing a teaching plan when it comes to *le* constructions, especially when teaching its two most basic functions, as illustrated in (6.18)–(6.19).

(6.18)   了 *le* used to express **the completion of an action**

a: 周末你们过得怎么样？

zhōumò nǐmen guòde zěnme yàng?

"How was your weekend?"

b: 我们看了一场电影，还去逛了商场。

wǒmen kàn le yìchǎng diànyǐng, hái qù guàng le shāngchǎng.

"We saw a movie and also did some shopping. (i.e., the actions of "watch" and "do shopping" were both completed at the time of this conversation.)

(6.19)   了 *le* used to express **a change of situation**

a: 你这两天觉得怎么样？

nǐ zhè liǎngtiān juéde zěnme yàng?

"How have you been feeling these last couple of days?"

b: 好多了。头也不疼了，肚子也不疼了。

hǎo duō le. tóu yě bù téng le, dùzi yě bù téng le.

"Much better (than before). (My) head does not hurt, nor does my stomach." (i.e., the situation with the "head" and "stomach" was different a couple of days ago.)

The only problem that some students may encounter when learning *le* constructions appears to be a lack of thorough comprehension of *le*'s functions in discourse. This is likely the result of the fact that although most contemporary grammar books explain the functions of both verb *le* and sentential *le* (e.g. Lǚ 1980, Li and Thompson 1981, Liu et al. 2002), few of them discuss how to teach students those functions. As a result, teachers all teach the two functions of *le* illustrated in (6.18) and (6.19) and in some cases add other functions as well; many students, however, either hesitate to use it due to concerns about making mistakes or they use it incorrectly.

To have a thorough understanding of *le*'s discourse functions, I suggest that teachers prepare their teaching plan according to the following guidelines:

- Illustrate the functions of *le* constructions in various discourse situations;
- Ask students to think about how to construct discourse situations where *le* would/might be used in their native language and explain the reason, meaning and difference;
- Focus on *le*'s basic yet unique discourse functions;
- Give students a topic or theme to write or talk about using *le* constructions whenever necessary;

These procedures should not be considered discrete activities, but rather connected with one another and pedagogically ordered. That is, discourse functions should be first introduced to students before asking them to think about how to construct the discourse where *le* might be used in their native language, focusing on *le*'s basic yet unique functions, and giving them a task to complete by using *le* constructions. Furthermore, when demonstrating *le*'s discourse functions, emphasis should be laid on where and when they are used, as illustrated in (6.20).

(6.20) Q: 今年夏天谁去中国？

   jīnnián xiàtiān shéi qù zhōngguó?

   "This summer who is going to China?"

   a: 去年我去了，今年就不去了。

   qùnián wǒ qù le, jīnnián jiù bú qù le.

   "I went last year, (so) I am not going this year."

   b: 我已经去了三次了，今年还想去。

   wǒ yǐjīng qù le sāncì le, jīnnián hái xiǎng qù."

   "I've been there three times. This year I still want to go."

   c: 我没去过，今年夏天打算去。

   wǒ méi qù guò, jīnnián xiàtiān dǎsuàn qù."

   "I've never been there before, (so) I plan to go this summer."

   d: 我想去，可是没有钱。

   wǒ xiǎng qù, kěshì méiyǒu qián.

   "I want to go, but (I) don't have money."

Among the four answers to the question "Who is going to China this summer?" in (6.20), two (6.20a and 6.20b) use the *le* construction and two (6.20c and 6.20d) do not, which is more natural in discourse than examples that all contain a *le* construction. Notice that (6.20a) uses *le* in two separate clauses: in the first clause it expresses the completed action of 去中国 "take a trip to China" and in the second clause, it expresses the idea that taking a trip to China is not going to happen this year or simply that the situation of going to China is changed, different this year. (6.20b), on the other hand, uses the verb *le* and sentential *le* in one sentence, with the verbal *le* expressing the idea that the action of "take a trip to China" is completed and the sentential *le* indicating that speaker has experienced the situation of going to China three times; different from those who have experienced the situation fewer times. Students should be informed that neither *le* in (6.20a) can be omitted because of the function required in the particular discourse situation. However, in (6.20b), either the verb *le* or the sentential *le* (but not both) could be omitted because of the overlapping function of the two *le*s in the one sentence, namely "complete the action of going to China". Let us examine more examples:

(6.21)   Q: 你怎么了？
              nĭ zĕnme le?
              "What's the matter with you?"

         a: 我饿了，今天没吃早饭。
              wŏ è le, jīntiān méi chī zăofàn.
              "I'm hungry (because) I did not eat breakfast this morning."

         b: 我女朋友请我吃饭，我高兴极了。
              wŏ nŭpéngyou qĭng wŏ chīfàn, wŏ gāoxìng jile..
              "My girlfriend invited me to dinner. I am so happy."

         c: 我奶奶死了，我得回家去。
              wŏ năinai sĭ le, wŏ dĕi huíjiā qù.
              "My grandma died, I have to go home."

Although the situation expressed by the answer of each student in (6.21) varies, the discourse function of *le* stays the same. That is the situation at the moment of conversation differs from the situation at other times. (6.21a) uses *le* to indicate that s/he is hungry now, but not before; (6.21b) is extremely happy now but this was not the case before; and (6.21c)'s grandma is not alive anymore.

Notice that whether the verb of the *le* sentence expresses an action as those in (6.20) or a stative situation as those in (6.21), the basic discourse function of the verbal (completion of action) and sentential (change of situation) *le* stays the same. Hence, teachers may not need to introduce students various grammatical terms to distinguish the types of verbs used with *le* as some textbooks and grammar books do (e.g. Li and Thompson 1981, Liu et al. 2002). With the understanding of *le*'s basic functions, students should be encouraged to use the *le* construction whenever they can and understand that it is inevitable to make mistakes in using the construction, or any newly acquired constructions; the most important process of learning is to learn from their mistakes and learn from using *le* in discourse.

6.3   Acquisition of Unique Sentences

By "unique sentence", I refer to those sentence constructions unique to Chinese either structurally or functionally or both. Based on their functions, two types of unique constructions will be discussed: (1) the *bǎ* (把) and *bèi* (被)constructions and (2) the focus constructions, including the *lián* (连)and *shì* (是) ... *de* (的) constructions. It should be noted that these two types of constructions do not mean to refer to all unique constructions in Chinese, but rather they are chosen to be representative and thereby to demonstrate the process of teaching and learning unique constructions. We know that there is no lack of linguistic research on these four selected unique constructions (Wang Huan 1957, 1983; Wang Li 1943–44; Thompson 1973, Tsao 1987, Xing 1993, Liu and Xu 1998) and most grammar books discuss them as well. The only aspect apparently lacking in the literature is the pedagogy of these constructions. Therefore, this section will focus on the procedure of teaching and learning the four constructions.

It is generally agreed among Chinese teachers that all four constructions must be learned by students of Chinese as FL either during the first and/or second year of Chinese classes due to the frequency of their occurrence in natural discourse and the importance of their discourse functions. Some textbooks (e.g. *Integrated Chinese* by Yao et al.) introduce all four constructions during first-year Chinese, while others (e.g. *New Practical Chinese Reader* by Liu et al.) do not do so until Book 2 (equivalent to second-year textbook in the US). It seems to me that since each of those constructions has certain discourse functions irreplaceable by other sentence constructions, students should learn them all at the elementary level.

6.3.1   *The* **bǎ (把)** *and* **bèi (被)** *construction*

In linguistic literature, many researchers discuss the *bǎ* construction along with the *bèi* constructions or when discussing the *bèi* construction, they mention and compare it with the *bǎ* construction (e.g. Wang Huan 1957, Li and Thompson 1981). Evidently, this situation contributes to the functional and syntactic similarity between the two constructions, which will be discussed in detail along with their unique functions. Perhaps another relevant question to be raised here is whether the two constructions should be taught simultaneously and, more importantly, whether they should be taught the same way in the classroom. It is my hope that teachers and students will have a better idea about these issues after reading the next two sections.

6.3.1.1   The *bǎ* (把) construction

The *bǎ* construction (agent + *bǎ* + patient + verb) is often referred to as a disposal construction by Chinese grammarians. The word "disposal" is used to describe the semantic property of the verb in the *bǎ* construction, namely the action expressed by the verb has the function of affecting the patient/object of the *bǎ* construction. Interestingly, for years teachers tried to avoid the term "disposal" when teaching the *bǎ* construction for fear of causing confusion of *bǎ*'s functions among students. However, my experiment of using the term in recent years provides some positive results. Students seem to understand the implication of "disposal" even though many of them laugh about it when first hearing it. Coupled with examples illustrating the disposal function, explanation of the syntactic, semantic, and discourse pragmatic functions should enable students to understand when, where, and why to use the *bǎ* construction. Consider the following examples:

(6.22)   Q: 他**把**书放在哪儿了？

*tā **bǎ** shū fàng zài nǎr le?*

"Where did she place the book?"

a: 他**把**书放在桌子上了。

*tā **bǎ** shū fàng zài zhuōzi shàng le*

"She put the book on the table."

b: *她放书在桌子上。

* *tā fàng shū zài zhuōzi shàng le*

(6.23)   Q: 你的饭呢？

nǐde fàn ne?

"Where is that food?"

a: 我把它放在冰箱里了。

*wǒ **bǎ** tā fàng zài bīngxiāng lǐ le.*

"I put it in the refrigerator."

b: *我放它在冰箱里了。

* *wǒ fàng tā zài bīngxiāng lǐ le.*

(6.24)   Q: 你的功课呢？

nǐde gōngkè ne?

"Where is your homework?"

a: 我**把**它交给王老师了。

*wǒ **bǎ** tā jiāo gěi Wáng lǎoshī le.*

"I gave it to Professor Wang."

b: *我交它给王老师了。

* *wǒ jiāo tā gěi Wáng lǎoshī le.*

The three examples in (6.22)–(6.24) may be used when first introducing the *bǎ* construction to students. Such questions as the one in (6.22) are highly recommended at the beginning of teaching the *bǎ* construction, because they give students an opportunity to think about the meaning of the question with the word *bǎ* and how to respond to it accordingly. If a student answered it with the remark in (6.22a), it means this student thought about the question and imitated the structure of the question for the answer — a great start for learning a new construction. If, however, a student answered the question with the remark in (6.22b), it is also encouraging (though it is ungrammatical and unacceptable) because the student clearly understand what was being asked and must have undergone the process of thinking about the question, comparing it with its English counterpart and responding to it with English structure. In either case, teachers may first comment on students' efforts positively and then explain why (6.22b) is unacceptable. Unlike some other constructions discussed so far in this chapter, the *bǎ* construction has a syntactic constraint. That is, when the verb takes an object and a complement of location as in (6.22)–(6.23), a complement of direction as in (6.24), or a complement of identification as in (6.25)–(6.26), the *bǎ* construction is mostly like to be used; other sentences such as those in (6.22b)–(6.26b) are not acceptable (cf. Xing 1993).

(6.25) Q: 老师，今天的功课是什么？
              lǎoshī, jīntiān de gōngkè shì shénme?
              "Professor, what's today's homework?"

        a: 把课文翻译成英文。
              bǎ *kèwén fānyì chéng yīngwén.*
              "Translate the text into English"

        b: *翻译课文成英文。
              * *fānyì kèwén chéng yīngwén.*

(6.26) Q: 你以为我是谁？
              nǐ yǐwéi wǒ shì shéi?
              "Who did you think I was?"

        a: 我把你看成他的太太了。
              wǒ ***bǎ*** *nǐ kàn chéng tā de tàitai le.*
              "I mistook you for his wife."

        b: *我看你成他的太太了。
              **wǒ kàn nǐ chéng tā de tàitai le.*

When students become consciously aware of this syntactic constraint and capable of distinguishing the *bǎ* construction from the unacceptable Chinglish sentences such as those in (6.22b)–(6.26b), they have acquired the basic (syntactic) function of the *bǎ* construction as mentioned in Chapter 3 and are ready to learn its commonly used function.

The commonly used function of the *bǎ* construction is primarily concerned with the discourse function of the object and semantic function of the verb in a given sentence. When the object is more important than a regular object in the subject-verb-object (SVO) construction, but is less important than regular subject, the *bǎ* construction is likely to be used, as shown in (6.27a) (Xing 1993). Meanwhile, the verb has to have the property of affecting or disposing of the object one way or another. In modern Chinese, this semantic property has to be expressed by a bi-syllabic verb or verb phrase (cf. Feng 1999). If the verb or verb phrase [underlined in (6.27)–(6.29)] has that semantic function, the *bǎ* construction can, but does not have to, be used, as shown in (6.27a–b). If the verb or verb phrase does not have that semantic function, the *bǎ* construction cannot be used, as shown in (6.28a) and (6.29a), unless a complement is added to make the verb phrase effectible as shown in (6.28b)–(6.29b).

(6.27) Q: 去中国的事儿办得怎么样了？
             qù zhōngguó de shìr bàn de zěnme yàng le?
             "What is the preparation for your trip to China?"

        a: 我刚**把**护照<u>办好</u>，还没办签证呢。
             *wǒ gāng **bǎ** hùzhào <u>bàn-hǎo</u>, hái méi bàn qiānzhèng ne.*
             "I just have the passport processed, but have not applied for visa yet."
        b: 我刚<u>办好</u>护照，还没办签证呢。
             wǒ gāng <u>bàn-hǎo</u> hùzhào, hái méi bàn qiānzhèng ne.
             "I just got my passport, but have not applied for visa yet."

(6.28) a: *这件事儿真把我<u>高兴</u>。
             zhè jiàn shìr zhēn **bǎ wǒ <u>gāoxìng</u>.* (verb: happy)
        b: 不对，你应该说"这件事儿真**把**我<u>高兴死了</u>。"
             *bú duì, nǐ yīnggāi shuō "zhèi jiàn shìr zhēn **bǎ** wǒ <u>gāoxìng-sǐ</u> le.* (verb: happy-death)
             "Not right. You should say 'this matter really makes me thrilled to death."

(6.29) a: *老师我**把**那个问题<u>懂了</u>。
             lǎoshī wǒ **bǎ nàge wèntí <u>dǒng</u> le.* (verb: understand)
        b: 你应该说"我**把**那个问题<u>弄懂</u>了。"
             *nǐ yīnggāi shuō "wǒ **bǎ** nàge wèntí <u>nòng-dǒng</u> le.* (verb: make-understand)
             "You should say 'I understood that problem.'"

The sentences in (6.27) demonstrate that the verb *bàn* "process" has the property of affecting or disposing the object *hùzhào* "passport" and is not restricted by the syntactic constraints discussed above; therefore, either the *bǎ* construction (6.27a) or SVO (6.27b) construction can be used to answer the question raised in (6.27Q). At this point, students may ask about the difference between using the *bǎ* construction and using the SVO construction. According to Xing (1993), the major difference between the two constructions is associated with the discourse status of the object *hùzhào* "passport". If the speaker intends to emphasize that the passport has been processed, the *bǎ* construction is preferred. If, on the other hand, the speaker simply wants to describe where s/he stands regarding the preparation of the trip to China (i.e., s/he got his passport but has not gotten his/her visa), then the SVO construction is more adequate. Notice that when determining whether the *bǎ* construction should be used, students have to first examine whether the syntactic and semantic constraints apply to a given sentence before taking into consideration the discourse status of the object.

The examples in (6.28)–(6.29) demonstrate another situation where the *bǎ* construction can or cannot be used. As just mentioned, to use the *bǎ* construction, students should first consider if the syntactic (the verb takes a complement of location, direction and so on) or semantic (the verb has the property of affecting the object) constraints apply to the verb in a sentence. If both syntactic and semantic constraints apply, only the *bǎ* construction can be used. If only the semantic constraint applies, either the *bǎ* construction or the SVO construction can be used. If neither the syntactic nor the semantic constraint applies, the *bǎ* construction cannot be used. With these rules in mind, students should be able to determine that the stative verbs, *gāoxìng* "happy" and *dǒng* "understand" cannot be used in the *bǎ* construction as shown in (6.28a) and (6.29a). However, if students are capable of changing the verb into a phrase which can convey the meaning of "affect something or somebody in some way", the *bǎ* construction can be used, as shown in (6.28b)–(6.29b). In (6.28), the verb *gāoxìng* "happy" is changed into *gāoxìng-sǐ le* "happy (thrilled) to death" and in (6.29), the verb *dǒng* "understand" is changed into *nòng-dǒng* "make understand". In both cases, the changed meanings indicate some sort of process of affecting somebody or something in some way. Therefore, the *bǎ* construction is acceptable.

Apart from the commonly used function just discussed, the *bǎ* construction also has special functions. As defined in Chapter 3, the special function is comprised of a special and idiomatic usage of a given construction. Consider the example in (6.30):

(6.30) Q: 这家人最近怎么了？
            zhè jiā rén zuìjìn zěnme le?
            "What happened to that family recently?"

        a: 听说把个孩子死了。
            *tīngshuō **bǎ** ge háizi sǐ le.*
            "It is said that a child died."

By the syntactic and semantic criteria discussed earlier, the verb *sǐ* "die" merely indicates the state of the subject and cannot affect something or somebody on its own, and therefore cannot be used in the *bǎ* construction. Yet, the *bǎ* construction in (6.30a) is acceptable. I consider this kind of usage a special function (as discussed in Chapter 3) when teaching students the *bǎ* construction and suggest that students learn this function case by case, that is, to treat this kind of *bǎ* construction as an idiomatic expression.

So far, I have shown the syntactic, semantic and discourse functions of the *bǎ* construction and when, where, and why the construction can or cannot be used in discourse. It has been suggested with supporting evidence that syntactic and semantic rules should be applied before discourse rules when using the construction. We may summarize the procedures of teaching the *bǎ* construction as follows:

- Illustrate the situations where the *bǎ* construction has to be used (i.e. the basic function) and briefly explain why;

- Provide discourse situations for students to use the construction and help them distinguish the *bǎ* construction from other commonly used constructions, such as the subject-verb-object construction;
- Demonstrate various situations where the *bǎ* construction is optionally used (i.e. the commonly used function) and briefly explain why;
- Ask students questions and encourage them to answer the questions with the *bǎ* construction;
- Based on students' comprehension, compare and explain the optionally used *bǎ* construction with other comparable constructions and provide further opportunity for students to practice and distinguish where and when the *bǎ* construction should be used;
- If asked, special functions of the *bǎ* construction may be explained at the advanced level of classes.

6.3.1.2   The *bèi* (被) construction

The *bèi* construction (patient + *bèi* + agent + verb) is referred to by some grammarians as the passive construction 被动式 (*bèidòngshì*) in Chinese (Wang L. 1943–44; Wang H. 1957, 1983). Similar to the *bǎ* construction, there has been no shortage of studies on the *bèi* construction. Being the subject of Chinese linguistic research for decades, the function of the *bèi* construction is not a mystery to most researchers anymore. However, as far as the instruction of this construction is concerned, teachers of different backgrounds may hold different opinions regarding what might be the most efficient way to teach the construction. In this section, I will present how I approach the construction in the hopes of providing some empirical materials for teachers and students who may find it useful in teaching or learning the construction. I will start with the function of the *bèi* construction. Whenever necessary, I will incorporate findings of linguistic research into the suggested process of teaching and learning.

Let us first begin with the process of teaching and learning the basic function of the *bèi* construction, and then explain the circumstances under which the *bèi* construction is used so that students know when to use it and when not to use it in natural discourse. Traditional analysis suggests that the primary function of the *bèi* construction is associated with the semantic property of the verb in the sentence. That is, when a bi-syllabic verb or verb phrase expresses the meaning of affecting something or somebody in a negative way, the *bèi* construction can be used, as shown in (6.31). Notice that the semantic property of the verb in the *bèi* construction is similar to that of the verb in the *bǎ* construction with only a minor difference between the two: the verb in the *bèi* construction expresses an adverse meaning, whereas the verb in the *bǎ* construction does not necessarily convey that meaning. Nevertheless, this minor distinction has become increasingly blurred in modern Chinese; the *bèi* construction in modern discourse does not have to have the adverse meaning, as shown in (6.32).

(6.31) Q: 你怎么啦？
   nǐ zěnme la?
   "What's the matter?"

a: 我**被**狗子那王八蛋<u>打了</u>。
   *wǒ **bèi** Gǒuzi nà wángbādàn dǎ le.* (verb: *da le* "hit")
   "I was hit by that bastard Gouzi."

b: 狗子那王八蛋**把**我打了。
   *Gǒuzi nà wángbādàn **bǎ** wǒ dǎ le.*
   "That bastard Gouzi hit me."

(6.32) Q: 他怎么那么高兴？
   tā zěnme nàme gāoxìng?
   "Why is he so happy?"

a: （他）刚**被**<u>提拔了</u>。
   *(tā) gāng **bèi** tíbá le.* (verb: *tíbá* "promote")
   "(He) was recently promoted."

b: （头儿）刚**把**他<u>提拔了</u>。
   *(tóu-er) gāng **bǎ** tā tíbá le.*
   "(Boss) just promoted him."

The sentence in (6.31a), with the verb *dǎ* "hit" expressing an adverse meaning, represents the basic prototypical function of the *bèi* construction. The sentence in (6.32a) also uses the *bèi* construction, however, its verb *tíbá* "promote" conveys a positive meaning. Furthermore, the same verb in (6.31) and (6.32) can be used in either the *bèi* or the *bǎ* constructions. This means that the semantic property of the verb in both constructions is quite similar, especially in modern Chinese. In other words, if the verb can be used in a *bèi* construction, it can also be used in the *bǎ* construction and vice versa, as shown in (6.31b–c) and (6.32b–c). A question to ask at this point is whether the *bèi* construction also has the same syntactic constraints (discussed in the previous section) as the *bǎ* construction. Linguistic investigations (e.g. Xing 1993) reveal that the two constructions indeed apply to the same syntactic constraint; however, differ substantially in terms of their discourse and pragmatic functions, as shown in (6.33)–(6.34).

(6.33) Q: 我们的午饭呢？
   wǒmen de wǔfàn ne?
   "Where is our lunch?"

a: （午饭）都**被**他<u>偷吃了</u>。
   *(wǔfàn) dōu **bèi** tā tōuchī le.*
   "(It) has been eaten by him without asking us."

(6.34) Q: 他怎么了？
              tā zěnme le?
              "What's the matter with him?"

        a: 他**把**我们的午饭都<u>偷吃</u>了。
              *tā **bǎ** wǒmen de wǔfàn dōu tōuchī le.*
              "He ate our lunch without asking us."

When the *bèi* construction is used, the focus of the conversation is on the patient or receiver of the action expressed by the verb in the sentence as in (6.33). When the *bǎ* construction is used, however, the focus of the conversation is on the agent as in (6.34). This functional difference clearly demonstrates the circumstances under which the two constructions should be used. One cannot switch the two constructions when answering the questions in (6.33)–(6.34) for reasons of discourse coherence maintenance, which will be discussed in detail in Chapter 7.

(6.35) Q: 美国在世界上的声誉怎么样？
              Měiguó zài shìjiè shàng de shēngyù zěnme yàng?
              "What is the reputation of the United States in the world?"

        a: 美国**被**世界上很多人<u>看成</u>最民主的国家。
              *Měiguó **bèi** shìjiè shàng hěnduō rén <u>kànchéng</u> zuì mínzhǔ de guójiā."*
              "The United States is considered the most democratic country by many people in the world."

        b: *世界上很多人看成美国最民主的国家。
              * *shìjiè shàng hěnduō rén <u>kànchéng</u> Měiguó zuì mínzhǔ de guójiā.*

(6.36) Q: 伊拉克人是怎么看待美国的？
              Yīlākè rén shì zěnme kàndài Měiguó de?
              "What do Iraqis think of the United States?"

        a: 不少伊拉克人**把**美国看成侵略者。
              *bùshǎo Yīlākè rén **bǎ** Měiguó kànchéng qīnlüèzhě.*
              "Many Iraqis consider the United States the occupier."

        b: *不少伊拉克人看成美国侵略者。
              * *bùsháo Yīlākè rén kànchéng Měiguó qīnlüèzhě.*

Notice that both the sentences in (6.35a) and (6.36a) have the verb *kànchéng* and a complement of identification (i.e. *zuì mínzhǔ de guójiā* "the most democratic county" and *qīnlüèzhě* "invader/occupier"). In this case, either the *bǎ* or the *bèi* construction can be used, but neither can use the SVO construction as shown in (6.35b) and (6.36b). This means the *bǎ* and the *bèi* construction apply the same syntactic rule to create grammatical sentences. Pragmatically, however, the *bèi* construction is used to place an emphasis or focus on the patient/receiver of the verb, whereas the *bǎ* construction focuses on the agent of the verb even though it also promotes the importance of the patient/receiver to a certain extent. The patient/receiver of the *bǎ* construction is definitely more important than that in the SVO construction (cf. Xing 1993).

Thus, the function of emphasis on the patient's discourse importance should be considered the commonly used function of the *bèi* construction. Students of elementary and intermediate levels, therefore, have to learn them well and thoroughly. For intermediate high and advanced students, some special functions of the *bèi* construction, as illustrated in (6.37) may also be introduced. The sentence in (6.37a) differs from other commonly used *bèi* constructions in that the noun phrase in the subject position is not the patient or receiver of the verb *shuāi* "trip and fall", but rather it is the agent of the verb, and the noun phrase after *bèi* is the reason why he is the agent of "trip and fall". As mentioned earlier, this *bèi* construction is not commonly used and therefore, students should learn it only as a special case.

(6.37)　Q:　你怎么啦？
　　　　　　　nǐ zěnme la"
　　　　　　　"What's the matter with you?"
　　　　a:　我**被**他摔了一个跟头。
　　　　　　　*wǒ **bèi** tā shuāi le yíge gēntou.*
　　　　　　　"I tripped and fell because of him."

The procedure for teaching students the construction, therefore, should start with the basic prototypical function, and then move on to the commonly used function and finally to the special function. Since these functions interact, in most cases corresponding with semantic, syntactic, and discourse pragmatic constraints, students should learn the functions along with those constraints. Following these learning steps, students should be able to understand when the *bèi* construction can or cannot be used and when it is preferred for use in discourse. If students learn the *bǎ* construction prior to the *bèi* construction, comparison between the two constructions can enhance and reinforce the acquisition of both constructions.

6.3.2　Focus constructions

The term "focus constructions" refers to those sentences that place an emphasis or focus on a certain element in a sentence. There are a number of ways to express focus/emphasis in modern Chinese. For instance, one may place the focused/emphasized part at the beginning of a sentence [i.e. topicalization, as illustrated in (6.38)], use intonation, or use a lexical element to mark focus or emphasis, as shown in (6.39)–(6.40).

(6.38)　Q:　你帮他找个女朋友，行吗？
　　　　　　　nǐ bāng tā zhǎo ge nǚ péngyou, xíng ma?
　　　　　　　"You help him to find a girlfriend, okay?"

a: 这种事儿，我向来不碰。
zhèi zhǒng shìr, wǒ xiànglái bú pèng.
"This kind of thing, I never get involved with."

(6.39)   现在经济不景气，很多人失业，**连**我们头儿**都**被解雇了。
***lián** wǒmen tóur **dōu** bèi jiěgù le.*
"Now the economy is not good, (so) many people have lost their jobs, even our boss has been laid off."

(6.40)   Q: 谁让你来**的**？
*(**shì**) shéi ràng nǐ lái **de**?*
"Who asked you to come?"
a: 是我们老板让我来找你的。
shì** wǒmen lǎobǎn ràng wǒ lái zhǎo nǐ **de。
"Our boss asked me to come find you."

The three sentences in (6.38a), (6.39) and (6.40a) all have a focused/emphasized part. The structural difference among them is that the focused/emphasized part in (6.38a) is marked by the position (i.e. the beginning of the sentence), whereas the two in (6.39)–(6.40) are marked by *lián ... dōu* and *shì ... de* respectively. In addition, the circumstances under which these constructions are used also vary, which will be explained in detail in the following two sections as well as when, where, and how to use these two constructions in discourse and how to teach them to students of Chinese as FL.

6.3.2.1   The *lián* (连) construction

The *lián* construction has to have either *dōu* 都 "all" or *yě* 也 "also" to express the meaning of focus/emphasis in modern Chinese (*lián* + focused element + *dōu/yě* + verb). Although *lián* has a number of other functions (e.g., it can be used as a preposition meaning "including" or an adverb meaning "continuously") both historically and in modern Chinese, its focus/emphatic function is the primary one in written discourse (Xing 2004: 99), hence it is important in Chinese acquisition. When examining the discourse in which the *lián* construction is found, I have realized that it is often used to further explain the situation discussed in the previous discourse, as demonstrated below:

(6.41)   房间太小，**连**电脑**都**放不下。   (Yao, et al. 1997: 113)
*fángjiān tài xiǎo, **lián** diànnǎo **dōu** fàng bú xià.*
"The room is very small. It does not even have room for my computer."

(6.42)   你这人怎么搞的？**连**这点儿小事**都**办不了。
*nǐ zhèi rén zěnme gǎo de? **lián** zhèi diǎn xiǎoshì **dōu** bàn bù liǎo.*

"What's wrong with you? You cannot even take care of this kind of trivial stuff."

(6.43)　　他天天都很忙，**连**周末**也**不休息。

tā tiāntiān dōu hěn máng, lián zhōumò yě bù xiūxi.

"He is busy every day; he does not even have spare time on the weekend."

(6.44)　a:　这个周末，到我们家来吧。

zhèige zhōumò dào wǒmen jiā lái ba.

"This weekend, please come to our house."

　　　b:　不去、不去。

bú qù, bú qù.

"(I'm) not going. (I'm) not going."

　　　a:　**连**你爸**都**来，你为什么不来？

lián nǐ bà dōu lái, nǐ wèi shénme bù lái?

"Even your father is coming. Why aren't you?"

In (6.41), the first sentence states, "the room is very small" followed by a *lián* construction that explains how small the room is, that is, "[it is so small that] there is no place in the room even for a computer." Apparently, the reason that "computer" is focused in this *lián* construction arises from the conventional wisdom which says that regular rooms normally have a place for such a common commodity. Similarly, in (6.42), the speaker complains in the first sentence about the way that the referent *nǐ zhèi rén* "you the person" does things and then uses a *lián* construction to further explain why the speaker complains, namely "even this trivial matter you cannot handle." In (6.43)–(6.44), both *lián* constructions are used to provide specific explanations of the general comments in the preceding discourse. Notice that although these *lián* constructions serve the same discourse function – providing further comments on the situation mentioned in the preceding discourse, their contexts vary. The one in (6.41) explains how small the room is, the one in (6.42) explains why the speaker complains, the one in (6.43) explains how busy he is, and the one in (6.44) explains why the listener should go to the speaker's house. Therefore, the focused part varies accordingly [i.e. "computer" in (6.41), "this trivial matter" in (6.42), "weekend" in (6.43), and "your father" in (6.44)]. Furthermore, both "computer" and "this trivial matter" are patients/receivers in the two sentences, whereas "weekend" functions as adverb and "your father" functions as the agent/subject of the *lian* construction. All these variations pose some problems for students in acquiring the *lián* construction.

When teaching students how to use the *lián* construction, it is common for teachers to explain the structure of the *lián* construction, and then give examples. As a result, students can identify and understand the *lián* construction, but cannot use it whenever necessary in discourse. Therefore, I suggest that teachers first explain when the *lián* construction is likely to be used in discourse, such as when a speaker gives a further explanation to a general comment given in the immediately preceding discourse, and then encourages students to create circumstances under which the *lián* construction may be used. When students become familiar with the discourse situation of the *lián* construction, teachers may proceed to explain and demonstrate what elements are most likely to be the focus of the *lián* construction.

By examining students' errors in using the *lián* construction, I find that it is more difficult for them to find an adequate focused element than to understand the general function of the *lián* construction, which seems to suggest that more explanation is needed as to the types of elements that can be focused on and the relationship between the focused elements and unfocused elements in the sentence and discourse. Taking the *lián* construction in (6.43) as an example, the focused element is *zhōumò* "weekend". Teachers may provide other elements that can be used in that context, as illustrated in (6.45).

(6.45)   a: 他天天都很忙，连吃饭的时间都没有。
             tā tiāntiān dōu hěn máng, **lián** *chīfàn de shíjiān* **dōu** *méiyǒu.*
             "He is very busy every day and does not even have time to eat."
         b: 他天天都很忙，这事儿他连想也没时间想。
             tā tiāntiān dōu hěn máng, zhèi shìr tā **lián** *xiǎng* **yě** *méi shíjiān xiǎng.*
             "He is very busy every day. This issue, he does not even have time to think about it"
         c: 他天天都很忙，连家都不回。
             tā tiāntiān dōu hěn máng, **lián** *jiā* **dōu** *bù huí.*
             "He is very busy every day and does not even go home."

All three *lián* constructions in (6.45) explain how busy the referent is: no time to eat in (a), no time to think about this issue in (b), and "no time" to go home in (c). This means all three *lián* constructions are used in the right discourse. If we look at the focused elements in these constructions "eating time", "thinking time", and "home time", we find that the speaker chooses the elements that are of importance in his/her life to focus on. In other words, "eat", "think" and "home" are all important concepts to the speaker, therefore, they are emphasized or focused on in the discourse using the *lián* construction. If, on the other hand, the focused element does not play any important role in the speaker or listener's life, then the *lián* construction may not be used, as shown in (6.46)–(6.47).

(6.46)   ??他天天很忙，连玩儿都没时间。
             tā tiāntiān dōu hěn máng, **lián** *wánr* **dōu** *méi shíjiān.*
             "He is very busy every day; he does not even have time to play."

(6.47)   a: *他天天很忙，连没有时间都看电影。
             * *tā tiāntiān dōu hěn máng,* **lián** *méiyǒu shíjiān* **dōu** *kàn diànyǐng.*
             Gloss: he every-day very busy, **lián** no time **dou** watch movie"

b:　他天天很忙，连看电影的时间都没有。

　　tā tiāntiān dōu hěn máng, **lián** *kàn diànyǐng de shíjiān* **dōu** *méiyǒu.*

　　"He is very busy every day. (He) does not even have time to watch a movie."

The acceptability of the *lián* construction in (6.46) depends on the understanding of the concept *wánr* "play". To some people, "play" cannot be possibly considered important in life; therefore, focusing on it using the *lián* construction is not acceptable. However, to many others, it is perfectly appropriate to focus on "play" in describing their lifestyles. In comparison, the *lián* construction in (6.47a) is totally unacceptable because the focused element is *méiyǒu shíjiān* "no time" which cannot be considered an important factor in anybody's life. However, if the focused element is changed into *kàn diànyǐng* "watch a movie" as in (6.47b), then the *lián* construction becomes acceptable.

To sum up this section, instead of discussing all *lián*'s functions, I have focused on its emphatic/focus function — the most commonly used function. It was demonstrated that the *lián* construction is most likely to be used to further explain or comment on the situation described in the immediately preceding discourse. When teaching this function, instructors may emphasize why some concepts can be focused on using the *lián* construction while others cannot, so that students have a clear understanding of the discourse pragmatic function, namely where and why the *lián* construction is used in discourse.

6.3.2.2　The *shi* (是) … *de* (的) construction

The *shì* … (*de*) construction (*shì* + focused element + verb + *de*) is often used to express the speaker's focus on a certain element mentioned in the previous discourse. Unlike the *lián* construction, the *shì* … *de* construction may focus on any elements known to the speaker and/or the listener, as illustrated in (6.48):

(6.48)　a:　春假的时候，我们去墨西哥了。

　　　　　chūnjià de shíhòu, wǒmen qù Mòxīgē le.

　　　　　"During the Spring break, we went to Mexico."

　　　　b:　你（是）怎么去的？[focusing on "how to get there"]

　　　　　*nǐ (**shì**) zěnme qù **de**?*

　　　　　"**How** did you get there?"

　　　　c:　我们（是）坐飞机去的。

　　　　　*wǒmen (**shì**) zuò fēijī qù de.*

　　　　　"We went there by airplane."

　　　　d.　你（是）谁跟一起去的？[focusing on "who went with you"]

　　　　　*nǐ (**shì**) gēn shéi yiqǐ qù **de**?*

　　　　　"**Who** went there with you?"

    e.   我（是）跟男朋友一起去的。

wǒ (shì) gēn nánpéngyou yiqǐ qù de.

"I went with my boyfriend."

(6.49) a: 你知道吗?他女儿已经大学毕业了。

nǐ zhīdào ma tā nǚér yǐjīng dàxué bìyè le?

"Do you know his daughter already graduated from college?"

    b: 不知道，他女儿是在哪儿上的（大学）？ [focusing on "where"]

bù zhīdào. tā nǚér shì zài nǎr shàng de (dàxué)?

"I don't know. **Where** did his daughter attend (the college)?"

    c: 她（是）在哈佛上的。

tā (shì) zài Hāfó shàng de.

"She attended Harvard University."

    d: 她是什么时候毕业的？ [focusing on "when"]

tā shì shénme shíhòu bìyè de?

"**When** did she graduate?

    e: 她（是）去年毕业的。

tā (shì) qùnián bìyè de.

"She graduated last year."

The mini-dialogues in (6.48) and (6.49) show that the speaker can focus on elements that provide information regarding who, whom, how, where and when in discourse. The situation described by the *shì ... de* construction always refers to an event that already happened. In natural oral discourse, *shì* is often omitted. Since both the function and the sentence structure of *shì ... de* construction is straightforward, it is relatively easy for students to acquire this construction in the classroom. When teaching this construction, teachers should make sure that students understand what constitutes a "focused element" and what can be placed in between *shì ... de*. Consider the following examples:

(6.50) a: 是她学（的）语言学。

shì tā xué (de) yǔyánxué

"**She** studied linguistics (implies: not other people)."

    b: *是她的学语言学。

* *shì tā de xué yǔyánxué*

    c: 她是学语言学的。

tā shì xué yǔyánxué de.

"Linguistics is what she studied."

    d: *她学是语言学的。

tā xué shì yǔyánxué de.

    e: 她是学的语言学。

tā shì xué de yǔyánxué.

"She indeed studied linguistics."

When focusing on the agent/subject of an action (i.e. who did something?), both the agent and its verb have to be placed in between *shì ... de*, as shown in (6.50a) because the basic function of the *shì ... de* construction is to focus on who, when, where, what, how relevant to an action described by the verb. Therefore, both the verb and the element related to the verb are the focused elements. This is why (6.50b)–(6.50d) are not acceptable; but (6.50c) is, in which the patient/object is focused (i.e. what is studied?) and both the verb and the patient/object are placed in between *shì ... de*. Students should also be aware that the action/verb itself can be focused too, as shown in (6.50e).

When learning the *shì ... de* construction, distinction may be made between the focus/emphasis function just discussed and the descriptive/confirmative function as shown in (6.51). In Chinese, to describe something with descriptive reduplicated adjectives such as *lánlán* "very blue" in (6.51a), the *shì ... de* construction has to be used (cf. Li and Thompson 1981). Without it, the sentence would be ungrammatical as shown in (6.51b). In comparison, it is optional to use the *shì ... de* construction to express focus or emphasis. The difference between the sentence with *shì ... de* and without is that the former has the focus function and describes an event that happened in the past (which may continue to the present) as in (6.52a), whereas the latter does not have the focus function and does not necessarily describe something that happened in the past as in (6.52b).

(6.51) Q 你说说海南怎么样？
      nǐ shuōshuō hǎinán zěnmeyàng?
      "Tell us how is Hainan?

    a: 不错，天是蓝蓝的，海也是蓝蓝的。
      *búcuò, tiān **shì** lánlán de, hǎi yě **shì** lánlán de.*
      "Not bad. The sky is every blue and the sea is also very blue."

    b; *不错，天蓝蓝，海也蓝蓝。
      * *búcuò, tiān lánlán, hǎi yě lánlán.*

(6.52) a: 是**她学**（的）语言学。
      shì *tā xué (de) yǔyánxué*。
      "**She** studied linguistics (implies: not other people)."

    b: 她学语言学。
      tā xué yǔyánxué.
      "She studies linguistics."

One other issue that students may have to deal with in learning the *shì ... de* construction concerns the translation of the *shì ... de* sentence into English or other languages. Notice that English does not have an equivalent to the *shì ... de* construction. To express the functional equivalent to the *shì ... de* construction, one has to use other means, such as intonation (i.e. placing an emphatic pitch on the focused elements) or use different sentence constructions. Due to this difference between Chinese and English, many native English speakers tend not to use the *shì … de* construction. Teachers, therefore, may have to explain the difference and possible equivalents in students' native language along with giving exercises that teach where and why the *shì … de* construction is used, so that students feel comfortable using it in discourse. We may summarize the procedures of teaching and learning the *shì … de* construction, as well as the *lián* construction as follows:

- Demonstrate the discourse functions of *shì … de* or *lián* construction in various discourse;
- Compare the emphatic construction with non-emphatic constructions;
- Compare the emphatic construction and its function with the equivalent in students' native language, if there is any;
- Focus on how to use the emphatic construction (e.g., what can be emphasized?)
- Create discourse situations for students to use the emphatic construction in class;
- Ask students to use the emphatic construction in both oral and written discourse/assignments.

6.4   Acquisition of Nominal Clauses

Chinese, similar to many other languages, has two major types of subordinate clauses: adverbial clauses modifying verbs and nominal clauses modifying nouns or used as noun phrases (NP). Compared with the unique constructions discussed in this chapter, subordinate clauses may be easier for students to acquire because they are all derived from regular sentences (including both basic and unique constructions). Naturally, this assumes that students have learned Chinese regular sentences well before using them as subordinate clauses. The only challenge that students may have appears to arise from the structural difference between nominal clauses in Chinese and those in students' native languages, such as English, because Chinese has a different word order in nominal clauses and modified noun phrases from that of English. Therefore, in what follows, I will examine the function and structure of nominal clauses and discuss students' errors in acquiring these clauses. Whenever appropriate, possible ways to help students use those clauses correctly in communication will be suggested. Adverbial clauses will not be discussed here due to the structural and functional similarity of these to those in other languages, such as English. Interested readers may consult Chapter 7 in which discourse connectors most likely to introduce adverbial clauses are discussed in detail.

   Chinese has the same basic word order as English, namely subject + verb + object (SVO); however, it has the opposite word order for nominal clauses and modified or head noun phrases.

Chinese: nominal clause + *de* (+ noun phrase)
English: (noun phrase +) nominalizer + nominal clause

Notice that in both languages, nominal clauses may or may not take a head noun phrase. The difference between the two languages lies in how clauses relate to their head nouns and other elements in a sentence. Chinese uses the nominalizer *de*, whereas English uses the nominalizer *that* or *which*. Chinese places nominal clauses before their head nouns, whereas English places them after. Consider the following examples:

(6.53) Q: 我们进去看看唱片吧。
        wǒmen jìnqù kànkàn chàngpiàn ba.
        "Let's go in to take a look at their CDs."

     a: 这家店卖的唱片都很贵。
        ***zhèi jiā diàn mài** DE chàngpiàn dōu hěn guì.*
        clause   DE NP   VP
     b: "The CDs **that this store sells** are all very expensive."
        NP   nominalizer clause   VP

(6.54) Q: 你喜欢谁的音乐？
        nǐ xǐhuān shéi de yīnyuè?
        "Whose music do you like?"

     a: 我喜欢朗朗弹的钢琴协奏曲。
        *wǒ xǐhuān **Láng Láng tán** **DE** gāngqín xiézòuqǔ.*
        V   clause   DE NP
     b: "I like the piano concerto **that Lang Lang played**."
        V   NP   nominalizer   clause
     c: *我喜欢钢琴协奏曲朗朗弹。
        * *wǒ xǐhuān gāngqín xiézòuqǔ **Láng Láng tán**.*
        V   NP   clause

The clause (bold-faced) in (6.53a) modifies the subject noun phrase *chàngpiàn* "music CDs" and the clause in (6.54a) modifies the object noun phrase *gāngqín xiézòuqǔ* "piano concerto". Both Chinese clauses use the nominalizer "*de*" and when translated into English, both use the nominalizer (underlined) "that". The only difference between Chinese and English is the word order within the clause and the head noun. In this case, most students have little difficulty learning these nominal clauses after teachers demonstrate and explain how to use them, except that a few students may makes mistakes like (6.54c) in which the Chinese clause uses the English word order. More students, however, make mistakes when the nominal clause does not have a head noun as shown in (6.55)–(6.56).

(6.55) Q: 她在哪儿工作？

"*tā zài nǎr gōngzuò?*"

"Where does she work?"

a: 我不知道他在什么地方工作。

wǒ bù zhīdào tā zài shénme dìfang gōngzuò.

"I don't know *where* he works."

b: *我不知道哪儿他工作。

wǒ bù zhīdào nǎr tā gōngzuò.

(6.56) Q: 她来不来？

tā lái bù lái?

"Is she coming or not?"

a: 谁知道他来不来。

shéi zhīdào tā lái bù lái.

"Who knows if/whether he will come or not!"

b: *谁知道如果他来还是不来

* *shéi zhīdào rúguǒ tā lái háishì bù lái.*

(6.57) Q: 我做饭，谁做菜？

wǒ zuò fàn, shéi zuò cài?

"I will cook the rice; who will cook the vegetables?"

a: 让王明做，他怎么做都好吃。

ràng Wáng Míng zuò. tā zěnme zuò dōu hǎo-chī.

"Ask Wang Ming to do it. However he cooks (it), (it) tastes good."

b: *怎么他做都好吃。

**zěnme tā zuò dōu hǎo-chī.*

The nominal clauses in (6.55a)–(6.56a) function as an object in the sentence and the one in (6.57a) serves as the subject of the sentence. Notice that all three clauses have an interrogative word/phrase (i.e. *nǎr* "where", *V-not-V* "whether … not", *zěnme* "how") and this is the place where students often have trouble with Chinese nominal clauses because they differ from their English counterparts structurally. Chinese places interrogative words/phrases in the same place they do in a statement, whereas English always places interrogative words at the beginning of a sentence regardless of whether they are in an interrogative sentence or nominal clause. If students do not remember this rule well, they may create ungrammatical Chinglish sentences as those in (6.55b), (6.56b) and (6.57b). When there is no interrogative word/phrase in a nominal clause nor a head noun for the clause as in (6.58a)–(6.59a), students do not seem to have any problem in acquisition because both Chinese and English use the same word order.

(6.58)   Q   他怎么说？
              tā zěnme shuō?
              "What did he say?"

         a: 他说**明天商店不开门**。
              *tā shuō **míngtiān shāngdiàn bù kāimén**.*
              "He told me **the shop would not open tomorrow**."

(6.59)   Q: 家长不应该这样对待孩子。
              jiāzhǎng bú yīnggāi zhèiyàng duìdài háizi.
              "Parents should not treat children like that."

         a: **家长教育孩子**是理所当然的。
              ***jiāzhǎng jiàoyù háizi** shì lǐ suǒ dāngrán de.*
              "**That parents discipline children** is what they are supposed to do."
              Or "Parents are supposed to discipline children."

I have shown so far that some Chinese nominal clauses are easier for native English speaking students to learn than others. Like other aspects of the Chinese language, the functions and structures of nominal clauses, if they exist in a student's native language, are easier for students to learn than those that do not exist in a student's native language. Hence, when teaching nominal clauses, teachers may first clarify the differences between Chinese nominal clauses and those in a student's native language, and then practice and use them in discourse. An interesting part of learning and practicing nominal clauses is that, like in English, theoretically there is no limit to the number of clauses in any given sentence; one can create a sentence with several embedded clauses in it, as shown in (6.60a).

(6.60)   Q: 你最喜欢什么？
              nǐ zuì xǐhuan shénme？
              "What do you like most?"

         a: 我最喜欢[我妈妈从一个[卖很多[儿童喜欢看的书]³的书店]²买的书]¹。
              wǒ zuì xǐhuan wǒ māma cóng yí ge mài hěnduō értóng xǐhuan kàn de shū de shūdiàn mǎi de shū.
              "I like the books ¹**that** my mother bought from a store² **where** they sell a lot of children's book ³**that** many children actually like to read."

There are three nominal clauses in (6.60a) marked by numerals. Apparently, the greater the number of embedded nominal clauses in a sentence, the greater the difficulty in understanding the meaning of the sentence and consequently the harder it is for students to learn it. Since, in real discourse, native Chinese speakers rarely use more than two nominal clauses in one sentence, students should not spend too much time on long sentences with many nominal clauses. Instead, they should focus on the basic structure when acquiring normal clauses.

Once students become fluent with the basics, they should be able to use it whenever they want and however they want in discourse. We may summarize the procedure of teaching Chinese nominal clauses as follows:

- Demonstrate primarily the structural difference between Chinese nominal clauses and those in students' native languages, since there is no functional difference between Chinese and other languages;
- Emphasize the position and usage of question words (e.g. 哪儿 *nǎr* "where", 谁 *shéi* "who") and nonexistence of conjunction words (e.g. 如果 *rúguǒ* "if") in nominal clauses;
- Ask students to use nominal clauses wherever they can in both oral and written discourse.

6.5   Conclusion

In this chapter, I have discussed three types of constructions: (1) the most commonly used constructions such as the topic-comment construction, the verb-complement construction, and the *le* construction, (2) the unique constructions including the *bǎ* and *bèi* construction and the *lián* and *shì ... de* construction, and (3) the nominal clause. Since all these constructions have different discourse structures and functions, various methods for acquisition of those constructions have also been introduced. Some teachers and students may find certain methods more appropriate for their teaching and learning style than others. In the end, I hope this chapter provides some guidelines for teachers to teach sentences. One can see that throughout the chapter I promote the teaching method that focuses on teaching when, where, and why a certain sentence is used in discourse and discourage any practice of teaching sentences apart from their discourse functions.

7 *Discourse and Pragmatics*

7.1 Introduction

Among numerous attempts made by researchers of different backgrounds and disciplines, the simplest definition of discourse regards discourse as a communicative unit consisting of at least two or more sentences (cf. Hymes 1974, Stubbs 1983, van Dijk 1985, Crystal 1985, Schiffrin 1994). This is a rather narrow and perhaps a slightly simplified notion of discourse. Nevertheless, it is still practical and useful for teachers and students of foreign languages, though some linguists may prefer a general and broad definition such as the one given by Blakemore (1988: 229): "the study of discourse belongs to the study of language in use." In addition to a straight definition of discourse, researchers interested in discourse analysis often discuss strategies in composing an easily comprehensible text. They use such terms as cohesion, coherence, connectedness, continuity, and interpretability to categorize their studies (Halliday and Hasan 1976, Hobbs 1979, Halliday 1987, Gernsbacher and Givón 1995, Bublitz et al. 1999, Kehler 2002). Speakers/writers who are capable of creating coherent and appropriate discourse are considered to have discourse competence. How, then, non-native speakers, that is, students of Chinese as a foreign language, acquire discourse competence, where even native Chinese people might not all have developed such a skill, is the focus of this chapter.

One question that often bewilders language teachers is whether discourse competence is, in fact, teachable. Studies on foreign/second language acquisition (e.g. Dunkel and Davis 1994, Dudley-Evans 1994, Silberstein 1994, Riggenbach 1998, Chun 2002), especially those on teaching English as a foreign language, provide some encouraging insight into that question. Cohesive devices or structures, such as turn-taking and intonation contour in conversation and transition in listening, reading and writing, can be explicitly taught. For Chinese discourse competence, there have not been many studies in the past. A few studies discuss discourse markers and Mandarin prosody in spoken and written texts (e.g. Feng, 2000, Chu 1998, Tao 1996, Shen 1990, Li and Thompson 1981, Tsao 1979, Chao 1968). Although these studies are not necessarily pedagogically oriented, the findings provide Chinese teachers with instrumental content for Chinese discourse and discourse devices to be used in teaching Chinese as a foreign language.

In recent years, we have seen an increasing interest in discourse devices (some researchers also use the term discourse elements) in the field of teaching and learning Chinese as a foreign language. Since discourse is such a broad area of study, Xing (1998) attempts to define the role of discourse elements and outline discourse content for Chinese language classes. Other researchers (e.g. Chu 2002, Li 2002, Tao 2005 [2002]) investigate specific discourse markers and structures and provide pedagogical procedures to facilitate the teaching of these markers. Cui (2003) suggests two stages in developing students' discourse competence: (1) enable teachers to introduce discourse devices and explain discourse functions to students; and (2) enable students to comprehend and apply discourse devices to listening, speaking, reading and writing Chinese. Clearly, both of these stages, or rather tasks, are challenging to Chinese language practitioners at the beginning of the twenty-first century, as Cui correctly pointed out, because many teachers, including some researchers, have not had a comprehensive understanding of discourse devices, let alone a comprehensive system of teaching discourse devices to students. In this situation, it is difficult for students to develop discourse competence.

To alleviate the challenge facing Chinese language teachers and students alike, the remainder of this chapter will first introduce various discourse devices and their discourse functions. Then, discourse models will be discussed to familiarize students with various formulas in understanding and in constructing clear, informative, and coherent discourse. In section 7.4, two major discourse styles will be discussed and pedagogical procedures will be suggested. Since discourse is so closely related to and interactive with the pragmatic, section 7.5 will be devoted to a discussion of the interpretation of different discourse by people of different backgrounds. The chapter will conclude with suggested procedures teachers may consult to help them in teaching different levels of discourse competence.

7.2   Discourse Devices

Similar to word structure and sentence structure, discourse can also be said to have various structures acting as the foundation for various discourse purposes. Discourse devices can be broken down into three levels: intonation, vocabulary, and grammar, although traditional understanding of discourse devices involves primarily in turns, episodes, paragraphs, etc., namely at the grammar level. In recent years, more and more researchers have realized that discourse devices and discourse pedagogy cannot and should not be limited to discourse grammar. Intonation and vocabulary patterns also constitute part of overall discourse structure. Only through these three discourse levels, can coherent texts be constructed that express different types of emotion, opinions, suggestions, suspicion, reasoning, etc. Clearly, discourse device functions as a means to convey discourse concepts, therefore, I will use the term *discourse device* throughout the chapter. Discourse device may be defined as a preferred means used by speaker/writer to express and achieve discourse coherence and ultimately communicative purpose. In the following three sections, I will discuss the three types of discourse devices mentioned above and their attendant discourse functions.

7.2.1 *Intonation*

Intonation is a discourse device that clearly only occurs in oral discourse, such as conversation, speeches, stories, and audio and video communications (e.g. broadcasting). The relationship between discourse and intonation has long been observed and discussed by phoneticians, discourse analysts, and researchers in foreign/second language acquisition (e.g. Chun 2002; Riggenbach 1999; Cruttenden 1997, Bolinger 1986, 1989; Cook 1979; Coulthard 1985). One consequence of the collaborative work between the two sub-fields of linguistics, phonetics/phonology (including intonation) and discourse analysis is the creation of a study on discourse intonation (e.g. Brazil 1975, Bradford 1988). According to Brazil (1975: 1–2), the perspective of discourse intonation probes the interrelationship between pitch configurations and their discourse meanings and a speaker's assessment and choice of one intonation pattern over another for the purpose of achieving coherence in discourse. This seems to suggest that pitch configuration is the means and coherence is the goal in the spectrum of discourse intonation. Most of these studies draw examples from Indo-European languages, especially from English, in which pitch configurations do not carry any lexical meanings, but rather convey only discourse meanings. For example, any single English word can be pronounced using any number of different pitches and still retain the same lexical meaning. This is not the case with Chinese, in which pitch configuration consists of two types: (1) tone contour (声调, *shēngdiào*), and (2) intonation contour (语调, *yǔdiào*) (cf. Chao 1933, 1968). Tone contour attached to Chinese characters is on lexicon so that characters with different tones convey different lexical meanings (see detailed discussed in Chapter 4). Intonation contour, on the other hand, functions at the sentence or discourse level to express a speaker's mood, opinion, attitude, etc. Due to this difference between Chinese and non-tonal languages, it is of vital importance that teachers of Chinese as a foreign language incorporate discourse intonation into their curriculum, so that students whose native language is non-tonal have a clear understanding of the function of pitch configuration in Chinese and apply intonation patterns appropriately in oral Chinese.

Although the dual existence of tone and intonation in Chinese has generated a number of theses in the past (Chun 1982, Shen 1990; Yang 1991, Tao 1996, Duanmu 2002), what seems to benefit teachers and students of Chinese most is the study of the discourse function of different intonations. Chun (2002: 37) summarizes the issues and questions relevant to language teachers and researchers regarding discourse intonation as follows:

- Which intonational cues mark stress?
- Which intonational cues mark contrast?
- Which intonational features signal speaker attitude and affective information?
- Which intonational features function as cues in the management of spoken interaction, such as interruption, asking for confirmation, or marking finality?

These are practical questions that Chinese language teachers may actually raise and discuss with students in their classroom and therefore they deserve adequate attention here. Stress is probably the most discussed discourse function of intonation among all languages of the world regardless of whether or not tones matter lexically in these languages. Chao (1968: 35) identifies three types of stress in Chinese based on the degree of pitch accent: normal (tone), weak stress, and contrastive. Normal stress falls on lexicon and is perceived as tonal contour. Weak stress, also known as the neutral tone, often falls on grammatical words (e.g. 的 *de*, 了 *le*) and particles (吧 *ba*, 吗 *ma*, 啦 *la*). Contrastive stress differs from the other two types in that it has a wider pitch range and greater intensity. When contrastive stress is absent in a sentence, the stress takes on the following intonation flow pattern:

(7.1)   STRONG STRESS   NORMAL STRESS   STRONGEST STRESS
我们的学生   都喜欢学   中文。
wǒmen de xuésheng dōu xǐhuan xué zhōngwén.
"Our students all like to study Chinese."

If a speaker adds the contrastive stress to *wǒmen* "we/our" or *xuésheng* "students", *zhōngwén* "Chinese" will not receive the strongest stress anymore, but if the contrastive stress is added to *zhōngwén*, which already has the strongest stress, then *zhōngwén* should be stressed even more. This is a general pattern in Chinese applicable not only in declarative statements but also interrogative statements with or without an interrogative marker, as shown in (7.2a)–(7.2b). In other words, the contrastive stress may overlap with the normal stress in any given flow of intonation pattern.

(7.2)   a.   STRONG STRESS   NORMAL STRESS   CONTRASTIVE STRESS.
你   是一个   好人？
nǐ   *shì yí gè*   *hǎo rén?*
"Are you a good person? (implication: I doubt you are a good person.)"

b.   STRONG STRESS   NORMAL STRESS   STRONGEST STRESS.

你   是一个好人   吗？

nǐ   *shì yí gè hǎo rén*   *ma?*

"Are you a good person? (No other implication)"

The presence and absence of the weak stress does not seem to affect the quality of the other two types of stress. However, it does affect discourse when it falls on sentence final particles in declarative or interrogative statements, the two commonly assumed intonation patterns, as shown in (7.3)–(7.4):

(7.3)   你走**呀**？

*nǐ zǒu **a**?*

"Why don't you go?"

(7.4)   这个礼物好**吧**？

*zhè gè lǐwù hǎo **ba**?*

"Isn't this a good present?"

(7.5)   他看的那本书能是你的**吗**？

*tā kàn de nà běn shū néng shì nǐ de **ma**?*

"How could the book he is reading be yours?"

(7.6)   今天晚上我们吃什么**呢**？

*jīntiān wǎnshàng wǒmen chī shénme **ne**?*

"What should we eat tonight?"

When attached to the bold-faced sentence-final particles in (7.3)–(7.6), the weak stress expresses speaker's attitude (7.3), opinion (7.4), suspicion (7.5), and reflection (7.6). Evidently, it functions at both the lexical level and the discourse level, unlike contrastive stress that only operates at the discourse level. It should be noted that even though all sentential final particles have weak stress, not all of them have the same discourse functions as exemplified above, nor do they have only one discourse function, as illustrated in (7.7)–(7.10) (cf. Lǚ 1980: 52–53):

(7.7)   不早了，你睡觉吧。

*bù zǎo le, nǐ shuìjiào **ba**.*

"Go to bed, it is late. "

(7.8)   我不想在家，我们出去玩儿吧？

*wǒ bù xiǎng zài jiā, wǒmen chūqù wánr **ba**?*

"I don't want to stay at home. Should we play outside?"

(7.9)   我不说话总可以了吧？

        *wǒ bù shuōhuà zǒng kěyǐ le **ba**?*

        "Is it okay if I don't say anything?"

(7.10)   今天不会是他的生日吧？

        *jīntiān bú huì shì tā de shēngrì **ba**?*

        "Today is not his birthday, is it?"(Or "Today can't be his birthday, can it?")

Ba with the weak stress expresses "order" in (7.7), suggestion in (7.8), concession in (7.9) and presumption in (7.10). Discourse functions of the other discourse markers can be found in Section 7.2.3.4 of this chapter. The multiple functions of discourse markers sometimes make it difficult for students to learn because these functions are not predictable. The positive side, though, is that all those discourse functions are expressed by the same intonation contour, namely the weak stress. This leads us to conclude that intonation patterns in Chinese are teachable. I have thus far introduced two major types of intonation patterns in Chinese: one is accomplished without using a particle and the other is accomplished using a particle, such as *ba*. Both types are regular in discourse, therefore, both can be taught to students of Chinese as a foreign language.

7.2.2   *Vocabulary*

Vocabulary is a basic discourse unit in every language including sign languages. Without it, communication would be impossible because vocabulary comprises the meaningful units of language. Vocabulary of different styles has evolved in most languages: formal versus informal, popular expressions versus traditional expressions, specialty terminology versus common words, etc. Socio-cultural variation in the use of vocabulary is also a frequent subject of discussion in discourse, sociolinguistic and foreign/second language acquisition research (e.g. Eisenstein 1993, Hatch and Brown 1995, Coady and Huckin 1997, Mey 1999, McCarthy et al. 1997, Celce-Murcia and Olshtain 2000). Hence, for language students, as well as for native speakers, it takes thought and a certain amount of perceptive skill to choose the right words for the right discourse situation. We may refer to this skill as discourse competence in vocabulary or *discourse vocabulary competence*. This skill might be easier for native speakers to develop because they are born into an environment that repeatedly provides sufficient discourse and pragmatic cues for using various types of vocabularies. For non-native speakers, such as students of Chinese as a foreign language, however, a simulated environment must be created in the classroom or for classroom use in order to teach students situation-determined vocabulary.

When conversing or writing a text, speakers/writers most likely have a communicative goal — and, therefore, a specific audience — in mind. To achieve this goal, they not only have to select words which accurately express their intended ideas, but, more importantly, identify the audience and its likes and dislikes. If the selected words and meanings match this audience's taste, identity, and ideology, it is likely that the intended communicative goal will be achieved. Otherwise, further explanation might be needed to avoid failure to communicate. Now the issue is how to accurately identify the target audience and its preference and then choose a compatible discourse set. One way for students of Chinese as a foreign language to accomplish this is for them to rely on their L1 acquisition experience of and identify the setting of discourse as being formal or informal. Formal discourse, such as that used in business meetings, job interviews, or appointments with a professor, may require students to use formal vocabulary in the conversation. For street talk and casual conversation with friends, informal vocabulary would be more appropriate and even more effective in achieving communicative goals. Although a good number of vocabulary items cannot be clearly classified as either formal or informal, others can be clearly differentiated as illustrated below:[1]

INFORMAL	FORMAL
你	您
nǐ "you"	*nín* "you"
爸爸、妈妈	父亲、母亲
bàba māma "dad mom"	*fùqin mǔqin* "father, mother"
老爷子	父亲
lǎoyézi "the old man"	*fùqin* "father"
老师	先生
lǎoshī "teacher"	*xiānsheng* "teacher"
问	请教
wèn "ask"	*qǐngjiào* "ask"
女的	妇女
nǚ de "woman"	*fùnǚ* "woman"
老婆	太太
lǎopo "wife"	*tàitai* "wife"
特别	别致
tèbié "special"	*biézhì* "special"
不同	区别
bùtóng "difference"	*qūbié* "difference"
好玩儿	有意思
hǎo wánr "interesting"	*yǒu yìsi* "interesting"
炒鱿鱼	解雇
chǎo yóuyú "get fired"	*jiěgù* "be laid off"
泡妞儿	跟女孩子在一起
pàoniūr "be with girl"	*gēn nǚ háizi zài yìqǐ* "be in the company of girls"
毛病	缺点
máobìng "shortcoming"	*quēdiǎn* "shortcoming"
打笛	坐出租汽车
dǎdī "take taxi"	*zuò chūzū qìchē* "take taxi"
你叫什么名字？	您贵姓？

nǐ jiào shénme míngzi?	*nín guì xìng?*
"What's your name"	"What is your honorable surname?"
你干吗？	你做什么？
nǐ gàn má?	*nín zài zuò shénme?*
"What are you doing?"	"What are you doing?"
早就听说过您。	久仰（久闻大名）。
zǎojiù tīng shuō guò nín	*jiǔ yǎng (jiǔ wén dàmíng)*
"I heard about you long ago."	"(I) have heard about your name long time ago."

Evidently, formal words are not necessarily the same as written, nor informal as spoken. In other words, formal words may be used in spoken discourse and likewise informal words can very well be used in written discourse such as letters and notes to be discussed in 7.4. In addition to formal versus informal words, students may also distinguish fashionable words from traditional words to enhance conversation. In recent years, native Chinese speakers are keen to use loan words and accented words borrowed from the dialects of economically prosperous regions (e.g. Taiwan, Hong Kong, Guǎngzhōu). By accented words, I refer to those words that are originally only used in non-Mandarin Chinese dialects. Speakers of Mandarin are considered fashionable if they use such vocabulary as those listed below:[2]

FASHIONABLE	TRADITIONAL
拜拜！	再见！
báibái "Bye bye"	*zàijiàn* "Good bye"
伊妹儿	电子邮件
yī màir "email"	*diànzǐ yóujiàn* "electronic mail"
老公	爱人、先生
lǎogōng "husband"	*àiren/xiānsheng* "spouse/husband"
老板	头儿、领导
lǎobǎn "boss"	*tóuer/lǐngdǎo* "head/leader"
下海	做生意
xiàhǎi "do business"	*zuò shēngyì* "do business"
小姐	服务员
xiǎojie "miss"	*fúwùyuán* "service person"
公司	单位
gōngsī "company"	*dānwèi* "work place"
跌股	没面子
diēgǔ "lose face/lose money in stock"	*méi miànzi* "lose face"
酷毙	很有吸引力
kùbì "extremely cool"	*hěn yǒu xīyǐn lì* "very attractive"
蹦迪	跳迪斯科
bèngdī "dance disco"	*tiào dísīkē* "dance disco"

Adequate use of fashionable words in discourse in appropriate situations may leave a positive impression as being refreshing and uplifting. However, overuse of this type of words or use with people who detest this type of language can lead to rejection and failure to communicate. For this reason, I suggest that Chinese teachers make a distinction between formal and informal and fashion and traditional words when introducing new vocabulary to students, even though the distinction among these types of words is not always transparent. Likewise, students should be conscientious when selecting different types of words in order to achieve communicative goals. It is our recommendation that teachers advise students to err on the side of "too formal" rather than "too informal" in discourse situations where there is some doubt as to appropriate register.

7.2.3   *Grammar and coherence*

The concept of grammar can be as broad as to refer to everything about a language or as narrow as to only refer to the rules of sentence and word structure. In this section, I use the term grammar to refer to rules of discourse structure. Since discourse consists of two or more sentences, any study of discourse grammar cannot avoid discussion of coherence and cohesion between or among sentences.[3] Halliday and Hasan (1976: 4) describe cohesion as follows:

> Cohesion occurs where the interpretation of some element in the discourse is dependent on that of another. The one presupposes the other, in the sense that it cannot be effectively decoded except by recourse to it. When this happens, a relation of cohesion is set up, and the two elements, the presupposing and the presupposed, are thereby at least potentially integrated into a text.

According to this definition, any device that relates one element in discourse to another leads to discourse cohesion/coherence.[4] Based on our understanding, the involved elements can be a word, a phrase or a sentence. After examining Chinese discourse grammar, I have selected the following list of discourse devices as core elements for Chinese discourse coherence and for teaching students of Chinese as a foreign language discourse competence.

- Topic chain (reference)
- Ellipsis
- Substitution
- Discourse connectors and discourse markers
- Word order variation
- Temporal sequence
- Foreground and background

Since each of these devices plays a unique role in constructing coherent discourse in Chinese, I will discuss them separately in the following seven sections.

7.2.3.1   Topic chain

Topic chain (话题链, *huàtí liàn*) refers to the continuity of a topic maintained by a number of consecutive clauses in discourse (cf. Tsao 1979, Li and Thompson 1981: 659, Haiman and Munro 1983, Givón 1983, Chu 1998: 324). Topic in Chinese most likely takes the subject position of a clause, as illustrated in (7.11).

> (7.11)   *我们*在中国学习的时候，一点儿都没有时间玩儿，每天除了学习就是学习，有时候连睡觉的时间都没有。
>
> ***wŏmen*** *zài zhōngguó xuéxí de shíhòu, yìdiănr dōu méiyŏu shíjiān wánr, mĕitiān chúle xuéxí jiùshì xuéxí, yŏu shíhòu lián shuìjiào de shíjiān dōu méiyŏu.*
>
> "When *we* were studying in China, (*we*) did not have any time for playing. Every day, (*we*) studied then studied some more. Sometimes (*we*) didn't even have enough time to sleep."

Wŏmen "we" is the topic of the paragraph in (7.11). Notice that this topic continues in the following three clauses after its first appearance in the first clause even though the topic is not visibly seen in the last three clauses. Despite these omissions, native Chinese speakers have no difficulty whatsoever understanding the topic of the three clauses. The continuity of the topic shared by the four clauses in (7.11) is one topic chain. Some Chinese researchers (e.g. Tsao 1979, Li 2002) believe that the topic chain is the basic discourse unit in Chinese for discourse coherence. Others (e.g. Shi 1989, Chu 1998) also consider the topic chain a syntactic unit: That is, a topic chain can be formed by a number of clauses that function as a part of sentence. For the convenience of students, I include topic chains that are formed among both sentences and clauses (i.e. subordinate clauses).

What makes the topic chain even more appealing to Chinese pedagogy specialists is the functional difference between its use in Chinese and other languages such as English. Comparing the Chinese paragraph in (7.11) with its English translation, we see that the same topic in the last three clauses cannot be omitted in English as it is in Chinese. This difference leads Chinese pedagogy specialists to explore possible strategies in teaching native English-speaking students how to compose a coherent Chinese discourse structure using topic chain cohesion. Li (2002) suggests that topic chains in Chinese code topic continuity through various syntactic constructions and predications, but topic chains in English are only used among certain constructions, such as the one expressing a temporal reference illustrated in (7.12).

(7.12a)　　"After finishing our homework, *we* went to a coffee shop."

做完功课以后，*我们*去了一家咖啡馆。

zuòwán gōngkè yǐhòu, wǒmen qù le yì jiā kāfēi guǎn.

(7.12b)　　* "After *we* finished our homework, went to a coffee shop"

*我们*做完功课以后，去了一家咖啡馆。

wǒmen zuòwán gōngkè yǐhòu, qù le yì jiā kāfēi guǎn.

(7.12c)　　After *we* finished our homework, we went to a coffee shop"

???*我们*做完功课以后，*我们*去了一家咖啡馆。

wǒmen zuòwán gōngkè yǐhòu, wǒmen qù le yì jiā kāfēi guǎn.

The three way comparison among (7.12a)–(7.12c) shows that the topic in Chinese topic chains can be omitted when there is one overt topic in that chain. The topic in an English topic chain, however, can only be omitted when it is in a subordinate clause expressing a temporary sequence. In addition, the appearance of the same topic in both clauses of (7.12c) is perfectly acceptable in English but is considered highly redundant, thus hardly acceptable in Chinese. Let us examine more topic chains:

(7.13)　　你不是不知道，有很多罪犯，前脚出了监狱，后脚就进枪店，买了枪就到处杀人。枪店也不查买枪的是什么人，不管他是不是杀过人放过火，脑子正常不正常，只要给钱，他们就卖。(From *Integrated Chinese II*, by Liu et al., 1997: 328)

Nǐ bú shì bù zhīdào, yǒu hěnduō zuìfàn, qián jiǎo chū le jiānyù, hòu jiǎo jiù jìn qiāng diàn, mǎi le qiāng jiù dàochù shā rén. qiāng diàn yě bù chá mǎi qiāng de shì shénme rén, bùguǎn tā shì bú shì shā guò rén fàng guò huǒ, nǎo zi zhèngcháng bú zhèngcháng, zhǐyào gěi qián, tāmen jiù mài.

"It is not that you do not know that many criminals enter a gun shop as soon as they are released from prison. The gun shop does not check their background, nor does (it) care about whether they (i.e. the buyers) ever killed anybody or whether (they) are mentally abnormal. They (i.e. the people in the gun shop) sell guns as long as (they) are paid."

There are different layers of topics and topic chains in the paragraph given in (7.13). The first layer has a topic 你 (*nǐ* "you"), but has no chain because the topic only occurs in one clause. The second layer has a topic 罪犯 (*zuìfàn* "criminals") and a chain, which introduces the third topic layer 枪店 (*qiāngdiān* "gun shops") and a chain. Within this third topic and chain layer, there is another chain layer with the topic, 他 (*tā* "he"), referring back to 罪犯 (*zuìfàn* "criminals"), namely the topic of the second layer. These intertwining chains and connections may be reiterated as follows:

First layer:　　　　　Topic *nǐ* "you", without a chain
Second layer:　　　　Topic: *zuìfàn* "criminal", with a chain

Third layer:	Topic: *qiāngdiàn* "gun shop" with a chain
Fourth layer:	Topic: *tā* "he (i.e. the buyer)", with a chain

These four layers of topics and topic chains provide instructional examples demonstrating that topic chains are not always arranged in linear fashion within discourse; rather, they interconnect with one another or they are "chain up" by layers. Each time a new layer is introduced, a new topic is born often in the object position, as illustrated and italicized in the following sentences.

You may not know that *many criminals* … (first layer)
They (i.e. criminals) enter *a gun shop*; (second layer)
The gun shop does not care who *the buy*er is; (third layer)
Or if he (the buyer) ever killed anybody … (fourth layer)

The way to develop a new topic is similar to that of the introduction of *new information* often discussed in discourse literature. Teachers interested in this subject may consult with Chu (1998) and Givón (1990). In addition to the development of multiple layers of topics and topic chains, it is also important to note that topics may be maintained, or rather chained, by a variety of sentence structures and means. Consider the situation in (7.14):

(7.14)   (a)女儿长大，(b)就要出嫁，(c)所以父母把她看成"别人家的人"，(d)是"赔钱货"。(From *Advanced Reader of Modern Chinese,* by Chou et al., 1993: 26)
(a) nǚ'ér zhǎngdà, (b) jiùyào chūjià, (c) suǒyǐ fùmǔ bǎ tā kànchéng "biérén jiā de rén", (d) shì "péiqián huò".
"When daughters grow up, they have to get married. This is why parents treat them as "non-family members" and "money losers"

The topic 女儿 (*nǚér* "daughter") is maintained throughout the remaining three clauses to form a topic chain. Notice that the first two clauses (a)–(b) have the regular "subject + verb" construction, the third clause (c) uses a *bǎ* construction, and the fourth one (d) uses a "subject + predicate" construction. These varied construction types do not seem to break up the flow of the topic and its chain. The English counterpart, however, behaves differently. From the English translation, we see two topic chains: one with topic 女儿 (*nǚér* "daughter") and the other with topic 父母 (*fùmǔ* "parent"). It is difficult to come up with a translation that reflects the original Chinese meaning and at the same time still keeps 女儿 *nǚér* as the sole topic. This difference between Chinese and English provides further evidence that topic chains are constructed differently in these two languages. Hence, teachers and students of Chinese as a foreign language should be aware of the rules and constraints in constructing topic chains for coherent discourse. We may summarize the rules and constraints on the omission of topic and construction of topic chains as follows:

- Chinese topic chains are formed by topics of a number of sentences/clauses referring to the same element and for the purpose of discourse coherence;
- In written discourse, topics in a topic chain can all be omitted except for the one located either in the first or second clause of the chain;
- In spoken discourse, all topics in a topic chain can be omitted if they refer to the speaker;
- New topics are likely to be introduced in the postverbal position;
- In Chinese, topics may be chained up even through different types of sentence structures; this is not necessarily the case in Indo-European languages.

7.2.3.2 Ellipsis

Ellipsis (省略, *shěnglüè*) is another discourse device that makes discourse more coherent and less redundant. Researchers consider it one of the strongest linking devices between sentences belonging to the same text (cf. Marello 1989). The question that probably concerns students and teachers of Chinese as a foreign language most is when ellipsis can occur in discourse and when it cannot. Consider the following advertisement:

(7.15)   《知音》(Zhīyīn), 2004: 4:60:

(a)投资 1.5 万元，请一个工人，在集贸市场租一个 5–10 平米左右的门面，半月就可开一家"唐林香烧烤鸡鸭连锁店"。因店面形象好，(b)特别是不需要回火可现吃，味道又美，(c)简直卖疯了！(d)当月投资，当月见效，一次投资，长期受益。

(a) tóuzī 1.5 wàn yuán, qǐng yíge gōngrén, zài jímào shìchǎng zū yíge 5–10 píngmǐ zuǒyòu de ménmiàn, bànyuè jiù kě kāi yìjiā "Táng Líng-xiāng shāokǎo jīyā liánsuǒdiàn". yīn diànmiàn xíngxiàng hǎo, (b) tèbié shì bù xūyào huíhuǒ kě xiànchī, wèidao yòu měi, (c) jiǎnzhí mài fēng le! (d) dāngyuè tóuzī, dāngyuè jiànxiào, yícì tóuzī, chángqī jiànxiào.

"Invest 10,000 dollars, hire one employee, rent a 5–10 square meter place at a market, and thus open a "roasted chicken and duck chain store". Since the store's reputation is good, especially (because there is) no need to warm (the cooked chicken and duck) and (customers) can eat freshly cooked (chicken and duck), (that) tastes delicious, and sells like crazy! Invest for one month and receive immediate profit. One-time investment, long-time benefit."

To save space and money, most advertisements omit all unnecessary elements as long as key information and purpose remain clear. This is the case in English as well. We see that in (7.15) all subjects are omitted regardless of whether they are part of a topic chain or whether they are coherent in the context. Yet, native speakers seem to have little difficulty understanding who "invests, hires, and rents", who "warms chicken and duck", who "tastes" and who "sells" because it is clear from the discourse itself — its content and style. In other words, clarity is the key for ellipsis especially with informal discourse; any element can be omitted as long as it is clear to the reader/listener from the context. Let us look at another short dialogue:

(7.16)   *Cháguǎn* "Tea House" by Lǎo Shě, p. 16

甲: 谭嗣同是谁？

      Tán Sì-tóng shì shéi?

A: "Who is Táng Sì-tóng?"

乙: 好像听说过！反正犯了大罪，要不怎么会问斩呢？

      hǎoxiàng tīngshuō guò! fǎnzhèng fànle dàzuì, yàobù zěnme huì wèn zhǎn ne?

B: "(I) might have heard (the name) before. (He) must have committed a big crime, otherwise how could (he) be sentenced to death?"

The omitted entities in (7.16B) are translated into English in parentheses. Notice that those omitted entities can either be a noun or pronoun, subject or object, which is clearly not the case in English where the presence of subject and object, noun and pronoun, is much less optional. This seems to suggest that clarity is again the key governing omission in the oral discourse. From the context of the dialogue, it is clear that the subject of "might have heard" is the speaker "I" and the object of "have heard" is the name of Táng Sì-tóng. As far as the subject of "have committed a big crime" is concerned, the discourse shows that it can be no one but Táng Sì-tóng, so it is omitted too. English, on the other hand, can omit the subjects "I" and "he", but not the object "the name" and the subject "he" in the interrogative sentence, even though they are clear to the speaker and listener in this conversation. This suggests that English is more rigid in ellipsis (cf. Asher 1993 and Kehler 2002, for detailed discussion on English ellipsis) than Chinese is. Nonetheless, notice that both examples given above are informal/oral texts. Is ellipsis so frequently used in Chinese written/formal discourse as in oral/informal discourse? Let us examine an example from somewhat more formal and written text:

(7.17)   *Mòzǐ* by Chen Wei, p. 118

比如美女，住在家里不出去，人们争着追求她；但如果她行走着自我兜售，那就没有谁娶她了。

bǐrú měinǚ, zhù zài jiālǐ bù chū qù, rénmen zhēngzhe zhuīqiú tā; dàn rúguǒ tā xíngzǒu zhe zìwǒ dōushòu, nà jiù méiyǒu shéi qǔ tā le.

"Taking a beautiful girl as an example, (if she) stays home and does not go out, men will pursue her. However, if she walks outside selling herself, then nobody will marry her."

In (7.17), ellipsis of a subject noun phrase occurs only once when the subject "a beautiful girl" is mentioned in the immediately preceding phrase. Unlike prounouns in (7.15)–(7.16), none of the other pronouns (e.g. *tā* "she/her") in (7.17) are omitted even though they could be if they were in an oral discourse. This seems to suggest that discourse type affects the use of ellipsis. Thus, we may summarize ellipsis in Chinese as follows: (1) In oral discourse, any noun phrases or pronouns may be omitted as long as they are conceptually clear to listeners; and (2) in written/formal discourse, pronouns in subject position are more likely to be omitted than those in object position. In other words, when teaching ellipsis, teachers and students should be aware that ellipsis may be used differently depending on the type of discourse. Conversational discourse, or rather spoken/informal discourse, may use it as much as possible, whereas written discourse or formal discourse, which lacks other linguistic cues such as intonation, body language, or visual aids, must use ellipsis more judiciously to achieve ultimate clarity.

7.2.3.3 Substitution

Substitution (替代, *tìdài*) refers to the situation when full nouns, phrases, or sentences are substituted with pronouns, demonstratives, or adverbial phrases of time, place, and manner, such as those categorized below:

Pronouns:	她 *tā* "she", 他 *tā* "he", 它 *tā* "it"
	它们/他们/她们 *tāmen* "they"
Demonstratives:	这 *zhè/zhèi* "this", 那 *nà* "that"
Adverbial phrases:	这样 *zhèyàng* "this way", 这么 *zhème* "so, this way"
	这儿 *zhèr* "here", 那儿 *nàr* "there"
	这会儿 *zhè huǐr* "now, at this moment"
	那会儿 *nà huǐr* "then, at that time"

Like ellipsis, substitution is often used to avoid repetition and redundancy in discourse for ultimate coherence (cf. Hobbs 1979). This is probably why some researchers do not make any distinction between the two. Among the rich body of English literature on substitution and ellipsis, most focus on pronoun reference and coreference using formal linguistic theories. Some researchers (e.g. Givón 1990) also discuss substitution from a discourse and cognitive point of view, but little research has been done regarding Chinese substitution and its uniqueness compared with other languages when teaching Chinese as a foreign language. Hence, the following discussion is based on our preliminary research on this subject.

For students of Chinese as a foreign language, Chinese referential pronouns are relatively easy to acquire because, except for 它 *tā* "it", they behave more or less the same as their counterparts in other languages, such as English. Often, teachers and students mistreat Chinese *tā* (它) as English *it* without realizing that the latter has a much broader function than the former. Consider the following discourse:

(7.18)   Rowling: *Harry Potter and the Philosopher's Stone*, p. 7
The Dursleys had everything they wanted, but they also had a secret, and their greatest fear was that somebody would discover *it*. They did not think they could bear *it* if anyone found out about the Potters.
"德斯雷一家想得到的东西都得到了，不过他们也有一个秘密，十分害怕别人发现这个秘密。他们觉得〔他们〕无法忍受任何人发现了哈里雷特一家这件事。"
Désīléi yijiā xiǎng dédào de dōngxi dōu dédào le, búguò tāmen yě yǒu yíge mìmi, shífēn hàipà biérén fāxiàn zhèige mìmi. tāmen juéde [tāmen] wúfǎ rěnshòu rènhé rén fāxiàn Hālíléitè yìjiā zhèijiàn shì.

"It" was used twice in the discourse given above. The first one refers to "secret" in the immediately preceding clause, and the second one refers to the event stated right after *it*, namely "anyone found out about the Potters." When translating this paragraph into Chinese, we find that both *it*s may not be translated into Chinese *tā*. Chinese either clearly states *it*s reference as in the case of the first *it* or does not use a referential pronoun at all as in the case of the second *it*. This difference between Chinese and English has created a lot of difficulty for students regarding when and when not to use substitution. Influenced by their native language, Chinese students of native English often overuse Chinese 它 *tā* in discourse. This makes it necessary for teachers to explain *tā*'s discourse function and its difference from English *it* at least in three different ways:

- Chinese does not have the referential pronoun equivalent to the so-called English dummy *it*;
- Chinese 它 *tā* is rarely used in the object position; and
- Unlike English *it*, Chinese, especially in written discourse, does not use 它 *tā*, especially in the object position, to refer to weather or event/ situation mentioned in a previous discourse.

When translating English *it,* Chinese often use definite article or demonstrative *zhè* "this" or *nà* "that" along with a noun just mentioned in the preceding discourse, as illustrated in (7.18). Let us look at another example:

(7.19)   Rowling: *Harry Potter and the Philosopher's Stone,* p. 8
[It was on the corner of the street that he noticed the first sign of something peculiar — a cat reading a map. For a second, Mr Dursley didn't realize what he had seen — then he jerked his head around to look again. There was a tabby cat standing on the corner of Privet Drive, but there wasn't a map in sight.] What could he have been thinking of? *It must have been a trick of the light.* Mr Dursley blinked and stared at the cat. *It stared back.*

他当时在想什么呢？**那**可能是光耍的花招。德斯雷先生眨了眨眼睛，盯着看那只猫。（**它**？）**猫**也盯着看他。

*tā dāngshí zài xiǎng shénme ne? **nà** kěnéng shì guāng shuǎ de huāzhāo. Désīléi xiānsheng zhǎ le zhǎ yǎnjīng, dīngzhe kàn nàzhī māo. **(tā?) māo** yě dīngzhe kàn tā.*

Examining the bold-faced English sentences in (7.19), we see that the first *it* refers several sentences back to the situation of "a cat reading a map". Chinese translation, however, has to translate *it* into 那 *nā* "that" because 它 *tā* "it" cannot be used to refer to a situation or event. The second English *it* in the last sentence of the paragraph seems to be similar to Chinese 它 *tā* "it" functionally, but stylistically, it is still better to repeat the noun that is just mentioned in the immediately preceding sentence, possibly because of the fact that another pronoun 他 *tā* "him" is already used in the sentence. This provides further evidence that English *it* enjoys a much broader usage than the Chinese 它 *tā* "it" in discourse. Chinese may use demonstratives and a full noun phrase in many of the places where English uses *it*. It is almost as if the "it" in English functions in a similar fashion to the omission of subject and object in oral Chinese; where these two grammatical items can be left out as long as clarity is not affected, in English these are most often replaced by "it."

Demonstratives are another type of word often used as reference for coherence in discourse. Although Chinese grammarians also consider those adverbial phrases listed at the beginning of this section as demonstrative pronouns, there are only two prototypical demonstratives in Chinese: *zhè/zhèi* (这 "this") and *nà* (那 "that"), from which the remaining demonstrative phrases are derived expressing time, place and manner of action or behavior mentioned in the previous discourse. *Zhè*, similar to English *this*, may be used to refer to a person, thing, event, or situation near the speaker and the listener with "near" implying either physical or temporal closeness, whereas *nà* can refer to the same entity but it is away from the speaker and the listener (cf. Fang 2002, Tao 1999). Because of the similarity between Chinese *zhè/nà* and English demonstratives *this/that*, students of Chinese who are native English speakers have little difficulty learning *zhè* and *nà*, no matter what they refer to or how far the distance from their antecedents, namely the person, thing, event, situation that they refer to in discourse, as shown in (7.20)–(7.21):

(7.20)　*Lóng Xū Gōu* by Lǎo Shě, p. 130

老街坊们，修沟的计划是先修一道暗沟；把暗沟修好，再填上那条老的明沟。**这**个，诸位都知道。

*lǎo jiēfangmen, xiūgōu de jìhuà shì xiān xiū yídào àngōu; bǎ àngōu xiūhǎo, zài tiánshàng nàtiáo lǎode mínggōu. **zhèige**, zhūwèi dōu zhīdào.*

"Old neighbors, (our) plan is to build an underground channel first. When finished with this project, (we) will fill up the old channel. ***This***, everyone knows."

(7.21)   *Four Generations Under the Same Roof* by Lǎo Shě, p. 45

甲：侵略者要是承认别人也是人，也有人性，会发火，它就无法侵略了！
日本人始终认为咱们都是狗，踢着打着都不哼一声的狗！

qīnlüèzhě yàoshi chéngrèn biérén yě shì rén, yě yǒu rénxìng, huì fāhuǒ, tā jiù wúfǎ qīnlüè le! rìběn rén shǐzhōng rènwéi zánmen dōu shì gǒu, tīzhe dǎzhe dōu bù hēng yìshēng de gǒu.

A: "If invaders admit other people are human, understand humanity, and have temper, they cannot invade (other people or countries) anymore. The Japanese always believe that we are all dogs, that do not make any noise when kicked or bitten."

乙：**那**是个最大的错误！"

nà shì ge zuìdà de cuòwù!

B: "**That** is the biggest mistake."

In (7.20), *zhè* (这 "this") refers to everything just said in discourse, so it is unlikely to be misunderstood or misinterpreted by students. Similarly, *nà* (那 "that") in (7.21) also clearly refers to the whole situation just described and should be easy for students to understand, imitate, and use in discourse. The same can be said about the demonstrative phrases expressing time (e.g. 这会儿 *zhè huǐr* "now" and 那会儿 *nà huǐr* "then") and place (这儿 *zhèr*/那儿 *nàr* "here/there") of an event and situation, as illustrated in (7.22a) and (7.22b). The ease in learning Chinese demonstrative phrases is undoubtedly contributed to by the fact that English also has demonstrative phrases that have the same or similar functions as their Chinese counterparts.

(7.22a)   *Beijinger* by Cáo Yǔ, p. 97

甲：老爷子，回屋去睡吧。

A: *lǎo yézi, huí wū qù shuì ba.*

"Master, (you) should go to your room and sleep."

乙：不，我要在**这儿**看看，你睡去吧。

*bù, wǒ yào zài **zhèr** kànkan, nǐ shuì qù ba.*

B: "No, I want to stay **here** and take a good look. You should go to sleep."

(7.22b)   甲：我刚从北京回来。

wǒ gāng cóng Běijīng huílai.

"I just came back from Beijing."

乙：你在**那儿**呆了几天？

*nǐ zài **nàr** dāi le jǐtiān?*

"How long did you stay **there**?"

甲：就一个礼拜。

jiù yíge lǐbài.

"Only a week."

However, other demonstrative phrases, such as 这么 (*zhème* "so, this way") and 这样 (*zhèyàng* "this way, in so doing"), that refers to the manner of an action or event mentioned in the previous discourse, do pose a challenge to students in acquisition. Let us look at a short dialogue:

(7.23)   *Lóng Xū Gōu* by Lǎo Shě, p. 126

甲：冲着人家这股热心劲儿，咱们应当回去帮忙！

   chòngzhe rénjiā zhèigǔ rèxīn jìnr, zánmen yīngdāng huíqù bāngmáng!

A: "Because of their enthusiasm, we should go back to help (them)."

乙：这话说得对！有我跟刘掌柜的在这儿，放心，人也丢不了，东西也丢不了。我说，四十岁以上的去舀水，四十以下的去挖沟，合适不合适？

   zhèi huà shuōde duì! yǒu wǒ gēn Liú zhǎngguìde zài zhèir, fàngxīn, rén yě diūbùliǎo, dōngxi yě diūbùliǎo. wǒ shuō, sìshí suì yǐshàng de qù yǎoshuǐ, sìshí yǐxiàde qù wāgōu, héshì bù héshì?

B: "You are right! Master Liu and I are here, so don't worry. We will take care of the people and things around here. I'd say those who are forty or older fetch water and those who are younger than forty dig the channel. Is that okay?"

丙：就**这么**办啦！

   *jiù **zhème** bàn la!*

C: "Let's do **it this way** (or *that)*."

In (7.23), 这么 *zhème* "this way" occurs in the last clause of this short dialogue. What it really refers to in the previous discourse may require students of Chinese who are not familiar with Chinese discourse structure and coherent structure to engage in a little bit of analysis because the previous discourse mentions a number of things: (1) a description of what the speaker will do; (2) a suggestion of what other people should do; and (3) a question for confirmation. Is *zhème* used to answer the question raised in the immediately preceding discourse? Or does it express agreement with Speaker B's suggestion of what other people should do? Or does it express agreement with what Speaker B's suggestion of what he himself should do? It turns out that since *zhème*'s discourse function is to flashback to the manner of an action or event that happened in the previous discourse, it cannot be used to refer to anything in the question raised by Speaker B. However, it fits well in referring to what people should do, including Speaker B. This seems to suggest that students need first understand the discourse function of *zhème*, that is, describing manner of action or event, before they are able to understand the discourse structure (i.e. where it occurs) and discourse coherence for which it is used.

Another reason that demonstrative phrases of manner pose problems for native English speaking students is that the English simple demonstratives *this/that*, can be used to refer to a manner of action or event, in addition to their other discourse functions discussed earlier. This is why *zhème* in (7.23) is translated into English "this way" or "that". Although students' linguistic knowledge of their native language is normally subconscious, their Chinese language performance, as that of any other foreign languages, is often affected by their L1 perception and production. For this reason, I suggest that teachers explain the difference in functions of demonstrative phrases between Chinese and students' native language so that they have the knowledge at least conceptually at the beginning and gradually work on production of the correct usage in Chinese.

7.2.3.4   Discourse connectors and discourse markers

In Chinese, the most commonly used and studied lexical items for discourse cohesion and coherence may be roughly classified into two types: (1) discourse connectors (篇章关联词 *piānzhāng guānlián cí*) and (2) discourse markers (语篇 标记 *yǔpiān biāojì*). Although it is sometimes difficult to distinguish these two types of discourse devices (cf. Jucker and Ziv 1998) because of the syntactic features they share (e.g., some adverbs can be used both as a discourse connector and discourse marker), most Chinese words can be classified as either discourse connectors or discourse markers, given a clear definition of these two terms. In what follows, I will first discuss discourse connectors and relevant issues involved in teaching them to students of Chinese as a foreign language and then focus on discourse markers, their roles in discourse coherence and in acquisition.

Discourse connectors are a favorite of many Chinese teachers and students because they are logical and coherent in meaning, stable in sentence construction, easily applicable and most importantly quite effective in communication. I use discourse connectors to refer to those elements that reflect the relationship between an utterance and previous/following discourse (cf. Levinson 1983) and they are likely realized as conjunctions or adverbs to link a logical relation (e.g. cause-result). For pedagogical purposes, we may further divide Chinese discourse connectors into two sub-types: concurrent connectors and simple connectors. Concurrent discourse connectors refer to those used in pairs, with one introducing the cause of a logical relation and the other introducing the result. Although many logical relations may be labeled as cause and result, Chinese uses different concurrent connectors to refer to different kinds of logical relations, as classified in Table 7.1:

For adult learners of Chinese, the concurrent discourse connectors listed in Table 7.1 are easy to learn not only because they encounter various logical relations in their daily life, but also because they use similar conjunctions to express the relations in their own language (cf. Couper-Kuhlen and Kortmann 2000). The only unique feature of Chinese is the concurrence of two connectors, a rare usage in Indo-European languages.[5] Nonetheless, since this type of connector is frequently used in discourse and relatively fixed in position within a sentence, students can begin learning them at the elementary level. By the time they finish second-year Chinese, students are quite familiar with the form and function of most of the concurrent connectors listed in Table 7.1. Hence, I will not explain how to use those connectors here; interested readers may consult grammar books such as 现代汉语八百词 (*Xiàndài Hànyǔ Bābǎi Cí*, Eight hundred Chinese words) by Lǚ (1980) or 实用现代汉语语法 (*Shíyòng Xiàndài Hànyǔ Yǔfǎ*, Practical modern Chinese grammar) by Liu et al. (2002).

Table 7.1 Logical relation expressed by paired discourse connectors

LOGICAL RELATION	CLAUSE 1	CLAUSE 2
Cause/result:	因为 *yīnwèi* "because"	所以 *suǒyǐ* "therefore"
	既然 *jìrán* "if"	那么 *nàme* "then"
Condition/transition	虽然 *suīrán* "although"	但是 *dànshì* "but"
	虽然 *suīrán* "although"	可是 *kěshì* "but"
	虽然 *suīrán* "although"	不过 *búguò* "however"
Condition/action	不管 *bùguǎn* "no matter"	都 *dōu* "all"
	只要 *zhǐyào* "as long as"	才 *cái* "so"
	无论 *wúlùn* "no matter"	都 *dōu* "all"
	不论 *búlùn* "no matter"	都 *dōu* "all"
	除非 *chúfēi* "unless"	才 *cái* "then"
Counterfactual/result	要是 *yàoshì* "provided that"	就 *jiù* "then"
	假如 *jiǎrú* "if"	就 *jiù* "then"
	如果 *rúguǒ* "if"	就 *jiù* "then"
	倘若 *tǎngruò* "suppose"	就 *jiù* "then"
Concession/result	虽然 *suírán* "although"	但是 *dànshì* "but"
	即使 *jíshǐ* "even if"	也 *yě* "also"
	哪怕 *nǎpà* "regardless of"	也 *yě* "also"
	就是 *jiùshì* "even if"	也 *yě* "also"
	固然 *gùrán* "It's true that"	可是 *kěshì* "however"
Succession/addition	不但 *búdàn* "not only"	而且 *érqiě* "but also"
	尚且 *shàngqiě* "not only"	何况 *hékuàng* "but also"

Simple discourse connectors, on the other hand, refers to those solo connectors often used to introduce new discourse, conclude discourse, or connect what has been said with what is to be said. It should be noted that this type of connector might not connect a logical relation, but could connect larger discourse units than concurrent connectors. Consider the following instances:

(7.24) "Character Stories" by Zhōu Guópín et al., p. 9

首先，我们必须分别给出图画和文字的定义：

***shǒuxiān*,** *wǒmen bìxū fēnbié gěichū túhuà hé wénzì de dìngyì:*

"***First of all***, we must clearly define and distinguish drawing and writing.

图画是指创作者用线条、颜色或事物创造出一种形象，以表达作者自身的感情、意识、和认知。

túhuà shì zhǐ chuàngzuòzhě yòng xiàntiáo, yánsè huò shìwù chuàngzàochū yìzhǒng xíngxiàng, yǐ biǎodá zuòzhě zìshēnde gǎnqíng, yìshi, hé rènzhī.

"Drawing refers to images that an author creates using lines, colors, and materials to express emotion, mentality and cognition."

文字...

wénzì ...

"Writing …"

(7.25)　"Character Stories" by Zhōu Guópín et al., p. 135

汉字的符号化使得汉字简化的步履越发轻快速捷了。...

hànzì de fúhàohuà shǐdé hànzì jiǎnhuà de bùlǚ yuèfā qīngkuài sùjié le.

"The symbolization of Chinese characters leads to the speedy process of simplification."

另外，由于汉字的抽象化和符号化，人们在使用时，可以大胆地省略掉字形中繁琐和重复的部分。...

lìngwài, yóuyú hànzì de chōuxiànghuà hé fúhàohuà, rénmen zài shǐyòngshí, kěyǐ dàdǎndi shěngluè zìxíng zhōng fánsuǒ hé chóngfú de bùfen. ...

"**In addition**, due to the abstractness of Chinese characters, people may omit complicated or repeated parts in characters with a little restriction."

(7.26)　"Character Stories" by Zhōu Guópín et al., p. 134

商代金文多象形字及由象形字合成的会意字，这些字多呈图画形 ...

Shāngdài Jīnwén duō xiàngxíngzì jí yóu xiàngxíngzì héchéng de huìyì zì, zhèixiē zì duō chéng túhuàxíng. ...

"The Brown Scriptures of the Shang Dynasty are mostly pictographs and ideographs developed from pictographs. Most of these characters have the shape of a picture."

然而，这种图画形文字如果要契刻在甲骨上显然是很不方便。

rán'ér, zhèizhǒng túhuàxíng wénzì rúguǒ yào qikè zài jiǎgǔ shàng xiǎnrán shì hěn bù fāngbiàn.

"**However,** this kind of pictograph is clearly difficult to carve on turtle shells."

(7.27)　"Character Stories" by Zhōu Guópín et al., p. 29

如前所述，要表示外出打猎，那么只要用一副鹿角、一根长矛便可以表示了；要是准备外出打猎三天，... 就在绳子上拴三块石头或者打三个节。

rúqián suǒshù, yào biǎoshì wàichū dǎliè, nàme zhǐyào yòng yífu lùjiǎo, yìgēn chángmáo biàn kěyǐ biǎoshì le; yàoshì zhǔnbèi wàichū dǎliè sāntiān, ... jiù zài shéngzi shàng shuān sānkuài shítou huòzhě dǎ sānge jié.

"**To summarize what has been said**, (we see that) if (people) want to express the idea of hunting, (they) only need an antler and a long bow to indicate that concept. To show that the hunt will last three days, (people) may tie three pieces of stone on a rope or tie three knots in it."

The discourse connectors highlighted in (7.24)–(7.27) are all used at the beginning of a paragraph either to introduce a new topic, add further explanation, transmit a point of view, or summarize what has been said in the previous discourse. From the English translation, we see that English has similar discourse connectors. This similarity, like any other similarities between Chinese and other students' native languages, certainly helps native English-speaking students learn this type of discourse connector. Examining the most commonly used simple connectors in Chinese reveals a number of discourse functions that teachers and textbook compilers may find useful in teaching students and in composing teaching materials. Table 7.2 lists eleven discourse functions and the discourse connectors used to express these functions.

The discourse functions and connectors listed in Table 7.2 comprise a large framework of discourse structure that we use for daily communication in both spoken and written forms. Because of their effectiveness, they are seen in all types of genres. This means that if students of Chinese as a foreign language want to list a number of things for discussion or essay, they should learn those discourse connectors having the function of *listing*. If, however, they want to arrange events and discussions according to the time when the events occur, they should learn discourse connectors of *temporal sequencing*, and so on. One criterion for well-organized and coherent discourse is the accurate use of discourse (connectors, especially for written discourse, although this is not the only criterion. For spoken discourse, discourse markers are more likely to be used, a point to which I will now turn our discussion).

Table 7.2 Discourse functions and discourse connectors

DISCOURSE FOUNCTION	DISCOURSE CONNECTOR
LISTING (of importance) 排列 *páiliè*	首先/第一 *shǒuxiān/dìyī* "first/most importantly" 其次/第二 *qícì/dì'èr* "next/secondly" 另外/此外 *lìngwài/cǐwài* "also/besides" 第三 *dìsān* "thirdly"
TEMPORAL SEQUENCING 时序 *shíxù*	最初 *zuìchū* "at the very beginning" 后来 *hòulái* "later on" 同时 *tóngshí* "at the same time" 从那以后 *cóng nà yǐhòu* "from that time on/since then" 以前/从前 *yǐqián/cóngqián* "before/once upon a time" 现在/目前 *xiànzài/mùqián* "now/currently" 将来/以后 *jiānglái/yǐhòu* "in the future/from now on"
ADDITION (further information) 附加说明 *fùjiā shuōmíng*	再说 *zàishuō* "furthermore" 另外/此外 *lìngwài/cǐwài* "in addition" 况且/何况 *kuàngqiě/hékuàng* "not to mention" 顺便说一下 *shùnbiàn shuō yixià* "by the way" 除此之外 *chúcǐzhīwài* "in addition"
SPECIFICATION 具体说明 *jùtǐ shuōmíng*	关于/至于 *guānyú/zhìyú* "as far as" 对于 *duìyú* "concerning" 就 … 来说/而言 *jiù ... láishuō/éryán* "speaking of ..." 具体来说 *jùtǐláishuō* "specifically speaking"

	这(也)就是说 *zhè (yě) jiùshìshuō* "this is to say"
	换句话说 *huànjùhuàshuō* "in other words"
CAUSE-RESULT	因此/因而 *yīncǐ/yīn'ér* "therefore"
结果 *jiéguǒ*	于是 *yúshì* "so"
EXPECTED-RESULT	果然 *guǒrán* "as expected"
预料结果 *yùliào jiéguǒ*	不出所料 *bùchūsuǒliào* "as expected"
CONCESSION	退一步说 *tuìyìbùshuō* "even if we step back"
让步 *ràngbù*	固然 *gùrán* "even if"
EXAMINATION	（另）一方面 *(lìng) yìfāngmiàn* "on one (the other) hand"
侧面考察 *cèmiàn guānchá*	从 … 方面看 *cóng ... fāngmiàn kàn* "looking from …"
TRANSITION	然而/不过 *rán'ér/búguò* "however"
转折 *zhuǎnzhé*	但是 *kěshì* "but"
	言归正传 *yánguīzhèngzhuàn* "come back to the topic"
COMPARISON	相比之下 *xiāngbǐzhīxià* "in comparison"
比较 *bǐjiào*	同样地 *tóngyàngdi* "similarly"
	而今 *érjīn* "today however"
	反之 *fǎnzhī* "on the contrary"
	与此相反 *yǔcǐxiāngfǎn* "conversely"
GENERAL STATEMENT	一般来说 *yìbān láishuō* "generally speaking"
概括说明 *gàikuò shuōmíng*	总的来说 *zǒngde láishuō* "overall"
GIVING FACTS	实际上 *shíjìshàng* "In fact"
说明真相 *shuōmíng zhēnxiàng*	实话说 *shíhuà shuō* "honestly speaking"
	不瞒你说 *bùmánnǐshuō* "honestly speaking"
	说句心里话 *shuōjùxīnlǐhuà* "tell you the truth from my heart"
REASONING	由此可见 *yóucǐkějiàn* "evidently"
推理 *tuīlǐ*	这说明 *zhèi shuōmíng* "this indicates"
	毫无疑问 *háowúyíwèn* "undoubtedly"
GIVING EXAMPLES	比如/例如 *bǐrú/lìrú* "for example"
举例 *jǔlì*	比方说 *bǐfāngshuō* "for example"
	拿 … 来说 *ná ... láishuō* "taking … as an example"
SUMMARIZING	综上所述 *zōngshàngsuǒshù* "to sum up"
总结 *zǒngjié*	总（而言）之 *zǒng(éryán)zhī* "to summarize"
	一句话 *yíjùhuà* "to summarize in one sentence"

Discourse marker is a rather familiar term among discourse researchers. However, it is rather vague (definitely vaguer than *connector*) so researchers often come up with their own terminology to describe this type of discourse device (e.g. pragmatic marker, discourse particle, pragmatic particle, connective, pragmatic expression) (see Schourup 1985; Schiffrin 1987, 1988, 1994; Clancy et al. 1996; Fraser 1996; Jucker and Ziv 1998; Blackmore 2002). I use discourse marker only to refer to those particles used in spoken discourse. It should be noted that the choice of discourse marker and its distinction from discourse connector is purely for descriptive and pedagogical purposes. While recognizing the difficulty of drawing a clear line between the two, I believe it is useful to distinguish them for students of Chinese as a foreign language, because the lower level Chinese classes emphasize more spoken discourse and competence, whereas the more advanced classes emphasize both spoken and written discourse and competence.

Unlike discourse connectors, discourse markers are more flexible in both contextual meaning and form. That is, a certain contextual meaning may be expressed by different discourse markers and a certain marker may be used to express multiple meanings. If examining discourse markers in spoken texts, we may categorize them based on their contextual meaning, as shown in Table 7.3.

Table 7.3   Discourse markers and their functions in spoken texts

DISCOURSE MEANING	DISCOURSE MARKERS
Agreement	好 *hǎo*, 对 *duì*, 嗯 *en*, 就是 *jiùshí*, 行 *xíng*
Disagreement	不 *bù*, 不对 *búduì*, 不过 *búguò*, 得了 *déle*, 哼 *heng*
Consequence	那 *nà*, 那么 *nàme*, 天哪 *tiānna*
Confirmation	的确 *díquè*, 是的 *shìde*, 当然 *dāngrán*, 对 *duì*
Transition	不过 *búguò*, 但是 *dànshì*, 就是 *jiùshì*, 可 *kě*
Sequence	那 *nà*, 然后 *ránhòu*, 后来 *hòulái*
Surprise	真的 *zhēnde*, 啊 *á*, 呵 *á*, 怪 *guài*, 哎呀 *aiya*
Drawing attention	瞧 *qiáo*, 嘿 *hèi*
Disbelief	哼 *heng*
Disappointment	唉 *ai*, 嗨 *hài*, 天哪 *tiānna*[6]
Interjection	对了 *duìle*, 得了 *déle*, 哎 *ai*, 嘿 *hèi*
Initiation	喂 *wéi*, 嘿 *hèi*, 你说 *nǐshuō*, 哎 *ai*
Responding	嗯 *en*, 嗳 *ai*, 啊 *a*[7]
Concluding	好吧 *hǎoba*, 好了 *hǎole*

Examining the list of discourse markers in Table 7.3, one may notice that this is not a traditional list of exclamations (感叹词, *gǎntàncí*), nor a list of interjections (插入语, *chārùyǔ*), but rather it includes a variety of markers used to introduce or express a variety of discourse modes in conversation. This way, I believe, students do not need to differentiate the part of speech of the markers included in the list, but only focus on their discourse meanings and functions, so when they want to express agreement, they may use 好 (*hǎo* "good"), 对 (*duì* "right"), 嗯 (*en* "right"), or 就是 (*jiùshì* "indeed"), as illustrated in (7.28a)–(7.28d).

(7.28a)   "Tea House" (茶馆) by Lǎo Shě, p. 33

     甲: 妈，等我长大了，我帮助你打！我不知道亲妈妈是谁，你就是我的亲
           妈妈！

mā, děng wǒ zhǎngdà le, wǒ bāngzhù nǐ dǎ! wǒ bù zhīdào qīn māma shì
shéi, nǐ jiùshì wǒ de qīn māma!

A: "Mother, when I grow up, I will help you fight! I don't know who my
biological mother is, so you are my mother!"

乙： **好！好！**咱们永远在一块儿，我去挣钱，你去念书！

hǎo! hǎo! zánmen yǒngyuǎn zài yíkuàir, wǒ qù zhèng qián, nǐ qù dúshū!

B: "**Okay! Okay!** We will be together forever. I will make money and you
will go to school!"

(7.28b)   "Tea House" (茶馆) by Lǎo Shě, p. 35

甲： 你说吧，你是大哥。

nǐ shuō ba, nǐ shì dàgē.

A: "Your are the big brother, so you talk."

乙： 那个，你看，我们俩是把兄弟！

nàge, nǐ kàn, wǒmen liǎng shì bǎxiōngdì!

B: "Then, you see, two of us are buddies!"

甲： **对！**把兄弟，两个人穿一条裤子的交情！

duì! bǎxiōngdì, liǎngge rén chuān yìtiáo kùzi de jiāoqíng!

A: "Right, buddies. (We) are so close: just like wearing the same pair of
pants."

(7.28c)   "Tea House" (茶馆) by Lǎo Shě, p. 36

甲： 你看我们是两个人吧？

nǐ kàn wǒmen shì liǎngge rén ba?

A: "You see we are two people."

乙： **嗯！**

en!

B: "Right!"

甲： 两个人穿一条裤子的交情吧？

liǎngge rén chuān yìtiáo kùzi de jiāoqíng ba?

A: "Two people having such a close friendship is just like wearing the same
pair of pants."

乙： **嗯！**

en!

B: "Right!"

甲： 没人耻笑我们的交情吧？

méi rén chīxiào wǒmen de jiāoqíng ba?

A: "Nobody will laugh at our friendship, right?"

乙： 交情嘛，没人耻笑！

jiāoqíng ma, méi rén chīxiào!

B: "A friendship, nobody will laugh at."

(7.28d)   "Tea House" (茶馆) by Lǎo Shě, p. 59

甲： 太不知好歹了，他门老老实实的，美国会送来大米、白面嘛！

> *tài bù zhī hǎodǎi le, wǒmen lǎolǎoshíshí de, měiguó huì sònglái dàmǐ,*
> *báimiàn ma!*

A: "(I) don't know what is good or bad. (If) they were honest and sincere, the US would send rice and flour!"

乙： ***就是****！*二位，有大米、白面，可别忘了我！以后给大家的坟地看风水，我一定尽义务。

> *jiùshi! èrwèi, yǒu dàmǐ, báimiàn, kě bié wàng le wǒ! yǐhòu gěi dàjiā de*
> *féndì kàn fēngshuǐ, wǒ yídìng jìn yìwù.*

B: "Indeed. You two, don't forget us when you have rice and flour! Let me know when you need someone to look at the *Fēng Shuǐ* for your grave. I will do OR try my best to do a good job."

Although all four discourse markers can be used to express agreement as illustrated above, they vary somewhat in discourse meaning because each has its own idiomatic meaning. 好 (*hǎo*), for instance, conveys the meaning of "favorably agree with what was said in the previous discourse" or rather "good". 对 (*duì*), on the other hand, confirms what has been said with its idiomatic meaning "correct". 嗯 (*en*) might be the least emphasized when expressing the meaning of "right", while 就是 (*jiùshi*) might be the most emphasized since its idiomatic meaning is "indeed". Because of the idiomatic meaning of these discourse markers, they are not always interchangeable in discourse. We see that *hǎo* in (7.28a) cannot replace *duì* in (7.28b); but *duì, en,* and *jiùshì* in (7.28b)–(7.28d) can be interchanged, even though the switched marker expresses a slightly different meaning in the conversation from the original marker.

We have seen that it is important to compare, distinguish and practice those discourse markers that share the same or similar discourse function and at the same time keep in mind their idiomatic meaning. In addition to that, students may find it helpful to practice and use those markers that have multiple discourse functions, such as 好 (*hǎo*) expressing "agreement" and "concluding", 是 (*shì*) expressing "agreement" and "confirmation", *duì* expressing "agreement" and "confirmation", and 那 (*nà*) expressing "sequence" and "consequence". In other words, students may ask the teacher how to distinguish the different functions of certain discourse markers. Teachers may use the examples such as those in (7.29) to demonstrate the functions of 得了 (*déle*).

(7.29a) 甲： 我觉得 …

> *wǒ juéde …*

A: "I think …"

乙： ***得了****，*你别说了，咱们先听听老大的意见吧。

> *déle, nǐ bié shuō le, zánmen xiān tīngting lǎodà de yìjiàn ba.*

B: "That's it! You stop. Let's first listen to Lao Da's opinion."

(7.29b)   甲： 这种事儿你得问我。我是专家。

           zhèi-zhǒng shìr nǐ děi wèn wǒ. wǒ shì zhuān jiā.

    A: "This kind of thing, you should ask me. I specialize in it."

    乙： ***得了***，我还不知道你？你知道什么呀？(disagreement)

           déle, wǒ hái bù zhīdào nǐ? nǐ zhīdào shénme ya?

    B: "You? You don't think I know you? What do you know?"

If students understand the context of 得了 (*déle*) in (7.29a)–(7.29b), they should have little difficulty understanding that the first *déle* expresses interjection and the second expresses the speaker's disagreement with what has been said in the previous discourse, although both convey a certain sense of rejection (i.e. "I don't like what you said. Stop talking."). Students may also use English translation to distinguish the two functions: one being something similar to "stop talking" and the other being "I don't agree with you". I believe that students can always take advantage of the knowledge that they already have about their own language when they learn Chinese.

When discourse markers have one special function, such as 瞧 (*qiáo* "look" – drawing attention) and 唉 *ai* (expressing disappointment), they are relatively easy to learn. Students may treat them the same as a new word with a special discourse meaning.

So far, I have discussed discourse connectors and discourse markers. The former is likely to have the syntactic function of a conjunction or adverbial phrase and the latter tends to be used as an exclamation and interjection in spoken discourse. It has been suggested that when learning discourse markers and connectors, students may learn their discourse functions first, and then compare and use them in various discourse situations. As far as which discourse markers and connectors should be learned at which level, I have indicated that the emphasis should be on discourse markers and concurrent discourse connectors at the lower levels and solo discourse connectors and more complicated discourse markers for overall discourse coherence at the more advanced level. This distinction should alleviate teachers' psychological burden of teaching all discourse markers and discourse connectors at a certain level, and at the same time give teachers and students a guideline regarding what discourse devices they should learn at what level.

7.2.3.5   Word order variation

Chinese, like English, has the SVO (agent + verb + patient) as its basic word order. It also has several alternative orders: (1) the 把 *bǎ* construction (agent + 把 *bǎ*/将 *jiāng* + patient + verb), (2) the *bèi* (被) construction (patient + *bèi* + agent + verb), (3) the *lián* construction (连 *lián* + agent/patient + verb) and 4) the topic constructions (patient + verb or patient + agent +verb). Most of these alternative constructions have patient in the preverbal position. Studies (Sun and Givón 1985, Xing 1993) show that approximately 90 percent of sentences in

Chinese written discourse consist of the SVO order and the remaining 10 use alternative orders. In Chapter 6, I have discussed the function of these alternative constructions. Here, I will only focus on word order alternation (语序变换, *yǔxù biànhuàn*) for the purpose of discourse coherence.

Assuming that students understand the syntactic function (e.g. some verbs have to use the *bǎ* construction) and semantic functions (e.g. verbs with stative meaning normally cannot be used in the *bǎ* construction) of the basic and alternative word order in Chinese (cf. Xing 1993), what they should learn next is to be able to alternate word order to produce a coherent discourse. Let us first consider the *bǎ* construction in (7.30):

(7.30) *Four Generations under the Same Roof* by Lǎo Shě, p. 232

光是你妈妈，我已经受不了，况且你妈妈又作了所长呢！可是话到了嘴边上了，*她把它截住*。她的人情世故使她留了点心 – 大赤包无论怎么不好，恐怕高低也不高兴听别人攻击自己的妈妈吧。

*guāng shì nǐ māma, wǒ yǐjīng shòubùliǎo le, kuàngqiě nǐ māma yòu zuò le suǒzhǎng ne! kěshì huà dào le zuǐbiān shàng le, **tā bǎ tā jiézhù**. tāde rénqíngshìgù shǐ tā liú le diǎn xīn – Dàchìbāo wúlùn zěnme bùhǎo, kǒngpà gāodī yě bù gāoxìng tīng biérén gōngjī zìjǐ de māma ba.*

"Your mother, I can barely stand to be with her, Not to mention that she has become a director. These words coming to her mouth, however, she did not say. Her life experience taught her to be cautious, because no matter how bad Da Chi-bao was, she would not like to hear other people attack her mother."

In the place where the bold-faced *bǎ* construction occurs in (7.30), the basic word order could be used as 她截住要说的话 *tā jiézhù yào shuō de huà* "She stopped what she wanted to say." The reason that the writer did not use the basic order is probably because the *bǎ* construction promotes the importance of the patient (i.e. the words she was going to say) in discourse, whereas the basic construction does not. This distinction has been supported by our previous studies of word order variation in both Chinese and English (e.g. Xing 1994, Myhill and Xing 1993), which suggest that the noun phrase in sentence initial position is the most important in discourse, that in preverbal position is very important, and that in postverbal position is the least important. We see that the writer places the patient (i.e. the words) in a very important position, but not as important as the agent (i.e. she) in the discourse. Nonetheless, the *bǎ* construction in (7.30) enables the patient to be closer to the topic of the previous discourse (i.e. the words), and hence makes the discourse more coherent. Acute readers may ask why the writer/speaker did not use the *bèi* construction that places the patient in the sentence initial position and the agent after the patient and before the verb. Technically, the *bèi* construction could be used in the place of the *bǎ* construction in (7.30). However, the writer/speaker did not seem to rate the patient being as important as the agent, which is understandable because the agent is a human figure, whereas the patient is nonhuman. The rule of thumb is that human referents have the tendency to have more importance than nonhuman referents in discourse (cf. Xing 1993).

(7.31)   *Four Generations under the Same Roof* by Lǎo Shě, p. 47

瑞宣大哥是那么有思想有本事，**可是被家所累**，没法子逃出去！在家里，对谁他也说不来，可是对谁他也要笑眯眯的像个当家人似的！

*Ruì-xuān dàgē shì nàme yǒu sīxiǎng yǒu běnshì, **kěshì bèi jiā suǒ lèi**, méi fázi táochū qù! zài jiā lǐ, duì shéi tā yě shuō bùlái, kěshì duì shéi tā yě yào xiào-mīmī de xiàng ge dāngjiā rén shìde!*

"Big brother Rui-xuan is such a thinker and so competent. However, he was burdened by family and could not escape from it. At home, he did not say no to anyone. He always smiled to everyone like a head of the household."

The *bèi* construction in (7.31) has to be used; otherwise, the topic (i.e. *Ruì-xuān*) and its chain in this discourse would be broken. We know that both the basic construction and the *bǎ* construction would have placed the agent (i.e. *jiā* "family"), instead of the patient (i.e. *Ruì-xuān*), in the sentence initial position, which is not desirable for the purpose of discourse coherence because the topic in this discourse is *Ruì-xuān*, not "family". Although the *bèi* construction has other functions as discussed in Chapter 6, coherence is the most important function in the discourse illustrated in (7.31). Following is another commonly used word order in Chinese.

(7.32)   *Four Generations under the Same Roof* by Lǎo Shě, p. 241

当天晚上，**门开了**，进来一个敌兵，打着手电筒。

*dāngtiān wǎnshàng, **mén kāi le,** jìnlái yíge díbīng, dǎ-zhe shǒudiàntǒng.*

"On that evening, the door opened and through it came an enemy soldier who had a flashlight in his hand."

In (7.32), there is a topic comment construction. I have discussed in Chapter 6 that the most common function of topic comment construction is either to promote the patient in discourse or to avoid the mention of the agent. The topic comment construction in (7.32) seems to play the role of the latter type. If we change this construction into the basic word order or the *bǎ* construction, we have to introduce an agent, namely "the person who opened the door". The problem with that is this would put the agent, a non-referential person (i.e. 一个敌兵 *yíge díbīng* "an enemy soldier"), in the topic position at the beginning of the discourse, which is not desirable for the purpose of coherence. It is better not to mention who opened the door and then introduce the person in a less prominent position (i.e. postverbal position) in the following discourse, just as the writer/speakers did in (7.32). Nonetheless, it is possible to use a *bèi* construction in the place of the topic comment construction as 门被一个敌兵打开了 *mén bèi yíge díbīng dǎkāi le* "the door was opened by an enemy shoulder." The only problem with this word order choice is that this would break the natural flow of the following discourse and the writer/speaker has to change the word order of the following discourse accordingly. This suggests that the original choice of the topic comment construction is the most appropriate.

(7.33)   *Four Generations under the Same Roof* by Lǎo Shě, p. 238
"你们捕了我来，我还不晓得为了什么。我应当问你们，我犯了什么罪！"
可是，**连这个*他也懒得说了**。看了看襟上的血，他闭了闭眼睛，...
*"nǐmen bǔ le wǒ lái, wǒ hái bù xiǎode wèile shénme. wǒ yīngdāng wèn nǐmen, wǒ fàn le shénme zuì!" kěshì **lián zhèige tā yě lǎnde shuō le**. kàn-le kàn jīnshàng de xiě, tā bìle bì yǎnjīng.*
" 'You arrested me, I don't even know why. I should ask you what crime I have committed.' However, even these words he did not want to say. Seeing the blood on his shirt, he closed his eyes."

The short discourse shown in (7.33) has a *lián* construction focusing or emphasizing the concept "these words" located in the sentence initial position. In addition to emphatic function, the *lián* construction, just like other constructions, is also used to connect ideas between discourses. We see that the emphasized element "these words" refers to the words quoted in the immediately preceding discourse. If we place the *lián* phrase after the agent and before the verb (i.e. 他连这个也懒得说了 *tā lián zhè ge yě lǎnde shuō le*), "these words" is still emphasized, but it is not as effective as it is in the sentence initial position. Besides, the insertion of the agent between the words — the antecedent and the reference — creates some distance for discourse coherence. This problem becomes even worse if other word order, such as the basic word order is used. Neither the *bèi* construction nor the *bǎ* construction is plausible in this spot because the *bèi* construction demotes the agent and the verb *shuō* "say" does not have the disposal function which is mandatory for the *bǎ* construction. The topic comment construction might be the only possible alternate construction as 这个他也懒得说了 only if the writer/speaker does not want to emphasize the patient "these words" as much as the original text demonstrates.

To summarize, in this section I have discussed several word order variations in Chinese and their discourse functions. Emphasis was laid on the alternation among the major word orders in discourse. It has been shown that the primary reason for word order alternation is to construct a coherent discourse and therefore students have to learn where, when, and why speakers/writers use one word order rather than another in discourse.

7.2.3.6   Temporal sequence

Temporal sequence (时间顺序, *shíjiān shùnxù*) is another discourse device used to arrange discourse structure in accordance with the time when actions and events occur in a real situation. Since Tai's (1985) study of temporal sequencing in word order, much interest has been directed at the role temporal sequencing plays in other aspects of the Chinese language (e.g. historical development of grammatical words, discourse structure, and discourse coherence). In this section, I will not discuss how words are arranged in sentences, but rather how sentences are arranged in discourse based on the time of the events and situations described by those sentences. Furthermore, I will compare the function of temporal sequence in Chinese discourse with its English counterpart so that students of Chinese can learn and benefit from their similarities and differences.

Let us first examine a written discourse from the novel *Four Generations under the Same Roof* by Lǎo Shě.

(7.34)   *Four Generations under the Same Roof* by Lǎo Shě, p. 239
手掌又打到他的脸上，而且是一连几十掌。他一声不响，只想用身体的稳定不动作精神的抵抗。打人的微笑着，似乎是笑他的愚蠢。慢慢的，他的脖子没有力气；慢慢的，他的腿软起来；他动了。左右开弓的嘴巴使他像一个不倒翁似的向两边摆动。打人的笑出了声。

shǒuzhǎng yòu dǎdào tā de liǎn shàng, érqiě shì yìlián jǐshí zhǎng. tā yìshēng bù xiǎng, zhǐ xiǎng yòng shēntǐ de wěndìng búdòng zuò jīngshén de dǐkàng. dǎ rén de wēixiào-zhe, sìhū shì xiào tā de yúchǔn. mànmande, tāde bózi méiyǒu lìqi; mànmande, tāde tuǐ ruǎn qǐlái; tā dòngle. zuǒyòu kāigōng de zuǐba shǐ tā xiàng yíge bùdǎowēn shìde xiàng liǎngbiān bǎidòng. dǎ rén de xiào chū le shēng.

"Slaps fell on his face again and continued for another dozen times. He did not respond. He only wanted to show his resistance by stabilizing his body. The hitter was laughing, as if he were an idiot. Slowly, his neck lost strength; slowly, his legs became weak. He moved. Slaps fell on both of his cheeks that made him swing from one side to the other. The hitter laughed loudly."

The discourse in (7.34) describes a scene in which a hitman continuously hits a resistant brave anti-Japanese person. Throughout the Chinese discourse, there is no single time expression, yet readers/listeners can follow the story sentence by sentence or one action after another without any difficulty, because all the actions involved are arranged in sequence. In other words, temporal sequence links sentences in Chinese to form a chronologically coherent discourse. Imagine if the above discourse were rearranged by ignoring the temporal sequence: readers/listeners would undoubtedly have trouble understanding the central meaning and progression of events in this paragraph.

English translation of the Chinese discourse in (7.34) demonstrates both some similar patterns and some differences from Chinese. We see that English uses the past tense throughout the paragraph and Chinese does not. This is simply because Chinese does not have a tense system. Although the tense system constitutes a significant difference between the two languages, it does not seem to affect the function of temporal sequencing in discourse of the two languages, because whether the series of actions are described by the past tense or without a past tense, they have to be in sequence. Without an adequate order of sentences, readers/listeners cannot understand the discourse. However, without a tense, readers/listeners seem not to have a problem. The English example in (7.35) further supports the analysis that temporal sequence functions the same in both languages with or without the use of the past tense.

(7.35)   *Harry Potter* by Rowling, p. 115

They pulled on their uniform-gowns, picked up their wands and crept across the tower room, down the spiral staircase and into the Gryffindor common-room. A few embers were still glowing in the fireplace, turning all the armchairs into hunched black shadows. They had almost reached the portrait hole when a voice spoke from the chair nearest them: 'I can't believe you're going to do this, Harry.'

"他们穿上他们的正式袍子，拿上他们的魔杖，悄悄的穿过塔屋，下了螺旋楼梯，走进格利菲多的教员公用室。有几块木炭还在壁炉里烧着，把手扶倚反射成罗锅一样的黑影。当他们就要到画像洞口的时候，一个声音从靠近他们的椅子那边传过来：'哈里，我不明白你们原来是要做这件事。'"

The English example in (7.35) again uses the past tense throughout the discourse and its Chinese translation does not, instead, it uses different complements (e.g. 了 *le*, 过 *guo*) right after verbs to indicate the completion of those actions. This difference does not seem to affect the natural coherent flow of the discourse governed by temporal sequence in either language.

The same discourse function of temporal sequencing in both Chinese and English makes it relatively easy for students of Chinese as a foreign language to use the device and produce coherent discourse. Nonetheless, students should be alerted that the same device behaves somewhat differently at the syntactic level between the two languages. Compare the following two simple sentences:

(7.36)   我 去 (在) 中国　学　中文。
Wǒ qù (zài) zhōngguó xué zhōngwén.
I study Chinese in China.

Chinese follows the principle of temporal sequencing in constructing the sentence in (7.36), whereas English does not. Tai (1985) convincingly argued that the order of the Chinese concepts in a sentence is concurrent with the order of the reality when these actions occur. As to the situation expressed by the sentence in (7.36), in order to fulfill temporal sequencing logic needs, 去中国 (*qù zhōngguó* "go to China") has to happen prior to 学中文 (*xué zhōngwén* "study Chinese"), not the other way around as illustrated by the English equivalent.

Another cue that students should know about temporal sequencing is the genre in which it tends to be used. Unlike other discourse devices discussed earlier, temporal sequence is highly likely to be used in narrative and descriptive genres. It is not common to see it in argument passages (to be discussed later) or expository essays.

For students of the lower level classes, using temporal sequence to describe a situation or scene that they encounter on a daily basis is always fun and challenging. Students may be asked to describe how to score for a certain sport or how students behave when their teacher is not in the classroom, etc. To avoid oversimplified or overcomplicated description, teachers may require or restrict students to produce a discourse demonstrating their level of Chinese proficiency by using certain number of words, expressions, and sentences and linking those sentences by temporal sequence.

7.2.3.7   Foreground and background

According to Hopper and Thompson (1980: 280), "In any speaking situation, some parts of what is said are more relevant than others. That part of a discourse which does not immediately and crucially contribute to the speaker's goal, but which merely assists, amplifies, or comments on it, is referred to as background. By contrast, the material which supplies the main points of the discourse is known as foreground." Although this is a rather general description of background (背景, *bèijǐng*) and foreground (前景, *qiánjǐng*), it gives us a general sense of how these terms are used in discourse analysis. Perhaps, the more intuitive distinction between the foreground and background discourse is simpler and easier for some teachers and students to understand than formal linguistic description, that is, foreground information is the most important and background information is supportive. One reason for me to introduce the concept of foreground and background to Chinese teachers and students is that they seem to correlate with specific discourse structures or discourse types.

Hopper (1979) was one of the first to propose the aspectual and cognitive characterization of foreground and background. He (1979: 223) claims that there is a strong statistical tendency for foregrounded events to have familiar, animate subjects, to be punctual rather than durative, to occur in sequence. In contrast, backgrounded situations tend to have less familiar subjects, to be durative or stative and not sequential. In the two decades since Hopper's study, Smith (2003) elaborated further on foreground and background; She points out (2003: 34–35) that foreground presents the main, sequential events of a narrative, while background provides the supporting and descriptive information. Foreground situations are usually events in sequence presented with the perfective viewpoint, while imperfectives and states are usually background. Comparing Hopper's and Smith's studies, we see that both of them agree on the relationship between aspect and foreground/background. However, Hopper links foreground and background with the familiarity of the speaker to the subject matter discussed in discourse, whereas Smith connects foreground and background with the discourse mode (e.g. descriptive or narrative discourse to be discussed in the next section). These studies are useful for pedagogy specialists and teachers of foreign languages because they explain the relationship between the discourse device foreground/background and discourse type/information type. Once this distinction is understood and acquired, students will be able to manage the flow of information for coherent discourse.

In discussion of foreground and background, two other terms are often mentioned in describing information flow of discourse: given information (已知 信息, *yǐzhī xìnxī*) and new information (新信息, *xīn xìnxī*). These two terms are defined and distinguished by the speaker based on whether discourse information is known to the listener/reader or not (cf. Brown and Yule 1983, Chu 1998), as illustrated in (7.37).

(7.37) *Four Generations under the Same Roof* by Lǎo Shě, p. 241

当天晚上，*门*开了，进来*一个敌兵*，打着手电筒。

dāngtiān wǎnshàng, **mén** *kāi le, jìnlái* **yige díbīng***, dǎ-zhe shōudiàntōng.*

"On that evening, the door opened and through it came an enemy soldier who had a flashlight in his hand."

In (7.37) 门 (*mén*) is given information assuming that the listener/reader knows to which door the speaker/writer refers. 一个敌兵 (*yígè díbīng*), on the other hand, is new information because this is the first time that the speaker introduces "an enemy soldier" into the discourse. Discourse analysts generally agree that there is a tendency for given information to be correlated with background and for the new information to be correlated with foreground. The only difference between given/new information and background/foreground, according to Chu (1998: 221), is that "the former pertains to the level of a phrase but the latter operates between clauses." In other words, the whole clause "the door opened" is a backgrounded event, while "entered an enemy soldier" is a foregrounded event. Concurring with Chu's distinction, I, henceforth, focus on the discourse pragmatic functions of background/foreground and their acquisition.

Following the Western tradition of discourse analysis that foreground generally pushes a narrative forward and is temporally ordered, while background describes stative situations or events, Chu (1998: 222) suggests the progression from background to foreground in discourse unless otherwise marked, as exemplified in (7.37). Furthermore, both Li and Thompson (1981) and Chu (1998) point out that background tends to correlate with the subordinate and relative clause and with clauses describing the cause-result relation, as illustrated in (7.38)–(7.39).

(7.38) Chu (1998: 230)

我*从图书馆借的*那本书结果不好看。

wǒ cóng túshūguǎn jiè de *nàběn shū jiéguǒ bùhǎo kàn.*

"That book *that I borrowed from the library* turned out to be boring."

(7.39) Li and Thompson (1981: 644)

(因为)我是美国人，所以我去中国需要护照。

(yīnwèi) wǒ shì měiguó rén*, suǒyǐ wǒ qù zhōngguó xūyào hùzhào.*

"*Because I am an American*, I need a passport to go to China."

The bold-faced subordinate clauses are background and the main clauses are foreground information/events. Let us look at another example:

(7.40)   *Open Country* by Cáo Yǔ, p. 45
甲：您从前见过？

nín cóngqián jià-guo?

A: "Have you seen (him) before?"

乙：*那还用说*。我告诉你，*要多丑有多丑，罗锅腰，灶王脸，粗大个，满身黑毛。*

nà hái yòng shuō. wǒ gàosu nǐ, yào duō chǒu yǒu duō chǒu, luóguō yāo, zàowáng liǎn, zū dàgè, mǎn shēn hēi máo.

B: "**Of course**. I can tell you (he) **is extremely ugly, hump-backed, stove-faced, and chubby with black hair all over his body.**"

The remark made by Speaker B starts with backgrounding (bold-faced) followed by a foreground clause and then again backgrounding (bold-faced). Notice that the second backgrounding is embedded in a subordinate clause, namely the object of the verb "tell", which confirms Chu's claim that background is marked by subordination. The only problem is that the second backgrounding is actually new information, which seems to go against the general tendency that background is correlated with given information. This seems to suggest that background can be identified by syntactic structure, but it cannot be clearly marked by information structure (i.e. given/new).

To summarize the discourse function of background and foreground discussed so far:

- Background tends to be marked by subordination
- Foreground correlates with new information
- Background precedes foreground
- Background sets up a scene or story
- Background describes stative events or situations
- Foreground describes sequential events or situations

Examining these tendencies and rules regarding background and foreground, we see that the first two tendencies occur at the sentence or phrase level but the remaining four generalizations are drawn from the discourse or paragraph level (i.e. concerning multiple sentences). The most important generalizations for Chinese students are probably the last two, which set background/foreground apart from discourse event/situation types in a way that other discourse devices I have discussed so far are incapable of doing. For this reason, I suggest that Chinese students learn all the generalizations but master the last two to enhance their discourse competence.

So far, I have discussed seven devices for discourse coherence: topic chain, ellipsis, abstraction, discourse connectors and markers, word order variation, temporal sequence and background/foreground. They all have their own unique discourse functions, yet they all seem to relate to one another — a true characteristic of discourse and discourse study. I hope that these devices will become tools for students to acquire discourse modes and eventually to enhance their discourse competence.

7.3   Discourse Modes

The notion of discourse mode (篇章模式, *piānzhāng móshì*) accounts for a variety of discourse passages in both spoken and written discourse (cf. Smith 2003). It is a larger discourse unit than the devices discussed in the previous section. Each mode has its own function. For instance, the opening mode starts a conversation, a story, an essay, or a report and the narrative mode describes sequential events. Based on my text analysis, I have selected six discourse modes to be examined and discussed in this chapter. Although the list given below is not exhaustive, it represents mainstream discourse; therefore, it is necessary for Chinese students to learn each item. The six modes are:

- Opening passage
- Narrative
- Description
- Notation
- Argument
- Conclusion

In general, discourse analysts do not seem to have a uniform way to assess discourse. Some classify and examine discourse by genres (e.g. Berger 1997), some by modes (e.g. Smith 2003), and others by function (e.g. Linde 1993). Clearly, the modes enlisted above are not selected and determined by genre. Other than narrative and description, the remaining modes normally only invoke a specific passage, rather than a text genre. In fact, all modes can be used in any genre: expository, narrative, descriptive, or conversational. Opening and conclusion modes are chosen because any discourse should include such passages. Narrative is chosen because it is, as explained later, the most basic component of any discourse genre. The descriptive is such a powerful mode in discourse that, without it, discourse would be dull, monotonous and less informative. Notation mode, often used in reports and documents, provides information that the listener/readers need for comprehension of certain concepts, situations, events, etc. Lastly, argument, which includes persuasion and negotiation, is the best mode for stating the speaker/writer's point of view in different circumstances. In the following sections, I will discuss these six modes in detail.

7.3.1   Opening passage

The opening passage might be the most important mode to use to attract the listener/reader's attention, regardless of discourse type — a speech, an announcement, or a conference presentation. "A good beginning signals a job half well done", as the Chinese are fond of saying. Let us first look at some examples:

(7.41a)   Opening passage of a ***note*** *Telling the Truth* by Bā Jīn, p. 45

我在《收获》上发表的《巴金全集》后记《最后的话》，就是我想对读者
说的话，我希望读者理解我。我这一生是靠读者养活的。我为读者写作，
我把心交给读者。

wǒ zài "Shōuhuò" shàng fābiǎo de "Bājīn Quánjí" hòujì "Zuìhòu de Huà",
jiùshì wǒ xiǎng duì dúzhě shuō de huà, wǒ xīwàng dúzhě lǐjiě wǒ. wǒ zhè yìshēng
shì kào dúzhě yǎnghuó de. wǒ wèi dúzhě xiězuò, wǒ bǎ xīn jiāogěi dúzhě.

"The postscript 'Final Words' from the *Complete Collection of Bā Jīn's Work*
that I have published in *Shōuhuò* is what I want to tell my readers. I hope readers
understand me. My whole life relies on readers. I write for them and give my
heart to them."

(7.41b)   Opening passage of a ***play,*** *Open Country* by Cáo Yǔ, p. 3

秋天的傍晚。

qiūtiān de bàngwǎn.

大地是沉郁的，生命藏在里面。泥土散着香，禾根在土里暗暗滋长。

dàdì shì chényù de, shēngmìng cáng zài lǐmiàn. nítǔ sànfāzhe xiāng, hégēn zài
tǔlǐ ànàn zīzhǎng.

"On an autumn evening, the globe in which life hides is mellow. The earth sends
out a charming fragrance, plant roots grow quietly under the ground."

(7.41c)   Opening passage of a ***Love Letter*** by Ān Dùn, p. 69

你好，别来无恙吗？

nǐ hǎo, bié lái wúwàng ma?

相识至今差不多四年了，一路走来，风风雨雨，有笑有累，有花有果，有
苦也有甜。而我，也从一个不谙世事的少女磨练成了独立自强的新女性。

xiāngshí zhì jīn chàbùduō sì nián le, yí lù zǒu lái, fēngfēngyǔyǔ, yǒu xiào yǒu lèi,
yǒu huā yǒu guǒ, yǒu kǔ yě yǒu tián. ér wǒ, yě cóng yíge bù ān shìshì de shàonǚ
móliàn chéng le dúlì zìqiáng de xīn nǚxìng.

"(Hello, Is there any change since we last parted? (We) have known each other
for about four years and have been through a lot together. We experienced many
ups and downs, laughter and exhaustion, joy and achievement, hardship and
happiness."

(7.41d) Opening passage of an *essay,* "On Women and Children" by Hú Shì, p. 1175

我的一个朋友对我说过一句很深刻的话：“你要看一个国家的文明，只需要考察三件事：第一，看他们怎么对待小孩子；第二，看他们怎么对待女人；第三，看他们怎么利用闲暇时间。”

wǒ de yíge péngyou duì wǒ shuōguò yijù hěn shēnkè de huà: "nǐ yào kàn yíge guójiā de wénmíng, zhǐ xūyào kǎochá sānjiàn shì: dìyī, kàn tāmen zěnme duìdài xiǎo háizi; dì'èr, kàn tāmen zěnme duìdài nǚrén; dìsān, kàn tāmen zěnme lìyòng xiánxiá shíjiān.

"One of my friends once said some profound words to me: If you want to find out how civilized a country is, you should check three things: first, find out how they treat children; second, see how they treat women, and third, see how they spend their spare time."

Although extracted from different genres, the types of opening passages illustrated in (7.41) are by no means all-inclusive. (7.41a) is the beginning of a brief note entitled "Telling the Truth" from a well-known author to his young followers; (7.41b) describes the opening scene of the play "Open Country"; (7.41c) shows the beginning of a love letter, and (7.41d) is the opening statement of an essay on women and children. We see that these beginning passages address different subjects, but what is more important to our discussion is that they employ quite different discourse strategies. The note on "Telling the Truth" starts by expressing the author's attitude and then moves on to give supporting evidence, a very effective way to give the reader/listener a clear idea of the author's position. In (7.b), it seems quite appropriate for the beginning of the prelude for the play "Open Country" to start with the description of the natural life of a country. As to the love letter, following the common format of letters, it starts with a casual greeting, and then proceeds to a summary of the life that the author has experienced with the addressee in the last four years, which makes the readers want to continue to read the letter and find out its real purpose. The last example, different from the rest, begins an essay by listing three issues that the author will discuss omitting the author's point of view to entice the reader to find it out by continuing to read the essay.

Comparing the four beginning passages, we see that the note uses a *statement*, simple, clear, straightforward and to the point — Telling the Truth. The play, on the other hand, opens with a vivid *description* of an open country, which other types of discourse (e.g. letters, essays, newspaper articles, etc.) would not often employ in a beginning passage, yet seems appropriate to begin a play entitled "Open Country". The love letter uses *metaphors* (i.e. using 'wind and rain" for "ups and downs" and "flowers and fruits" for "joy and achievement") to describe the romantic relationship that the author has with the addressee. The essay starts with a generic *proposition* using the discourse structure "if (you want to find out this, you do that)". These four ways of pursuing the opening mode may be summarized as follows:

- Simple statement for a note
- Vivid description for a play

- Metaphors for a love letter
- Generic proposition for an essay

Although these patterns may not apply to all other discourse of similar genres (i.e., notes, plays, love letters, and essays), they seem at least to suggest that the opening mode relies on the type of discourse. For a simple note, it would be strange to start with a vivid description. Likewise, a play may sound blunt if started with a straightforward statement or a generic proposition. Therefore, I recommend that teaching and learning the opening mode be tied with discourse type (e.g. note, letter, story and essay) and discourse strategies (e.g. statement, metaphor, description and proposition). Students may learn one discourse opening strategy at a time and gradually accumulate others to achieve high fluency in creating opening passages.

7.3.2 Narrative

Berger (1997: 4) describes narrative as "a story, and stories tell about things that have happened or are happening to people, animals, aliens from outer space, insects – whatever." This description seems quite adequate in reflecting the characteristics of narrative in discourse, namely simplicity and commonality. It seems natural that these characteristics would make narrative the most basic and most studied of all discourse passages (cf. Linde 1993, Norrick 2000). For language students whose foreign language learning goal is to communicate about things that happen to people, animals, insects, etc., it is inevitable — and necessary — to learn and master narrative and style.

Questions and issues relevant to narrative passages (i.e. both spoken and written) often focus on: (1) the nature of narrative, (2) narrative structures, and (3) teaching and learning narrative passages. Considering the focus of this book, I will only discuss narrative acquisition and the relationship between narrative and discourse structures. Let us first examine a narrative passage from an oral interview:

(7.42) "Love Stories" by Ān Dùn, p. 143
[1]他拖着箱子**找到我**住的地方时，我正在一个朔料模特的头上修剪假发，[2]房东把他**领进门**，[3]说："这个人在门外一家一户地打听你住在哪里。"[4]我特别**高兴**。手里拿着剪刀，身上穿着围裙，手都不知道往哪里放。[5]房东**离开**了，[6]我们俩面对面傻**站着**，半天，[7]我**说**："你坐啊。"[8]他才**放下**箱子。[9]看了我好一会儿，[10]说："你比原来好看了。"

[1]*tā tuōzhe xiāngzi **zhǎo dào wǒ** zhù de dìfang shí, wǒ zhèngzài yíge suòliào mótè de tóu shàng xiūjiǎn tóufa,* [2]*fángdōng bǎ tā **lǐng jìn mén**,* [3]*shuō: "zhèige rén zài ménwài yìjiā yíhù di dǎting nǐ zhù zài nǎlǐ."* [4]*wǒ tèbié **gāoxìng.** shǒulǐ názhe jiǎndāo, shēnshàng chuānzhe wéiqún, shǒu dōu bù zhīdào wǎng nǎlǐ fàng.* [5]*fángdōng **líkāi** le,* [6]*wǒmen liǎng miàn duì miàn shǎ **zhànzhe**, bàntiān,* [7]*wǒ*

shuō: "nǐ zuò a." [(8)]*tā cái fàngxià xiāngzi.* [(9)]*kàn le wǒ hǎo yíhuìr,* [(10)]*shuō: "nǐ bǐ yuánlái hǎokàn le."*

"When he dragged in his luggage and **found me** at my apartment, I was practicing cutting hair on a plastic model. My landlord **led him in** and **said** 'This is the person who was looking for you door to door in the neighborhood.' I **was extremely happy.** I had scissors in my hand and an apron covering my clothes so I did not know where to put my hands. The landlord **left.** We **were standing** face to face. After a while, I **said**, 'Why don't you sit down?' Only then, did he **put his suitcase down.** After **staring at me** for a while he **said**, 'You look prettier than before.'"

The speaker tells the interviewer ***how*** she first saw her boyfriend at her new place after several years of separation from him. We may summarize the procedure into nine steps based on the action involved as diagrammed below. These steps are also numerically marked in the passage.

找到我	*zhǎodào wǒ*	"(he) found me"
进门	*jìn mén*	"(he) enter (my apartment)"
说	*shuō*	"(I) said"
高兴	*gāoxìng*	"(I) was happy"
离开	*líkāi*	"(landlord) left"
站着	*zhàn zhe*	"(we) were standing"
说	*shuō*	"(I) said"
放下箱子	*fàngxià xiāngzi*	"(he) put down his suitcase"
看	*kàn*	"(he) looked at (me)"
说	*shuō*	"(he) said"

Observant readers may quickly realize that there is a pattern in this narrative passage. That is, the ten steps proceed in sequence: "find" => "enter" => "say" => "be happy" => "leave" => "stand" => "say" => "put down" => "look at" => "say". Listeners and readers do not need to worry about when the ten actions happen, but simply follow the train of actions to understand the sequence and whole process of how the speaker reunites with her boyfriend. English demonstrates a similar pattern in narrative passage (see Linde 1993, Berger 1997, and Smith 2003), which is good news for native English speaking students of Chinese. However, English has an aspect and tense system expressing the time when actions occur (e.g. past tense, present progressive tense etc.) that Chinese lacks. We see that of the ten actions in (7.42) only the first sentence is marked by a time expression indicating the meaning of "when he found me, I was doing …" and the remaining sentences all use bare verb phrases without any indication of when the actions happen. This is not acceptable in languages with a tense system. What makes the Chinese passage more interesting, though, is that listeners and readers do not seem to have any problem understanding the Chinese passage in (7.42) and the sequential actions. It appears that once the time of the first action is established at the beginning of the discourse, there is no need to mention time for the subsequent actions anymore. This suggests that sequence is built into narrative discourse in Chinese. In other words, unless clearly specified in discourse, narrative structures are arranged in temporal sequence and understood by Chinese speakers. This general rule is naturally acquired by native speakers. For nonnative speakers whose native language has a tense system, however, the rule has to be learned in the language classroom.

Linde (1993) convincingly argues that narrative order (i.e. sequence) is the basis for the two major coherence principles of life stories: causality and continuity. We have seen in the previous paragraph that narrative order is definitely the basis for continuity in Chinese discourse. Even though causality is not as typical as continuity in Chinese narrative, it is still seen, as illustrated in (7.43).

(7.43)   *Open Country* by Cáo Yǔ, pp. 28–29

你记着，大星头一天不在家，今天晚上，门户要特别小心。**(1)今天进了贼，**
(2)掉了东西，(3)我就拿针戳烂你的眼，叫你跟我一样的瞎，听见了没有？

nǐ jìzhe, Dàxīngtóu yìtiān bú zài jiā, jīntiān wǎnshàng, ménhù yào tèbié xiǎoxīn.
(1)jīntiān jìn le zéi, (2)diào le dōngxi, (3)wǒ jiù ná zhēn cuōlàn nǐ de yǎn, jiào nǐ
gēn wǒ yíyàng de xiā, tīngjiàn le méiyǒu?

"Remember, the Star Head [nickname] is out for the day. Be vigilant tonight. *(1)*
(If) a **thief breaks in and** *(2)***robs the house,** *(3)***I will poke your eyes with a needle**
and make you blind just like me. Do you hear me?"

In this narrative passage, three clauses are highlighted. The first two present the cause of the action expressed in the third clause. That is, the reason "I will poke your eyes with a needle is if you let thief break in and steal things from the house". To mark the causality in narrative, Chinese often use the adverb 就 (*jiù*) or 才 (*cái*) in the result clause, which is roughly translated into English "(if) ..., then". This seems to suggest that since Chinese does not have a tense system marking the time when actions occur, a logical order of actions based on their sequence and cause-result becomes the key in shaping the structure of discourse. In other words, discourse structure, particularly narrative structure, coincides with the chronology of actual events/situations perceived by speakers/writers and listeners/readers.

Thus, when acquiring the narrative mode in Chinese, students should pay attention to the following generalizations:

- Narrative passages are ordered by temporal sequence;
- Temporal sequence is not marked by tense, but is built in to the discourse structure;
- Narrative passage can be cause-result and the result may be marked by 就 (*jiù*);

7.3.3 Description

Description is used to describe a thing, person, an event or a situation. If narrative is a story, then description may be considered a picture showing what a person or a place looks like. What makes description even more useful is that it can be inserted into a story, a journal, a report or a dialogue to make them sound more interesting and informative. It appears that Chinese has a lot in common with descriptive discourse in other languages, such as English. Consider the following descriptive passages:

(7.44) *Beijinger* by Cáo Yǔ, p. 51

他身材不高，宽前额，丰满的鼻翼，一副宽大的厚嘴唇，唇上微微有些黑髭，很漂亮的。他眼神有些浮动，和他的举止说话一样。"

tā shēncái bù gāo, kuān qián'é, fēngmǎn de bíyì, yífù kuāndà de hòu cuīchún, chún shàng wēiwēi yǒu xiē hēi zī, hěn piàoliang de. tā yǎnshéng yǒu xiē fúdòng, hé tā de jǔzhǐ shuōhuà yiyàng.

"He is not tall. He has a wide forehead, a full-grown nose, and a pair of thick lips with some light hair over them, very pretty. His eyes are lively, just like his words and deeds."

(7.45) *Beijinger* by Cáo Yǔ, p. 5

这间小花亭是上房大客厅和前后院朝东的厢房交聚的地方，屋内一共有四个出入的门路。屋左一门通大奶奶的卧室，前门悬挂一张精细无比的翠绿纱帘，屋后一门通入姑奶奶的睡房，门前没有挂着什么，门框较小，也比较脏，似乎里面的物资也不甚讲究。

zhèi jiān xiǎo huātíng shì shàngfáng dà kètīng hé qiánhòu yuàn cháo dōng de xiāngfáng jiāojù de dìfang, wūnèi yígòng yǒu sìge chūrù de ménlù. wū zuǒ yì mén tōng dà nǎinai de wòshì, qiánmén xuánguà yì zhāng jīngxì wúbǐ de cuìlǜ shā diào, wū hòu yì mén tōng rù gūnǎinai de shuìfáng, mén qián méiyǒu guàzhe shénme, ménkuàng jiǎoxiǎo, yě bǐjiào zāng, sìhū lǐmiàn de wùzī yě búshèn jiǎngjiu.

"This small flower pavilion sits in between the main guest hall and bedrooms of both the front and back yards facing the east. There are four exit/entrance doors altogether. The door on the left leads to the first lady's bedroom. There is a delicate unique green curtain hanging on the door. The door on the back leads to the aunt's bedroom. There is nothing hanging in front of the door. The door's frame is relatively small and dirty which seems to suggest that things inside are not tasteful either."

The passage in (7.44) portrays a handsome person and the one in (7.45) describes a family compound. Unlike narrative discourse, descriptive passages are built with static spatial advancement (cf. Smith 2003). In other words, descriptive discourse is not ordered in sequence, but rather arranged via spatial orientation. From the two passages in (7.44)–(7.45), it is also evident that descriptive discourse correlates to two Chinese constructions: (1) [place + stative verb (*zhe* 着)] and (2) [subject + predicate (*yǒu* 有 "exist")]. Since both constructions are primarily used to indicate the stativeness of the topic (i.e. place or object) described in the discourse (cf. Li and Thompson 1981), it is only natural that they repeatedly appear in the two descriptive passages given above. Thus, we see two characteristics of descriptive mode: the spatial orientation and the correlation with stative constructions.

These two features of descriptive mode, I believe, can be effectively used in classroom teaching. Students of Chinese may learn the cognitive characteristic — the spatial orientation — of descriptive mode faster and more easily because it exists in all languages. Students may use their native intuition to learn how to use descriptive mode in Chinese discourse. The syntactic characteristic of descriptive mode, on the other hand, appears to be Chinese-specific because other languages use different syntactic constructions to describe a place, a person, an object, etc. Therefore, students have to learn the two constructions. As a matter of fact, the two constructions are rather simple from a pedagogical viewpoint so that they can be easily acquired at lower levels of Chinese learning. The challenge that students may encounter is linking a number of the stative constructions together to form a coherent discourse. Notice that the description in (7.44) begins the passage with the person's overall height, then moves to forehead, nose, mouth, lips and finally focuses on the eyes at the end of the passage. Clearly, the writer/speaker did not arrange the discourse randomly, but rather constructed it from top (i.e. "forehead") to bottom (i.e. "lips"), from general (i.e. "height") to specific (e.g. "forehead", "nose", "lips"), from less significant to more significant feature (i.e. "eyes"). Furthermore, the writer/speaker diversifies the discourse with different discourse devices. Ellipsis happens in several clauses and word order variation is employed for emphasis (i.e. the first clause uses "subject + predicate" construction, but second clause does not employ the same construction in order to emphasize the "wide forehead".) These strategies are hard to learn at once, they have to be acquired one by one in a systematic way.

Another challenge that students may encounter in learning the descriptive mode is the use of descriptive words and phrases. Sometimes students find it difficult to identify the appropriate word to describe one's face, eyes, nose or lips in Chinese either because they have a limited vocabulary or because they have a limited knowledge of the Chinese aesthetic.[8] Unfortunately, there is no quick fix for this. Students have to gradually acquire and build up those two types of knowledge to achieve advanced Chinese competence.

7.3.4   Notation

The notation mode provides explanation and information for readers and listeners to help them understand the subject matter discussed in discourse. We may describe notation as an almanac and without it, language would lose at least half of its power of communication. We use this mode every time we introduce a new term or concept throughout this book; parents and teachers use it all the time in educating their children and students; and partners, friends, and co-workers cannot communicate well without it. This is why the notation mode may occur in different genres and styles of discourse. Consider the following example:

(7.46) *Love Stories* by Ān Dùn, pp. 169–70
我们俩结婚的时候，真是一贫如洗，什么也没有。我在洮南，我姐姐给我寄来两个花被面，我自己做了两条被子，他带来了辽宁产的苹果。结婚不能再穿打补丁的衣服了，他就穿一身学生装。… 其实那也不叫结婚，就是大家见个面认识一下，领导给了一间小平房，我们住进去就完了。

wǒmen liǎng jiéhūn de shíhòu, zhēn shì yìpínrúxǐ, shénme yě méiyǒu. wǒ zài Táonán, wǒ jiějie gěi wǒ jì lái liǎng ge huā bèimiàn, wǒ zìjǐ zuò le liǎngtiáo bèizi, tā dàilái le Liáoníng chǎn de píngguǒ. jiéhūn bù néng zài chuān dǎ bǔdìng de yīfu le, tā jiù chuān yìshēn xuésheng zhuāng. … qíshí nà yě bú jiào jiéhūn, jiùshì dàjiā jiàn ge miàn rènshi yíxià, lǐngdǎo gěi le yìjiān xiǎo píngfáng, wǒmen zhù jìnqu jiù wán le.

"When we got married, we were penniless and had nothing. I was at Táonán. My sister sent me two floral comforter covers and I made two comforters. He came from Liáoníng and brought some apples. Since we could not wear our patched clothes at the wedding, he wore a student uniform … Actually, that was not a wedding. We just introduced everyone and moved into a one-room apartment that the manager at work assigned to us. That's it."

The first sentence in (7.46) introduces a concept "we were penniless and had nothing" and the remaining discourse explains this concept. This is the typical structure for the notation mode. Towards the end of the passage in (7.46), the writer/speaker introduces another concept "actually, that was not a wedding" and proceeds to explain why (i.e. "we just introduced everyone and moved into an apartment"). We see that the discourse structure of notation mode is rather straightforward, similar to the sentence structure of the topic comment construction: topic + comment. The only difference between the two is that the topic and comment in the notation passage are both expressed by one or several sentences, whereas those in the topic comment constructions are expressed by one or more phrases.

Compared with the narrative mode and the descriptive mode, the notation mode does not strictly proceed in sequence, nor does it employ spatial orientation. It may mix some narrative sentences and stative ones while applying different discourse devices (e.g. foreground and background), as illustrated in (7.47).

(7.47) *Beijinger* by Cáo Yǔ, p. 91
我这兄弟最讲究喝茶。他喝起茶来要洗手，漱口，焚香，静坐。他的舌头不但尝得出这茶叶的性情，年龄，出生，做法，他还分得出这杯茶用的是山水，江水，井水，雪水还是自来水，烧的是炭火，煤火，或者柴火。

wǒ zhèi xiōngdì zuì jiǎngjiu hē chá. tā hēqǐ chá lái yào xǐshǒu, sùkǒu, fénxiāng, jìngzuò. tā de shétou búdàn chángdechū zhèi cháyè de xìngqíng, niánlíng, chūshēng, zuòfǎ, tā hái fēndechū zhèi bēi chá yòng de shì shānshuǐ, jiāngshuǐ, jǐngshui, xuěshuǐ háishì zìláishuǐ, shāode shì tànhuǒ, méihuǒ, huòzhe cháihuǒ.

"This brother is very fastidious about drinking tea. When he drinks tea, he has to wash hands, brush teeth, burn incense and meditate. His tongue is so sensitive that it can not only tell tea's characteristics, age, production location and processing method, but also the type of water used in making it: mountain water, ocean water, well water, snow water or pipe water, as well as how the water is boiled whether on a coal fire or a wood fire."

Notice that the topic in (7.47) is "this brother is very fastidious about drinking tea" and the remaining discourse comments on the topic. Among the comments, there are narrative lines, such as "wash hands, brush teeth, burn incense, and meditate" and there are descriptive lines as well, such as "his tongue is so sensitive that it can distinguish not only ...". This mixed feature of the notation mode may not stand out at first sight, however, since its structure is so straightforward and its function is so convenient, students will soon realize that this mode is probably the most useful mode in any given discourse.

When learning the notation mode, students may first engage in how to introduce a topic using the strategies discussed in 7.3.1 and then work on comments using the discourse devices introduced in 7.2 for discourse coherence. They may also borrow some lines from other discourse modes for a certain type of discourse. A successful control of these two parts should lead to an effective use of the notation mode in communication.

7.3.5 Argument

Smith (2003: 33) points out that an argument passage brings something to the attention of the reader/listener, makes a claim, comment, or argument and supports it in some way. In daily communication, we hear argument at home, work, shopping and almost everywhere we go, and read it in letters, essays, proposals, journal articles, etc.

(7.48)   *Love Stories* by Ān Dùn, p. 166

我说"不就是关节炎吗？我愿意伺候她。不就是一个药罐子吗？我愿意替她背着。我一个人，什么都能承受，这么多年了，家里穷，外面乱，我不是也还好好的吗？更何况结婚以后我们就是两个人了，没有什么困难是我们应付不了的。"我反反复复就是这么几句话，把老人说急了，他们就说"你们将来别后悔！"我说"你们放心，我不后悔！"

wǒ shuō "bú jiùshì guānjiéyán ma? wǒ yuànyì cìhou tā. bú jiùshì yíge yào guànzi ma? wǒ yuànyì tì tā bēizhe. wǒ yíge rén, shénme dōu néng chéngshòu, zhèime duō nián le, jiālǐ qióng, wàimian luàn, wǒ búshì yě hái hǎohǎode ma?

gèng hékuàng jiéhūn yǐhòu wǒmen jiùshì liǎngge rén le, méiyǒu shénme kùnnan

shì wǒmen yìngfu bù liǎo de." wǒ fānfǎnfúfú jiùshì zhèime jǐjù huà. bǎ lǎorén
shuō jí le, tāmen jiù shuō "nǐmen jiānglái bié hòuhuǐ!" wǒ shuō "nǐmen fàngxīn,
wǒ bú hòuhuǐ!"

"I said 'It isn't because of arthritis, is it? I am willing to wait on her. It isn't
because (she) take a lot of medicine, is it? I am willing to accept that. I can
handle everything by myself. In the past several years, we've experienced
poverty at home and chaos outside the home, but aren't we all fine? Not to
mention that after we got married, we were two people. We can overcome any
difficulties.' I repeatedly said these words. When I really got on the elders'
nerves, they would say 'Don't regret things later.' I would say 'Don't worry, I
won't.' "

The argument in (7.48) is made by the speaker to defend his decision to
marry a girl who has a poor health. The argument consists of several facts (e.g.,
"She is sick; I can take care of her", "We are poor; but I am fine with that")
expressed by rhetorical questions and answers and an implied proposition: "I want
to marry her". This is a simple argument structure: facts + proposition, in which
facts are invoked through questions + answers. Argument may also be used in
negotiation or persuasion, as illustrated in (7.49)–(7.50).

(7.49)   A conversation at a morning market in Beijing
        甲： 黄瓜怎么卖？
        A: *Huángguā zěnme mài?* "How much is the cucumber?"
        乙： 一块五。
        B: *yí kuài wǔ.* "A dollar fifty"
        甲： 太贵了，便宜点儿卖了。
        A: *tài guì le, piányi diǎnr mài le.* "(It's) too expensive. (I'll) buy if cheaper."
        乙： 要多少？
        B: *yào duōshǎo?* "How much (do you) want?"
        甲： 两、三斤。
        A: *liǎng-sān jīn.* "Two to three Jin (approximately equal to 1.1 pound)."
        乙： 买五斤，要你五块，反正该收摊儿了。
        B: *mǎi wǔ jīn, yào nǐ wǔ kuài, fǎnzhèng gāi shōu tānr le.*
              "Then, you have to buy at least five Jin. Five dollars. I have to close
              anyway."
        甲： 行，来五斤。
        A: *xíng, lái wǔ Jīn.* "Okay, (I'll) buy five Jin."

(7.50) *Beijinger* by Cáo Yǔ, p. 57
        你现在快做母亲了，要成大人了，为什么想不要孩子呢？有了孩子，他就
        会慢慢待你好的。顺着他点儿，他还是个小孩子呢。
        nǐ xiànzài kuài zuò mǔqin le, yào chéng dàrén le, wèishénme xiǎng bú yào háizi
        ne? yǒule háizi, tā jiù huì mànmàn dài nǐ hǎo de. shùnzhe tā diǎnr, tā háishì ge
        xiǎo háizi ne.

"Now you are about to become a mother and grow up. Why don't you want a child? When you have a baby, he will gradually treat you well. Do what he wants you to do. He is still a youngster."

The conversation in (7.49) shows that both speakers hold their own subjective goals in mind (i.e., Speaker A aims to buy the cucumber one dollar per *Jin*; whereas Speaker B only sells the cucumber for one dollar per *Jin* if the buyer buys at least five *Jin*s.) and both attempt to achieve their goals with their arguments and facts (i.e. "It's too expensive." and "It's time I should close."). The passage in (7.50), on the other hand, shows that only the speaker has her subjective agenda, "Why don't you want a child" meaning "You should have a child", and the listener does not have the same mind set as the speaker. To support her proposition, the speaker also provides supporting facts (i.e. "you have grown up" and "he will treat you well") hoping that the listener will be convinced to have the baby.

Notice that several cognitive components are involved in the argument mode: facts, proposition, and the subjective goal of the speaker and listener. Evidently, these components are the basis of argument passages. Without facts, it would be difficult to convince listeners/readers; and without a proposition or a subjective goal, there would be no argument. Examine the examples in (7.48)–(7.50), it is also noticeable that some of the facts presented in the arguments are invoked through rhetorical questions and answers. Whether this kind of structure has a strong correlation with the argument mode is yet to be proved. However, my text analysis seems to suggest that "question + answer/fact + proposition" is the format of the discourse structure for the argument mode in Chinese, which is also supported by studies of argumentative texts in Western languages (e.g. Connor and Kaplan 1987, Toulmin 1958). That is to say that for the argument mode, one has to have a question, problem, or issue in mind, and then provide the answer/solution to the question/problem or facts to explain the issue. Through the process of question and answer, problem and solution, or issue and fact, a proposition demonstrating the speaker's subjective goal should emerge. Furthermore, the speaker's subjective proposition can be presented at the beginning, the middle, or the end of the argument mode, and it can be either verbally expressed as in (7.50) or nonverbally as the one in (7.48).

The examples in (7.48)–(7.50) also demonstrate a logical relationship between fact and proposition: cause => result. It is interesting, though, that either a proposition or fact can function as cause or result. In (7.48) the proposition, i.e. I want to marry her, is the cause of the fact "we can overcome any difficulties" whereas in (7.50) the proposition, "you should have a child" is the result of the fact "you have grown up".

Compared with other discourse modes discussed so far, the argument mode does not progress throughout the passage in temporal sequence as the narrative mode, nor with spatial advancement as the descriptive mode, but rather it appears to mix narrative and descriptive structure and use the mixed structure for facts and use the general statement for the speaker's subjective proposition. These characteristics of the argument mode, as outlined below, may be used as guidelines for Chinese students in learning the mode.

- Argument passages have to have a proposition;
- Argument passages have to include some facts to support the proposition;
- Facts can be realized as questions and answers or problems and solutions;
- The proposition must be clearly stated or understood through facts;
- The proposition may be located at the beginning, the middle or the end of the passage;
- The proposition and fact have a logical cause-result relation;
- Both the proposition and fact can function as cause or result.

7.3.6 *Concluding passage*

The concluding passage is considered by some the most important section of essays, reports, newspaper articles, proposals, etc. As graduate students, we were told to read only the beginning and concluding paragraphs of research papers for a preliminary screening of references. Although this advice does not apply to all readings in communication, it at least gives us a hint of the consensus on the status of the concluding passage in discourse. Following are three concluding passages from different types of discourse.

(7.51) *Love Stories* by Ān Dùn, p. 108

我们在网上说"我爱你"，每次都说，每次都知道说了也没有实际用处。我觉得这就是我认识的互联网。它也许无所不能，但他永远不是我们需要的那个世界。

wǒmen zài wǎngshàng shuō "wǒ ài nǐ", měi cì dōu shuō, měi cì dōu zhīdào shuō le yě méiyǒu shíjì yòngchu. wǒ juéde zhèi jiùshì wǒ rènshi de hùliánwǎng. tā yěxǔ wúsuǒbùnéng, dàn tā yǒngyuǎn búshì wǒmen xūyào de nàge shìjiè.

"Every time we write an email message, we say 'I love you', even though we all know it doesn't mean anything. I think this is what we understand about the Internet. It can take us everywhere, except to the world we really need."

(7.52) *Collection of Reflections* by Bā Jīn, p. 89

"讲真话，掏出自己的心。"这就是我的座右铭，希望读者根据它来判断我写出的一切，当然也包括所有的佚文。…

"jiǎng zhēnhuà, tāochū zìjǐ de xīn." zhèi jiùshì wǒde zuòyòumíng, xīwàng dúzhě gēnjù tā lái pànduàn wǒ xiě chū de yíqiè, dāngrán yě bāokuò suǒyǒu de yìwén.

"Tell the truth and open my heart" is my motto. I hope readers will use this motto to judge my works, including all my anecdotal notes and essays."

(7.53)   *On Modern Issues* by Féng Yǒulán

… 在这种情况下，夫妻在一块儿共同生活，谁也不是谁的附属品，妇女问题就自然解决了。

… *zài zhèizhǒng qíngkuàng xià, fūqī zài yíkuàir gòngtóng shēnghuó, shuí yě búshì shuíde fùshǔpǐn, fùnǚ wèntí jiù zìrán jiějué le.*

"… In this circumstance, husband and wife live together with equal rights; no one belongs to the other. Only then will women's problems be automatically resolved."

The passage in (7.51) is taken from a summary of an interviewer's note about "Love on the Internet"; the passage in (7.52) is from the postscript of *The Complete Collection of Bā Jīn's Work*; and the passage in (7.53) is the conclusion of an essay on women. Although these three concluding passages do not seem to belong to the same genre, they all share the same discourse structure and function. That is, they use a specific example to draw a general conclusion showing the writer/speaker's point of view on the subject of the writing. We see that the passage in (7.51) uses the situation of Internet users, who often write "I love you" in their email to their lovers but they cannot feel the love, as a way of illustrating that, in reality, people cannot use the Internet to experience the love they long for from their lovers. Similarly, the author in (7.52) quotes the words that he often says as a motto to guide readers' understanding and assessment of his literary works. The passage in (7.73) may be more formal in terms of style because it is the conclusion of an expository essay written by a well-known literary critic, however, its discourse structure appears the same as that of the two passages just discussed. That is, after giving a specific example (i.e. this circumstance), the author uses a general statement to draw the conclusion (i.e. "women's problems will be automatically resolved."), which may be diagrammed as "specific example + general conclusive statement". We may also summarize the discourse structure and discourse function of the three concluding passages as a process of metaphorical extension, using a specific/concrete concept (e.g. situation, motto, saying) to signify an abstract idea or point of view (e.g. the relationship between Internet and love, between truth and literary writing, and between a situation and women's status). However, this does not mean all concluding passages share this structure and function. Consider the following discourse:

(7.54)   *Love Stories* by Ān Dùn, p. 204

忘了告诉你，我马上就要 39 岁了，这月初三是我的生日。我应该是比你大很多吧。我请你吃饭，你有空吗？

wàng le gàosu nǐ, wǒ mǎshàng jiùyào sānshíjiǔ suì le, zhèi yuè chūsān shì wǒde shēngrì. wǒ yīnggāi shì bǐ nǐ dà hěnduō ba. wǒ qǐng nǐ chīfàn, nǐ yǒu kòng ma?

祝福新年。

zhùfú xīnnián.

"I forgot to tell you that I will be 39 soon. January 3 is my birthday. I must be much older than you. I will treat you to dinner. Do you have free time?"

"Best wishes for a happy new year."

(7.55) *A Vegetable Garden* By Shěn Cóngwén, p. 122
玉家菜园改称玉家花园是主人儿子死去三年的事儿。这妇人沉默寂寞的活了三年，到儿子生日那一天，天落大雪，想这样活下去日子已够了，春天同秋天不用再来了，把一点家产全分派给几个工人，忽然用一根丝绦套在颈子上，便溢死了。

Yùjiā Càiyuán gǎichéng Yùjiā Huāyuán shì zhǔrén érzi sǐqù sānnián de shìr. zhèi fūrén chénmò jìmò de huóle sānnián, dào érzi shēngrì nà yìtiān, tiān luò dàxuě, xiǎng zhèiyàng huó xiàqu rizi yi gòule, chūntiān tóng qiūtiān bú yòng zài lái le, bǎ yìdiǎn jiāchǎn quán fēnpàigěi jǐge gōngrén, tūrán yòng yìgēn sītāo tào zài bózi shàng, biàn yìsǐ le.

"Yu's family vegetable garden became a flower garden when her son had been dead for three years. This woman lived quietly by herself for 3 years. Then on her son's birthday, the snow was falling heavily. She did not want to live like that anymore, nor did she feel the need to wait for the spring and fall's coming. She divided her limited properties, gave them to several of her workers, and then suddenly hanged herself with a silk ribbon. She died."

The passage in (7.54) comes from a letter written to an interviewer with whom the writer was eager to share her story. The passage in (7.55) is the ending of a short story entitled "A Vegetable Garden". Evidently, the two endings use quite different discourse structures and devices: the letter ends with an inviting question to the addressee, whereas the story ends with a description of how the leading character died, which led to the end of her vegetable garden. Furthermore, the letter appears to employ the spoken style of discourse (e.g. omission of subject, use of spoken discourse markers such as 吧 (*ba*), and colloquial words such as 马上 *mǎshàng* "soon" and an interrogative sentence); whereas the story uses the written style (e.g. complicated descriptive words). Both endings may be thought-provoking to readers, yet the letter may invoke a simple process of thinking, namely, whether the reader should accept the dinner invitation while, the ending of the story may lead to much deeper and more abstract thought process about life and death and the symbolic meaning of a garden. Another similarity between the two ending passages is that both contain the most important or most powerful message that the writers intend to pass to readers. This is probably because if the information is not given in the concluding passage, readers may not have time to think about or may not pay sufficient attention to the issues raised in the passage. Whatever the reason, it is safe to say that the concluding passages do not have a uniform discourse structure, but they do seem to share the same discourse function; they all serve to provide readers with the most important information relevant to the topic. This information may reflect the writer's subjective point of view or the purpose of the writing. Also information given in concluding passages often has a greater impact and longer standing effect upon the reader since it is the last thing s/he reads.

These results should help students learn how to produce concluding passages. With the knowledge that discourse structures and styles may vary while the discourse function stays the same in concluding passages, students may focus on the process of identifying appropriate discourse structures and style in their acquisition of concluding remarks. It is well known that English writers try every way to find the perfect punch line for the ending of their writing. The Chinese writings discussed above seem to demonstrate the same trend.

So far, six discourse modes have been discussed: opening passage, narrative, description, notation, argument, and concluding passage. The opening and concluding modes differ from the remaining four modes categorically. We have seen that the opening and concluding modes do not limit their use to certain discourse structures or genres but have their own unique discourse function. The remaining modes, in comparison, all seem to correlate with certain discourse structures. The narrative mode tends to describe an event or a situation in temporal sequence; the descriptive mode tends to depict a stative situation with stative constructions such as "place + verb 着 *zhe*/有 *yǒu*"; the notation mode often gives a topic and then comments on it just like an extended "topic + comment" structure; and the argument mode always consists of two components: facts and proposition. These two components are not linear in order; either may occur first depending upon the writer/speakers' own preference.

In acquisition of discourse modes, I suggest that teachers first introduce their discourse functions and discourse structures discussed in this section, and then ask students to use specific discourse patterns and structures to construct a particular mode. Students may start with one mode in their writing first and then gradually add more modes into their compositions.

7.4   Discourse Style

Although the term "style" may be used to refer to a wide scope of linguistic concepts and is often vaguely defined, I choose the term "discourse style" to specifically refer to two discourse types: oral and written discourse. Chinese may use *yǔtǐ* (语体, "genre") to convey the meaning of style and *kǒuyǔ yǔtǐ* (口语语体) for oral/spoken discourse and *shūxiě tǐ* (书写体) or *shūmiàn yǔtǐ* (书面语体) for written discourse. These two discourse styles may not be clearly identifiable in many discourses, yet there are sufficient differences between the two that they merit a discussion of their own in this book.

7.4.1   Spoken discourse

Spoken discourse competence may be equivalent to Chinese 说话能力 (*shuōhuà nénglì,* "speakability"). I use spoken discourse interchangeably with oral discourse. Chinese people often use the term 会说话 (*huì shuōhuà*) to describe those who possess the ability of using language skillfully in oral communication to achieve his/her communicative goals. Interestingly, this ability is not necessarily measured by a speaker's educational background, but rather by a speaker's discourse and pragmatic knowledge, namely, knowing how and what to say and when and to whom to say it. In this section, I will focus on one component of speakability (oral discourse knowledge), leaving the other component (pragmatic knowledge) for discussion in Section 7.5.

Oral discourse may be roughly divided into two different types: (1) conversation or dialogue between two or more speakers, (2) interviews, debates, and business negotiation between two or more parties. Although both types share the key features of oral discourse — involving both speakers and listeners — conversation has been considered the most basic form of language use and requires the least linguistic skill in communication (cf. Svennevig 1999, Lerner 1989, Garvey and Berninger 1981, Goodwin 1981, Jefferson 1973), for which reason, our discussion will focus only on conversation.

One question often raised among Chinese language teachers is the authenticity of textbook dialogues. Are they good conversational materials for students to learn and imitate? Some teachers (e.g. Tao 2004, 2005) suggest that students must be exposed to and use real-time spontaneous conversation to develop their oral language competence. However, most others seem to be concerned about the idea of using real-time conversation as teaching materials because of the constant use of discourse particles (e.g *ba* 吗, *me* 么, *ne* 呢, etc.) and repetition in real-time natural conversation. I share this concern and suggest that teachers spend their limited classroom time on constructed conversations, such as those provided in textbooks, and at the same time provide students with opportunities to listen, observe, and practice real-time conversations outside classroom. This is because constructed dialogues provide students with crucial linguistic knowledge about oral discourse, while real-time conversations present reinforcement for oral discourse coherence.

When working on either constructed conversation or real-time conversation, teachers and students may focus on some of the most important strategies frequently employed in constructing conversations.

- Initiation (of a conversation)
- Repetition
- Alternation (Taking turns)
- Interjection (Sentential particles)
- Conclusion (End of conversation)

These five modes of conversation are also the most frequently discussed topics in the study of oral discourse. To help students develop their oral discourse competence, I will briefly discuss the discourse function of each of those five modes, and then suggest some enhancing and reinforcement exercises for students to practice.

Initiation of a conversation can be seen in a variety of forms: starting a phone conversation as in (7.56), a casual conversation with a good friend on street or at lunch as in (7.57), a conversation with a teacher or co-worker as in (7.58), or a formal conversation with a respected scholar as in (7.59).

(7.56)　甲：喂，王鹏在吗？

　　　　　wéi, Wáng Péng zài ma?

　　　　A:　"Hello, is Wang Peng in?"

　　　　乙：我就是，您那位？

　　　　　wǒ jiùshì, nín nǎ wèi?

　　　　B:　"I am Wang Peng. May I ask who this is?"

(7.57)　甲：嘿，肖云，你怎么在这儿？

　　　　　hei, Xiāo Yún, nǐ zěnme zài zhèir?

　　　　A:　"Heh, Xiao Yun, how come you are here?"

　　　　乙：今天没事儿，所以跑出来逛逛。

　　　　　Jīntiān méi shìr, suǒyǐ pǎo chūlái guàngguang.

　　　　B:　"I am free today, so I am just wandering around."

(7.58)　甲：老师，您现在有空吗？我想问一个问题。

　　　　　lǎoshī, nín xiànzài yǒu kòng ma? wǒ xiǎng wèn yíge wèntí.

　　　　A:　"Teacher, are you free now? I want to ask you a question."

　　　　乙：现在不行，我得去开会，不过下午你可以到我的办公室来。

　　　　　xiànzài bù xíng, wǒ děi qù kāihuì, búguò xiàwǔ nǐ kěyǐ dào wǒ de bàngōngshì lái.

　　　　B:　"Not now, I have to go to a meeting, but you may come to my office   this afternoon."

(7.59)　甲：王老，久仰久仰，拜读过您的很多文章，很荣幸今天有机会见到您。

　　　　　Wánglǎo, jiǔyǎng jiǔyǎng, bàidú guò nín de hěnduō wénzhāng, hěn róngxìng jīntiān yǒu jīhuì jiàndào nín.

　　　　A:　"Elder Wang, I have heard a lot about you. I have also read many of your articles. It's an honor to have the opportunity to meet you today."

　　　　乙：你是 …

　　　　　nǐ shì …

　　　　B:　"You are …"

How to start a conversation seems primarily dependent on three major facts: Who are the speaker and the listener? What is the relationship between the speaker and the listener? And what is the situation under which the conversation occurs? The beginning of the phone conversation in (7.56) evidently uses different discourse strategies from the other three beginnings (7.57)–(7.59) in that the speaker and the listener of the phone conversation cannot see each other so that they have to identify themselves first before carrying on the conversation further. The conversations in (7.57)–(7.59), on the other hand, all begin by using the position where the speaker stands (e.g. see someone on street, see teacher after class or at the teacher's office) to lead to further conversation. The difference among them is that the speaker chooses different discourse markers and expressions to start the conversation with different addressees (e.g. friend, teacher, well-known scholar), so that each conversation is conducted appropriately from pragmatic, cultural and sociolinguistic points of view. Unlike English, Chinese normally do not greet teachers by 嘿 (*hèy* "hello"), nor should they use such an informal expression as 你怎么在这儿？(*nǐ zěnme zài zhèir?* "How come you are here?") in a formal discourse setting. In most cases, the degree of formality in Chinese is measured by the choice of expressions (e.g.你 *nǐ* vs. 您 *nín* "you", 久仰 *jiǔyǎng* "heard a lot about you" vs. 好久不见 *hǎojiǔ bújiàn* "long time no see") and sometimes the choice of discourse structures (e.g. short sentences vs. long sentences). Using these criteria, we may say that the degree of formality increases from the example in (7.57) to that in (7.59).

Thus, when teaching students the strategies of starting a conversation, we may lay out the following procedures:

- Identify the speaker/listener;
- Identify the situation under which the conversation occurs;
- Choose appropriate expressions based on the identity of the speaker/listener and on the speaker/listener's own point of view;
- Choose adequate discourse structures

If students can accurately identify the person involved in the conversation and choose appropriate linguistic tools accordingly to initiate a conversation, they are capable of starting a conversation successfully and ready to move on to another phase of conversation. For some students, it is easy to identify the person to whom the speaker is talking, however, it is hard for them to find or remember various ways to initiate a conversation. In this case, teachers may familiarize students with different situationally constructed dialogues such as those in (7.58)–(7.61) in the classroom and encourage them to practice with native Chinese outside the classroom.

Repetition is a typical characteristic of oral discourse. This is why many researchers investigate its form and function. Tannen (1989: 47–52) who discusses repetition in much of her research endeavor (e.g. Tannen 1982, 1984, 1986, 1987, 1989, 1993) claims that repetition serves four functions: It enables a speaker to produce language in a more efficient, less energy-draining way, facilitates a listener's comprehension, evinces a speaker's attitude, and gives a speaker the opportunity to manage discourse (e.g. showing listenership, providing back-channel response, gearing up to answer or speak). When discussing repetition in Chinese, Chen (1984: 170–84) also lists four functions: (1) preparing a speaker to speak, (2) reiterating what has been said to confirm listeners' comprehension, (3) emphasizing, and (4) expressing a speaker's attitude. Comparing Tannen's assessment with Chen's, we see they overlap substantially with the only difference being that Tannen's assessment is more detailed and possibly somewhat more inclusive. Nonetheless, these studies provide us with guidelines for the function of repetition in teaching and learning oral discourse. In other words, we may teach students repetition in Chinese conversation by demonstrating the major functions discussed by both Tannen and Chen with examples and simple explanations, as follows:

- Give a speaker some time to think of what to say next by repeating words such as:
  这个、这个 *zhège* "this" or "so"
  嗯、嗯 *en*
- Confirm a listener's comprehension by repeating *duì* or *shì*
  对对对 *duì* "correct" or "right"
  是、是、是 *shì* "indeed" or "that's right"
- Emphasize the focused concept;
  e.g. 滚，滚，滚！*gǔn* "go away!"
- Express a speaker's attitude
  e.g. 别拉着，讨厌，别拉着我！
  bié lā zhe, tǎoyàn, bié lāozhe wǒ
  "Don't interfere. Disgusting. Don't interfere with my business."

The most common ways for Beijingers to prepare a speaker to speak or give a speaker some time to think what to say next is to repeat the expression *zhège* or *en* and the most frequently heard expression when confirming a listener's understanding of what a speaker says is to repeat *duì* or *shì*. When emphasizing a certain concept or idea in conversation, a speaker can simply repeat the word that expresses the concept or idea. Since it often takes more than one word to express one's attitude, a speaker may repeat a phrase or sentence which clearly expresses his/her attitude. Once these four functions of repetition are explained and demonstrated in the classroom and practiced outside the classroom, students should not have difficulty using repetition in natural conversation. Another advantage for students in learning repetition is that repetition is a feature of all languages. Even though the means or the lexical elements used to express repetition vary, its functions seem to be the same or similar across languages.

Alternation (*Taking turns*) is another unique property of conversational discourse. Sack et al. (1974) is probably the most cited work regarding turn-taking in conversation. According to them, turn-taking must account for, among other facts, the following: (1) the occurrence and recurrence of speaker change, (2) the overwhelming tendency for only one party to talk at a time, (3) the comparative absence of gaps and overlaps, and (4) the variability of turn size, turn order, turn distribution, turn content, and number of participants. Although a number of researchers (e.g. Power 1986, O'Connell et al. 1990) have challenged the model created by Sacks et al., many more either use Sack et al.'s model as a guideline for further study or modify the model so that it becomes more comprehensive (e.g. Garvey and Berninger 1981, Duncan and Fiske 1985, Ford and Thompson 1996).

Many of the research activities on turn-taking have been carried out in the Western hemisphere, but a few researchers (Biq 1990; Tao 1996; Du-Babcock 1996, 1997; Li et al. 2001) have ventured to initiate similar investigations into Chinese conversational discourse. Based on these studies and my own investigation of turn-taking in Chinese conversation, I find that for pedagogical purpose, it is useful to categorize turn-taking into two types: (1) turn-taking in formal conversation, and (2) turn-taking in casual conversation. By formal conversation, we refer to spoken discourse most likely occurring at a formal setting such as business meetings with people of little familiarity or with someone of a higher social status, as demonstrated in (7.60). Informal conversation, however, is most likely to occur among friends, family members, or co-workers at the same professional level, as shown in (7.61).

(7.60)   *Da Zhai Men* by Guo, pp. 884–5

郑：　七老爷！

Zhèng: qī lǎoyé! "Master VII!"

白：　吃饭了吗？

Bái: chī fàn le ma? "Have you eaten?"

郑：　吃了。

Zhèng: chī le. "(I) have."

白：　还能吃吗？

Bái: hái néng chī ma? "Can (you) eat more?"

郑：　能！

Zhèng: néng! "(I) can."

白：　过来，把这桌子菜都给我吃喽！（郑伸了伸筷子又缩了回来。）

Bái: guòlái, bǎ zhèi zhuōzi cài dōu gěi wǒ chī lou! (Zhèng shēn le shēn kuàizi yòu suō le huílái.)

"Come here. Eat all the food on this table for me ! (Zheng was about to eat with chopsticks, then stopped.)"

白：　怎么啦？

Bai: zěnme la? "What's the matter?"

郑：　这碗太小。

Zhèng: zhèi wǎn tài xiǎo. "This bowl is too small."

白：　（笑了）给他拿大碗！（刘妈拿过一个盆来）

Bái: (xiào le) gěi tā ná dà wǎn! (Liú mā náguò yíge pén lái)

"(Laughing) Give him a large bowl! (Nanny Liu brings over a washbasin.)"

白：　胡闹，怎么洗碗的盆儿都上来了。

Bai: húnào, zěnme xǐwǎn de pénr dōu shàng lái le.

Nonsense, how could a washbasin be used.

郑：   挺好。这盆合适。

Zhèng: tǐnghǎo. zhèi pén héshì. "Good. This washbasin is just right."

白：   坐下好好吃！

Bái: zuòxià hǎohǎo chī!

"Sit down and eat well!"

郑：   蹲着好！（大口大口地吃着）

Zhèng: dūnzhe hǎo! (dàkǒu dàkǒu de chīzhe)

Squatting is good! (Devouring the food ravenously)

白：   （高兴极了）哈哈—痛快！痛快！你们都看见了吗？啊？这才叫吃饭。

Bái: (gāoxìng jíle) haha – tòngkuai! tòngkuai! nǐmen dōu kànjiàn le ma? a? zhèi cái jiào chīfàn.

"(Extremely happy) haha-Great! Didn't you all see that? This is what eating is supposed to be."

(7.61)   *Da Zhai Men* by Guo, pp. 813–4

金：   你是哪屋的？没见过！

Jīn: nǐ shì nǎ wū de? méi jiànguo!

"Which (family) unit are you from? (I) have not seen you before!"

水：   我是二爷二奶奶屋的，新来的，乌梅姐姐嫁人了。

Shuǐ: wǒ shì èryé èrnǎinai wū de, xīnlái de, Wū-méi jiějie jiàrén le.

"I am from the Master II and Lady II's unit. (I) just came here, (because) sister Wu-mei got married.

金：   嫁人了？嘿 – 七爷还说赏我个丫头，怎么都嫁人了？

Jīn: jiàrén le? hei – qīyé hái shuō shǎng wǒ ge yātou, zěnme dōu jiàrén le?

Married? Master VII said he would award me a servant girl. How come all girls got married?

水：   就你长的这丑八怪样儿，谁跟你呀！

Shuǐ: jiù nǐ zhǎngde zhèi chǒubāguài yàngr, shéi gēn nǐ a!

"You are so ugly, who would marry you!"

金：   反正七爷答应过我，他说话不能不算数。

Jīn: fǎnzhèng qīyé dāyìng guò wǒ, tā shuōhuà bù néng bú suànshù.

"Master VII indeed promised me. He cannot break his promise."

水：   真的？

Shuǐ: zhēnde? "Really?"

金：   可不真的！

Jīn: kě bu zhēnde! "Of course!"

水：   哎呀，可别把我给你，吓死我！

Shuǐ: aiya, kě bié bǎ wǒ gěi nǐ, xiàsǐ wǒ!

"Oh, my goodness, (I hope he) will not award me to you."

金：   我就跟七爷要你吧，我长得丑可什么都不缺。（说着一把搂着水葱）

Jīn: wǒ jiù gēn qīyé yào nǐ ba, wǒ zhǎngde chǒu kě shénme dòu bù quē.

(shuōzhe yibǎ lǒuzhe Shuǐ-cōng)

"I'll ask Master VII to let me marry you. I am ugly but (I) have all the necessary equipment. (While saying this, he grabbed Shui-cong)

水： 撒手撒手！你缺德不缺德！

Shuĭ: *sāshŏu sāshŏu! nĭ quēdé bù quēdé!* "Stop it, stop it! You are so wicked!

金： 你就跟了我吧啊？

Jīn: *nĭ jiù gēn le wŏ ba a?* "Would you marry me?"

In the dialogue given in (7.60), Bai, the master of a household, clearly dominates the conversation and selects the next speaker (i.e. Zheng, a servant) to speak what he wants to hear. In (7.61), however, the situation is different. Both Jin and Shui have the same social status (i.e. servant in a wealthy household), therefore, both have the same right in taking turns during the conversation. They frankly express their own opinions (e.g. "I'll ask the Master to allow me to marry you.") and even insult each other smoothly (e.g. "You are so ugly; who would marry you?), using strategies such as giving a signal (e.g. "Really？", "Would you marry me?").

It appears that alternation or taking turns is more rigid during a formal conversation: that is, the current speaker must send signals to the speaker s/he selects to speak next, the so-called "current speaker selects next" technique (e.g. Sachs et al. 1974). Without the go-ahead signal, the next speaker should not speak (cf. Du-Babcock, 1996, 1997). Such a speaker-dominated conversation appears directly related to socio-cultural norms of Chinese tradition. The Chinese traditionally teach their children to keep quiet when adults, elders, teachers, etc. talk. Even when children grow up, they have to listen to the elders, teachers, leaders and authorities to show respect regardless of whether what they say is correct or not. Certainly, whether they obey elders is a different story, but at least, they are trained to be quiet in the presence of a speaker with higher authority, rather than interrupt with a linguistic or nonlinguistic signal, such as asking a question, or showing signs of inattention, which are considered some of the characteristics of initiating a turn in conversation in many other languages. When nobody interrupts, asks a question, or sends a signal to stop a speaker, it becomes natural for the speaker to continue talking or select the next speaker, which shapes the characteristic of turn-taking in formal conversation.[9] In comparison, an informal conversation does not involve a participant who acts as an authority figure, so all conversation participants have the equal right to initiate a turn, select a next speaker, or take turns in the conversation. In this case, conversation turns tend to be smoother, natural, and unnoticeable, similar to strategies of turn-taking discussed by discourse analysts in the West (e.g. Sacks et al. 1974, McLaughlin 1984, Furo 2001), which may be summarized as follows:

- A current speaker is willing to yield to the next speaker by giving various signals, such as either a rising or falling intonation, a hand gesture, the direction of head, or an utterance as *nĭ shuō ne* (你说

呢？ "What do you think?"); *jiù nàme huishì* (就那么回事儿 "Well, that's how things go");
- A participant tries to fill pauses;
- A participant volunteers information or opinions.

Since conversation happens between a speaker and listener(s), turn-taking can be initiated by either the current speaker or listener as described above. In fact, these strategies of turn-taking in conversation are valid across languages; only the transitional utterance varies from language to language. Hence, students of Chinese as a foreign language may simply learn those utterances that initiate a turn, pass it to next speaker, and conclude a turn, and apply them the same way as they do in their native language.

Interjections (*Sentential particles)*, such as 吧 (*ba*), 了 (*le*), 么 (*me*), and 呢 (*ne*), are often used in Chinese conversations to express the speaker's point of view or to connect discourse structures, along with discourse markers discussed in 7.2.3.4. Chao (1968), Li and Thompson (1981), and Chu (1998) all discuss sentence final particles and their discourse functions. The only problem is that teachers cannot introduce all the findings reported in those works to students, because some of them are not as important as others for foreign language acquisition. As a result, we have to prioritize the functions of particles and determine which functions of which particles should be included in classroom teaching.

Chu (1998), following Chao (1968) and Li and Thompson (1981), provides a detailed analysis of six types of sentence final particles: *ma* 吗, *ba* 吧, *a* 啊/*ya* 呀, *me* 么, *le* 了, *ne* 呢. We may summarize the three researchers' findings in Table 7.4.

Table 7.4   Discourse functions of sentence final particles (cf. Chu 1998:185, Li and Thompson 1981, Chao 1968)

PARTICLES	DISCOURSE FUNCTIONS
吧 *ba*	Soliciting agreement (i.e. suggestion, modesty, supposition, agreement)
啊/呀 *a/ya*	Reduced forcefulness (i.e. confirmation, command, warning, impatience)
么 *me*	Insistence (i.e. obviousness, assurance, exhortation)
了 *le*	End of discourse
呢 *ne*	Coherence (i.e. response to expectation, turn-taking signal)

Since the final particle *ma* 吗 limits its function to interrogative, a syntactic function, I exclude it from our current discussion. Considering the common use of the remaining five particles in conversation, I suggest that students of Chinese as a foreign language learn them at the lower level of their classes. Notice that most of them have a general discourse function and several specific functions. Teachers may start by introducing the general function first, then provide examples to demonstrate each specific function as in (7.62)–(7.65).

(7.62)   吧 *ba* **used to "solicit agreement"**

     a.   Expressing SUGGESTION

          我们走吧。(Chu 1998: 133)

          *wǒmen zǒu **ba***. "Let's go."

     b.   Expressing SUPPOSITION

          孩子都大了吧。(Chu 1998: 133)

          *háizi dōu dà le **ba*** "The children are all grown up, I guess."

     c.   Expressing AGREEMENT

          好吧，就这么办吧。(Chu 1998: 134)

          *hǎo **ba**, jiù zhème bàn **ba***. "All right, (we'll) do it this way."

(7.63)   啊/呀 *a/ya* **used to "reduce or soften a tone"**

     a.   Expressing CONFIRMATION

          你不去啊？ (Chu 1998: 140)

          *nǐ bú qù **a**!* "You are not going?"

     b.   Expressing COMMAND

          走啊，咱们都走啊! (Chu 1998: 140)

          *zǒu **a**, zámen dōu zǒu **a**!* "Let's go! Let's all go!"

     c.   Expressing WARNING

          你对他要小心点儿啊。(Chu, 1998: 142)

          *nǐ duì tā yào xiǎoxīn diǎnr **a**.* "You've got to be careful with him."

     d.   Expressing IMPATIENCE

          这到底是怎么回事啊?

          *zhè dàodǐ shì zěnme huíshì **a**?*

          "What has really happened?"

(7.64)   么 *(me)* **used to express "insistence"**

     a.   Expressing OBVIOUSNESS

   甲： 他好像从来不需要背的 … (Chu 1998: 177)

          tā hǎoxiàng cónglái bù xūyào bèi de

          "He never seems to need to recite (anything)."

   乙： 不需要么。这是我们的，这个，这个，教育方法么。

          *bù xūyào **me**. zhè shì wǒmen de, zhège, zhège, jiàoyù fāngfǎ **me**.*

          "Of course, there is no need. This is our way of education."

     b.   Expressing ASSURANCE

   甲： 我今天晚上吃得太多，… (Chu 1998: 152)

          wǒ jīntiān wǎnshàng chīde tài duō … "I ate too much tonight …"

   乙： 你要上一号，就好了么。

          *nǐ yào shàng yīhào, jiù hǎo le **me**.*

          "You'd be OK if you went to the bathroom"

     c.   Expressing EXHORTATION

          哎呀，你才喝了那么一点儿酒，怎么会醉呢？再喝一杯么。

          (Chu 1998: 150)

*aiya, nǐ cái hēle nàme yīdiǎnr jiǔ, zěnme huì zuì ne? zài hē yībēi **me**.*

"Well, you've had very little wine, how can you be drunk? (You sure) can have another drink."

(7.65)　呢 (*ne*) used to express "coherence"
　　a.　Expressing RESPONSE TO EXPECTATION
　　　　我还得写一篇论文呢。(Li and Thompson 1981: 303)
　　　　*wǒ hái dě xiě yīpiān lùnwén **ne**.*
　　　　"I still have to write a dissertation
　　b.　Linking DISCOURSE STRUCTURES (INVITING SOMEONE TO TALK)
　　　　你说呢？
　　　　*nǐ shuō **ne**?*
　　　　"What do you think?"

Examples for the discourse function of *le* are not given, because they overlap with those of *le*'s sentential function, namely, change of state or situation, which we have discussed in Chapter 6. I also discourage teachers from introducing all the discourse functions of any given sentence particle at once, to avoid overwhelming students with too much information in one class. Furthermore, my teaching experience suggests that it is not necessary to spend valuable class time teaching students the minor functions of final particles, such as the exclamation function in (7.66). Interested students should be able to learn them on their own outside the classroom.

(7.66)　啊 (*a/ya*) used to express exclamation
　　a.　你还没上床啊？
　　　　*nǐ hái méi shàng chuáng **a**?*
　　　　"Aren't you in bed yet?"
　　b.　喂，先生啊！
　　　　*wèi, xiānsheng **a**!* "Hey, mister!"

Since minor functions are difficult to distinguish even for native speakers, students should not be burdened by the requirement to learn these functions. They should, instead, concentrate on the primary functions listed in Table 7.4. With the development of students' discourse competence, their ability to interpret, distinguish and use sentential final particles should improve accordingly.

The last conversational mode is **conclusion** or how to end a conversation. Similar to European cultures and languages, there are many different ways to lead to the closing of a conversation in Chinese. One may use body language such as looking at his/her watch or just give a general statement summarizing what has been talked about during the conversation. Following are a few traditional techniques used to close a conversation.

(7.67)   **End of a conversation**

    a.   Using time as a signal, such as:

         时间不早了，我该走了。

         shíjiān bùzǎo le, wǒ gāi zǒu le

         "It's late; I have to go."

    b.   Giving a summary statement, such as

         就那么回事吧　。

         jiù nàme huíshì ba

         "Well, that's life."

    c.   Expressing gratitude such as

         谢啦。

         xiè la.

         "Thank you."

    d.   Expressing gratitude for someone who will do you a favor, such as

         拜托(啦)。

         bài tuō (la).

         "(I'm) counting on you."

Notice that all the examples in (7.67) show that the speaker willingly ends the conversation. Presumably, listeners may lead to the end of conversation as well by looking at their watches, or by showing signs of fatigue or boredom. When a speaker understands the sign(s), it is likely that s/he would end the conversation the same way as they do, willingly.

So far, I have discussed five different conversational modes: initiating a conversation, repetition, turn-taking, sentence-final particle, and closing a conversation. Each of these modes has its own unique function in conversation and each contributes to the development of students' oral proficiency. I suggest that students start to learn these modes from the beginning level and gradually progress and master the techniques before they reach the advanced level on the scale of ACTFL guidelines (1986).

7.4.2   Written discourse

Unlike oral/spoken discourse, written discourse has only one and a half participants, the writer — an active participant and his/her projected readers — a half participant (cf. Wang 2003, Ford and Thompson 1996). Therefore, the technique involved in written discourse deals primarily with how the writer writes for various communication purposes. For practical and pedagogical purpose, I chose two types of written discourse to discuss: (1) letters and notes (including email messages), and (2) essays and reports. Letters and notes are less formal than essays and reports, although the former can be formal depending upon the status of the addressee. In what follows, I first describe the characteristics of the two types of written discourse and then give some suggestions for teaching and learning them in the classroom.

Letters and notes are seen everywhere in our daily life. I classify them into the same category of discourse type because they share the same format and similar communicative function, namely informing an addressee of something. There are some differences between them, such as: letters can be formal, whereas notes are generally not considered a formal discourse; letters can be very long, whereas notes are often short. However, these differences seem categorically minor. The salient teaching features for letters and notes might be format, beginning and end of the discourse (cf. Wang 2003).

Letter and note format consists of two parts: envelope format and content format. To write an envelope, the writer has to arrange two components: the addressee's address and name and the sender's address and name. Chinese places the addressee's address on the topic or left side of the envelope and name in the middle and the sender's address and name at the bottom or right side of the envelope. There is a major difference between the Chinese format and the American format in addressing envelopes: the order of writing the address. Chinese arranges address locations from big place to small place as illustrated in (7.68), whereas English reverses the order.

(7.68)

中国、　　北京市、　北京大学、中文系
Zhōngguó, Běijīngshì, Běijīng dàxué, zhōngwénxì
"China, City of Beijing, Beijing University, Chinese Department"

王怡文　　先生　　　　收
Wáng Yíwén xiānsheng　　*shōu*
Wang Yiwen mister　　　　receiver

美国、华盛顿州、北临海、西华盛顿大学、外语系; 邢
Měiguó, huáshèngdùnzhōu, běilínhǎi, xīhuáshèngdùn dàxué, wàiyǔxì; xíng
USA, WA, Bellingham, WWU, Foreign Language Department; Xing

As far as the layout of letters is concerned, it starts with the addressee's name, and then follows with an opening statement, the body part of the letter, closing remarks, writer's signature and date. Notice that Chinese letter does not include addressee's address in the letter. Another difference between Chinese and English letters is that Chinese dates the letter at the end of the letter, while English does it at the beginning.

To begin a letter/note, the writer has to know or decide: (1) how to address the addressee, and (2) what to say first. Consider the following samples of writing:

(7.69)　　**Beginning of a Letter/Note**:

a.　　TO PARENTS
爸爸、妈妈，

现在打电话，写电子邮件很方便，所以很少给你们写信了。不过有些话我还是觉得写信说得比较清楚。…

bàba, māma,

xiànzài dǎ diànhuà, xiě diànzǐ yóujiàn hěn fāngbiàn, suǒyǐ hěnshǎo gěi nǐmen xiěxìn le. búguò yǒuxiē huà wǒ háishì juéde xiěxìn shuō de bǐjiào qīngchu ...

"Dear Dad and Mom,

I rarely write to you anymore because it is so convenient to call or send an email. However, for certain things, I still think it is clearer to explain them in a letter."

b.   TO A BOY/GIRL FRIEND

红红，

很想你，你现在做什么？想什么？是在想我吗？真想跟你在一起，分开的日子实在难过，你什么时候会给我一个惊喜，突然出现在我的面前？

Hóng-hong,

hěn xiǎng nǐ, nǐ xiànzài zuò shénme? xiǎng shénme? shì zài xiǎng wǒ ma? zhēn xiǎng gēn nǐ zài yìqǐ, fēnkāi de rìzi shízài nánguò, nǐ shénme shíhòu huì géi wǒ yíge jīngxǐ, tūrán chūxiàn zài wǒde miànqián?

"Dear Hóng-hóng,

I miss you. What are you doing and thinking right now? Are you thinking about me? I really want to be with you. It's so hard to be alone. When are you going to surprise me by suddenly appearing here in front of me?"

c.   TO A TEACHER

王老师，您好！

很久没跟您联系了，我还在读研究生，今年夏天毕业。我知道您很忙，不过还是想求您点儿事儿。

Wáng lǎoshī, nín hǎo!

hěnjiǔ méi gēn nín liánxì le, wǒ háizài dù yánjiūshēng, jīnnián xiàtiān bìyè. wǒ zhīdào nín hěnmáng, búguò háishì xiǎng qiú nín diǎnr shìr.

"Dear Professor Wáng,

I have not contacted you for a while. I am still working on my graduate degree and plan to graduate this summer. I know you are busy, but I would like to ask you for a favor ..."

d.   TO A PROSPECTIVE EMPLOYER

…公司经理：

在报纸上看到贵公司招聘管理方面的人才，我认为自己在各方面都具备贵公司所提的条件，为此特提出申请，望贵公司考虑。

我曾在 …

... gōngsī jīnglǐ:

zài bàozhǐ shàng kàndào guì gōngsī zhāopìn guǎnlǐ fāngmiàn de réncái,
wǒ rènwéi zìjǐ zài gè fāngmiàn dōu jùbèi guì gōngsī suǒtí de tiáojiàn,
wèicǐ tèbié tíchū shēnqǐng, wàng guì gōngsī kǎolù.
wǒ céng zài ...

"Dear Managers of the Company,

   I have learnt from the newspaper that your company is currently hiring management specialists. I am writing to apply for the position because I believe that I am fully qualified for the position. Please consider my application.

   My working experience …"

These letters/notes are addressed to different people with different relationships to the writer. However, all the beginning remarks seem to lead to a reason why the letter/note is written (i.e., "It is clearer to explain things in a letter"; "I miss you"; "I want to ask you for a favor"; and "I am applying for a position in your company.") Presumably, when addressed to a prospective employer, it has to be a letter; but when addressed to a friend, a teacher, or parents, it can be a letter, a note, or an email message. Comparing the Chinese letters/notes with their corresponding English translation, the major difference between the two languages is the use of the word "dear" when addressing the receiver of the letter. Unlike English, Chinese does not use 亲爱的 (*qīnàide* "dear") in any of the letters/notes. Exceptions to this rule is an indication of influence by Western culture or tradition. The addition of "dear" to the English translation in (7.67) is intended for English idomaticity. Discussion about the body of letters/notes is omitted in this section for two reasons: One is that I have already discussed discourse modes in section 7.3, with which interested readers should consult when writing this part of letters/notes. The second reason arises from the fact that letter/note discourse has a great deal in common across languages; students may apply the same techniques they use in writing in their native language to writing Chinese letters.

We now turn to the closing of a letter/note. Chinese, like many other languages, has some formulaic endings. Which form is chosen, it then, depends largely upon the relationship between the writer and the addressee, as illustrated in (7.70).

(7.70)   **Concluding a letter/note**

   a.   TO PARENTS
        就写到这儿。匆此，问安！
        jiù xiědào zhèir. cōngcǐ, wèn'ān!
        儿敬上
        ér jìngshàng
        十月一日
        shí yuè yī rì
        "I'll just stop here. Wish you everything well!

Respectfully,

Your son

October 1, 2004"

b.   TO BOYFRIEND/GIRLFRIEND

我爱你！祝你做个好梦！

wǒ ài nǐ! zhù nǐ zuò ge hǎo mèng!

彤彤

Tóng-tóng

八月十五

bā yuè shíwǔ

"I love you. I wish you a pleasant dream!

Tóngtóng

August 15"

c.   TO A TEACHER

就这些，实在是不好意思又麻烦您。如果您有什么需要我帮忙的，请
及时跟我联系。

jiù zhèixiē, shízài shì bù hǎo yìsi yòu máfan nín. Rúguǒ nin yǒu shénme
xūyào wǒ bāngmáng de, qǐng jíshí gēn wǒ liánxì.

春祺

chūnqí

　教安！！

　jiào'ān!

学生王晓其敬上

xuéshēng Wáng Xiǎoqí jìngshàng

三月三十一日

sān yuè sānshíyī rì

"That's all. I am sorry to bother you again. If I can help you with anything,
please let me know.

Best wishes for the Spring season. Best wishes for smooth teaching.

Respectfully yours,

Student, Wáng Xiǎoqí

March 31"

d.   TO A PROSPECTIVE EMPLOYER

如果您有什么问题，请及时跟我联系。我的手机电话是… 恭候您的
回音。

rúguǒ nín yǒu shénme wèntí, qǐng jíshí gēn wǒ liánxì. wǒ de shǒujī
diànhuà shì ... gōnghòu nín de huíyīn.

祝贵公司事业兴旺！

zhù guì gōngsī shìyè xīngwàng!

王虎城

Wáng Hǔ-chéng

六月八日

liù yuè bā rì

"If you have any questions, please contact me. My cell phone number
is … (I) look forward to hearing from you.

Best wishes for the prosperity of your company.

Wáng Hǔ-chéng

June 8"

All the closing remarks in (7.70) express the writers' wishes to the addressee.
They only differ somewhat in terms of formality. When writing to parents and a
teacher, the writer uses expressions showing respect to them (e.g. 问安 *wèn'ān*
"Wish you peace!", or 教安 *jiào'ān* "Best wishes for smooth teaching!") and
sincerity (e.g. 实在是不好意思又麻烦您 *shízài shì bù hǎo yìsi yòu máfan nín* "I
am so sorry to bother you again …") When closing a letter of application for a job,
the writer uses a formal expression as 恭候您的回音 *gōnghòu nín de huíyīn* "(I)
look forward to hearing from you" and 祝贵公司事业兴旺 !"*zhù guì gōngsī shìyè
xīngwàng* "Best wishes for the prosperity of your company." The closing remarks
to a friend, on the other hand, appear less formal, but more personal (i.e. 我爱你！
祝你做个好梦！*wǒ ài nǐ, zhù nǐ zuò ge hǎo mèng.* "I love you and wish you a
pleasant dream!")

Furthermore, the writer's signature varies as well. The signature on the
parents' letter contains the word 儿 *ér*, "son" and 敬上 *jìngshàng*,
"respectfully"; the signature to a boy/girlfriend's letter uses only the writer's
nickname; however, the signature on a letter to a teacher or business company
includes the full name of the writer (i.e. last name followed by first name.) These
variations clearly reflect the interpersonal relationship that the writer has with
those addressees: closeness to parents and girl/boyfriend and seriousness with a
teacher and prospective employer. Such reflection, however, does not exist in
essays and reports.

Essays and reports are probably the most commonly requested written
discourse in schools and at work, and this category includes reflections on a
certain subject recently discussed in class, term papers, and newspaper/journal
articles. Since essays and reports usually use some, if not all, the discourse modes
that I have discussed in Section 7.3, I will not discuss this subject further here.
Students who have the desire to learn and improve their writing skills should
begin to write short simple essays or reports from the elementary level. They may
begin writing by imitating the lessons they have learned and gradually add more
complicated discourse structures, discourse devices, and discourse modes
discussed earlier in this chapter. With the progression of their discourse
competence, students' writing competence should develop accordingly. Teachers
and students may also consult with Feng (2000) who provides numerous phrases
commonly used in written discourse and Luo (2002) who compiles many
examples and exercises for practicing writing skills.

7.5 Interpretation and Pragmatics

So far, I have devoted most of our attention to the production of discourse. In this section, I briefly discuss the other side of the coin, interpretation of discourse. It is well known that accurate interpretation of a given discourse (both spoken and written) requires pragmatic knowledge, which is defined by many as the relationship of signs to interpreters (Morris 1971, Levinson 1983). Such knowledge ranges from common sense, code switching (from one language to another, from one dialect to another, from one style to another), idiosyncrasies (personal preference and traits) to social/cultural tradition (authority and gender). In other words, accurate interpretation of discourse has to be derived from understanding of location, time, and purpose of discourse and the status of people involved in discourse. Failure to identify these traits on the part of either the speaker or listener could lead to a misinterpretation of discourse, as illustrated by the following story:

(7.71) 有一个主人请客，同时请了两位客人。到吃饭的时候，只来了一个，另一个没来，主人着急，就跟来了的客人说：怎么该来的还没来呢？客人听了，很不高兴，没吃饭就走了。后来第二个客人来了，主人便对这位客人说：怎么不该走的走了呢？客人听了，也很不高兴，没吃饭也走了。主人不知道为什么，便对太太说：怎么该吃饭的都走了？太太听了非常生气地说"你的意思是说我和你都不应该吃饭吗？"

yǒu yige zhǔrén qǐngkè, tóngshí qǐngle liǎngwèi kèrén. dào chīfàn de shíhou, zhǐ láile yíge, lìngyíge méilái, zhǔrén zhāojí, jiù gēn láile de kèrén shuō: zěnme gāiláide hái méi lái ne? kèrén tīngle, hěn bù gāoxìng, méi chīfàn jiù zǒu le. hòulái dì èrge kèrén lái le, zhǔrén biàn duì zhèwèi kèrén shuō: zěnme bù gāi zǒude zǒule ne? kèrén tīngle, yě hěn bùgāoxìng, méi chīfàn yě zǒule. zhǔrén bù zhīdào wèishénme, biàn duì tàitai shuō: zěnme gāi chīfànde dōu zǒule? tàitai tīngle fēicháng shēngqì di shuō "nǐ de yìsi shì shuō wǒ hé nǐ dōu bú yīnggāi chīfàn ma?"

"One day, a host invited two guests for dinner. When dinner was ready, only one guest showed up. The host said with concern on his face "How come the one that should have come has not come yet?" Upon hearing this, the guest who had come left unhappily and without eating dinner. Later, when the second guest arrived, the host asked him "How come the one that should not have left, left already?" The second guest was not happy either upon hearing this remark and also left without eating dinner. The host could not understand why both guests left, so he asked his wife "How come the two who should have eaten here left?" The wife looked at him and said angrily "Do you mean to say that you and I should not eat here?"

The answer to the wife's question is obviously "No, that is not what I mean." Then, the question is whether both guests misinterpreted the host's remarks. Some may say yes, while others may say no, depending on how much extra linguistic information they have and how they interpret the meaning beyond discourse structures. If a listener knows that the host is an honest person and people should take his words at face value, then s/he might not have left upon hearing what he said. On the other hand, if the speaker knows that the listener is a sensitive person and often reads between lines, then s/he should be careful not to use ambiguous expressions to avoid possible misinterpretation. Since both the speaker and the listener failed to identify those pragmatic factors involved in discourse, there was a failure to communicate.

For students of Chinese as a foreign language, it is more a challenge to acquire pragmatic competence in the classroom than discourse competence primarily because pragmatic information depends on context, and has little to do with linguistic structure (Levinson 1983: 9). One way to reduce students' pragmatic competence burden is to encourage those who have studied Chinese for two years to go to China and live in a natural Chinese language environment for a semester or two. This should give them the opportunity to observe and imitate native speakers, practice with native speakers, and apply pragmatic knowledge that they have learned from native speakers to real-time communication.

7.6   Conclusion

This chapter has discussed three major areas relevant to the development of students' discourse competence: discourse devices, discourse modes, and discourse styles. It has demonstrated seven types of discourse devices (topic chain, ellipsis, substation, word order variation, discourse connectors and markers, temporal sequence, and background/foreground), six discourse modes (opening passage, narrative, description, notation, argument, and closing passage), and two discourse styles (spoken and written). Evidently, to acquire all these skills for discourse competence cannot be accomplished in a week, a month, a semester, or even a year; students have to commit to a long-term systematic training to be able to speak, understand, read, and write advanced or native discourse. Considering the volume of skills involved in developing discourse competence, I suggest the following procedures for different levels of Chinese students.

At the elementary level, students should concentrate on learning most of the basic discourse devices. By basic, I refer to discourse intonation, simple ellipsis, simple substitution, simple discourse connectors and discourse markers, and simple alternation between the main word order and other word orders, etc. Elementary students should also have a good understanding of the style of spoken discourse and as well as the basic discourse modes such as simple narrative and description passages.

At the intermediate level, students should continue to learn discourse devices but focus more on complicated discourse connectors and other means for discourse coherence. Exercises may be designed to practice how to connect sentences with the same topic to form a topic chain, how to use ellipsis and substitution to form a closely netted discourse, how to alternate word order to avoid something one does not want to mention in discourse, etc. At this stage, spoken discourse may still be the primary style for students to learn, however, some traits of written discourse should be introduced to students as well. Basic discourse modes and functions, such as opening and closing passage, narrative, description and notation, should all be explained and incorporated into classroom teaching and practice.

For advanced students, the focus should be on the development of the skill in managing overall discourse. This involves not only the skill of creating and connecting different passages (e.g., produce and link paragraphs, turn-taking in conversation, etc.) but also the skill of correctly identifying and interpreting different styles (both spoken and written) of discourse. Students should also be required to learn, practice and use the argument mode to express their opinions, negotiate or persuade others to come to agree with them. At this stage, spoken and written discourse should be equally emphasized.

Due to the broad range of issues relevant to discourse teaching and learning, it is difficult, if not impossible, to discuss every issue in detail. Nonetheless, I hope this chapter provides teachers and students alike with the basic knowledge about discourse and acquisition of discourse competence.

8 Culture in Teaching and Learning Chinese as a Foreign Language

8.1 Introduction

Culture has been a subject of discussion among researchers in the field of humanities and social sciences for centuries, yet for laypeople and even some college language teachers, it is still an abstract concept, difficult to pin down. Examining the definitions of culture in literature, we find that there are numerous ways to define and describe this elusive concept. Sapir, widely believed to be America's most brilliant anthropologist and linguist, defines culture in the following way:

> The cultural conception we are now trying to grasp aims to embrace in a single term those general attitudes, views of life, and specific manifestations of civilization that give a particular people its distinctive place in the world. Emphasis is put not so much as on what is done and believed by a people as on how what is done and believed functions in the whole life of that people, on what significance it has for them. (Sapir 1949: 83)

In the last several decades, students of sociology, anthropology, sociolinguistics and foreign/second language acquisition have attempted to interpret the concept of culture in relation to their own disciplines of study:

> Culture patterns — social facts — provide a template for all human action, growth, and understanding. Cultural models thus derive from the world in which we live, and at the same time provide a basis for the organization of activities, responses, perceptions, and experiences by the conscious self. (Rosaldo 1984: 140)

> Culture is difference, variability, and always a potential source of conflict when one culture enters into contact with another. (Kramsch 1993: 1)

These are typical definitions of the so-called *major culture* or "Big C" (大文化, *dà wénhuà*). Some students classify culture into different types: ethnic culture, local culture, academic culture, and disciplinary culture (e.g. Flowerdew and

Miller 1995, Scollon and Scollon 1995, Lü 1999) and even consider teaching and learning norms as classroom culture. Hinkel (1999: 1) points out that

> Even within the explorations and the teaching of language, the term *culture* has diverse
> and disparate definitions that deal with forms of speech acts, rhetorical structure of text,
> social organizations, and knowledge constructs. Culture is sometimes identified with
> notions of personal space, appropriate gestures, time, and so forth.

Lü (1999: 18) lists various types of Chinese culture from a narrow sense, or the "small C" (小文化, *xiǎ wénhuá*) labeled by some anthropologists, such as, 饮食文化 (*yǐnshí wénhuá*, "food culture"), 酒文化 (*jiǔ wénhuà*, "liquor culture"), 茶文化 (*chá wénhuá*, "tea culture"), etc.

Given these definitions of culture from a wide range of perspectives, it is important for language teachers to understand and narrow down the scope and content of the culture that they teach in language classes. Clearly, teachers cannot teach everything relevant to culture in language classes. For this reason, the current chapter aims to first discuss the relationship between culture and language and the connected, almost inseparable relationship between culture and language teaching and learning, and then to discuss the content of culture in teaching and learning Chinese as a foreign language (FL) and how it can be classified into the same three levels as the language skills themselves, namely, elementary, intermediate, and advanced. Sections 8.4–8.5 will demonstrate activities recommended for teaching and learning Chinese through Chinese culture; Section 8.6 discusses means of assessing students' culture proficiency and Section 8.7 concludes this chapter with the implication of the current work, future research and practice of teaching and learning culture in the language classroom.

8.2   Culture Content and Language Proficiency

Native speakers of any a given language can communicate both effectively and efficiently because they know the culture and understand the society in which they live, the people they interact with, and the social norms they are obligated to obey. When speakers of a language, including native speakers, lack knowledge in those areas, their language proficiency tends to stagnate at a certain level and cannot be further developed. Ochs and Schieffelin (1984) claim that "The process of becoming a competent member of society is realized to a large extent through language, by acquiring knowledge of its functions, social distribution, and interpretations in and across socially defined situations, i.e. through exchanges of language in particular social situations." This is probably why national standards established by the ACTFL (1996) for foreign languages (i.e. the five goal areas: communication, culture, connections, comparisons, and communities) enlist culture as a core component in language acquisition. Among foreign language teachers, the current consensus appears to be that it is difficult to achieve high proficiency in any language without a concomitant awareness, indeed, almost adoption, of the culture in which the language is used.

8.2.1 *Culture and language*

The direct relationship between cultural awareness and language proficiency stated above mirrors the close tie between culture and language. If culture and language are "inseparable and constitute a single universe or domain of experience" as claimed by Kramsch (1991: 217), then neither culture nor language can stand on its own in the research of language pedagogy. In other words, one cannot discuss a language without talking about its interaction with culture, nor can one study the development of culture without the assistance of language. Other scholars have made similar observations, however, from different angles:

> Language is becoming increasingly valuable as a guide to the scientific study of a given culture. In a sense, the network of cultural patterns of a civilization is indexed in the language which expresses that civilization. (Sapir 1949: 68)

> In second language classrooms, language and culture are inextricably intertwined. Culture is negotiated in large part through language, and language codifies many cultural assumptions and values." (Brody 2003: 40)

> Language organizes and expresses a whole range of cultural information and interpretations of concepts and ways of life that have acquired their specific form as part of the development of the specific community of language users. (Bryam 1989: 147)

Lǚ, a Chinese pedagogy specialist, suggests a similar relationship between culture and language, except that he adds "Language is the foundation of culture [语言是文化的基础 *yǔyán shì wénhuà de jīchǔ*]" (Lǚ 1999: 20–21), a position on which I disagree with him. I believe that the relationship is the reverse, that is, culture is the foundation of the development of a language. Without this foundation, we may not or need not have a language.

Thomas (1983, 1984) also discusses the relationship between language and culture, although he emphasizes the inappropriateness of language usages derived from lack of cultural awareness:

> Nonnative speakers are often perceived to display inappropriate language behaviors and often are not even aware that they do. Inappropriateness in interactions between native and nonnative speakers often leads to socio-pragmatic failure, breakdown in communication, and the stereotyping of nonnative speakers.

Thomas appears to believe that appropriateness is the key in associating language with culture. That is, if one can communicate using appropriate language, this person then has the appropriate cultural knowledge. Without the appropriate cultural knowledge, the purpose of communication cannot be fulfilled. Evidence supporting this point of view can be found in all languages and cultures, Chinese language and culture being no exception. Take politeness, for example. There are many different ways of expressing politeness in Chinese, some of which are listed below:

- Using honorific forms to address elders (e.g. 您 *nín*);
- Letting other people enjoy/do things first (e.g. eat, speak, etc.);
- Avoiding showing off or flattering oneself;
- Showing respect to elders;
- Showing modesty when praised

Whether the above listed behaviors are expressed verbally or through body language, their correct deployment should enable speakers to achieve their communicative goals in normal social interaction with Chinese people. Lack of awareness of or disregard for these so-called proper behaviors can lead to failure of communication. This makes us believe that a language class in which communicative skills are taught cannot be totally successful without also incorporating key cultural components.

8.2.2 *Role of culture in language teaching and learning*

Kramsch (1993: 8) points out "If language is seen as social practice, culture becomes the very core of language teaching. Cultural awareness must then be viewed both as enabling language proficiency and as being the outcome of reflection on language proficiency." Byram and Fleming (1998: 1–2) suggest that when language teaching begins to take seriously the concept of learning a language as the means of communication and interaction with people of another society and culture, it turns to ethnography to provide a description of context in which the language is used. Assuming that all language teachers consider teaching a language as a means of communication, the question facing them is how they balance culture and language components in the foreign language classroom. Is language proficiency or cultural proficiency the goal of teaching and learning or both? If one or both is the goal, how should teachers integrate them into teaching and learning?

During the first half of the twentieth century, the first question was easy to answer because culture was not taken seriously by any language teachers. The second half of the twentieth century and the early twenty-first century, however, have seen an increasing interest in inclusion of culture in language teaching and learning (Brooks 1960, Seelye 1976, Damen 1987, Kramsch 1993, Seelye 1994, Byram and Fleming 1998, Lange and Paige 2003). This movement coincides with an increase in the number of students interested in learning a foreign language due in part to economic globalization. As a result, a new field of study has emerged, intercultural communication, which probes the principle and practice of communication among people with different cultural backgrounds. Currently, if asked about the role of culture in teaching and learning a foreign language, teachers and students may give different answers depending upon their understanding of the interrelationship between language and culture. For teachers who have knowledge of the theory and practice of intercultural communication, culture is considered an important component in teaching and learning a language. However, for students whose motive for learning a foreign language is to acquire language competence, cultural competence is considered less important than language competence. If we combine the two beliefs, we get a good picture of the position of culture in the language classroom in recent years. That is, some teachers ignore cultural components in language teaching or consider culture a separate, though related, skill from language learning, while others know that culture is inextricably connected to language, but may not be sure how to implement cultural components into language teaching. Based on earlier research of intercultural communication and case studies (e.g. Allen 1985, Hymes 1989, Kramsch 1993, Kubler 1997a, Liu and Ao 1998, Byram and Fleming 1998, Lü 1999, Hinkel 1999, Myers 2000, Christensen and Warnick 2004) of teaching culture in the language classroom, including teaching Chinese as FL, I propose the following guidelines for culture and language proficiency in teaching Chinese as FL.

- Language proficiency is the primary goal of teaching and learning a foreign language.
- Culture as a concept should be introduced and explained to students whenever it enhances language learning and advances language proficiency.
- Language proficiency progresses along with the development of cultural awareness.

Although culture may be inseparable from language, cultural proficiency, in my view, does not necessarily imply language proficiency. However, the reverse situation can be true, that is, true language proficiency implies cultural proficiency. For instance, a graduate of Chinese civilization, history or literature studies may have learned a great deal about Chinese society, people, and social norms and often knows more about Chinese culture than ordinary Chinese people, but his/her Chinese language proficiency level can be rather low. Yet another graduate of Chinese language studies, having attained a high proficiency in the language, is most likely to also have a thorough knowledge of the Chinese culture. Because of this difference between culture and language, culture should only be considered a means for students to achieve language proficiency in the language classroom. Furthermore, with the development of students' language competence, their cultural awareness should increase accordingly. Therefore, the following section will focus on different levels of cultural proficiency and their correlation with language proficiency.

8.3   Teaching and Learning Chinese Culture in Language Classes

Culture, especially Chinese culture, is very much a complex and multifaceted subject for scholars, educators and students alike to study, teach, and learn. Chinese culture embodies over five thousand years of recorded history and more than fifty ethnic groups, with their own traditions, beliefs, and social norms. With this dimension of culture, it is impossible for language teachers to include everything in the language curriculum. This challenges pedagogy specialists to investigate and determine the content — and amount — of Chinese culture that can or should be included in language classrooms. In recent years, some Chinese educators (e.g. Zhang 1990, Lǚ 1999) in Mainland China have promoted cultural communication information[1] (语言交际文化 *yǔyán jiāojì wénhuà* in language teaching), similar to the idea of multicultural communication developed by Western researchers. According to Lǚ (1999: 21), cultural communication information conveys psychological attitude, value systems, living styles, moral standards, customs, ethnicity, and interests of an ethnic group of people, which are expressed through words, sentences and the socio-pragmatic system of the Chinese language. These studies are useful for us to gain a general understanding of the content of (Chinese) culture, however, they are not instrumental in helping teachers to identify those cultural elements necessary for language teaching and learning. To accomplish that, I propose the following criterion:

Criterion for selection of culture content for Chinese language classes:

Any traditions, attitudes, rituals, beliefs, behaviors that are unique to Chinese society and people and crucial to learning and understanding the Chinese language, the people and their behaviors may be considered as part of the Chinese culture content to be taught and learned by non-native students of the Chinese language.

This criterion correlates with the one recommended in Chapter 2 for selecting grammatical elements for teaching and learning Chinese as FL discussed in Chapter 2. The focus of both criteria is on the uniqueness and importance of a given cultural or grammatical element to the learning of the Chinese language. However, unlike grammatical elements, cultural elements are more abstract and therefore more difficult to pinpoint. Take *Chinese tradition* as an example. If asked, a teacher has to think for a moment to name some instances that can be considered elements of Chinese tradition. In comparison, grammatical elements are relatively easy for any teacher to name. For the purpose of convenience in teaching and learning, we may break Chinese culture into five categories: tradition, attitude, ritual, belief, and social behavior. It should be noted the elements included in those five categories are not meant to be exclusive. Teachers are encouraged to add more to these categories in their teaching to enhance students' learning.

Tradition
- Personal names
- Formation of Chinese characters
- Festivity
- Legendary figures
- Influential historical events
- Painting
- Music
- Martial arts
- Medicine
- Family

Attitude
- Friendship
- Respect
- Modesty
- Manhood
- Female virtue
- Interpersonal relationships
- Family
- Social status
- Patriotism
- Education (e.g. learning)

Ritual
- Weddings (or Marriage)
- Funerals (or Death Rituals)
- Birth of a child
- Kinship
- Courtship

Belief
- Life and death
- Confucianism
- Daoism
- Buddhism
- Marriage
- Education

Social Behavior
- Eating
- Drinking (liquor, tea)

- Social gathering and interaction
- Working
- Learning

Examining the elements within these five categories, one may notice that certain elements do not belong exclusively to one particular category. Fortunately, this is not important to the learning of Chinese culture in language classes. The important task is to identify the elements and to determine when and how these cultural elements can be integrated into language classes and become instrumental in the advancement of students' Chinese language competence.

According to the theory of learnability discussed in Chapters 1–3, students learn language/linguistic elements most effectively and efficiently if they are given learning materials that progress from simple to complicated, from concrete to abstract and from most commonly used to less commonly used in communication. As far as cultural elements are concerned, there has not been much discussion regarding the procedures of teaching and learning at different levels of language proficiency, although among researchers interested in cultural acquisition, there seems to be a consensus that second culture (C2) proficiency is difficult to obtain (e.g. Byram 1989: 42, Kramsch 1991: 220, Robinson 1991: 115). Assuming that students' cultural proficiency progresses with their language proficiency, I suggest applying the same theory of learnability in language learning to cultural learning: That is to group cultural elements based on the degree of difficulty in learning, just as we have done with grammatical elements in Chapter 2. This way not only can language elements and cultural elements of parallel difficulty levels be acquired simultaneously, but, more importantly, students' language proficiency and cultural proficiency can be improved at the same time.

8.3.1   Elementary Level

At the elementary level, language students, or rather Chinese language students, most likely focus on acquisition of pronunciation, words/characters and their discourse and pragmatic functions (see discussion in Chapters 2–5). How, then, should cultural concepts be integrated into Chinese teaching and learning at this level? This section aims to answer this question by discussing the approach, content and goal of learning culture in elementary Chinese language classes.

When discussing acquisition of vocabulary, Myers (2000), following Wierzbicka (1997), suggests a *key word* approach in teaching and learning Chinese culture, although he does not specify the level at which the suggested approach is most effective. According to Wierzbicka (1997: 4), key words represent distinctive categories that reflect important cultural characteristics, such as ways of living and ways of thinking of people in a given society. Since it is extremely difficult if not impossible to find words in the second/foreign language that are the exact equivalents of the ones in the first language (Wang 1954: 18),

Myers (2000) recommends an integrated approach explaining key words as polysemes: words with several different but related meanings (see definitions and explanations of the polyseme by Lakoff 1987, Cheng and Tian 1989, Traugott and Dash 2002). With explanations of distinctive Chinese polysemes, non-native speakers of Chinese gain an enhanced appreciation of Chinese culture (Meyer 2000: 7).

The key word method is valid and in fact has already been used by some Chinese teachers, although the current teaching materials do not seem to show that it has become a mainstream method for teaching culture, as pointed out by Myers (2000: 21). Since the key word method is for learning culture through words/characters, it seems most appropriate to use it primarily for students of elementary Chinese. (Of course, this does not mean that students of higher levels cannot also benefit from this method; rather that students with higher proficiency may benefit more from other methods to be introduced in Sections 8.3.2 to 8.3.3.) In addition to the key word method, cultural learning, I suspect, should focus on *understanding* at the elementary level. With various polysemes for a concept such as greeting, students may not only learn how to say "hello 你好 *nǐ hǎo* ! " but also understand that 早 *zǎo*, 早晨好 *zǎochén hǎo*, 你好 *nǐ hǎo*, 怎么样 *zěnme yàng* or 老师早 *lǎoshī zǎo* can all be interpreted as "good morning!" while 晚安 *wǎnān,* 好好休息 *hǎohǎo xiūxi* or 再见 *zàijiàn* may all convey the meaning of "good night!" The functional differences among these sets of expressions are of social and pragmatic nature. Lack of understanding of these differences may lead to failure of communication. A simple illustration is that when a Chinese person says "怎么样 *zěnme yàng*", the listener does not necessarily have to elaborate how s/he has been doing in the last several days; rather a simple response, such as "很好 *hěn hǎo*" can be sufficient, much as "How are you?" is used in English. After determining the method we wish to use to integrate culture into language learning, we should then identify the cultural elements to be acquired by students of elementary Chinese. As mentioned in the preceding section, I suggest that cultural content elements, as with grammatical elements, be selected and taught according to the theory of learnability derived from both first and second/foreign language acquisition. Knowing that concrete concepts are more easily conceived and understood than abstract concepts and commonly used concepts are more important than less commonly used in communication, I have proposed the following list of cultural concepts for Chinese classes at the elementary level:

- Chinese names (formation, meaning, implication)
- Chinese characters (formation, development)
- Chinese standard language and dialects
- Color terms
- Four precious articles for intellects
- Chinese food and drink
- Chinese family
- Chinese zodiac

- Simple interpersonal relationships
- Simple habitual activities (greeting, praising, expressing gratitude, etc.)

By no means exclusive, this list represents some cultural elements of concrete, specific, and common characteristics that are attainable for students of elementary Chinese. For instance, in the process of acquiring Chinese names, students may learn the structure of Chinese names, major family names, significance of different names, implications of particular names during different social-political periods, variations among people of different social and economic backgrounds (e.g. names convey meanings of prosperity, politics, history, geographic location, belief, generation etc.) Similarly, by learning the formation of Chinese characters, students also learn the principles behind the creation and development of Chinese characters, which evidently enhances the learning of Chinese characters.

For all students taking Chinese, it is essential for the instructor to find out whether they have some prior knowledge of the standard dialect — Mandarin — or other Chinese dialects (i.e. Wú, Mǐn, Yuè, Xiāng, Gàn, Hakka, and Mandarin, see Norman 1988) so as to be able to help students understand the geographic, social, linguistic, and political implications of their prior knowledge of Chinese.

To add color to Chinese classes both figuratively and literally, teachers can easily teach color terms and their semantic and pragmatic functions in communication (e.g., *red* symbolizes happiness; *white* conveys the meaning of sadness; etc.) and compare Chinese color associations with those in students' native language (e.g 戴绿帽子 *dài lǜ màozi* "wear a green hat" meaning one's wife is not faithful. English has the expression "feeling blue"). Four precious articles (i.e. brush, ink stick, paper, and ink stone) may also be explained in language classes so that students understand their significance of learning in Chinese history. Other elements mentioned in the list exemplify either the distinctive manners of Chinese daily activities or historical influence over Chinese people's lives. Whether it is Chinese cuisine, family structure and relations, birth year, eating, working or interacting with people, they are all concrete perceptions of basic Chinese culture.

Observant readers may have noticed that one characteristic shared by all the cultural elements listed for elementary Chinese classes is to enhance the learning of Chinese language, especially learning Chinese words/characters and their communicative functions. Indeed, this characteristic, I believe, should be the primary goal of teaching culture at the elementary level of Chinese classes. To achieve this goal, we must, as demonstrated above, first select cultural elements that match the language elements in terms of their degree of difficulty and their degree of importance in communication; then we must teach those elements using key words so that students understand the significance of those cultural elements in communication.

8.3.2   *Intermediate Level*

It is discussed in Chapter 2 that the focus of Chinese language learning at the intermediate level is on when, where and why sentences are used in discourse. The best way to strengthen this focus might be to first identify the culture-linked language in Chinese — for instance, the use of 我们再考虑考虑吧 *wǒmen zài kǎolùkǎolù ba* "Let us think about it further" as a polite rejection — and then to integrate these culture-linked linguistic elements into the intermediate Chinese language classroom. Now the question is *how* to select and teach cultural elements that are appropriate for intermediate language students. This section aims to develop a list of cultural elements for intermediate Chinese students and to introduce a teaching method that can infuse cultural elements into the language classroom.

The acquisition of some concrete, specific and common cultural elements at the elementary level should instill in students an ongoing desire to learn more about the distinctiveness of Chinese culture at the intermediate level. Therefore, I suggest that at the intermediate level teachers introduce to students as many concrete and straightforward cultural elements as possible along with some abstract concepts relevant to Chinese culture. On the concrete to abstract and simple to complicated continuum cultural elements at the intermediate level may be considered as falling exactly in the middle. That is students at this level should be introduced to cultural elements of some concrete and some abstract concepts, which are relatively simple and easy to learn but not as easy as those introduced at the elementary level. Consider the following list:

- Chinese festivals and their implications
- Chinese ethnic groups and their characteristics
- Chinese family life (e.g. marriage, family relationships, etc.)
- Interpersonal relationships (e.g. friendship, respect)
- Education
- Major events and figures in modern history (e.g. the cultural revolution, Máo Zédōng, Dèng Xiǎopíng)
- Chinese food and its characteristics
- Chinese thoughts (e.g. Confucianism, Daoism, Buddhism)
- Chinese living standards and social status
- Chinese fine arts (e.g. Beijing Opera, painting, musical instruments)
- Chinese civilization (e.g. Chinese medicine)
- Sports (e.g. martial arts)
- Current affairs

All the elements listed above can be taught and learned as either concrete or abstract concepts depending on students' language proficiency level. For intermediate-low students who have not yet learned to express abstract concepts in Chinese, only concrete facts should be taught. For instance, what do Chinese people do at the major festivals? What are the major differences between the Han ethnic group and other Chinese ethnic groups? What constitutes the Chinese family? How do Chinese people show respect for and get along with one another? What is the structure of the Chinese educational system? When and why did the Cultural Revolution take place? What are the names and characteristics of the major Chinese cuisines? These are all factual issues that will be relatively easy for students to talk about and comprehend. For intermediate-high students, however, simple abstract concepts should be introduced, such as, the reasons for celebrating different festivals, relationship between family members, friends, and co-workers, a general understanding of Chinese traditional thoughts, etc. These topics can be associated with simple abstract concepts that students can easily relate to their own lives and compare with their own culture. Although the list is not meant to be exclusive, it should give teachers a general idea of the type of cultural elements that can and should be included in intermediate Chinese language classes.

Now let us turn to the method of teaching and learning cultural elements at the intermediate level. Inspired by the key word approach suggested by Wierzbicka (1997) and Myers (2000), I propose a *key sentence* approach for intermediate Chinese students to learn cultural concepts and improve language proficiency. This approach states that key sentences, distinctive grammatical structures in Chinese as those discussed in Chapter 6, be used to express cultural characteristics of Chinese tradition, attitude, ritual, belief and behavior. Since Chinese is a typologically different language from Indo-European and other world languages (Greenberg 1966, Li and Thompson 1975, Shi 2000), Chinese is, thus, likely to use a different sentence structure to express an idea or a thought in comparison to other languages. Furthermore, since the sentence is the minimum unit for expressing a complete idea, using key sentences is a natural vehicle to express Chinese ideas and thoughts.

Using the topic-comment structure as an example, intermediate level students may use this structure to describe or comment on a Chinese festival or even to engage in a debate about it, as illustrated below:

(8.1)   *Describing the Mid-Autumn Festival*:

(a)   中秋节是阴历八月十五。

   zhōngqiūjié shì yīnlì bā yuè shíwǔ.

   "The Mid-Autumn Festival is on the fifteenth day of the eighth month of the lunar calendar"

(b)   这一天，中国人吃很多好吃的东西，还特别要吃月饼。

   zhèi yi tiān, zhōngguó rén chī hěnduō hǎochī de dōngxi, hái tèbié yào chī yuèbǐng.

   "On this day, Chinese people eat a lot of good food, especially moon cakes."

(c)   月饼常常是圆的，是一种点心，有时候做得很甜，我不太喜欢吃。

   yuèbǐng chángcháng shì yuán de, shì yìzhǒng diǎnxīn, yǒushíhòu zuò de hěn tián, wǒ bú tài xǐhuan chī.

"Moon cakes are a kind of dessert often in a round shape. I do not like very sweet moon cakes."

(d) 吃月饼的时候，人们常常坐在外面赏月。

chī yuèbǐng de shíhòu, rénmen chángcháng zuò zài wàimiàn shǎng yuè.

"People often sit outside and admire the full moon when they eat moon cakes."

(e) 这就是为什么中秋节有时候也叫月饼节。

zhè jiùshì wèishénme zhōngqiūjié yǒushíhòu yě jiào yuèbǐng jié.

"This is why the Mid-Autumn Festival is sometimes also called the Moon Cake Festival."

In this short paragraph describing the Mid-Autumn Festival, sentence (c) is a typical topic-comment construction commonly used by native Chinese speakers. The topic in this sentence is 月饼 *yuèbǐng* "moon cake" and the remaining three parts are comments. An English translation, however, cannot use the topic-comment construction simply because it does not have such a grammatical construction; instead, two sentence structures have to be used to express the same idea as the topic-comment construction.

(8.2) *Comment on the Mid-Autumn Festival:*

(a) 月饼难吃极了，里面有很多糖，皮儿有很多油。

yuèbǐng nánchī jíle, lǐmiàn yǒu hěnduō táng, pír yǒu hěnduō yóu.

"Moon cakes do not taste good at all. There is a lot of sugar inside them and a lot of oil in the crust."

(b) 不过在那天，请几个朋友来一起在月亮下面喝喝酒，吃点东西，聊聊天儿还不错。

buguò zài nà tiān, qǐng jǐge péngyou lái yìqǐ zài yuèliàng xiàmiàn hēhe jiǔ, chī diǎn dōngxi, liáoliao tiānr hái búcuò.

"However, on that day it is a good idea to invite a few friends over for a drink, food, or chat."

Both sentences (a) and (b) use the topic-comment construction. The topic in the first sentence is 月饼 *yuèbǐng* "moon cakes" and the one in the second sentence is 请几个朋友来喝喝酒，吃点儿东西，聊聊天儿 *qǐng jǐge péngyou lái hēhē jiǔ, chī diǎr dōngxi, liáoliáo tiānr* "to invite a few friends to come over for drink, food, or chat". The comments are 里面有很多糖，皮儿有很多油 *lǐmian yǒu hěnduō táng, bír yǒu hěnduō yóu* "there is a lot of sugar inside them and a lot of oil in the crust" and 还不错 *hái búcuò* "not bad" respectively. Evidently, Chinese and English use quite different constructions to express these comments on moon cakes and things that people do on the Mid-Autumn holiday. In this case, the key word method recommended by Myers (2000) may help students understand the meaning of moon cakes, but not be quite so effective in explaining the festival and its impact on Chinese people's social activities as the key sentence method.

(8.3)   *Debate about moon cakes:*

甲：现在的月饼越来越难吃，跟过去的月饼比差远了。

xiànzài de yuèbǐng yuèláiyuè nánchī, gēn guòqù de yuèbǐng bǐ chà yuǎn le.

"Nowadays, moon cakes have become much worse than ever before."

乙：瞎说！以前月饼什么样？现在月饼什么样？以前的月饼一共也没几样，现在中秋节到商店看看，满柜台都是各种各样的月饼。

xiāshuō! yǐqián yuèbǐng shénme yàng? xiànzài yuèbǐng shénme yàng? yǐqián de yuèbǐng yígòng yě méi jǐyàng, xiànzài zhōngqiūjié dào shāngdiàn kànkan, mǎn guìtái dōushì gèzhǒnggèyàng de yuèbǐng.

"Nonsense! What did moon cakes taste like in those days? What do they taste like nowadays? In the old days, there were only a few kinds of moon cakes, but nowadays if you go to shops before the Mid-Autumn Festival, you will see store counters full of different kinds of moon cakes."

甲：你说得对，品种是多了，但是质量差远了。现在吃什么月饼吃两口就不想吃了，可过去的提浆月饼，吃多少都不够。

nǐ shuō de duì, pǐnzhǒng shì duō le, dànshì zhìliàng chà yuǎn le. xiànzài chī shénme yuèbǐng chī liǎng kǒu jiù bù xiǎng chī le, kě guòqù de Tíjiāng yuèbǐng, chī duōshǎo dōu búgòu.

"You are right, there are more varieties now, but the quality is pretty bad. I can only eat a bit nowadays, whereas in the past, I could not get enough Tijiang moon cakes."

乙：那是你的嘴变了。提浆月饼现在给你，你也不爱吃。

nà shì nǐ de zuǐ biàn le. Tíjiāng yuèbǐng xiànzài gěi nǐ, nǐ yě bú ài chī.

"That's because your tastes have changed. If I were to give you a Tijiang moon cake right now, you wouldn't like it either."

There are a number of topic-comment constructions in this mini-dialogue, through which Chinese people's opinion about moon cakes and their quality in comparison with the past are clearly expressed. Furthermore, the topic-comment construction enables speakers to focus on the topic of their conversation and communicate effectively. It should be noted that even though the key sentence method can be effective in expressing cultural concepts, overuse of a particular sentence structure in one paragraph can lead to incoherence in discourse (detailed discussion on coherence is given in Chapter 7). Therefore, teachers' guidance is central to a balanced procedure of learning both cultural and language components at the intermediate level.

Notice that the major difference between the key word method and key sentence method lies in the function of these two methods: The key word method uses polysemes — two or more words with related meaning — to reflect cultural concepts, whereas the key sentence method uses a particular sentence structure (e.g. topic comment) to express cultural concepts. Furthermore, cultural concepts are embedded in key words, but not in key sentences. In other words, key words are used to convey a certain cultural concept, but a key sentence may be used to convey many different cultural concepts in different communicative situations. Because of this difference, mastering the use of key sentences undoubtedly enhances cultural proficiency. Nonetheless, it is not clear whether key sentences, such as topic-comment constructions, bear any cultural implication in and of themselves. Can we tell non-native students of Chinese that Chinese people first state a topic and then comment on it? Unfortunately, we cannot: in no language does any native speaker always speak one way or another and furthermore there is no conclusive research on this aspect, even though it is true that being able to choose from an inventory of ways to express the same thought is one of the things that separate native or native-like from non-native speakers. Before sociolinguists discover the answer, we can only assume that the topic-comment construction is one of the many key sentences in Chinese and can be filled with cultural information and used effectively in communication.

8.3.3   Advanced Level

After students complete two years of Chinese language training, they should be able to handle successfully most uncomplicated communicative tasks and social situations and to sustain understanding over longer stretches of connected discourse on a number of topics pertaining to different times and places (ACTFL Chinese Proficiency Guidelines 1990). At this level of language proficiency, students are prepared to explore Chinese culture in a more in-depth way. I propose that advanced level students of Chinese language learn a wide range of cultural elements through abstract concepts. Without doubt, this stage of learning is challenging, but at the same time, it can be interesting and stimulating because abstract concepts convey ideas or thoughts that cannot be seen; they can only be understood or felt in many cases. To students, it is a joy and a milestone to be able to understand and communicate about something that is not visible. Following is a list of cultural elements that are full of abstract concepts:

- Family value
- Morality
- Ethnicity
- Chinese Ideology (e.g. Chinese philosophy)
- Food and health
- Life and longevity
- Protocol
- Education
- Influential historical events and figures
- Childbirth
- Women's issues
- Social issues

- Religion
- Aesthetics (e.g. elegance, beauty)
- Art (e.g. painting, literature)
- Current affairs (e.g. politics, economy)

Experienced teachers may add more elements to this list. The more challenging task for language teachers, however, is to develop a suitable method so that those abstract cultural concepts can be integrated into the language classroom. Our experience in teaching and creating textbooks for advanced learners indicates that cultural concepts at the advanced level have to be tied up with genre of discourse, that is, the style of discourse (see Swales 1990 for detailed discussion of English genre analysis in academic and research settings). Whether the communicative task is a narrative story, a letter, an advertisement, an expository essay on social problems, a dialogue between business partners, or a healthy debate on religious issues, the genre of discourse has to be explained and learned in the language classroom. For this reason, I suggest a *key genre* method for teaching and learning cultural elements at the advanced level of language proficiency. This method advocates teaching and learning cultural elements through various genres of discourse. Earlier studies indicate the following relationship between written discourse and culture:

> The structure of written discourse and rhetorical paradigms is based on cultural frameworks, derived from different stylistic, religion, ethical, and social notions, all of which comprise written discourse conventions. Rhetorical constructs are often determined by the conceptualizations of the purpose of writing, the text's audience, and notions of what represents good writing. All these are bound up with the culture of the writer and the audience for which a text is created. (Hinkel 1999: 71)

If written discourse has such a close relationship with culture, it would be difficult to say that oral discourse has a different or lesser tie with culture. I argue that oral discourse may reflect more of a speaker's style, beliefs, morality, and understanding of society than written discourse because oral discourse takes place in a given place and time often with the assistance of body language and other situational cues that do not normally accompany written discourse. If this is true, then both written and oral discourse patterns are important for students to know in order to acquire cultural knowledge. In the following, let us examine three commonly used discourse genres and their integration with cultural content.

(8.4)   *The narrative genre: "My Grandma: A Story"*

(a)   在我的记忆中，奶奶给我留下的印象最深。小的时候，因为爸爸、妈妈都忙着工作，没有时间管我，所以把我送到乡下跟奶奶一起住。

　　　　zài wǒ de jìyì zhōng, nǎinai gěi wǒ liúxià de yìnxiàng zuì shēn. xiǎo de shíhou, yīnwèi bàba, māma dōu mángzhe gōngzuò, méiyǒu shíjiān guǎn wǒ, suǒyǐ bǎ wǒ sòngdào xiāngxià gēn nǎinai yìqǐ zhù.

(b) 我没见过爷爷，只知道他很早就去世了，奶奶三十刚出头，就守了寡。

    wǒ méi jiànguo yéye, zhǐ zhīdao tā hěn zǎo jiù qùshì le, nǎinai sānshí gāng chūtóu, jiù shǒule guǎ.

(c) 后来我才知道那个时候丈夫死了，家族的人是不允许奶奶再嫁人的，因为有失体面。

    hòulái wǒ cái zhīdao nà ge shíhòu zhàngfu sǐ le, jiāzú de rén shì bù yǔnxǔ nǎinai zài jià rén de, yīnwèi yǒu shī tǐmiàn.

(d) 奶奶似乎整天就知道做工。她每天天不亮就起床做早饭，吃了早饭，去地里干活。中午有时候在地里吃午饭，一直干到太阳下山才回家。这样她可以跟男人一样挣全工分。

    nǎinai sìhū zhěngtiān jiù zhīdào zuògōng. tā měitiān tiān bú liàng jiù qǐchuáng zuò zǎofàn, chī le zǎofàn, qù dìlǐ gànhuó. zhōngwǔ yǒushíhòu zài dìlǐ chī wǔfàn, yìzhí gàndào tàiyang xiàshāng cái huíjiā. zhèiyàng tā kěyǐ gēn nánrén yíyàng zhèng quán gōngfēn.

(e) 奶奶不仅自己每天做工，还总是要求他身边的人也不能闲着。

    nǎinai bùjǐn zìjǐ měitiān zuògōng, hái zǒngshì yāoqiú tā shēnbiān de rén yě bù néng xiánzhe.

(f) 她常说："能做工是有福的人。我就希望我能这样做下去，等到哪一天做不动了，一躺倒就死了，是我最大的福分。"

    tā cháng shuō: "néng zuògōng shì yǒu fú de rén. wǒ jiù xīwàng wǒ néng zhèiyàng zuò xiàqù, děngdào nǎ yìtiān zuò bú dòng le, yi tǎngdǎo jiù sǐ le, shì wǒ zuì dà de fúfèn."

(g) 奶奶的确就是这样离开我们的。

    nǎinai díquè jiùshì zhèiyàng líkāi wǒmen de.

"In my memory, grandmother has left the deepest impression. When I was little, my parents were busy with their jobs and had no time to take care of me, so they sent me to the countryside to live with my grandmother. I never met my grandfather because he died when my grandma was only a little over thirty years old. She never married again. Later on, I learned that to maintain filial piety and continue to honor the husband's family women back then were not supposed to remarry after their husbands died. Grandma seemed to work all the time. She got up very early every day to cook breakfast. After breakfast, she went to work in a field and often had lunch there. She did not come home until sunset. This way, she could earn the same labor credit as men. Aside from working all day long herself, she also demanded that the people around her work as hard as she did. She used to say 'Being able to work means good fortune. I only hope that I can continue working like this and die when I can no longer work.' Indeed, this is how grandma left us."

In this short story, the narrator mentions at least three culturally relevant issues: family relations (i.e. I live with grandma), a traditional Chinese widow (i.e. women should not remarry), and the concept of work in the mind of this country woman (i.e. Work means good fortune). With the narrative genre, these three cultural concepts seem to have been nicely knitted into the story. Hearing the story, listeners can understand the who, when, where, and why of the story — a reason why the narrative genre is often used in communication.

(8.5)   *The expository genre: "Etiquette – A must lesson for children: An essay"*

(a)   礼，是中国文化很重要的一部分。礼来自人与人之间的日常相处，是传达人们情意的桥梁。

Lǐ, shì zhōngguó wénhuà hěn zhòngyào de yíbùfen. Lǐ láizì rén yǔ rén zhījiān de rìcháng xiāngchǔ, shì chuándá rénmen qíngyì de qiáoliáng.

(b)   人的外在表现大致分为两种：一是语言，一是动作。遇到身份不同的人，我们的立场也相对变化，立场一变，外在表现也就跟着改变。所以语言、动作表达合宜的人，不仅是有教养的人，几乎称得上是艺术家。

Rén de wàizài biǎoxiàn dàzhì fēnwéi liǎng zhǒng: yī shì yǔyán, yī shì dòngzuò. Yùdào shēnfèn bùtóng de rén, wǒmen de lìchǎng yě xiāngduì biànhuà, lìchǎng yíbiàn, wàizài biǎoxiàn yě jiù gēnzhe gǎibiàn. Suǒyǐ yǔyán, dòngzuò biǎodá héyí de rén, bùjǐn shì yǒu jiàoyǎng de rén, jīhū chēngde shàng shì yìshùjiā.

(c)   因为他知道在某一种特定的情况下，该表达什么，怎么表达，不能失言，也不能失态，否则就失礼了。

Yīnwèi tā zhīdào zài mǒu yizhǒng tèdìng de qíngkuàng xià, gāi biǎodá shénme, zěnme biǎodá, bù néng shīyán, yě bù néng shītài, fǒuzé jiù shīlǐ le.

(d)   《论语》里有一个故事：有一次，子路迷了路，向一位老先生打听孔子去向，老先生瞧不起孔子，没回答，却留子路在家住了一宿，又杀鸡又做饭，还叫他的两个儿子出来跟子路打招呼，说一声"子路叔叔好！"这就是"礼"。

"Lúnyǔ" lǐ yǒu yíge gùshi: yǒu yicì, Zǐlù mí le lù, xiàng yíwèi lǎo xiānsheng dǎting Kǔnzǐ qùxiàng, lǎo xiānzheng qiáobùqǐ Kǔnzǐ, méi huídá, què liú Zǐlù zài jiā zhùle yi xiǔ, yòu shā jī yòu zuòfàn, hái jiào tā de liǎng ge érzi chūlái gēn Zǐlù dǎ zhāohu, shuō yìshēng "Zǐlù shūshu hǎo!" Zhèi jiùshì "lǐ".

(e)   遗憾的是现在大学生到处可见，可懂得其礼的人并不那么多。

Yíhàn de shì xiànzài de dàxuéshēng dàochù kějiàn, kě dǒngde qí lǐ de rén bìng bù nàme duō.

"Etiquette is an important part of Chinese culture. It is derived from daily interaction among people and functions as a transmitter of people's feeling. People's appearance may be evaluated in two ways: language and behavior. Our attitude changes with the change of people's status. When that happens, our behavior changes accordingly. Therefore, people with proper language and behavior are not only considered educated, but almost artistic because they know what to say and how to say it under certain circumstances. They guard against slips of the tongue, they do not forget themselves, lest they lose their etiquette. There is a story in *The Analects of Confucius*: Once upon a time, Zilu lost his way, so he asked an old man if he knew where Confucius had gone. The old man looked down upon Confucius, so he did not answer Zilu's question, instead, he let Zilu stay for the night. Then he killed chickens and cooked dinner for Zilu and also called in his two sons to greet Zilu with 'Welcome, Uncle Zilu!' This is etiquette, which is unfortunately not known by many young people anywhere anymore. (This essay is based on an article written by Gao 1990: 26–28)

The expository genre can be used effectively to explain, discuss and argue about a subject or one's point of view. In the short essay given above, "etiquette" is the topic. The author first explains what etiquette is and how it is reflected in people's language and behavior. Then a story from *The Analects of Confucius* is cited to illustrate the importance of teaching etiquette to children, in this case, how to treat the guest Zilu, even though the host does not like the person that the guest is associated with. The author ends with regret that there is an obvious lack of teaching etiquette in modern times.

Notice that in this expository essay, a short narrative story is inserted to further explain or illustrate what etiquette is. This shows that once students learn some of the basic genres of discourse, they can use one or more in an essay depending upon the purpose of communication. If the purpose is to tell a story of what Chinese people do during the Spring Festival, the narrative genre may be sufficient. However, if the purpose is to convince a teacher to reconsider a student's grade, this student may have to try every effort to combine arguments and narrative discourse.

(8.6) *The Dialogue Genre: A conversation between a teacher and a student*

老师： 请进！找我有什么事儿吗？

qǐng jìn! zhǎo wǒ yǒu shénme shìr ma?

"Come in please! Are you looking for me?"

学生： 我想问问老师这个学期我的成绩怎么样。

wǒ xiǎng wènwen lǎoshī zhèige xuéqī wǒde chéngjì zěnmeyàng?

"I want to know my grade for this quarter.

老师： 不太好。你为什么缺了那么多课？这次考试也考得不太好。

bú tài hǎo. nǐ wèishénme quē le nàme duō kè? zhèi cì kǎoshì yě kǎo de bú tài hǎo.

"Not very good. Why did you miss so many classes? You did not do well on the last exam either."

学生： 对不起，老师！这个学期家里有很多事儿，加上我个人的事儿，心情一直不太好。

duì bù qǐ, lǎoshī! zhèige xuéqī jiālǐ yǒu hěnduō shìr, jiāshàng wǒ gèrén de shìr, xīnqíng yìzhí bú tài hǎo.

"I am sorry, teacher. I have many family and personal matters to take care of this quarter. Because of that, I have been depressed for a while."

老师： 你是学生。学生最重要的事儿是上课、学习。家里的事儿和个人的事儿都不应该影响学习。

nǐ shì xuésheng. xuésheng zuì zhòngyào de shìr shì shàngkè, xuéxí. jiālǐ de shìr hé gèrén de shìr dōu bú yīnggāi yǐngxiǎng xuéxí.

"You are a student. The most important responsibility for students is to attend school and study. Family and personal things should not affect your studies."

学生： 可是我奶奶死了，我得回家去。还有我跟女朋友吹了。我们俩好了好几年，她一直对我很好，可是有一天我去她的宿舍找她，看到她正跟另一个男的谈情说爱。一气之下，就跟她吹了。自那以后，我每天都不想起床，不想吃饭，更不想到学校来上课。这就是为什么我缺了那么多课。

*kěshì wǒ nǎinai sǐ le, wǒ děi huíjiā qù. háiyǒu wǒ gēn nǚ péngyou chūi le. wǒmen liǎ
hǎo le hǎo jǐnián, tā yìzhí duì wǒ hěn hǎo, kěshì yǒu yìtiān wǒ qù tā de sùshè zhǎo tā,
kàndào tā zhèng gēn lìng yíge nán de tánqíngshuōài. yìqì zhīxià, jiù gēn tā chūi le. zì
nà yǐhòu, wǒ měitiān dōu bù xiǎng qǐchuáng, bù xiǎng chīfàn, gèng bù xiǎng dào
xuéxiào lái shàngkè. zhèi jiùshì wèishénme wǒ quē le nàme duō kè.*

"But my grandma died and I had to go home. Besides, I broke up with my girlfriend.
We had been together for several years. She was very good to me. But one day,
when I went to her place to look for her, I found she was talking love with another
guy. I could not stand it and broke up with her. Since then, I do not want to get up in
the morning, do not want to eat, not to mention go to school. That's why I missed so
many classes."

老师：　这些事儿，我都帮不了你啊。

　　　　zhèixiē shìr, wǒ dōu bāng bù liǎo nǐ a.

　　　　"I cannot help you with that."

学生：　您可不可以给我一个补考的机会？或者让我再写一篇长长的文章。如果给我一个
　　　　机会，我一定让您满意。

　　　　*nín kě bù kěyǐ gěi wǒ yíge bǔkǎo de jīhuì? huòzhě ràng wǒ zài xiě yìpiān chángcháng
　　　　de wénzhāng. rúguǒ gěi wǒ yíge jīhuì, wǒ yídìng ràng nín mǎnyì.*

　　　　"Can you give me a chance to retake the test? Or let me write a really long essay. I
　　　　promise that I will do a good job."

老师：　那你就写一篇文章吧，题目自己定，不过得写 500 字以上。

　　　　nà nǐ jiù xiě yìpiān wénzhāng ba, tímù zìjǐ dìng, búguò děi xiě wǔbǎi zì yǐshàng.

　　　　"Then why don't you write a long essay? You may choose a topic of your own, but it
　　　　has to be at least 500 characters long."

There are a number of linguistic and sociolinguistic characteristics in this
teacher-student conversation. Since it is a conversation, it inevitably reflects the
style of oral Chinese, such as the use of verb reduplication (问问 *wènwen*),
sentence particle (吗 *ma,* 吧 *ba,* 啊 *a*), and substitution (e.g. 那 *nà*). (See detailed
discussion on spoken and written discourse in Chapter 7.) Notice that the teacher
and student are clearly distinguished by their way of talking: the teacher is direct
(e.g. 你为什么缺那么多课？*nǐ wèi shénme quē nàmen duō kè?* "Why did you
miss so many classes?"), straightforward (e.g. 不太好。*bú tài hǎo* "Not very
good"), and authoritative (e.g. 题目自己定，不过得写 500 字以上 *tímù zìjǐ dìng,
búguo děi xiě wǔbǎi zì yǐshàng* "You choose your own topic. However, you have
to use at least 500 characters"), while the student is polite (by using the honorary
form 您 *nín*), tentative (by using V + not + V structure: 可不可以 *kě bù kě yǐ*
"may or may not"), and persuasive (providing specific facts: 我奶奶死了，我得
回家去。还有我跟女朋友吹了 *wǒ nǎinǎi sǐ le, wǒ děi huí jiā qù. Háiyǒu wǒ gēn
nǚ péngyou chūi le* "My grandma died and I had to go home." "I broke up with
my girlfriend."). One may argue that those characteristics of the Chinese teacher
and student represent the interaction of conversational genre and interpersonal
relationships in Chinese society. Scollon and Scollon (1995: 41) point out that
"most Asians are quite conscious in any interaction who is older and who is

younger, who has a higher level of education, who is in a higher institutional or economic position and who is lower, or who is teacher and who is student." Once speakers know the identity of the person to whom they speak, then they can determine the genre of discourse to be employed in their communication. Let us examine another genre of discourse commonly used in our daily life.

(8.7)   *The Personal Letter Genre: Excerpt from a letter to a close friend*

(a)   我一直不敢跟她说我们分开吧。我们两个人其实早就知道不行了，但是谁也不忍心说出分开的话来。我舍不得，她和我一样。

wǒ yìzhí bù gǎn gēn tā shuō wǒmen fēnkāi ba. wǒmen liǎngge rén qíshí zǎojiù zhīdào bùxíng le, dànshì shuí yě bù rěnxīn shuō chū fēnkāi de huà lái. wǒ shě bù dé, tā hé wǒ yíyàng.

(b)   我恨我自己，我给她造成了那么大的伤害，在她的家乡，很多人都见过我们在一起，知道我们是要结婚的，可是她现在还是一个人，我已经有了自己的孩子……

wǒ hèn wǒ zìjǐ, wǒ gěi tā zàochéng le nàme dà de shānghài, zài tā de jiāxiāng, hěnduō rén dōu jiànguò wǒmen zài yìqǐ, zhīdào wǒmen shì yào jiéhūn de, kěshì tā xiànzài háishì yíge rén, wǒ yǐjīng yǒule zìjǐ de háizi ...

(c)   我一直有一种感觉，我这个人很卑鄙，我做了卑鄙的事情，我是一个军人，每天讲的都是责任感和道德，我是一个从农村出来的、穷人家的孩子，农家孩子讲的是不能背信弃义，要忠厚老实，可我都干了些什么？

wǒ yìzhí yǒu yìzhǒng gǎnjué, wǒ zhèige rén hěn bēibǐ, wǒ zuò le bēibǐ de shìqin, wǒ shì yíge jūnrén, měitiān jiǎng de dōushì zérèngǎn hé dàodé, wǒ shì yíge cóng nóngcūn chūlái de, qióngrén jiā de háizi, nóngjiā háizi jiǎng de shì bù néng bèixìnqìyì, yào zhōnghòu lǎoshi, kě wǒ dōu gàn le xiē shénme?

(d)   我从来没有跟别人说过这件事，放在心里，特别压抑。我要用一辈子来对她道歉，为她祝福。(An 2000: 182)

wǒ cónglái méiyǒu gēn biérén shuō guò zhèijiàn shì, fàng zài xīnlǐ, tèbié yāyì. wǒ yào yòng yí bèizi lái duì tā dàoqiàn, wèi tā zhùfú.

"For a long time, I hesitated to break up with her. Even though both of us knew that it would not work out, neither of us wanted to say it. I could not do it, nor could she. I hate myself because I caused her so much pain. In her hometown, many people saw us together and thought that we would get married. Yet, she is still single, and I already have my own children … Because of that, I have always felt that I am despicable. I am a soldier who should be responsible and moral. I come from a poor family in the countryside where youngsters are honest and loyal, not betrayers. Look what I did. I have never talked about this matter with anyone before but I feel so depressed about it. I feel that I have to apologize to her and pray for her for the rest of my life."

This type of letter genre is similar to colloquial speech. From the excerpt given above, we see that the writer wrote the paragraph following the thread of thinking and a way of talking. Unlike formal speeches, letters often use first person as a narrator, many colloquial expressions (e.g. 其实 *qíshí* "in fact", 早就

zăojiù "long ago", 干了些什么 *gàn le xiē shénme* "what have I done") and repetition or omission of subjects (see further discussion on this subject in Chapter 7). Through letters, students may learn not only how to write informal essays and notes, but more importantly how to follow Chinese people's conversation or discussion about their life — dating (e.g. many villagers saw us together which meant we would get married), morality (e.g. I am despicable because I did not marry her), responsibility (e.g. Soldiers are responsible and moral), values (e.g. In the countryside, youngsters are honest and loyal), etc.

Comparing the key genre method with the key sentence method, we see that both use a linguistic unit, one is the sentence and the other is a discourse unit, to convey cultural or other concepts. It should be noted that earlier research has not suggested any direct relationship between sentence structures and culture concepts, although there are studies showing a correlation between Chinese discourse and culture. Scollon and Scollon (1995) demonstrate that for the expository essay, Chinese tends to explain the reason first and draw the conclusion at the end, whereas English tends to state the purpose/goal or result of research at the beginning before explaining procedures and arguments to reach that goal.

This chapter, so far, has discussed the content and methodology of teaching three levels of cultural elements in Chinese language classes. It has been suggested that cultural elements be classified and taught according to their degree of difficulty, importance, abstraction and contextualization. At the elementary level, most cultural elements are concrete and common concepts so that they are easy for students to learn and understand. At the intermediate level, both concrete and abstract cultural concepts are introduced to students, although the emphasis is still on concrete cultural concepts with some integration of simple abstract concepts. When students finish two years of language classes, they should be ready to tackle most commonly discussed abstract cultural concepts. In teaching these three different layers of cultural elements, I have proposed a key word, key sentence and key genre system as guiding principles at the elementary, intermediate, and advanced levels. The key word method emphasizes learning cultural elements through understanding key words and their communicative function at the elementary level. With the progression of students' language proficiency, the teaching and learning method becomes increasingly context-based. Hence, for students at the intermediate level, the key sentence method is recommended for learning cultural concepts in Chinese, while for those at the advanced level, the key genre method is recommended so that students can learn relatively complicated cultural concepts through different genres of discourse. It should be noted that each of these three methods is not meant to be discrete from the other two; rather each should be used as a primary method at its designated level and the remaining two as assisting methods.

8.4 Learning Activities

The growth of the global economy and promotion of multiculturalism have generated unprecedented opportunities for students to learn and understand Chinese culture regardless of where they are and who they are. We may characterize these opportunities as being of two types: one-way interaction and two-way interaction. The one-way interaction refers to learning activities in which students interact with objects or electronic machines, such as computers, television, books, etc. The two-way interaction, on the other hand, refers to learning activities in which students directly interact with other speakers of Chinese, both native and non-native. Most Chinese teachers generally think that the two-way interaction is better than the one-way interaction in terms of the effectiveness of learning. In either case, it can be a challenge for teachers with limited resources to design interesting and enjoyable activities that help students actually learn cultural elements in language classes. In the following paragraph, a few activities of both types will be discussed, some of which are traditional cultural activities, while others are relatively new and use modern technology.

Traditionally, in addition to classroom learning, students spend time watching Chinese movies or reading Chinese books to learn about Chinese culture. More recently, however, with the advance of computer technology and easy access to the Internet, students are more likely to be found in a computer lab or on their own computer reading email, Internet articles, or instant messages after class. Both the traditional and modern-day student activities are one-way interactions,[2] yet the computer activities are so popular and enticing to students that they leave teachers no other choice but to incorporate the technology into the teaching of cultural and language competence. For this purpose, I recommend using the *Blackboard* learning system, a web-based software that allows teachers to interact with students (e.g. through discussion lists, real-time chat, email, group file exchange), access students' activities (e.g. assignments, tests/quizzes, surveys), and publish course materials (e.g. syllabus, handouts, readings, essays). With this system, teachers can manage their courses easily and interact with students effectively. If teachers, for instance, want their students to learn about Chinese cuisines, they can not only send messages to students with links to various websites containing pictures and explanations of Chinese dishes, but also lead a discussion among students about the subject. All messages and discussions can be typed in Chinese. According to Blackboard Inc., there are more than 2,000 institutions in the United States using the Blackboard learning system in teaching and (long-distance) learning in 2004. It appears that this is a trend in teaching and learning foreign languages and Chinese is not an exception. It appears that this learning system is especially beneficial for learning and understanding cultural concepts — information-based concepts, in comparison with skill-based concepts, such as teaching and learning pronunciation. After all, the World Wide Web provides us with so much information about any given cultural concept that constant exploration should guarantee students' understanding of the commonly discussed topics in Chinese culture.

As far as the activities involved in two-way interaction are concerned, classroom teaching and learning comes first. Then total immersion programs, such as study abroad programs. After-school interaction with Chinese people may be one of the most popular activities for two-way interaction. Since classroom time is limited, to gain a good understanding of Chinese culture requires continued practice of cultural competence. Participating in a Chinese study program in China is an effective way to acquire the knowledge of Chinese culture by total immersion in a Chinese environment. For students who cannot participate in a study abroad program, making friends with Chinese people and learning Chinese culture from them can be an alternative. After all, it is not difficult to find a nice Chinese person no matter where you are.

In recent years, a newly developed two-way interaction using computer and satellite technology has also attracted the interest of many Chinese programs. This is long-distance teaching and learning programs, which allow native Chinese teachers at one end and students at the other to interact just as they would in a real-time classroom. An apparently very successful long-distance program is the Cross-Cultural Distance Learning (CCDL) program established by Waseda University, Japan. According to Professor Sunaoka, director of this program, CCDL has been developed as a learning network with the participation of students and teachers from 34 universities and colleges around the world (Sunaoka 2003). Through this program, students can directly interact with native speakers, discussing cultural issues, while practicing their language skills. For institutions that have technology support and are located in the same or similar time zone as China, this kind of long distance learning is certainly worthwhile. However, for institutions in North America with 12–16 hours time difference from China, it is difficult to arrange for students and teachers on both sides of the Pacific Ocean to meet and interact effectively.

8.5   Teaching Strategies

In the literature of cultural acquisition, there has been a debate over how cultural instruction should be conducted and how second culture (C2) competence can be developed. Some researchers (Byram 1991, Kordes 1991) suggest that the goal of culture instruction cannot be accomplished unless an intercultural (native cultural and second cultural) understanding, or even multicultural understanding (Kramsch 1993), has been developed in a traditional classroom setting. For teachers whose native culture (C1) is students' C2, intercultural understanding might be attained relatively easily in the classroom, if the teacher has a good understanding of students' C1, and explains and compares students' C1 with their C2 adequately. However, if the teacher lacks a comprehensive understanding of either students' C1 or C2, it would be very difficult to help students understand

C2, not to mention help them develop their ability to behave like members of C2. Some Western researchers (e.g. Lantolf 1999, Byram and Morgan 1994) argue that it is more important to investigate the possibility of people becoming cognitively like members of other cultures than to investigate the development of the ability to understand other cultures. Although this is a valid argument, it seems to me that Western students' ability to understand Eastern culture, such as Chinese culture, has to be studied and developed first before attempting to study and develop their ability to behave like members of an Eastern culture. After all, Westerners have different appearance (e.g. skin, hair, face) and cultural roots (e.g. ideology) from Easterners. Even if they have a good command of an Eastern language, it can be very difficult, if not impossible, for them to behave like or be received as a member of an Eastern culture. For this reason, I agree with Kramsch (1993) that in the classroom setting, it is necessary to develop an understanding of a third culture (C3) which is derived from distinctive traits and discourse modes of C1 and C2.

Now the question is how to develop students' competence within this newly created C3. It should be noted that students with different ethnic backgrounds might have to acquire different C3s. For instance, to Western students of Chinese, their C3 is derived from Chinese and Western cultures, whereas to Eastern students of Chinese their C3 is derived from Chinese and another Eastern (e.g. Korea, Japanese) culture. Furthermore, one C3 might be easier to acquire than another one due to the degree of difference or similarity between C1 and C2. Nonetheless, I suggest four phases of learning for the development of students' competence in C3: identifying, understanding, comparing and practicing. In a regular language class, a common practice of cultural instruction is that teachers identify C2 elements, and then explain them in the hopes that students will understand them and practice them in communication. In a real language environment (e.g. communication in Chinese with Chinese in China), however, we see a different picture: that is, the student identifies C2 elements, seeks explanation about them, understands them, and may eventually practice them. Comparing these two ways of learning, we see that the teacher-initiated learning (i.e. teachers identify cultural elements for students) is less effective than the student-initiated learning (i.e. students identify cultural elements by themselves). This leads us to ask how teachers can create a classroom environment that mimics authentic communication so that students are motivated to learn cultural elements needed in real-life communication. According to Robinson-Stuart and Nocon's (1996) report, it is possible for students to develop cultural communicative competence as a result of an instructional program that brings students into meaningful interaction with members of the second culture. Based on our experience in teaching Chinese culture in Chinese language classes, we know that Chinese teachers can help students develop their cultural communicative competence by developing a C3, as illustrated by the following four steps using class activities to develop students' cultural competence in interacting with Chinese people about a Chinese festival:

262 *Teaching and Learning Chinese as a Foreign Language*

Step 1: *Identifying C2*
- What do Chinese people eat at the Spring Festival?
- What do Chinese people do at the Spring Festival?

Step 2: *Understanding C2*
- Why do Chinese people eat what they eat at the festival?
- Why do Chinese people do what they do at the festival?

Step 3: *Comparing C1 with C2*
- Does students' C1 have a similar festival to the Chinese Spring Festival?
- If so, what are the similarities and differences between C1 and C2?
- If not, what characteristics of the Spring Festival are uniquely Chinese?

Step 4: *Practicing C3*
- How do non-native students with a knowledge of the Spring Festival interact with Chinese people about this festival?

C3 in this case is the cultural knowledge needed to interact successfully with Chinese people during the Spring Festival. In developing this C3, identifying and understanding C2 — Steps 1 and 2 — play an indispensable role. Without these two steps, it would be impossible to compare C1 and C2, let alone practice C3. Therefore, I suggest that in the development of students' cultural competence of C3 in communication, teachers follow the four steps and design activities in line with questions such as those given above. Certainly, these steps are only general procedures; whether a student's cultural competence can be developed and successfully practiced in communication depends, to a great extent, upon how teachers design the activities and ultimately how students react toward those activities.

8.6   Assessment

Evaluation and assessment of cultural proficiency is commonly viewed as a difficult and complicated task. Some researchers (e.g. Kramsch 1993, Hinkel 1999) point out that it is more difficult to assess cultural proficiency than linguistic proficiency, while others (Byram 1997) have made efforts to lay out specific procedures for evaluating intercultural competence. Reviewing Byram's (1997: 87) suggestion that "assessment should focus on the objectives of intercultural communication only, i.e. on determining how far learners have reached the competence described by those selected objectives," we find that the assessment of (inter)cultural competence may not be so complicated and difficult as perceived and the fact that many seem to believe that it is difficult to assess cultural competence is because researchers and teachers have not paid enough attention to the importance of cultural instruction and assessment. The key factor involved in assessment, according to Byram, is the objectives of intercultural competence. Once these objectives are clearly identified and selected by curricular designers, the task left for teachers is to find out how to assess the cultural competence described in the objectives of a curriculum.

Suppose that the objectives for Chinese language students at the elementary, intermediate, and advanced level include, but are not limited to, the understanding and practicing of the cultural elements in communication listed in Section 8.3. Teachers of these three levels may use the list as a basis for both oral and written tests to evaluate students' understanding, speaking, reading, and writing competence of those cultural concepts. This kind of assessment of cultural competence is pedagogically no different from the assessment of language competence. Yet, we have not seen it become a common practice in Chinese language classes. Perhaps, language teachers are waiting for guidance from professional organizations, such as the ACTFL. In the field of teaching Chinese as FL, we all know that there is a general lack of research on the role of culture in the acquisition of the Chinese language and I hope that the recommendations given in this chapter shed some light on the understanding of the place of culture in Chinese language teaching and learning.

8.7   Conclusion

Although this chapter is the last content-specific chapter in this book, it is, nonetheless, a critical one. Compared with the earlier chapters on language/linguistic aspects, this culture chapter serves a unique purpose for the discussion of teaching and learning Chinese as a FL. Traditionally, culture was not a subject of discussion among language pedagogy specialists because culture was not considered an integral part of language teaching. Now, many researchers and teachers, including Chinese teachers, recognize the importance of culture, but hesitate to act, namely, to implement the introduction of cultural elements into language teaching and assessment. I have proposed that culture teaching, including both content and methodology, should be systematic and integrated with language teaching so that students' cultural competence can be developed along with their language competence. It should be noted that this is a preliminary study of the place of culture in language teaching and learning. Future study may focus on the effectiveness of the methods recommended earlier in this chapter, exploration of other methods appropriate to different levels of language and cultural acquisition, and accurate assessment of Chinese cultural competence.

9 *Conclusion*

9.1 Introduction

As mentioned at the beginning, the primary goal of this book is to help teachers and students understand the theoretical and practical models in Chinese language pedagogy and acquisition. By the time readers reach this chapter, they may realize that some issues are considered conclusive, while many others remain open for further discussion or investigation. Chapter 2 and Chapters 4–8 have discussed substantially the content that students at different levels should learn in the Chinese language classroom and Chapters 3–8 have provided various teaching and learning methods based on reports of teachers' experiences and the research of pedagogical specialists. Nevertheless, some issues relevant to these subjects, such as policies and attitudes toward the Chinese language both inside and outside China and the interrelationship between teaching and learning, were only briefly mentioned. We, therefore, devote this last chapter to further discussion of these issues. In addition, this chapter discusses some of the resources for teaching and learning Chinese and offers a look at the direction of future work.

9.2 (Un)commonness of Chinese

Is Chinese a common language? For non-native Chinese, the answer to this question is primarily derived from the policy implemented in teaching Chinese as a foreign language (FL) by a nation and the attitude of the people toward the language. In countries, such as Singapore or Korea, Chinese may be considered a common language along with English. In the United States, however, Chinese is still labeled and statistically supported[1] as a "less commonly taught language" in comparison with such commonly taught foreign languages as Spanish and French. Some teachers may attribute the situation to the lack of students interested in learning Chinese. We would argue that the situation actually reflects China's political, economical and social status in the global forum and China's relationship with other countries. In the 1960s and 1970s, China almost completely closed its door to the outside world; so not many people were interested in learning the language or about the culture. Even if some people had the desire to learn the language, if their government had a strained relationship with the Chinese government, it was forbidden. This, in fact, was the situation in Malaysia in the 1960s and 1970s. In this case, it is not a surprise that Chinese would be considered an un-common language by the Malays.

Although the situation in the twenty-first century United States differs from that of Malaysia in the 1960s and 1970s, (that is, the US government does not impose any policies on its citizens preventing them from learning Chinese), many Americans still have not realized the pragmatic importance of the Chinese language, therefore do not encourage their children to learn the language. "When there is no demand, there is no Chinese class" as one of the middle school principals in the state of Washington put it. Presumably, this is one of the major reasons why many middle schools and high schools in the United States do not offer Chinese as a foreign language. When investigating the mindset of Americans toward learning Chinese, we find that only those who are exposed to international affairs and point of views are likely to realize the potential role the Chinese language will likely play in their children's future and hence encourage their children to learn the language. For a majority of Americans who do not learn much from media reports about Chinese culture, history, economy and social development in the last decade, however, Chinese is merely an extremely difficult language to learn and China is still an underdeveloped communist country. To this group of Americans, there is no compelling reason to learn. This misperception, as with all misperceptions, will require time and effort if it is to be changed.

It appears that to change the image of Chinese from an undesirable to a desirable language in the world — to shift its status from an "uncommonly taught language" to a "commonly taught language" in other words — requires the cooperation and collaboration of both the Chinese government and people and the government and people of interested countries. In recent years, the Chinese government has indeed made noticeable efforts to promote the study of Chinese as FL both inside and outside China by establishing the China National Office for Teaching Chinese as a Foreign Language (*Hànbàn*), by building Confucius Institutes around the world, and by setting up centers world-wide that organize and oversee the Hànyǔ Shuǐpíng Kǎoshì (HSK) "Chinese Assessment Test". Since its establishment, *Hànbàn* has organized various activities both for training teachers and for exciting students' interest in learning Chinese, helped pedagogy specialists develop teaching materials (e.g. *New Practical Chinese Reader* by Liu Xun et al.), and negotiated with the College Board of the United States regarding ways to use Chinese language credits for US college admission and credits (e.g. SAT II Chinese Test). This year 2005, the US National Security Education Program (NSEP) announces a new major effort as part of its National Flagship Language Initiative (NFLI) and chose Chinese as the prototype for this effort. This project, the *Chinese K-16 Flagship*, will for the first time focus on the development in the US of an articulated K-16 student pipeline with the goal of graduating students of Chinese who are linguistically and culturally competent.

All these endeavors have clearly affected some people's perception of the Chinese language in the United States and around the world. Clearly, there is much more work to do to further promote the teaching and learning of Chinese as FL. Not surprisingly however, the ultimate force that could drive the Chinese language to attain as internationally recognized status as English and to become a commonly taught foreign language in the world, would be China's economic development and China's strengthening ties to the world community. As China's economy grows, the Chinese language becomes a more commonly used language in the world economic community; when the Chinese government maintains a friendly and healthy relationship with other countries, the Chinese language is looked upon more favorably as a means of communication among people of these countries.

9.3   Further Remarks on Teaching and Learning

Throughout this book, I have discussed issues relevant to teaching and learning Chinese as FL. However, no part of the book has thus far clearly discussed and stated the characteristics and the interrelationship between teaching and learning. Therefore, I will, in this section, first compare the characteristics of teaching and learning Chinese, or rather any language, as a foreign language and then discuss how the two aspects of pedagogy interact with each other in classroom.

The role of teaching may be described as serving two functions: (1) preparing teaching materials and (2) enabling student learning. One deals with what to teach and the other with how to teach. Chapter 2 was exclusively designed to discuss what to teach and Chapter 3 how to teach. One may have noticed that both aspects of teaching seem to exist independently, yet a close look at them reveals that they do not only depend on each other, but also interact closely with each other. It was suggested in Chapter 2 that teaching materials should be determined based on their commonality, importance, and uniqueness in both spoken and written discourse. When teaching any aspect of a language, teachers have to ponder what makes each one common, important, or unique in communication and then how to effectively teach students the properties of a given linguistic sign (e.g. the *bǎ* construction). In other words, teaching method largely relies on and is determined by the content of teaching. For instance, when teaching tones, teachers may use listening and pronunciation as the primary activities in classroom. However, when teaching characters or sentences, teachers may have to design and give students some discourse situations where those characters and sentences are used to help them understand and use them in real discourse. In this case, listening exercises may also help, but they are not the only aspect of teaching. This becomes even more evident when teaching is assessed by the success of student learning. Among teachers, it is a common feeling that a successful foreign language learning experience involves training in the four skills: listening, speaking, reading and writing. Omitting any aspect of this training when teaching a sentence implies inadequacy and, in a way, unfairness to the student who needs all to become a successful FL speaker.[2] A successful and effective teacher is capable of integrating what to teach with how to teach and thereby pass on language competence to students and enable students to use it in communication.

Learning, on the other hand, focuses on how to acquire and use communicative competence. Since both actions (acquiring and using language competence) are initiated and executed by learners, it is imperative for teachers and learners to be aware of and understand the various factors affecting learners' performance in learning and using a language. In Chapter 3, several factors considered critical were mentioned; these affect the process of students' acquisition of communicative skills, among which psychological, environmental and instructional factors are considered to be some of the most important. Psychological factors refer to a student's learning attitude and include the reason why they are learning a foreign language and whether they are interested in learning or not. Environmental factors refer to where students acquire and use the language in communication. Instructional factors relate to how students are taught. Some may consider student intelligence a factor in foreign language acquisition. It is excluded from our list because we do not believe that this is among the most important factors in learning a language. Our experience in the last decade suggests that almost all students can learn Chinese as long as their minds and hearts are in it. Occasionally, we are pleased to find some students exceptionally fast in the acquisition of Chinese. Yet, can we be sure that these students are more intelligent than other students? It's hard to say; an adequate argument that proves these students to be more intelligent has yet to be made.

In most cases, it does not take long for teachers and learners to become familiar with the salient psychological, environmental, and instructional factors involved in learning Chinese. Along with a clear idea of why students are learning it and how they can learn it best, the learning process becomes apparent. Teachers will soon recognize and identify learning preferences in their classes and using this information, implement class-wide learning exercises that target each group from the passive learners to the motivated ones; no student, no matter what group s/he falls in, can be hurt by more practice.

Teachers and students together create the classroom atmosphere and nowhere more so than in a Chinese classroom where the language can be so different from a student's own. Both students and teacher must cooperate and collaborate to keep this atmosphere learning-conducive.

9.4   Resources for Learning Chinese

There have never been more resources for learning Chinese than there are in this computer age. Computers help to compile textbooks and reference books easily and to create multimedia courseware that students may interact with to acquire the listening, speaking, reading and writing skills. In what follows, four types of resources relevant to teaching and learning Chinese as FL will be discussed and commented on: textbooks, reference books, websites, and study abroad programs. It should be noted that most of these resources are commonly used by students of Chinese as FL in North America.

9.4.1 Textbooks

The Chinese textbooks currently available to students of Chinese as FL, can be categorized into three types: (1) grammar-structure oriented, (2) topic-discussion oriented, and (3) interactive oriented. The most representative textbook of the first type could be the conversation and reading series compiled by DeFrancis (see #1 in Appendix IV). Although some of the expressions used in the two series are out of date, the two series may still be considered the best structured in terms of vocabulary, grammar, and reading texts among all textbooks available in the market nowadays. In comparison, the second type of textbooks, which is most commonly seen in the twenty-first century, emphasizes topics that students will be interested in talking about in Chinese. C-P Chou's *Intermediate Reader* (1992) and *Advanced Reader* (1993) may be among the first few such textbooks published in the US. The *Intermediate Reader* includes lessons on job application, rape and stealing, living together, abortion and drugs, love and marriage, the generation gap and women's rights, etc. The advantage of using this type of textbook is that in every lesson, students learn new expressions to use in the discussion of controversial contemporary issues related to their life, environment, families and friends, and society. One drawback of this type of textbook, though, is that it tends to lack a comprehensive system in building up students' linguistic or grammatical competence, aspects which DeFrancis' books integrated so well. However, whether this will affect students' long-term learning goals and language competence has not yet been studied. The third type of textbook refers to those coupled with some kind of computer programs so that students may learn Chinese not only through traditional lecturers in classroom, but more importantly via interactive practice and exercises on the computer. This is also known as multimedia courseware. An example of this type of textbook would be *Chinese Breakthrough: Learning Chinese through TV and Newspapers* compiled by Jin et al. Because compiling this type of courseware requires both technical support and pedagogical experience, there is not yet sufficient courseware of this type available to different levels of Chinese students. This situation should be changed in the near future.

Appendix IV provides a list of Chinese textbooks. Although by no means exhaustive, those on the list were included either because they are commonly used in North America or because they are familiar to the author. They are listed alphabetically by title and therefore the order does not necessarily reflect this author's preference.

As indicated in Chapter 2, it is important to choose adequate teaching materials for different levels of students. However, in my view, teaching methodology is even more important. Given the teaching materials available today, a good teacher with an adequate teaching methodology can be just as successful, perhaps even more so, in helping their students learn a great deal of Chinese, than even a good teacher without an adequate teaching methodology.

9.4.2   References

Two types of reference books are provided alphabetically by author(s)' last name in Appendix V: grammar books and books on teaching and learning Chinese. In choosing these books in Appendix V, one criterion I used was accessibility: Are these books informative, simple and clear enough so that typical Chinese teachers would be able to understand their content material without difficulty and use it effectively to teach Chinese as FL? Teachers may find that different reference books can be used for different pedagogical purposes. For information about functions of a certain grammatical element, teachers may consult books such as Lǚ's 《现代汉语八百词》 (*Eight hundred words of modern Chinese*) or Li and Thompson's *Mandarin Chinese*. For information about the etymology of Chinese characters, one should consult the on-line dictionary *Wenlin* or Wieger's *Chinese Characters*. For pedagogical theory and practice, one may consult Lǚ, Bi-song's 《对外汉语教学概论》 (*Introduction to teaching Chinese as a foreign language*) or this book. Since the current work discusses various aspects of teaching and learning Chinese as FL, the author hopes that it will be considered a reference book by Chinese language teachers. Teachers may also find it easier to use books written by someone who has the same educational background as they do. For instance, if a teacher receives his/her higher education in the West, they may find the reference books written by Chao (1968) or Li and Thompson (1981) painless to use while a teacher in China may find the book by Lǚ (1980) or Liu (2002) straightforward. Nonetheless, a well-informed teacher knows exactly where to find the information needed in teaching.

9.4.3   Internet resources

The Internet might be the fastest way to obtain information in this Computer Age. Internet resources on teaching and learning Chinese may be classified into two types: (1) websites offering information and practice regarding teaching and learning Chinese, and (2) discussion lists and chat rooms where teachers and students may exchange information, raise questions and discuss them with other Chinese language practitioners. Due to the constant change and development of new websites, it is difficult to provide a comprehensive list of websites. Appendix VI is only a preliminary attempt to list those websites that the author often uses or hears from colleagues in the field. Anyone interested in surfing the Internet or joining a discussion list should be able to find those sites by simply typing a keyword such as "learning Chinese" or "Chinese characters" into a search engine, such as Google, Yahoo, or MSN. To get started, one may first try the website put together by Professor Marjorie Chan, who teaches Chinese and Chinese linguistics at the Ohio State University, which has links to more than 600 websites about Chinese language and linguistics: http://chinalinks.osu.edu.

9.4.4 Study abroad programs

It was mentioned in the previous chapters that students who are determined to acquire advanced competence in Chinese must participate in at least one study-in-China program. Appendix VII lists a number of popular study-in-China programs among American students. There are many other relatively small study-in-China programs[3] sponsored by colleges and universities in the United States. Students and teachers interested in those programs may search the Internet to locate the program sponsor, host institution in China, and detailed information about their programs.

Before choosing a study-in-China program, students should first ask themselves following questions:

- What is my purpose for going to study in China?
- Where do I want to study?
- How long do I want to study (just summer or through a complete academic year)?
- What kind of program do I want to be enrolled in?
- How much can I afford to pay for a program?

Once students have clear answers to these questions, it becomes relatively easy to choose a program from among the many available in China. If a student is highly capable, highly motivated and determined to improve his/her Chinese, and financially solvent, this student should try to get into a highly competitive program such as *Princeton in Beijing, Associate College in China* (ACC). However, if a student's primary reason for going to China is to gain Chinese experience or learn Chinese culture and at the same time to learn some Chinese, it may be most appropriate for this student to apply to a program such as *EducAsia* or *School for International Training* (SIT). In recent years, more and more universities and colleges have established their own study-in-China programs. Students of these schools may first consider their own program before applying for programs outside their school. This is because faculty members know their own program best in terms of the appropriateness for their own students.

Although in recent years, an increasing number of students choose to study Chinese in Mainland China, some students still go to Taiwan to learn Mandarin at such well-known places, as the Chinese Center at the National Taiwan Normal University or National Taiwan University, where many Chinese teachers currently teaching Chinese at US universities acquired their advanced Chinese competence.

Since Taiwan has an excellent pool of Chinese teachers resulting partially from a relatively large number of foreign students in the 1960s–1980s, students should consider with all relevant information about the programs in Taiwan and as well as those in Mainland China before making a decision. Choosing a suitable program can mean the difference between a successful Chinese study abroad experience and a disappointing one.

9.5   Directions for Future Work

Throughout this book, I have shown that the field of teaching and learning Chinese as FL is growing faster than ever before. However, compared with research on the acquisition of other languages, especially English, the study of Chinese acquisition is still underdeveloped. Among the five aspects of teaching and learning Chinese discussed in Chapters 4–8 (i.e. pronunciation, characters, sentences, discourse and pragmatics, and culture), the acquisition of characters and sentences has been studied longer and more thoroughly than the remaining three areas. In other words, teachers are better informed or trained in teaching Chinese characters and sentences than teaching Chinese pronunciation, discourse and pragmatics and culture.

As far as the acquisition of the Chinese pronunciation system is concerned, there is a general lack of a systematic study concerning students' perception and production of tones and pīnyīn. As teachers, we may know how to pronounce Chinese, or rather Mandarin sounds, but many of us do not know for sure how to teach them so that students perceive them and produce them accurately. For instance, when teaching the falling tone, should we tell students "Start with a high pitch and make it fall as low as possible"? or "The falling tone sounds like the pitch accent used in such English exclamations as "Out!" or "Go!""? Or should we simply give students the pitch value (i.e. the level tone: 55, the rising tone: 25, the low falling and rising tone: 214, and the falling tone: 51) and ask them to imitate us, the teachers? We do not have definitive answers to these questions, nor do we know which method may be better than another in teaching students the pronunciation system. As a result, we hear many students, at least half if not more, speak Chinese with an English accent even after two or three years of learning Chinese. Therefore, research in this area is not only necessary but also imperative.

Acquisition of discourse competence is another area where there is a lack of sufficient research. Although Chapter 7 (by far the longest chapter) of this book is intended to clarify many issues relevant to teaching and learning discourse devices in Chinese, a substantial number of questions remain unanswered. For instance, we do not know how students' discourse competence in their first language interacts with the acquisition of discourse competence in Chinese, nor do we know the most efficient method to use to teach students to connect different sentences together to make a coherent discourse. Should students learn discourse structures, such as coherent devices, by analyzing written discourse and/or oral discourse? Or should they just listen to native speakers and see how they use them in communication? A better understanding of these questions would certainly help us teach students Chinese discourse competence more efficiently.

How to develop student's Chinese cultural competence along with Chinese language competence is the third area that cries out for further study. In Chapter 8, we suggested three different ways (i.e. key word method, key sentence method, and key discourse structure method) and four steps (i.e. identify, understand, compare and practice) to develop a student's comprehension of Chinese culture. It should be noted that these methods are the preliminary results of this author's investigation of teaching culture in Chinese language class and therefore should be put into practice, assessed and revised based on the results of using them in the classroom. Presumably, some of the methods suggested in Chapter 8 may not be as effective as other methods suggested in the same chapter. They are mentioned in this book in order to inspire further discussion and generate better ideas for teaching and learning cultural knowledge along with the acquisition of language competence.

One limitation of this book is reflected in the imbalance of perspective as relates to teachers and students on the teaching and learning of Chinese as FL. Clearly, I have contributed more sections discussing the teacher's point of view throughout the book. This limitation is the result of the author's background. A corresponding book examining the process of learning Chinese from the student's point of view would certainly be a valuable addition to our understanding of the field of teaching and learning Chinese as a foreign language.

Appendix I

Sample Syllabus and Schedule for *Elementary Chinese*

I. INSTRUCTORS

II. REQUIRED MATERIALS
1. *Integrated Chinese* 《中文听说读写》, Level 1, Part 1 Textbook [TEXT] Tao-chung Yao and Yuehua Liu. Boston: Cheng and Tsui.
2. *Workbook* [WKB] *Integrated Chinese*, Level 1, Part 1
3. *Character Workbook* [CW] *Integrated Chinese*, Level 1, Part 1

III. LANGUAGE LEARNING MATERIALS
A. **AUDIO TAPES:** For Recording Textbook Lessons
1. Take the blank tape to the department office of **Textbook:** Practice: Introduction, Lessons 1 and 2
    Tape 3: *Integrated Chinese*, Level 1, Part 1: **Textbook**: Lessons 3 through 6
B. **AUDIO TAPES**: For Recording Student's Voiceodern and Classical Languages, HU 230. Fill out forms requesting the lessons you want copied, as below:
    Tape 1: *Integrated Chinese*, Level 1, Part 1: **Workbook**: Introduction through Lesson 11
    Tape 2: *Integrated Chinese*, Level 1, Part I: **T**
C. **VIDEO**: View Chinese film clips and feature films in the Language Media Center, Haggard Hall 113–114.
D. **COMPUTER PROGRAMS:** [In the Language Media Center in Haggard Hall 113–114]
1. **Multimedia Companion to Integrated Chinese** Level 1/1 to learn listening, speaking, reading, and writing
2. **Pronunciation Modules** to learn the Chinese pronunciation system
3. **Wenlin** to learn Chinese characters;
4. **Microsoft Word 2000** to write Chinese homework and essays;
5. Websites: <http://eastasia.hawaii.edu/tedyao/icusers/> containing a variety of exercises for students using *Integrated Chinese* to practice listening, speaking, reading and writing skills.

IV. LEARNING OBJECTIVES

The course is designed as an integrated study of Chinese usage. Students are expected to gain a beginner's proficiency in areas of listening, speaking, reading and writing Chinese.

- Listening Skills: ability to distinguish the sounds and tones of spoken Standard Chinese, known as *putonghua* or Mandarin; ability to comprehend simple sentences, short speeches, and dialogues.
- Speaking Skills: ability to produce the basic sounds of spoken Chinese, including the distinct pronunciation of tones; ability to respond to questions and to initiate simple dialogues. The first several weeks of the quarter will focus on the acquisition of pronunciation and speaking skills.
- Reading Skills: ability to recognize approximately 200 Chinese characters and to learn their use in combination; ability to read prepared texts.
- Writing Skills: knowledge of principles in the formation of Chinese characters; ability to write all characters learned in the texts; ability to write dialogues and short essays.

V. EVALUATION

A. Evaluation will be made on the basis of proficiency and participation
B. Grading:

30%	Unit examinations
15%	Weekly quizzes, dictation and essays
20%	Homework assignments, Workbook, and Chinese Character Book
15%	Class attendance and quality of participation
10%	Oral tapes, oral review and oral presentation
10%	Final examination
100%	

C. Grades will be assigned as follows:
    A: 100–97; A: 96–95; A-: 94–91; B+: 90–87; B: 86–85; B-: 84–81;
    C+: 80–77; C: 76–75; C-: 74–71; D+: 70–77; D: 66–65; D-: 64–61; F: 60 and below.
D. Class Participation will be graded as: A: Well prepared; B: Well prepared; good performance; C: Some evidence of preparation; D: Present for class; unprepared for class; F: Absent

- Notes: You will use a form to record your own attendance, assignments and examination scores. Make-up examinations will be given only in the case of excused absences. Three or more absences could result in the lowering of the student's grade by one full letter grade.
- Each student will meet with instructors to evaluate progress at least twice during the quarter. If you have any questions regarding the course, features of the Chinese language, or your own progress, please see the instructors during their office hours. Welcome to the class! Good luck in your studies!
- Chinese will be the primary medium of instruction for the course. Students will be addressed by their Chinese names as soon as these have been

determined. If you would like to participate in the selection of your Chinese name, please consult with instructors; you may also refer to a website: http://www.mandarintools.com/chinesename.html

SAMPLE OF SPECIFIC ASSIGNMENTS AND PROCEDURES

Day 1
1. Introduction to course: Syllabus and materials
2. IC (Integrated Chinese): Textbook [Introduction and Lesson 1] (Transparencies); Chinese Pronunciation, pp. 1–3; Chinese Characters, pp. 14–16; Text and Dialogue, pp. 21–23
3. Assignment: Study pronunciation (pp. 1–3); copy audio tapes and listen to them ; write characters: CW (Character Workbook) pp. 1–2 [Radicals]: 人, 刀, 力, 口, 女 ; study dialogue, TEXT (Textbook) pp. 21–23: 你好! 你叫什么名字?

Day 2
1. *Integrated Chinese*, Introduction and Lesson 1: Greetings
2. TEXT: Introduction, pp. 1–5; Pronunciation Drills; Tones, p. 10; Module I: Unit 1
3. TEXT: Text and Dialogue: pp. 21–23
4. CW: Chinese characters: Radicals, pp. 1–5; characters, pp. 17–21
5. Assignment: Study pronunciation; listen to tapes; write characters, CW, pp. 1–5 ; read dialogues, pp. 22–23

Day 3
1. IC: Introduction and Lesson 1: Greetings
2. TEXT: Lesson 1: Grammar, pp. 26–27
3. CW: Chinese characters: pp. 17–21
4. TEXT: Introduction, pp. 1–7 ; Pronunciation and pinyin: Module I: Unit 2
5. **PRE-TEST:** pronunciation: pinyin and tones [not graded; used for diagnosis only]
6. Assignment: Study pronunciation; listen to tapes; practice pronunciation Modules in LAB, Haggard Hall 113; Write Chinese characters, CW, pp. 17–18; Read and practices dialogues, TEXT, pp. 22–23; review grammar, pp. 26–27

Day 4
1. IC: Introduction and Lesson 1: Greetings
2. TEXT: Introduction, pp. 1–10: Pronunciation, pinyin and tones: Module I: Unit 3
3. CW: Chinese Characters, Radicals, pp. 6–7; Lesson 1: pp. 19–20
4. WKB, pp. 13–15: Review of Lesson 1, Dialogue #1
5. Assignment: Prepare for Chinese character quiz [Dialogue #1; vocabulary #1–13]

Appendix II

Sample Syllabus and Schedule for *Intermediate Chinese*

I. INSTRUCTOR

II. REQUIRED MATERIALS (Available at the university bookstore)
1. **Books**
    (a) 《中文听说读写》 *Integrated Chinese* Level II: Textbook
    (b) 《中文听说读写》 *Integrated Chinese* Level II: Workbook
    (c) DICT — Chinese/English; English/Chinese Dictionary
2. **Audio Tapes**
Go to the Department of Modern & Classical Languages and fill out a form requesting the lessons you want copied. For the Winter quarter, you should request the following CDs:
    CD #1: Lessons 1–4 *(Integrated Chinese* Level II)
    CD #2: Lessons 5–8 *(Integrated Chinese* Level II)
    CD #6: Workbook: Lessons 1–20 *(Integrated Chinese* Level II)

III. OTHER LANGUAGE LEARNING MATERIALS (available at the Language Lab)
1. **Video**
    (a) Chinese New Year
    (b) Chinese feature films
2. **Computer Software**
    (a) Microsoft Word 2000 (Chinese word processor on IBM)
    (b) Wenlin (Chinese Dictionary on IBM)
3. **Related Webpages**
    (a) http://www.ac.wwu.edu/~chinese (Chinese program homepage at Western)
    (b) http://nts.lll.hawaii.edu/tedyao/icusers (for *Integrated Chinese* users)
    (c) http://www.csulb.edu/~txie/online.htm (Popular page for learning Chinese)
    (d) http://deall.ohio-state.edu/chan9/c-links.htm (Links to Chinese related pages)

IV. OBJECTIVES OF THIS COURSE

Students are expected to gain intermediate proficiency in the areas of listening, speaking, reading, writing and translating Chinese.

- **Aural Skills**: The ability to distinguish the sounds and tones of spoken Standard Chinese; ability to comprehend short speeches, dialogues and stories.
- **Oral Skills:** The ability to respond to questions and to initiate dialogues; ability to narrate, to describe, and to compare different situations with correct tones and intonation.
- **Reading Skills**: The ability to read variety of short speeches, dialogues, and stories; ability to use a dictionary to expand vocabulary and to determine meanings of words in context.
- **Writing Skills**: The ability to write all characters learned in the texts; ability to write sentences, paragraphs, and essays that use materials learned in texts.
- **Translation Skills**: Recognition of the basic word order and grammatical patterns in Chinese; awareness of differences between English and Chinese sentence structures and common expressions.

V. REQUIREMENTS AND GRADING

1. Requirements

Before coming to class, prepare the material to be covered on that day (i.e. memorize vocabulary, write characters, listen to audio tapes, go through text and reading material, and do homework); Chinese is the ONLY language used in classes.

2. Grading

(a) Written exams (4)	20%
(b) Oral exams (4)	20%
(c) Weekly dictation	15%
(d) Class participation*	10%
(e) Homework (essays and handouts)	20%
(f) Final exam	15%

NOTES: Make-up exams will be given only in the case of excused absences. Three or more absences could result in the lowering of the student's grade by one full letter grade.

3. Grades will be assigned as follows:

A: 94–100; A-: 90–94; B+: 88–90; B: 84–88; B-: 80–84; C+: 77–80; C: 74–77 C-: 70–74; D: 60–69; F: 0–59

You will be scheduled at least two individual sessions with me discussing your performance and progress in this class. If you have questions, be they regarding the course, your progress or the language itself, please come to see me during my office hours or by appointment. Good Luck!

SAMPLE OF SPECIFIC SCHEDULES AND PROCEDURES

一月四日：星期二
1.   Course Introduction: Syllabus and Materials
2.   Integrated Chinese — Textbook (课本) 第二册，第一课：生词和语法
3.   作业/功课：学习，听第一课的生词和课文

一月五日：星期三
1.   第一课：课文和语法
2.   做练习：课本，第 14–15 页
3.   作业：准备听力练习：Integrated Chinese — Workbook (本子)，第 1–3
     页：做语法练习；本子第 8–10 页；写作文：开学的第一天

一月六日：星期四
1.   第一课：语法和听力
2.   做语法练习：本子第 8–10 页
3.   听力练习：本子第 1–3 页
4.   **交作文#1**
5.   作业：(a) 准备口语练习；本子第 3 页 — 怎么介绍自己；(b) 准备
     听写

一月七日：星期五
1.   **第一课: 听写**
2.   口语练习：本子第 3 页
3.   阅读练习：本子第 4–7 页
4.   作业：（1）准备翻译练习；本子第 11–12 页；（2）作 Handout 的
     练习

一月十日：星期一
1.   第一课：翻译练习
2.   **交 Handout**
3.   **复习：准备第一次笔试**

一月十一日：星期二
1.   **笔试#1**
2.   作业：准备第二课：听课文和生词的录音带，看懂语法

一月十二日：星期三
1.   第二课：课文和语法
2.   作业：（1）做练习：课本第 30–32 页；听力练习：本子第 13–14 页；
     （2）作 Handout

Appendix III

Sample Syllabus and Schedule for *Advanced Chinese*

CHINESE 330: CHINESE FILM AND LITERATURE
中国电影文学
西华盛顿大学中文 330 课表

一、 老师： 邢老师
办公室： HU215
电话： 650-3926
电脑信箱： Janet.Xing@wwu.edu
上课时间： 星期一下午，三点到五点半
上课地点： HU109
办公室时间：星期一、星期三和星期五， 十二点或者跟老师预约

二、 教材：（本课用的电影都在学校的图书馆）
《马路天使》、《小城之春》、《雷雨》、《骆驼祥子》
《芙蓉镇》、《菊豆》、《秋菊打官司》、《红高粱》
《大红灯笼高高挂》、《黑炮事件》、《错位》、《活着》

三、 教学目的：
1、学习文学剧本和电影语言；
2、中国电影历史；
3、了解中国文化、历史、习俗；
4、学习"书面语"和"口语"的不同；
5、学习"俗语"和"成语"的用法。

四、 上课内容和方式：
讲解和讨论文学作品、电影的题材、内容、语言、历史等问题。看电影。学生每个星期要看电影、写一个一页纸的小作文。学期中有一个期中考试、期末有一个期末考试。

Appendix IV

List of the Commonly Used Textbooks in North America

TEXTBOOKS

1. *Beginning Chinese Reader* (1966), *Intermediate Chinese Reader* (1967), *Advanced Chinese Reader* (1968) by John DeFrancis. New Haven: Yale University Press. Professor DeFrancis also compiled a conversation series: *Beginning Chinese (in pinyin)/Character Text for Beginning Chinese*, *Intermediate Chinese (in pinyin)/Character Text for Intermediate Chinese*, and *Advanced Chinese (in pinyin)/Character Text for Advanced Chinese*, published by Yale University Press (1976, second edition). All lessons contain dialogues, vocabulary, pronunciation, sentence, grammar drills and exercises, and notes.

2. *Beyond the Basic: Communicative Chinese for Intermediate/Advanced Learners* by Bai, Song, and Xing. Boston: Cheng and Tsui Publications (1996). This book is designed for intermediate-high and advanced-low students according to the ACTFL proficiency rating. All lessons have a text (in both simplified and traditional characters), discussion questions, vocabulary, sentence patterns, grammar notes, supplementary vocabulary for discussion, a composition related to the topic of every lesson, and extended exercises to develop speaking, reading and writing skills.

3. *Chinese Breakthrough: Learning Chinese through TV and Newspapers* (Textbook, Workbook, CD ROM, video and audio tapes) by Hong-gang Jin et al. (1998, third edition). Boston: Cheng and Tsui Publications. This book appears suitable for third-year Chinese students. Professor Jin and her team also compiled *China Scene: An Advanced Chinese Multimedia Course Textbook and Workbook* (2000) and *Shifting Tide* (2002) published by Cheng and Tsui.

4. *Chinese Text for a Changing China* by Irene Liu and Shaoqi Liu. Boston: Cheng and Tsui Publications (1996). This book is the revised edition of *A New Text for a Modern China*. The updated edition includes the most recent developments in Chinese society and language.

5. *Communicating in Chinese* Series: *An Interactive Approach to Beginning Chinese* by Cynthia Ning. New Haven: Far Eastern Publications (1993). This series contain Student's Book: Listening and Speaking, Picture Cards (Listening/Speaking), Teacher's Activity Book, Student's Book: Reading and Writing, and Teacher's Activities and Reference Book for Reading and Writing.

6. *Integrated Chinese (IC), Level 1–2* by Ted Yao et al. Boston: Cheng and Tsui (1997). This two-level IC series come with three books at each level: Textbook, Workbook, and Character Workbook (simplified and traditional). This two-level series might be the most common textbook used in the United States in the twenty-first century.

7. *Intermediate Reader of Modern Chinese* (1992) and *Advanced Reader of Modern Chinese: China's Own Critics* (1993) by Chi-ping Chou et al. Princeton: University of Princeton Press (1992). Professor Chou's team also compiled an advanced textbook possibly used by fourth-year Chinese students: *Advanced Reader of Modern Chinese: Literature and Society* (1999) published by Princeton University Press.

8. *Interactions I–II: A Cognitive Approach to Beginning Chinese* by Jennifer L-C Liu and Margaret Yan. Bloomington: Indiana University Press (1997). This textbook series is accompanied by Workbook and Teacher's Manual.

9. *Making Connections: Enhance Your Listening Comprehension in Chinese* (simplified/traditional edition and audio CD) by Madeline Spring. Boston: Cheng and Tsui Publications (2002). This book may be used to develop student's listening competence and used in conjunction with the lessons in *Integrated Chinese Level 1.*

10. *Mandarin Primer*: An Intensive Course in Spoken Chinese by Chao Yuan-ren. Cambridge: Harvard University Press (1948). Some teachers may consider this book too old to be used with twenty-first-century students, yet others still find it useful for information about the properties of the Chinese language.

11. *New Practical Chinese Reader (PCR) 1–4* by Liu Xun et al. Beijing: Beijing Language and Cultural University Press (2002–2004). This is an upgraded and revised (both in vocabulary and lesson topics) series of the *Practical Chinese Reader* by the same author originally published in 1976. The New PCR (1–4) series may be the most informative and instructive textbooks compiled by native Chinese speakers.

12. *Taiwan Today* by Teng and Lo. Boston: Cheng and Tsui Publications (1999, second edition). This book may be used by high intermediate students. It has 12 chapters (in both simplified and traditional characters) that present various aspects of Taiwan's culture.

13. *Zhongwen* (中文) series by Yi-min Jia (ed.). Guangzhou: Jinan University Press (1997). This series, different from all the textbook introduced above, is designed for K-12 students in North America and aims to help young students build a foundation in listening, speaking, reading and writing.

Appendix V

List of the Commonly Used Reference Books in North America

1. Chao, Yuan-ren (1968) *A Grammar of Spoken Chinese*. Berkeley/Los Angeles: University of California Press. Its Chinese translation (汉语口语语法) was published in 2001 by Shangwu Yinshu Guan (商务印书馆).

2. Chao, Yuan-ren (1948a and 1948b) *Mandarin Primer: An Intensive Course in Spoken Chinese*. Cambridge: Harvard University Press. [Although this book is generally considered a textbook, the first two parts provide teachers and students with necessary information about the Chinese language and the method of teaching and learning the language. Hence, it may be considered a reference book as well.]

3. Li C. and S. Thompson (1981) *Mandarin Chinese: A Functional Reference Grammar*. Berkeley/Los Angeles: University of California Press.

4. Liu, Yue-hua (刘月华), W. W. Pan (潘文娱), and W. Gu (故玮) (2002) 《实用现代汉语语法》(Practical Grammar of Modern Chinese, extended edition). Beijing: Shangwu Yinshu Guan (商务印书馆).

5. Lu, Bi-song (吕必松) (1999) 《对外汉语教学概论》 (Introduction to Teaching Chinese as a Foreign Language). Beijing: National Education Board (国家教委).

6. Lu, Shu-xiang (吕叔湘) (1980) 《现代汉语八百词》 (Eight-hundred Words of Modern Chinese). Beijing: Shangwu Yinshu Guan (商务印书馆).

7. Wieger, L (1965) *Chinese Characters*. New York: Dover Publications, Inc. (This book gives a list of 224 traditionally used radicals, explains the origin, etymology, creation, history, classification, and significance of these primitives in both Chinese and English).

8. *Wenlin* (http://www.wenlin.com/) on-line dictionary and software for learning Chinese created by Wenlin Institute, Inc.

Appendix VI

List of Websites on Teaching and Learning Chinese

- **CLAP**: http://www.sinologic.com/clas/ Chinese Learner's Alternate Page, from SinoLogic; updated weekly.
- **Tianwei Xie's webpage**: http://www.csulb.edu/~txie/online.htm. Containing the most extensive set of Chinese learning exercises and links to online Chinese learning software and vendors.
- **Chinese Language Teaching and Learning Aids**: http://www.wfu.edu/~moran/. Course materials developed by Patrick Moran: Macintosh CAI , CAL, CALL applications, printable flashcards, printable calligraphy practice sheets, etc.
- **ChiNews-On-Web Course:** http://chinews.hawaii.edu/. Prof. Ying-che Li's extensive, multimedia website for computer-assisted language learning (CALL).
- Chinese Online Reading Assistant (CORA) Project: http://www.lang.uiuc.edu/chinese/reading. Browse Prof. Chin-chuan Cheng's website to practice reading the online Chinese materials (encoded in GB and Big5), accompanied by online glosses. Real-time (RealAudio) sounds will eventually be included with most, if not all, of the lessons.
- **Chinese Character Lists**: http://www.afpc.asso.fr/. These are available from the French Chinese Language Teachers Association (Association Française des Professeurs de Chinois [AFPC]) website.
- **Hanyu Shuiping Kaoshi (HSK)**: http://people.cohums.ohio-state.edu/chan9/c-links3.htm#hsk. Hanyu Shuiping Kaoshi (HSK). China's HSK homepage (GB/Eng).
- **Internet Based Chinese Learning and Teaching:** http://chinese.bendigo.latrobe.edu.au/. La Trobe University's pay-to-enroll, online Chinese language courses; sample lessons; sample audio files in RealAudio format.
- **Multimedia Inside CHINESE Language Lab:** http://peijean.ficnet.net.tw/. Page Lin's colorful site for online pronunciation lessons using real-time (RealAudio) sounds.
- **Online Chinese Resources:** http://www.lsa.umich.edu/asian/chinese/online/index3.html. University of Michigan's links to resources to aid in the learning of the Chinese language and culture.
- **Speak Mandarin Campaign:** http://www.gov.sg/spkmandarin/. Singapore government's colorful and sophisticated multimedia-based website for

promoting use of Mandarin Chinese; includes language lessons; vocabulary lists; cartooned Chinese fables and parables; stroke order, evolution and pronunciation of Chinese characters, etc.

- **Study Mandarin Chinese using VOA**: http://www.ocrat.com/ocrat/voa/. Aimed at intermediate-level students of Mandarin and updated weekly, this site provides sentence-by-sentence sound clips from Mandarin-language newscasts, along with transcripts (GB, Big5, or graphics), Pinyin, and vocabulary lists.
- **CHINESE List** maintained by Prof. Bai (bai@kenyon.edu) at Kenyon College, "established to promote communication among teachers, researchers and students of the Chinese language."

Appendix VII

List of Study Abroad Programs Commonly Used by Students in North America

1. *Associated Colleges in China* (ACC) directed by Professor Hong-gang Jin, sponsored by Hamilton College, Williams College, and Oberlin College, and hosted by the Capital University of Economy and Trade, Beijing. This rigorous total immersion program appears best suited to students who are highly devoted to learning Chinese while in China. It offers courses in summer and fall (http://www.hamilton.edu/academic/eal/Abroad_link.html).

2. *CET Academic Program*, headquartered in Washington DC, not affiliated with any colleges or universities. CET has three locations in China: Beijing, Harbin, and Nanjing and offers courses in summer, fall and spring (http://www.cetacademicprograms.com/ChinaPrograms/).

3. *Columbia Summer Language Program in Beijing*, directed by Le-ning Liu, sponsored by Columbia University and hosted by Tsinghua University, Beijing. This program also developed an internship section in Shanghai for its students (http://www.ce.columbia.edu/beijing/apply.cfm).

4. *Council on International Educational Exchange* (CIEE), headquartered in New York, not affiliated with any colleges or universities. It has three locations in China: Beijing (summer, fall, and spring), Shanghai (summer, fall, and spring), and Nanjing (fall and spring) (http://www.ciee.org/).

5. *Harvard Academy in Beijing*, directed by Shengli Feng, sponsored by Harvard University, and hosted by Beijing Language University. This is the most recently established program, yet it is probably one of the most promising programs in the years to come (http://www.fas.harvard.edu/~clp/HBA/).

6. *Hopkins-Nanjing Center for Chinese Study*, jointly administered by Nanjing University and the Johns Hopkins University. The Center offers a one-year graduate-level program in Chinese. Since the Center also offers master's degree in Chinese and American Studies, students who wish to receive an MA degree or transfer humanity credits above and beyond Chinese may find this program more attractive (http://sais-jhu.edu/Nanjing/index.html).

7. *Inter-University Program for Chinese Language Studies at Qinghua* (IUP) managed by the IUB Advisory Board, headquartered at University of California at Berkeley. This program intended for students who aspire to attain advanced competence is known for its small-size classes and individual attention from teachers. It offers classes in spring, summer and fall semester (http://ieas.berkeley.edu/iup/).

8. *Mandarin Training Center*, National Taiwan Normal University. The Center has become the largest and best-known institution in Taiwan dedicated to the teaching of Chinese as a second language. In addition to all levels of Chinese language courses all year round, students may also take classes in painting, Chinese martial arts, folk singing, among others, in the afternoon according to individual interests (http://www.mtc.ntnu.edu.tw/indexe.html).

9. *Princeton in Beijing*, directed by Professor C-P Chou, sponsored by Princeton University, and hosted by Beijing Normal University. This program is probably the largest intensive summer program sponsored by a US university with an enrollment of over 100 students. Many students who participate in the program consider it challenging, yet rewarding in the end (http://www.princeton.edu/~pib).

Notes

Chapter 1

1   Some researchers use the term "acquisition" to refer to the process of acquiring a language naturally (e.g. the situation in acquiring learners' first language) and use the term "learning" to refer to other language learning experience. This book does not distinguish the two terms and use them interchangeably.

2   This book uses the term "Chinese as a foreign language (FL)," instead of "Chinese as a second language," to refer to all situations in which Chinese is not the students' native language.

3   The ACTFL Proficiency Guidelines' Speaking section was revised in 1999 and published in *Foreign Language Annals*, Vol. 33(1), 13–18. The revised version adds a low advanced level to the original guidelines published in 1986. Chinese Proficiency Guidelines have not been accordingly modified at the time of this work.

Chapter 2

1   In Taiwan and Singapore, traditional/complicated characters are still used in all official settings and schools even though some simplified characters have penetrated the colloquial usage.

2   Content of this section and section 2.3.2 builds on Xing (2003).

3   English has verbal structures like "walk out of classroom," "walk downstairs" for 走出教室 *zǒu chū jiàoshì* and 走下楼 *zǒu xià lóu*. However, English grammarians label "out of classroom" as a prepositional phrase modifying "walk" and downstairs an adverb modifying the verb, whereas Chinese grammarians consider both 出教室 *chū jiàoshì* and 下楼 *xià lóu* as directional complements modifying the verb.

4   I am grateful to Professor C-P Chou and Gregory Jiang for providing some of these examples.

Chapter 3

1   Parts of this chapter, especially 3.1 and 3.4.1, build on Xing (2003).
2   The results in Table 3.1 are derived from the author's visits to a number of classes at the Northwest Chinese School, Seattle Chinese School, Lakeside Schools, Snohomish High School, and Bellevue High School in the state of Washington, USA.
3   It should be noted that 上来/下去 *shànglái/xiàqù* originally conveyed the concept of spatial direction. Later, through metaphorical extension, 下去 acquired the meaning of "continue." What should be emphasized here is that the "end" meaning of 下 is limited to situations in which it follows a verb only (e.g., 停下), and not situations in which it is used with the directional verbs, such as 来/去.

Chapter 4

1   Norman (1988: 141) explains, "The three retroflex sounds are pronounced with the front of the tongue retracted to a position just behind the alveolar ridge." Before vowels such as *i*, Norman further points out, "retroflex sounds are pronounced with spread lips, which contrary to the English speaker's habit of pronouncing *j, ch, sh*." According to Norman (on the same page), the three palatal sounds, on the other hand, are "articulated with the blade of the tongue placed against the front part of the palate; simultaneously the free front part of the tongue is raised toward the alveolar ridge. The English sounds *ji, chi*, and *shi* fall somewhere between the Chinese retroflexes and the palatals, and the typical English-speaking student of Chinese has a difficult time learning to distinguish Chinese pairs like *shǎo* and *xiǎo*."
2   *S* can be used either at the beginning or at the end of a syllable as in *say* [sei] and *mass* [mæs].
3   If this analysis holds, then the confusion between the two tones is not a result of the pitch value shared by the two tones as reported in the literature (e.g. Repp and Lin 1990), but rather resulted from the uncertainty of the application of tone 3 sandhi rules.
4   The front rounded vowel *ü* often has its two dots omitted after the palatal sounds because the back front vowel *u* never occurs after the palatal sounds.
5   The *i* sound after *zhi, chi, shi* is a low front vowel; it is different from the *i* after the palatal sounds (*ji, qi, xi*).

Chapter 5

1   The pronunciations of radicals given in Table 5.3 are the commonly used pronunciation in modern Chinese, which may not be the same as the original

sound of those radicals. For instance, originally, the radical ﹅ given in the table is pronounced "*zhŭ*" meaning "stop"; however, we choose the commonly used term "*diăn*" meaning "dot" to refer to this radical.

Chapter 7

1   Some of the examples come from *Pop Chinese: A Cheng and Tsui Guide to Colloquial Expressions* by Feng et al. (2004). It should be noted that the distinction between the two pairs is sometimes more than formal versus informal; some may have a wider scope of meaning and some may differ in terms of their grammatical or discourse pragmatic functions.

2   Jiāo (2003) has a substantial discussion on the new vocabulary developed in recent years in China. Numerous popular and fashionable expressions are also provided in his article. Footnote 1 is also applied here.

3   This section builds on Xing (2005).

4   Halliday and Hasan (1976) introduced the notion of *cohesion* and for a decade or so since that time, researchers did not clearly differentiate between cohesion and coherence in discourse. However, in the last two decades, an increasing number of researchers have addressed the different functions played by the two concepts (cf. Carrell 1982, Cooper 1988, Campbell 1995, Bublitz 1999). Due to the nature of the current work, we use coherence throughout the book unless it is part of quotation or custom usage such as "lexical cohesion".

5   There are a few concurrent discourse connectors in English (e.g. "*not only ...,* *but also ...*"), German (e.g. *nicht nur ..., aber auch*) and French (e.g. *non seulement ..., mais également*). Most discourse connectors in these languages are used individually, which introduces either cause or result. Chinese also has solo connectors marking a logical relation, such as 从而 *cóngér* "so that", 于是 *yúshì* "as a result", 因此 *yīncǐ* "therefore", 免得 *miǎnde* "in order to avoid" etc.

6   天哪 *tiānna* may be used for two discourse functions: "consequence" and "disappointment". There is no apparent difference with the sound and form when serving for these two functions.

7   The character 啊 may also be used to serve for two discourse functions. When pronounced with a neutral tone, it signals a common "response" of the listener; when pronounced with a rising pitch, it expresses "surprise" of the listener.

8   Traditionally, Chinese aesthetic view on women is largely derived from their face, namely whether a person has large eyes with double-layered eyelid, bridged nose, or small mouth, quite different from the modern American aesthetic emphasizing on the figure of women and their breasts and hips.

9   It should be noted that the characteristics of formal conversation just discussed differ from that of business negotiation, another type of oral

discourse mentioned at the beginning of this section. Readers interested in business negotiation may consult Ulijn and Li (1995).

Chapter 8

1   The term "cultural communication information" is used by Lǚ and some other Chinese researchers. It might be convenient — and more appropriate — to use the English expression "multicultural communication" developed by Western researchers.
2   Some teachers may consider instant messages as a two-way interaction activity. I argue that even though the respondent is another human being, the student is reading messages on the screen, not directly interacting with the person, namely hearing the sound of the language and making an oral response right away. Therefore, the interaction is still one way, not two ways.

Chapter 9

1   According to a national survey conducted by Draper and Hicks, American Council on the Teaching of Foreign Languages (2002) on "Foreign Language Enrollments in Public Secondary Schools," among almost seven million students enrolled in foreign language courses in 2000, less than 0.1% students were enrolled in Chinese, while majority of the students were enrolled in Spanish (68.7%) and other languages (French 18.3%, German 4.8%, Latin 2.7%, Italian 1.2%, etc.).
2   This would exclude special situations when a class is designed to train students' competence in certain particular area(s), such as speaking or reading.
3   When SARS broke out in 2003, the office of the International Programs and Exchanges at Western Washington University received information from associated institutions that more than 500 schools (including primary and secondary schools) in the United States canceled their study abroad programs in China.

References

ACTFL. 1989. *Oral Proficiency Interview*. White Plains: Language Testing International.

ACTFL. 1990. *Chinese Proficiency Guidelines*. New York: ACTFL Materials Center.

Alber, C. 1996. Citizens of a global village: Information technology and Chinese language instruction – A search for standards. In S. McGinnis (ed.), *Chinese Pedagogy: An Emerging Field*, Chinese Language Teachers Association Monograph Series, No. 2, pp. 229–53. Columbus, OH: Foreign Language Publications.

Allen, W. 1985. Toward cultural proficiency. In A. C. Oeaggio (ed.), *Proficiency, Curriculum, Articulation: The Ties That Bind*, pp. 137–66. Middlebury, VT: Northeast Conference on the Teaching of Foreign Languages.

An, D. (安顿). 2000.《情证今生》(Love letter). Haikou, China: Hainan Chuban Gongsi.

Arnold, J. (ed.) 1999. *Affect in Language Learning*. Cambridge: Cambridge University Press.

Asher, N. 1993. *Reference to Abstract Objects in Discourse*. SLAP 50, Dordrecht: Kluwer.

Ba, J. (巴金). 1995.《再思录》(Retrospection). Shanghai: Yuandong Chubanshe.

Bachman, L. F. 1990. *Fundamental Considerations in Language Testing*. Oxford: Oxford University Press.

Bachman, L. F. and A. D. Cohen. 1998. *Interfaces between Second Language Acquisition and Language Testing Research*. New York: Cambridge University Press.

Bai, J. 2003. Making multimedia an integral part of curricular innovation. *Journal of the Chinese Language Teachers Association* 38(2): 1–16.

Bai, J., R. Song and J. Xing. 1996. *Beyond the Basic: Communicative Chinese for Intermediate/Advanced Learners*. Boston: Cheng and Tsui.

Baller, F. W. 1912. *Lessons in Elementary Wen-Li*. Shanghai: China Inland Mission and Presbyterian Mission Press.

Bar-Lev, B. 1995. Does the home make a difference? A comparison of home-exposure and non-home-exposure students of Mandarin. *Journal of the Chinese Language Teachers Association* 30(3): 55–68.

Bar-Lev, Z. 1991. Two innovations for teaching tones. *Journal of the Chinese Language Teachers Association* 26(3): 1–24.

Beck, M.L. (ed.) 1998. *Morphology and Its Interfaces in Second Language Knowledge.* Amsterdam: John Benjamins.

Bellassen, J. 2004. Teaching and learning Chinese in France. *The First International Symposium on Teaching and Learning Chinese as a Second Language,* December 26–28, Zhongshan University, Guangzhou, China.

Bellassen, J. and P. P. Zhang. 1997. *A Key to Chinese Speech and Writing.* Beijing: Sinolingua.

Berger, A. A. 1997. *Narratives in Popular Culture, Media, and Everyday Life.* Thousands Oaks: Sage Publications.

Berns, M. 1990. *Contexts of Competence: Social and Cultural Consideration in Communicative Language Teaching.* New York and London: Plenum Press.

Bialystok, E. (ed.). 1991. *Language Processing in Bilingual Children.* Cambridge: Cambridge University Press.

Biq, Y. O. 1990. Conversation, continuation, and connectives. *Text* 10(3): 187–208.

Blackney, R. B. 1935. *A Course in the Analysis of Chinese Characters.* Shanghai: The Commercial Press.

Blakemore, D. 1988. The organization of discourse. In F. J. Newmeyer (ed.), *Linguistics: The Cambridge Survey,* Vol. IV, pp. 229–50. Cambridge: Cambridge University Press.

Blakemore, D. 2002. *Relevance and Linguistics Meaning: The Semantic and Pragmatic of Discourse Markers.* Cambridge, UK: Cambridge University Press.

Bley-Vroman, R. 1988. The fundamental character of foreign language learning. In W. Rutherford and M. Sharwood-Smith (eds.), *Grammar and Second Language Teaching: A Book of Readings,* pp. 19–30. New York: Newbury House

Bley-Vroman, R. 1989. What is the logical problem of foreign language learning? In S. Gass and J. Schachter (eds.), *Linguistic Perspectives on Second Language Acquisition,* pp. 41–72.

Blicher, D. L., Diehl, R. L. and L. B. Cohen. 1990. Effects of syllable duration on the perception of the Mandarin Tone2/Tone3 distinction: Evidence of auditory enhancement. *Journal of Phonetics* 18: 37–49.

Bloomfield, L. 1942. *Outline Guide for the Practical Study of Languages.* Baltimore: Linguistic Society of America.

Bolinger, D. 1986. *Intonation and Its Parts: Melody in Spoken English.* Stanford: Stanford University Press.

Bolinger, D. 1989. *Intonation and Its Uses: Melody in Grammar and Discourse.* Stanford: Stanford University Press.

Boltz, W. G. 1994. *The Origin and Early Development of the Chinese Writing System*. New Haven: American Oriental Society.

Brazil, D. 1975. *Discourse Intonation*. University of Birmingham: English Language Research.

Breitenbach, S. 2003. *Francisco Varo's Grammar of the Mandarin Language (1703): An English Translation of 'Arte de la lengua Mandarina'*. Amsterdam/Philadelphia: John Benjamins.

Brooks, N. 1960. *Language and Language Learning: Theory and Practice*. New York: Harcourt, Brace and World.

Brown, G. and G. Yule. 1983. *Discourse Analysis*. New York: Cambridge University Press.

Brumfit, C. 1984. *Communicative Methodology in Language Teaching*. Cambridge: Cambridge University Press.

Brumfit, C. J. and K. Johnson. 1979. *The Communicative Approach to Language Teaching*. Oxford: Oxford University Press.

Bublitz, W., U. Lenk, and E. Ventola. 1999. *Coherence in Spoken and Written Discourse*. Amsterdam/Philadelphia: John Benjamins.

Byram, M. 1989. *Cultural Studies in Foreign Language Education*. Clevedon/Philadelphia: Multilingual Matters.

Byram, M. 1991. *Cultural Studies and Language Learning: A Research Report*. Clevedon: Multilingual Matters.

Byram, M. 1997. *Teaching and Assessing Intercultural Communicative Competence*. Clevedon: Multilingual Matters.

Byram, M. and M. Fleming. (ed.) 1998. *Language Learning in Intercultural Perspective*. Cambridge, UK: Cambridge University Press.

Byram, M. and C. Morgan. 1994. *Teaching-and-Learning Language-and-Culture*. Clevedon, UK: Multilingual Matters.

California College in China Foundation (CCCF). 1943 [Reprint]. *Chinese Language Lessons*《华文初阶》. Stanford: Stanford University Press.

Campbell, K. S. 1995. *Coherence, Continuity, and Cohesion. Theoretical Foundations for Document Design*. Hillsdale: Erlbaum.

Cao, Y. (曹禺). 1994a.《原野》(Open country). Beijing: Renmin Wenxue Chubanshe.

Cao, Y. (曹禺). 1994b.《北京人》(Beijinger). Beijing: Renmin Wenxue Chubanshe.

Carr, M. 1981. Pedagogy, radicals, and grapho-semantic fields. *Journal of the Chinese Language Teachers Association* 16(3): 51–66.

Carrell, P. 1982. Cohesion is not coherence. *TESOL Quarterly* 16: 479–88.

Celce-Murcia, M. and E. Olshtain. 2000. *Discourse and Context in Language Teaching*. New York: Cambridge University Press.

Cen, Q. X. (岑麒祥). 1990.《汉语外来语辞典》(Chinese loan-word dictionary). Beijing: Shanwu Yinshu Guan.

Chan, M. K. M. 2002. Concordances and concordances: Tools for Chinese language teaching and research. *Journal of the Chinese Language Teachers Association* 37(2): 1–58.

Chan, M. K. M. 2003. The digital age and speech technology for Chinese language teaching and learning. *Journal of the Chinese Language Teachers Association* 38(2): 49–86.

Chan, S. W. 1942 [Reprint]. *Chinese Reader for Beginners*《中国国语入门》. Stanford: Stanford University Press.

Chao, D. L. 1997. Chinese for Chinese-Americans: A case study. *Journal of the Chinese Language Teachers Association* 32(2): 1–14.

Chao, Y. R. 1933. Tone and intonation in Chinese. *Bulletin of the Institute of History and Philology* 4: 121–34.

Chao, Y. R. 1948a. *Character Text for Mandarin Primer.* Cambridge, MA: Harvard University Press.

Chao, Y. R. 1948b. *Mandarin Primer.* Cambridge, MA: Harvard University Press.

Chao, Y. R. 1967. *Mandarin Primer: An Intensive Course in Spoken Chinese.* Cambridge, MA: Harvard University Press.

Chao, Y. R. 1980 [1930]. A system of tone letters. *Fangyan* 2: 81–83.

Chao, Y. R. 2001[1968]. *A Grammar of Spoken Chinese* (Originally published by University of California Press and later translated by S. Lu). Beijing: Shangwu Chubanshe.

Chen, J. M. (陈建民). 1984.《汉语口语》(Spoken Chinese) Beijing: Beijing Press.

Chen, M. Y. 2000. *Tone Sandhi: Patterns Across Chinese Dialects.* Cambridge, UK: Cambridge University Press.

Chen, Q. H. 1997. Toward a sequential approach for tonal error analysis. *Journal of the Chinese Language Teachers Association* 32(1): 21–39.

Chen, Q. H. 1998. Business Chinese education: A challenging and promising endeavor into the twenty-first century. *Journal of the Chinese Language Teachers Association* 33(2): 1–22.

Chen, Q. H. 2003. Variables and solutions in Business Chinese curriculum development. *Journal of Language for International Business* 14(1): 34–44.

Chen, W. (陈伟). 1993.《墨子：兼爱人生》(Mozi on love of life). Wuhan: Changjiang Wenyi Chubanshe.

Cheng, C. 1973. A quantitative study of Chinese tones. *Journal of Chinese Linguistics* 1: 93–110.

Cheng, X. H. and X. L. Tian. 1989.《现代汉语》(Modern Chinese grammar). Hong Kong: San Lian.

Chi, R. 1989. Observations on the past, present, and future of teaching Mandarin Chinese as a foreign language. *Journal of the Chinese Language Teachers Association* 24(2): 109–22.

Chi, T. R. 1996. Toward a communicative model for teaching and learning Chinese as a foreign language: Exploring some new possibilities. In S. McGinnis (ed.), *Chinese Pedagogy: An Emerging Field*, Chinese Language

Teachers Association Monograph Series, No. 2, pp. 135–58. Columbus, OH: Foreign Language Publications.

Chinese Language Association for Secondary Schools. 1990. *Guidelines for Chinese Language Teaching in Secondary Schools.* Washington, DC: National Foreign Language Center.

Chomsky, N. 1965. *Aspect of the Theory of Syntax.* Cambridge: MIT Press.

Chou, C. P. 1992. *Intermediate Reader Chinese.* Princeton: Princeton University Press.

Chou, C. P. (ed.) 1999. A summary of the 1999–2000 Chinese enrollment survey. *Secondary School Chinese Language Center Newsletter* 11(1): 4–8.

Christensen, M. B. and J. P. Warnick. 2004. *Performed Culture: An Approach to East Asian Language Pedagogy,* manuscript.

Chu, C. 1998. *A Discourse Grammar of Mandarin Chinese.* New York: Peter Lang.

Chu, C. 2002. Relevance theory, discourse markers and the Mandarin utterance-final particle *a/ya. Journal of the Chinese Language Teachers Association* 37(1): 1–42.

Chu, C. Z. 2001. Learning and teaching Chinese characters: Toward a component-orientated net-weaving approach. Paper presented at the Annual Meeting of CLTA, Washington, DC.

Chu, C. Z. 2004. A reflection on traditional approaches to Chinese character teaching and learning. In Yao et al. (eds.), *Studies on Chinese Instructional Materials and Pedagogy.* Beijing: Beijing Language University Press.

Chu, M. 1999. Curricular design. In M. Chu (ed.), *Mapping the Course of the Chinese Language Field,* pp. 3–23. Kalamazoo, MI: Chinese Language Teachers Association, Inc.

Chun, D. M. 1982. A contrastive study of the suprasegmental pitch in modern German, American English, and Mandarin Chinese. PhD dissertation, University of California at Berkeley.

Chun, D. M. 2002. *Discourse Intonation in L2: From Theory and Research to Practice.* Amsterdam/Philadelphia: John Benjamins.

Clancy, P., S. A. Thompson, R. Suzuki, and H. Tao. 1996. The conversational use of reactive tokens in English, Japanese, and Mandarin. *Journal of Pragmatics* 26: 355–87.

Coady, J. and T. Huckin. (eds.) 1997. *Second Language Vocabulary Acquisition.* New York: Cambridge University Press.

Connor, U. 1996. *Contrastive Rhetoric: Cross-cultural Aspects of Second-language Writing.* New York: Cambridge University Press.

Connor, U. and R. Kaplan. (eds.) 1987. *Writing across Languages: Analysis of L2 Text.* Menlo Park, CA: Addison-Wesley Publishing Company.

Cook, V. 1979. *Using Intonation.* London: Longman.

Cook, V. 2001. *Second Language Learning and Language Teaching.* Oxford: Oxford University Press.

Cooper, A. 1988. Given-new: Enhancing coherence through cohesiveness. *Written Communication* 5: 352–67.

Coulmas, F. 2003. *Writing Systems: An Introduction to Their Linguistics Analysis.* Cambridge, UK: Cambridge University Press.

Coulthard, M. 1985. *An Introduction to Discourse Analysis.* London: Longman.

Couper-Kuhlen, E. and B. Kortmann (eds.) 2000. *Cause-Condition-Concession-Contrast: Cognitive and Discourse Perspectives.* New York: Mouton de Gruyter.

Cruttenden, A. 1997. *Intonation.* Cambridge: Cambridge University Press.

Crystal, D. 1985. *A Dictionary of Linguistics and Phonetics.* Oxford: Basil Blackwell.

Cui, S. R. 1993. Conceptualizing language proficiency. *Journal of the Chinese Language Teachers Association* 22(2): 1–24.

Cui, S. R. (崔颂人). 2003. 〈浅谈篇章语法的定义与教学问题〉(Discussion on discourse grammar and teaching). *Journal of the Chinese Language Teachers Association* 38(1): 1–24.

Damen, L. 1987. *Culture Learning: The Fifth Dimension in the Language Classroom.* Reading, MA: Addison-Wesley Publishing Company.

DeFrancis, J. 1964. *Intermediate Chinese Reader.* New Haven: Yale University Press.

DeFrancis, J. 1968. *Advanced Chinese Reader.* New Haven: Yale University Press.

DeFrancis, J. 1977 [1963]. *Beginning Chinese Reader.* New Haven: Yale University Press.

DeFrancis, J. 1984. *The Chinese Language: Fact and Fantasy.* Honolulu: University of Hawaii Press.

Dew. E. J. 1997. The frequency factor in graded vocabulary for textbooks. *Journal of the Chinese Language Teachers Association* 32(2): 83–106.

Ding, S. S. et al. (丁声树等). 1961.《现代汉语语法讲话》(Discussion on modern Chinese grammar). Beijing: Shangwu Yinshuguan.

Dörnyei, Z. and R. Schmidt (eds.) 2001. *Motivation and Second Language Acquisition.* Manoa: University of Hawaii Press.

Doughty, C. and J. Williams (eds.) 1998. *Focus on Form in Classroom Second Language Acquisition.* New York: Cambridge University Press.

Duanmu, S. 2002 [2000]. *The Phonology of Standard Chinese.* Oxford: Oxford University Press.

Du-Babcock, B. 1996. Topic management and turn taking in professional communication: First versus second language strategies. *Perspectives* 8(1): 1–39.

Du-Babcock, B. 1997. A comparative analysis of topic management and turn-taking in professional communication. *Perspectives* 9(2): 36–77.

Dudley-Evans, T. 1994. Variation in the discourse patterns favored by different disciplines and their pedagogical implications. In J. Flowerdew, (ed.)

Academic Listening: Research Perspectives, pp. 146–58. New York: Cambridge University Press.

Dulay, H. and Burt, M. 1974. Natural sequences in child second language acquisition. *Language Learning* 24: 37–53.

Dulay, H., M. Burt and S. Krashen. 1982. *Language 2*. London: Oxford University Press.

Duncan, S. and D. W. Fiske. 1985. The turn system. In S. Duncan and D. W. Fiske (eds.), *Interaction Structure and Strategy*, pp. 43–65. Cambridge: Cambridge University Press.

Dunkel. P and J. Davis. 1994. The effects of rhetorical signaling cues on the recall of English lecture information by speakers of English as a native or second language. In J. Flowerdew (ed.), *Academic Listening: Research Perspectives*, pp. 55–74. New York: Cambridge University Press.

Eckman, F. R. and A. J. Hastings (eds.) 1977. *Studies in First and Second Language Acquisition*. Rowley, MA: Newbury House.

Eckman, F. R., D. Highland, P. W. Lee, J. Mileham and R. R. Weber (eds.) 1995. *Second Language Acquisition Theory and Pedagogy*. Mahwah, NJ: Lawrence Erlbaum Associates.

Einsenstein, M. 1993. *The Dynamic Interlanguage: Empirical Studies in Second Language Variation*. New York: Plenum Press.

Ellis, R. 1985. *Understanding Second Language Acquisition*. Oxford: Oxford University Press.

Ellis, R. 1997. *Second Language Acquisition*. Oxford: Oxford University Press.

Ellis, R. 1999. *The Study of Second Language Acquisition*. Oxford: Oxford University Press.

Ellis, N. C. and A. M. Hooper. 2001. Why learning to read is easier in Welsh than in English: Orthographic transparency effects evinced with frequency-matched tests. *Applied Psycholinguistics* 22(4): 571–99.

Everson, M. 1988. Speed and comprehension in reading Chinese: Romanization vs. characters revisited. *Journal of the Chinese Language Teachers Association* 23(2): 1–20.

Everson, M. 1998. Word recognition among learners of Chinese as a foreign language: Investigating the relationship between naming and knowing. *The Modern Language Journal* 82(2): 194–204.

Everson, M. E. and C. R. Ke. 1997. An inquiry into the reading strategies of intermediate and advanced learners of Chinese as a foreign language. *Journal of the Chinese Language Teachers Association* 32(1): 1–20.

Fang, M. (方梅). 2002. 〈指示词这和那在北京话中的语法化〉 (Grammaticalization of the demonstratives *zhe* and *na* in Beijing dialect). *Zhongguo Yuwen* 4: 343–56.

Fei, J. C. (费锦昌). 1996. 〈现代汉字部件探究〉(Study on the parts of Chinese characters). 《语言文字应用》(Application of language and words), Vol. 2.

Feng, S. L. 2000.《汉语韵律句法学》(Prosodically constrained syntax in Chinese). Shanghai: Jiaoyu Chuban She.

Feng, S. L. 2003a. 〈书面语语法界教学的相对独立性〉,《语言教学与研究》 (Language teaching and research), Vol. 2, pp. 53–63.

Feng, S. L. 2003b. 〈韵律制约的书面语与听说为主的教学法〉,《世界汉语教学》 (Chinese teaching in the world), Vol. 1, pp. 87–97.

Feng, S. L. 2004. Prosodic structure and its implications for teaching Chinese as a second language. *Journal of the Chinese Language Teachers Association* 39(1): 1–24.

Feng, Y. 2000. *A Learners' Handbook of Modern Chinese Written Expressions.* Hong Kong: The Chinese University Press.

Feng, Y. et al. 2004. *Pop Chinese: A Cheng & Tsui Guide to Colloquial Expressions.* Boston: Cheng and Tsui.

Feng, Y. L. (冯友兰). 1940.《新事论 — 谈儿女》(On new issues: Children). Changsha: Shangwu Yinshu Guan.

Fitzgerald, J. et al. 2002. *Maximizing Australia's Asia Knowledge: Repositioning and Renewal of a National Asset.* Australia: Asian Studies Association of Australia, Inc.

Flowerdew, J. and L. Miller. 1995. On the notion of culture in L2 lectures. *TESOL Quarterly*, 29(2): 345–73.

Flynn, S. and S. & Martohardjono, G. 1996. Second language acquisition: Theoretical and experimental issues in contemporary research. *Behavioral and Brain Sciences* 19: 677–738.

Ford, C. E. and S. A. Thompson. 1996. Interactional units in conversation: Syntactic, intonational, and pragmatic resources for the projection of turn completion. In E. Ochs, E. Schegloff, and S. Thompson (eds.), *Interaction and Grammar*, pp. 134–84. Cambridge: Cambridge University Press.

Fox, R. A. and Y. Y. Qi. 1990. Context effects in the perception of lexical tone. *Journal of Chinese Linguistics* 18(2): 261–84.

Fraser, B. 1996. Pragmatic markers. *Pragmatics* 6(2): 167–90.

Fries, C. C. 1945. *Teaching and Learning English as a Foreign Language.* Ann Arbor: University of Michigan Press.

Fu, Y. H. (傅永和).1992. 〈汉字部件出现的结构部位〉(Structural positions of parts of Chinese characters).《语言文字应用》(Application of language and words), Vol. 2.

Furo, H. 2001. *Turn-Taking in English and Japanese: Projectability in Grammar, Intonation, and Semantics.* New York: Routledge.

Gallagher, M. 1999. Special curricula for English-speaking learners at Chinese community schools. In M. Chu (ed.), *Mapping the Course of the Chinese Language Field*, pp. 313–30. Kalamazoo, MI: Chinese Language Teachers Association, Inc.

Gao, D. W. (高大威). 1990.《永恒的叮咛》(Forever advice). Taipei: Central Daily.

Gardner, R. and W. Lambert. 1972. *Attitudes and Motivation in Second-Language Learning.* Rowley, MA: Newbury House.

Garvey, C. and G. Berninger. 1981. Timing and turn taking in children's conversation. *Discourse Processes* 4: 27–57.

Gass, S. 1979. Language transfer and universal grammatical relations. *Language Learning* 29: 327–44.

Gass, S. M. and J. Schachter. 1989. *Linguistic Perspectives on Second Language Acquisition.* New York: Cambridge University Press.

Gass, S. and J. Schachter (eds.) 1995. *Linguistic Perspectives on Second Language Acquisition.* Cambridge: Cambridge University Press.

Gass, S. M. and L. Selinker. 2001. *Second Language Acquisition: An Introductory Course.* Mahwah, NJ: Lawrence Erlbaum Associates.

Gersbacher, C. and T. Givón. 1995. *Coherence in Spontaneous Text.* Amsterdam/Philadelphia: John Benjamins.

Gibson, O. 1887. *Easy Questions for Beginners.* Foochow: M. E. Mission Press.

Giles, H. A. 1872. *Chinese without a Teacher*《汉言无师自明》. Shanghai: Kelly and Welsh, Ltd.

Givón, T. 1983. Topic continuity in discourse: The function domain of switch-reference. In J. Haiman and P. Munro (eds.), *Switch Reference and Universal Grammar*, TSL2, pp. 51–82. Amsterdam/Philadelphia: John Benjamins.

Givón, T. 1988. The pragmatics of word-order: Predictability, importance and attention. In M. Hammond, E. A. Moravcsik and J. R. Wirth (eds.), *Studies in Syntactic Typology*, pp. 243–84. Amsterdam/Philadelphia: John Benjamins.

Givón, T. 1990. *Syntax: A Functional-Typological Introduction*, Vol. II. Amsterdam/Philadelphia: John Benjamins.

Goodwin, C. 1981. *Conversation Organization: Interaction between Speakers and Hearers.* New York: Academic Press.

Greenberg, J. H. 1966. *Universal of Language.* Cambridge, MA: MIT Press.

Gregg, K. W. 1989. Second language acquisition theory: The case for a generative perspective, pp. 15–40. In S. Gass and J. Schachter (eds.), *Linguistic Perspectives on Second Language Acquisition.* Cambridge: Cambridge University Press.

Guo, B. C. (郭宝昌). 2001.《大宅门》(Gate of a big residence). Beijing: Renmin Wenxue Chubanshe.

GYUWGWH (国家语言文学工作委员会汉字处).1989.《现代汉语常用字频度统计》(Frequency rate of the commonly used modern Chinese characters). Beijing: Yuwen Chuban She.

Haiman, J. and P. Munro (eds.) 1983. *Switch Reference and Universal Grammar*, TSL2. Amsterdam/Philadelphia: John Benjamins.

Halliday, M. 1987. Spoken and written modes of meaning. In R. Horowitz and S. Samuels (eds.), *Comprehending Oral and Written Language.* San Diego: Academic Press.

Halliday, M. and R. Hasan. 1976. *Cohesion in English.* London: Longman.

Hanzi Shuxing Zidian《汉字属性字典》(Character property dictionary). 1989. Beijing: Yuwen Chuban She.

Harbaugh, R. 1998. *Chinese Characters: A Genealogy and Dictionary*《中文字谱》. Zhongwen.com.

Harley, B. et al. (eds.) 1990. *The Development of Second Language Proficiency*. New York: Cambridge University Press.

Hatch, E. and C. Brown. 1995. *Vocabulary, Semantics, and Language Education*. New York: Cambridge University Press.

Hayes, E. 1987. The relationship between Chinese character complexity and character recognition. *Journal of the Chinese Language Teachers Association* 22(2): 45–57.

Hayes, E. 1990. The relationship between 'word length' and memorability among non-native readers of Chinese Mandarin. *Journal of the Chinese Language Teachers Association* 25(3): 31–41.

Healy, A. F. and L. E. Bourne. (eds.) 1998. *Foreign Language Learning: Psycholinguistic Studies on Training and Retention*. Mahwah, NJ: Erlbaum.

Higgs, T. V. (ed.) 1984. *Teaching for Proficiency, the Organizing Principle*. Lincolnwood, IL: National Textbook Company.

Hillier, W. C. 1909–1910. *Chinese Language and How to Learn it*. London: K. Paul.

Hinkel, E. 1999. *Culture in Second Language Teaching and Learning*. New York: Cambridge University Press.

Hobbs, J. R. 1979. Coherence and co-reference. *Cognitive Science* 3: 67–90.

Hong, W. 1996. On developing business Chinese. *The Journal of Language for International Business* 7(2): 28–37.

Hong, W. 1997. Sociopragmatics in language teaching: With examples of Chinese requests. *Journal of the Chinese Language Teachers Association* 32(1): 95–107.

Hong, W. 2002. How does power affect Chinese politeness? *Journal of the Chinese Language Teachers Association* 37(2): 59–73.

Hopper, P. 1979. Aspect and foregrounding in discourse. In T. Givón (ed.), *Discourse and Syntax, Syntax Semantics*, 12. New York: Academic Press.

Hopper, P. J. and S. A. Thompson. 1980. Transitivity in grammar and discourse. *Language* 56(2): 251–99.

Hu, S. (胡适). 1930.《胡适文存》(Collections of Hu Shi essays). Shanghai: Yadong Tushuguan.

Huang, P. R. (黄沛荣). 2003.《汉字教学的理论与实践》(Theory and practice of Chinese character teaching and learning). Taipei: Lexue Shuju.

Hymes, D. H. 1971. *On Communicative Competence*. Philadelphia: University of Pennsylvania Press.

Hymes, D. H. 1972. Toward ethnographies of communication: The analysis of communicative events. In P. Giglioli (ed.), *Language and Social Context*, pp. 21–43. Harmondsworth: Penguin.

Hymes, D. H. 1974. Why linguistics needs the sociologist. In *Foundations in Sociolinguistics: An Ethnographic Approach*, pp. 3–28. Philadelphia: University of Pennsylvania Press.

Hymes, D. 1995 [1989]. The ethnography of speaking. In Ben Blount (ed.), *Language, Culture, and Society*, pp. 248–82. Prospect Heights: Waveland Press.

Hymes, D. H. (ed.) 1964. *Language in Culture and Society: A Reader in Linguistic and Anthropology*. New York: Harper and Row.

Imbault-Huart C. 1889. *Langue Chinoise Parlée*《京话指南》. Paris: E. Leroux.

Inhoff, A. W. and Liu, W. (1998). The perceptual span and oculomotor activity during the reading of Chinese sentences. *Journal of Experimental Psychology: Human Perception & Performance 24:* 20–34.

Jefferson, G. 1973. A case of precision timing in ordinary conversation overlapped tag-positioned address terms in closing sequences. *Semiotics* 9: 47–96.

Jiao, X. X. (焦晓晓). 2003.〈近年来中国境内出现的新词语及其对海外汉语教学的挑战〉(New vocabulary developed in recent years in China and its challenge to teaching Chinese as L2). *Journal of the Chinese Language Teachers Association* 38 (1): 97–126.

Jin, H. et al. 2000. *China Scene: An Advanced Multimedia Course Textbook and Workbook*. Boston: Cheng & Tsui.

Johns, K. M. 1988. *How Children Learn a Second Language*. Bloomington, IN: Phi Delta Kappa Educational Foundation.

Johnson, D. W. and R. T. Johnson. 1979. Conflict in the classroom: Controversy and learning. *Review of Educational Research* 49(1): 51–70.

Jucker, A. H. and Y. Ziv (eds.) 1998. *Discourse Markers: Descriptions and Theory*. Amsterdam/Philadelphia: John Benjamins.

Kanno, K. (ed.) 1999. *The Acquisition of Japanese as a Second Language*. Amsterdam/Philadelphia: John Benjamins.

Ke, C. R. 1998. Effects of strategies on the learning of Chinese characters among foreign language students. *Journal of the Chinese Language Teachers Association* 33(2): 93–112.

Ke, C. R. 1996. An empirical study on the relationship between Chinese character recognition and production. *Modern Language Journal* 80: 340–50.

Kehler, A. 2002. *Coherence, Reference, and the Theory of Grammar*. Stanford: Center for the Study of Language and Information.

Kiriloff. C. 1969. On the auditory perception of tones in Mandarin. *Phonetica* 20: 2.4.

Kirkpatrick, A. 1996. Using authentic texts to teach languages: With special reference to modern standard Chinese. *Journal of the Chinese Language Teachers Association* 31(1): 17–32.

Kordes, H. 1991. Intercultural learning at school: Limits and possibilities. In D. Buttjes and M. Bryam (eds.), *Mediating Languages and Cultures*, pp. 17–30. Clevedon, England: Multilingual Matters.

Kotenbeutel, C. 1999. National standards for foreign language teaching: The Chinese connection. In M. Chu (ed.), *Mapping the Course of the Chinese Language Field*, pp. 257–70. Kalamazoo, MI: Chinese Language Teachers Association, Inc.

Kramsch, C. 1991. Culture in language learning: A view from the States. In K. de Bot, R. B. Ginsberg, and C. Kramsch (eds.), *Foreign Language Research in Cross-Cultural Perspective*, pp. 217–40. Amsterdam: John Benjamins.

Kramsch, C. 1993. *Context and Culture in Language Teaching*. New York: Oxford University Press.

Krashen, S. 1982. *Principles and Practice in Second Language Acquisition*. Oxford: Pergamon Press.

Krashen, D. Stephen, R. C. Scarcella and M. H. Long. (eds.) 1982. *Child-adult Differences in Second Language Acquisition*. Rowley, MA: Newbury House Publishers.

Kubler, C. 1993. Teaching advanced conversation and comprehension through Xiangsheng. *Journal of the Chinese Language Teachers Association* 28(1): 1–12.

Kubler, Co. 1997a. A framework for basic Chinese language programs. *Journal of the Chinese Language Teachers Association* 32(3): 41–50.

Kubler, C. 1997b. Study abroad as an integral part of the Chinese language curriculum. *Journal of the Chinese Language Teachers Association* 32(3): 15–30.

Kumaravadivelu, B. 2003. *Beyond Methods: Macrostrategies for Language Teaching*. New Haven: Yale University Press.

Lakoff, G. 1987. *Women, Fire, and Dangerous Things: What Categories Reveal about the Mind*. Chicago: University of Chicago Press.

Lan, H. R. 1994. Her beauty is EATable: A culturo-linguistic study. *Journal of the Chinese Language Teachers Association* 29(3): 79–98.

Lange, D. L. and R. M. Peige. (eds.) 2003. *Culture as the Core: Perspectives on Culture in Second Language Learning*. Greenwich, CT: Information Age Publishing.

Lantolf, J. P. 1999. Second culture acquisition: Cognitive considerations. In Eli Hinkel (ed.), *Culture in Second Language Teaching and Learning*, pp. 28–46. Cambridge, UK: Cambridge University Press.

Lantolf, J. P. (ed.) 2000. *Sociocultural Theory and Second Language Learning*. Oxford: Oxford University Press.

Lao, S. (老舍). 1994.《茶馆》(Tea house) and《龙须沟》(Longxue village). Beijing: Renmin Wenyi Chubanshe.

Lapkin, S. (ed.). 1998. *French Second Language Education in Canada: Empirical Studies*. Toronto: University of Toronto Press.

Larsen-Freeman, D. 1986. *Techniques and Principles in Language Teaching*. Oxford: Oxford University Press.

Leech, Geoffrey and Jan Svartvik. 1994. *A Communicative Grammar of English*. London: Longman.

Lerner, G. H. 1989. Notes on overlap management in conversation: The case of delayed completion. *Western Journal of Speech Communication* 53: 167–77.

Levinson, S. C. 1983. *Pragmatics*. Cambridge: Cambridge University Press.

Li, A. M. 1999. Agency: A cultural perspective implicit in language use. In M. Chu (ed.), *Mapping the Course of the Chinese Language Field*, pp. 71–101. Kalamazoo, MI: Chinese Language Teachers Association, Inc.

Li, Charles N. (ed.) 1975. *Word Order and Word Order Change*. Austin: University of Texas Press.

Li, C. N. and S. A. Thompson. 1975. Subject and topic: A new typology of language. In Li and Thompson (eds.), *Subject and Topic*, pp. 459–89. New York: Academic Press.

Li, C. N. and S. A. Thompson. 1977. The acquisition of tones in Mandarin-speaking children. *Journal of Child Language* 4(2): 185–99.

Li, C. N. and S. A. Thompson. 1981. *Mandarin Chinese: A Functional Reference Grammar*. Berkeley: University of California Press.

Li, W., H. Zhu and Y. Li. 2001. Conversational management and involvement in Chinese-English Business talk. *Language and Intercultural Communication* 1(2): 135–50.

Li, W. D. 2002. Clause-integration in discourse: Criteria and mechanisms in Chinese and English. *Proceedings of the Fourteenth North American Conference on Chinese Linguistics*, pp. 208–22.

Liang, H. H. (梁新欣). 2004.〈从师生互动谈如何上好单班课〉(Interaction between teachers and students at individual conference). *Journal of the Chinese Language Teachers Association* 39(1): 63–84.

Lin, Y. 2000. Vocabulary acquisition and learning Chinese as a foreign language. *Journal of the Chinese Language Teachers Association* 35(1): 85–108.

Linde, C. 1993. *Life Stories: The Creation of Coherence*. New York: Oxford University Press.

List of the Frequently Used Characters《现代汉语常用字表》. 1988. Beijing: Yuwen Chubanshe.

Little, D. 1994. Words and their properties: Arguments for a lexical approach to pedagogical grammar. In T. Odlin (ed.), *Perspectives on Pedagogical Grammar*. Cambridge: Cambridge University Press.

Liu, D. Q. and L. J Xue. 1998.〈焦点与背景、话题及汉语"连"字句〉(Focus and background, topic and the *lian* construction in Chinese). *Zhongguo Yuwen* 4: 243–52.

Liu, N. S. (刘乃叔) and G. H. Ao. (敖桂华) 1998.〈对外汉语教学中文化渗透之我见〉(Our views on culture permeating Chinese language teaching and learning for non-native speakers).《汉语学习》(Chinese language learning) 104: 43–45.

Liu, X. (刘珣). 2002.《汉语作为第二语言教学简论》(Introduction to teaching and learning Chinese as a second language). Beijing: Beijing Language and Cultural University.

Liu, X. et al. (刘珣主编). 1981.《实用汉语课文》(Practical Chinese reader). Beijing: Commercial Press.

Liu X. et al. (刘珣主编). 2003.《新实用汉语课文》(New practical Chinese reader). Beijing: Beijing Language University Press.

Liu, Y. H. (刘月华). 1998.〈关于中文教材语法的编写〉(On grammatical elements in Chinese teaching materials). *Journal of the Chinese Language Teachers Association* 33(3): 51–62.

Liu Y. H. et al. (刘月华等). 2002 [1983].《实用现代汉语语法》(Practical modern Chinese grammar). Beijing: Shangwu Chubanshe.

Lu, B. F. 1997. Computer-aided training in reading Chinese. *Journal of the Chinese Language Teachers Association* 32(2): 57–82.

Lu, X. X. (陆锡兴). 2003.《汉字的隐秘世界》(Secret world of Chinese characters). Shanghai: Cishu Chubanshe.

Lǔ, B. S. (吕必松). 1981. Integrating structure, meaning, and function in language pedagogy. *Journal of the Chinese Language Teachers Association* 16(2): 1–16.

Lǔ, B. S. (吕必松). 1999a.《对外汉语教学概论》(Introduction to teaching and Learning Chinese as a Second Language). Beijing: Education Bureau.

Lǔ, B. S. (吕必松) (ed.) 1999b.《汉字与汉字教学研究论文集》(Chinese characters and characters teaching). Beijing: Beijing University Press.

Lǔ, S. X (吕叔湘). 1980.《现代汉语八百词》(Eight hundred Chinese function words). Beijing: Shangwu Chuban She.

Lundelius, O. 1992. Pinyin vs. tonal spelling. *Journal of the Chinese Language Teachers Association* 28 (3): 93–108.

Luo, Q. S. (罗青松). 2002.《对外汉语写作教学研究》(Study on teaching and learning writing skill of Chinese as L2). Beijing: Zhongguo zhehui kexue chubanshe.

Ma, J. H and R. Smitheram. 1996. *Pronunciation Module*. Boston: Cheng and Tsui.

Ma, J. H. 1999. *Drills and Quizzes in Mandarin Chinese Pronunciation* Audio Cassette. Boston: Cheng and Tsui.

Ma, J. Z. (马建忠). 1983 [1898].《马氏文通》(Chinese grammar by Mr Ma). Beijing: Shangwu Chubanshe.

Marello, C. 1989. Ellipsis between connexity and coherence. In M. Conte et al. (eds.) *Text and Discourse Connectedness*, pp. 119–36. Amsterdam/Philadelphia: John Benjamins.

McCarthy, M., F. O'Dell, and E. Shaw. 1997. *English Vocabulary in Use: Upper Intermediate Reference in Practice for Students of North American English.* New York: Cambridge University Press.

McDonald, E. 1999. Teaching grammar through text: An integrated model for a pedagogical grammar of Chinese. *Journal of the Chinese Language Teachers Association* 34(2): 91–120.

McDonald, E. 2000. Teaching grammar through text: An integrated model for a pedagogical grammar of Chinese. *Journal of the Chinese Language Teachers Association* 34(2): 91–120.

McGinnis, S. 1992. Stanley Mickel: Reading Chinese newspapers: Tactics and skills. *Journal of the Chinese Language Teachers Association* 27(3): 111–7.

McGinnis, S. 1994. Cultures of instruction: Identifying and resolving conflicts. *Theory Into Practice* 33(1): 16–22.

McGinnis, S. 1996. Tonal distinction errors by beginning Chinese language students. In S. McGinnis (ed.), *Chinese Pedagogy: An Emerging Field*, Chinese Language Teachers Association Monograph Series, No. 2, pp. 81–91. Columbus, OH: Foreign Language Publications.

McGinnis, S. 1997. Tonal spelling versus diacritics for teaching pronunciation of Mandarin Chinese. *The Modern Language Journal* 81(2): 228–36.

McGinnis, S. 1999. Students goals and approaches. In M. Chu (ed.), *Mapping the Course of the Chinese Language Field,* pp. 151–88. Kalamazoo, MI: Chinese Language Teachers Association, Inc.

McLaughlin, B. 1984. *Second-language Acquisition in Childhood.* Hillsdale, NJ: Lawrence Erlbaum Associates.

McLaughlin, M. L. 1984. *Conversation: How Talk Is Organized.* Beverly Hills, CA: Sage.

Mey, J. L. 1999. *When Voice Clash: A Study in Literary Pragmatics.* Berlin: Mouton de Gruyter.

Mickel, S. 1991. *Reading Chinese Newspapers: Tactics and skills.* New Haven: Far Eastern Publications.

Miracle, W. C. 1989. Tone production of American students of Chinese: A preliminary acoustic study. *Journal of the Chinese Language Teachers Association* 24(3): 49–65.

Moore, S. 1996. Intervention strategies for the development of pre-collegiate Chinese. *Journal of the Chinese Language Teachers Association* 31(2): 23–36.

Moore, S. J., A. R. Walton, and R. D. Lambert. 1992. *Introducing Chinese into High Schools: A Dodge Initiative.* Washington, DC: National Foreign Language Center.

Morris, C. W. 1971. *Writings on the General Theory of Sings.* The Hague: Mouton.

Myers, D. 1997. Teaching culture with language: Words of foreign origin and linguistic purism. *Journal of the Chinese Language Teachers Association* 32(2): 41–56.

Myers, D. 2000. Teaching culture with key words in Chinese as a foreign language: The state of the field. *Journal of the Chinese Language Teachers Association* 35(3): 1–28.

Myhill, J. and Z. Xing. 1993. The discourse functions of patient fronting: A comparative study of Biblical Hebrew and Chinese. *Linguistics* 31: 25–57.

Nation, I. S. P. 2001. *Learning Vocabulary in Another Language*. New York: Cambridge University Press.

Newmark, L. and D. Reibel. 1968. Necessity and sufficiency in language learning. *International Review of Applied Linguistics in Language Teaching* 6: 145–64.

Newmyer, F. and S. Weinberger. 1988. The ontogenesis of the field of second language learning research. In S. Flynn and W. O'Neil (eds.), *Linguistic Theory in Second Language Acquisition*, pp. 34–45. Dordrecht: Kluwer Academic Press.

Ning, C. 1993. *Communicating in Chinese: A First-year Curriculum*. Yale University: Far Eastern Publications.

Norrick, N. R. 2000. *Conversational Narrative: Storytelling in Everyday Talk*. Amsterdam/Philadelphia: John Benjamins.

Norman, J. 1988. *Chinese*. Cambridge, UK: Cambridge University Press.

Norment, N. 1994. Contrastive analyses of cohesive devices in Chinese and Chinese ESL in narrative and expository written texts. *Journal of the Chinese Language Teachers Association* 29(1): 49–82.

Ochs, E. and B. B. Schieffelin. 1984. Language acquisition and socialization. In R. Shweder and R. LeVine (eds.), *Cultural Theory*, pp. 276–320. Cambridge: Cambridge University Press.

O'Connell, D. C., S. Kowal, and E. Kaltenbacher. 1990. Turn-taking: A critical analysis of the research tradition. *Journal of Psycholinguistic Research* 19: 345–73.

Odlin, T. (ed.) 1994. *Perspective on Pedagogical Grammar*. New York: Cambridge University Press.

Omaggio, A. C. 1986. *Teaching Language in Context: Proficiency Oriented Instruction*. Boston: Heinle and Heinle.

Packard, J. 1989. High-versus low-pressure methods of Chinese language teaching: A comparison of test results. *Journal of the Chinese Language Teachers Association* 24(1): 1–18.

Packard, J. 1990. Effects of time lag in the introduction of characters into the Chinese language curriculum. *The Modern Language Journal* 74(2): 167–75.

Perfetti, C. A. and L.-H. Tan (1998). The time course of graphemic, phonological, and semantic activation in visual Chinese character identification. *Journal of Experimental Psychology: Learning, Memory, and Cognition* 24: 101–18.

Perfetti, C. A. and S. Zhang (1991). Phonemic processes in reading Chinese words. *Journal of Experimental Psychology: Learning, Memory, and Cognition* 17: 633–43.

Phillips, J. K. (ed.) 1999. *Foreign Language Standards: Linking Research, Theories, and Practices*. Lincolnwood, IL: National Textbook Company.

Phillipson, R., E. Kellerman, L. Selinker, M. S. Smith, and M. Swain (eds.) 1991. *Foreign/Second Language Pedagogy Research*. Clevedon, Avon: Multilingual Matters.

Power, R. J. and M. F. Dal Martello. 1986. Some criticisms of Sacks, Schegloff, and Jefferson on turn-taking. *Semiotica* 58(1–2): 29–40.

Prabhu, N.S. 1987. *Second Language Pedagogy*. Oxford: Oxford University Press.

Quirk, R. et al. 1985. *A Comprehensive Grammar of the English Language*. London: Longman.

Ramsey, R. S. 1987. *The Language of China*. Princeton: Princeton University Press.

Ratay, J. P. 1927. *Current Chinese*《适用新中国话》. Shanghai: Kelly and Welsh, Ltd.

Repp, B. H. and H. Lin 1990. Integration of segmental and tonal information in speech perception: A cross-linguistic study. *Journal of Phonetics* 18: 481–95.

Richards, J. and D. Nunan (eds.) 1990. *Second Language Teacher Education*. Cambridge: Cambridge University Press.

Richards, J. and T. S. Rogers. 1986. *Approaches and Methods in Language Teaching: A Description and Analysis*. New York: Cambridge University Press.

Riggenbach, H. 1998. Evaluating learner interactional skills: Conversation at the micro level. In R. Yong and A. He (eds.), *Language Proficiency Interviews: A Discourse Approach*, pp. 53–67. Amsterdam/Philadelphia: John Benjamins.

Riggenbach, H. 1999. *Discourse Analysis in the Language Classroom*. Ann Arbor: University of Michigan Press.

Rivers, W. M. 1981[1968]. *Teaching Foreign Language Skills*. Chicago: University of Chicago Press.

Rivers, W. M. 1983. *Communicating Naturally in a Second Language: Theory and Practice in Language Teaching*. New York: Cambridge University Press.

Robinson, G. 1991. Second culture acquisition. In J. E. Alatis (ed.), *Linguistics and Language Pedagogy: State of the Art*, pp. 114–22. Washington, DC: Georgetown University Press.

Robinson-Stuart, G. and H. Nocon. 1996. Second culture acquisition: Ethnography in the foreign language classroom. *Modern Language Journal* 80: 431–49.

Romírez, A. G. 1995. *Creating Contexts for Second Language Acquisition: Theory and Methods*. New York: Longman Publishers.

Rosaldo, M. 1984. Toward an anthropology of self and feeling. In R. Shweder and R. LeVine (eds.), *Cultural Theory*, pp. 137–57. Cambridge: Cambridge University Press.

Rose, K. R. and G. Kasper. (eds.) 2001. *Pragmatic in Language Teaching*. New York: Cambridge University Press.

Ross, A. 2003. Syllabus: Third-year Chinese. Lakeside Schools, Washington.

Ross, C. 1997. The framework for post-basic Chinese. *Journal of the Chinese Language Teachers Association* 32(3): 51–56.

Rutherford, W. 1987. *Second Language Grammar: Learning and Teaching*. London: Longman.

Sachs, H., E. A. Schegloff, and G. Jefferson. 1974. A simplest systematics for the organization of turn taking for conversation. *Language* 50: 695–737.

Samimy, K. and Y. A. Lee. 1997. Beliefs about language learning: Perspectives of first-year Chinese learners and their instructors. *Journal of the Chinese Language Teachers Association* 32(1): 40–60.

Sapir, E. 1949a [1921]. *Culture, Language, and Personality*. Berkeley: University of California Press.

Sapir, E. 1949b. *Language*. San Diego: Harcourt Brace Jovanovich.

Schachter, J. 1988. Second language acquisition and its relationship to universal grammar. *Applied Linguistics* 9(3): 219–35.

Schiffrin, D. 1987. *Discourse Markers*. New York: Cambridge University Press.

Schiffrin, D. 1988. Conversation analysis. In F. Newmeyer (ed.), *Linguistics: The Cambridge Survey*, pp. 251–76. Cambridge: Cambridge University Press.

Schiffrin, D. 1994. *Approaches to Discourse*. Cambridge: Blackwell.

Schmidt, R. and C. McCreary. 1977. Standard and super-standard English. *TESOL Quarterly* 11: 415–30.

Schourup, L. C. 1985. *Common Discourse Particles in English Conversation*. New York: Garland.

Scollon, R. and S. W. Scollon. 1995. *Intercultural Communication: A Discourse Approach*. Oxford, UK and Cambridge: Blackwell.

Seelye, H. N. 1976. *Teaching Culture: Strategies for Foreign Language Education*. Skokie, IL: National Textbook Company.

Seelye, H. N. 1994. *Teaching Culture: Strategies for Intercultural Communication*. Lincolnwood, IL: National Textbook Company.

Sergent, W. and M. Everson. 1992. The Effects of frequency and density on character recognition speed and accuracy by elementary and advanced L2 readers of Chinese. *Journal of the Chinese Language Teachers Association* 27(1/2): 29–44.

Shen, C. W. (沈从文). 1993. 《沈从文名作欣赏》 (Sheng Congwen's works). Beijing: Zhongguo Heping Chubanshe.

Shen, H. S. 2000. The interconnections of reading text-based writing and reading comprehension among college intermediate learners of Chinese as a foreign language. *Journal of the Chinese Language Teachers Association* 35(3): 29–48.

Shen, X. S. 1989. Toward a register approach in teaching Mandarin tones. *Journal of the Chinese Language Teachers Association* 24(3): 27–47.

Shen, X. S. 1985. Pitch range of tone and intonation in Beijing dialect. In Lin, T. and L-J. Wang (eds.), *Working Papers in Experimental Phonetics*. Beijing: Beijing University Press.

Shen, X. S. 1990. *The Prosody of Mandarin Chinese*. Berkeley and Los Angeles: University of California Press.

Shi, D. X. 1989. Topic chain as a syntactic category in Chinese. *Journal of Chinese Linguistics* 17(2): 223–62.

Shi, D. X. 2000. Topic and topic-comment constructions in Mandarin Chinese. *Language* 76(2): 383–408.

Shi, Y. W. (史有为). 2000.《汉语外来词》(Chinese loan words). Beijing: Shangwu Yinshu Guan.

Shi, Z. Q. 1988. *The Present and Past of the Particle le in Mandarin Chinese*. PhD dissertation, University of Pennsylvania.

Silberstein, S. 1994. *Techniques and Resources in Teaching Reading*. New York: Oxford University Press.

Smith, C. S. 2003. *Modes of Discourse*: *The Logical Structure of Texts*. Cambridge: Cambridge University Press.

Soothill, W. E. 1942. *The Student's Four Thousand Zi 字 and General Pocket Dictionary*. London: Kegan Paul.

Spring, M. 1999. Improving reading instruction in upper-level Chinese courses: Challenges and possibilities. In M. Chu (ed.), *Mapping the Course of the Chinese Language Field,* pp. 51–69. Kalamazoo, MI: Chinese Language Teachers Association, Inc.

Stubbs, M. 1983. *Discourse Analysis*. Chicago: University of Chicago Press.

Sun, C. F. 1996. *Word Order Change and Grammaticalization in the History of Chinese*. Stanford: Stanford University Press.

Sun, C. F. and T. Givón. 1985. On the so-called SOV word order in Mandarin Chinese: A quantitative text study and its implications. *Language* 61.2: 329–51.

Sunaoka, K. 2003.〈以提升交际能力为目的之汉语教学以及水平测验〉(Chinese language teaching, learning and testing for communicative competence). The Third International Conference on Internet Chinese Education, October, Taipei.

Svennevig, J. 1999. *Getting Acquainted in Conversation*. Amsterdam/Philadelphia: John Benjamins.

Swales, J. M. 1990. *Genre Analysis: English in Academic and Research Settings*. Cambridge, UK: Cambridge University Press.

Tai, J. 1985. Temporal sequence and Chinese word order. In J. Haiman (ed.) *Iconicity*. Amsterdam: John Benjamins.

Tang, Y. F. 1996. Linguistically accurate and culturally appropriate: The use of authentic video in Chinese language instruction. In S. McGinnis (ed.), *Chinese Pedagogy: An Emerging Field*, Chinese Language Teachers Association Monograph Series, No. 2, pp. 285–314. Columbus, OH: Foreign Language Publications.

Tannen, D. 1982. Oral and literate strategies in spoken and written narratives. *Language* 58(1): 1–21.

Tannen, D. 1984. *Conversational Style: Analyzing Talk among Friends*. Norwood, NJ: Ablex.

Tannen, D. 1986. *That's Not What I Meant!: How Conversational Style Makes or Breaks Your Relations with Others*. New York: William Morrow, Ballantine.

Tannen, D. 1987. Repetition in conversation: Toward a poetics of talk. *Language* 63(3): 574–605.

Tannen, D. 1989. *Talking Voices: Repetition, Dialogue, and Imagery in Conversational Discourse*. Cambridge: Cambridge University Press.

Tannen, D. (ed.) 1993. *Framing in Discourse*. Oxford: Oxford University Press.

Tao, H. Y. 1996. *Units in Mandarin Conversation: Prosody, Discourse, and Grammar*. Amsterdam/Philadelphia: John Benjamins.

Tao, H. Y. 1999. The grammar of demonstratives in Mandarin conversational discourse: A case study. *Journal of Chinese Linguistics* 27(1): 69–103.

Tao, H. Y. 2002. The gap between natural speech and spoken Chinese teaching material: Toward a discourse approach to pedagogy. Paper presented at the Harvard Symposium on Chinese Language Pedagogy, April. Harvard University. Later published in the *Journal of the Chinese Language Teachers Association,* 2005, 40: 2, pp. 1–24.

Tao, H. Y. 2004. Delay and repair strategies in conversation and spoken language teaching. Paper presented at the Annual Meeting of the Chinese Language Teachers Association, Chicago, November 18–21.

Teng, S. H. 1997. Towards a pedagogical grammar of Chinese. *Journal of the Chinese Language Teachers Association* 32(2): 29–40.

Teng, S. H. 1998. Sequencing of structures in a pedagogical grammar. *Journal of the Chinese Language Teachers Association* 33(2): 41–52.

Teng, S. H. 2002. 〈对外汉语语法点难易度的评定〉(Assessment of pedagogical grammar of Chinese). In M. Ren (ed.), 《对外汉语教学语法探索》(Studies of pedagogical grammar of Chinese), pp. 102–11.

Teng, Shou-hsin and Yeh Deming. 2001. 《东亚地区语文使用与教学现况之比较研究 — 华语教育实施情况》(Comparative study of the language practice and teaching at the East Asian countries – Report on Chinese education). Taipei: Institute of Teaching Chinese as a Second Language, National Taiwan Normal University.

Thomas, J. 1983. Cross-cultural pragmatic failure. *Applied Linguistics* 4(1): 91–112.

Thomas, J. 1984. Cross-cultural discourse as "unequal encounter": Toward a pragmatic analysis. *Applied Linguistics* 5(2): 226–35.

Thompson, S. 1973. Transitivity and some problems with the *ba* construction in Mandarin Chinese. *Journal of Chinese Linguistics* 1.2: 208–21.

Times Books International. 1985. *Simplified Chinese Characters*. Singapore: Times Books International.

Titone, B. and M. Danesi. 1985. *Applied Psycholinguistics: An Introduction to the Psychology of Language Learning and Teaching*. Toronto: University of Toronto Press.

Tomlin, R. S. 1994. Functional grammars, pedagogical grammars, and communicative language teaching. In T. Odlin (ed.), *Perspectives on Pedagogical Grammar*, pp. 140–78. London: Cambridge University Press.

Toulmin, S. E. 1958. *The Uses of Argument*. Cambridge: Cambridge University Press.

Traugott, E. C. and R. B. Dasher. 2002. *Regularity in Semantic Change*. Cambridge, UK: Cambridge University Press.

Tsao, F. F. 1979. *A Functional Study of Topic in Chinese: The First Step Toward Discourse Analysis*. Taipei: Student Book Co.

Tsao, F. F. 1987. A topic-comment approach to the *ba* construction. *Journal of Chinese Linguistics* 15.1: 1–50.

Tsao, F. F. 1990. *Sentence and Clause Structure in Chinese: A Functional Perspective*. Taipei: Student Book Co.

Tzeng, O. J.-L., D. L. Hung and, W. S.-Y. Wang. 1977. Speech recoding in reading Chinese characters. *Journal of Experimental Psychology: Human Learning and Memory 3*: 621–30.

Ulijn, J. M. and X. L. Li. 1995. Is interrupting impolite? Some temporal aspects of turn-taking in Chinese-Western and other intercultural business encounters. *Text* 15(4): 589–627.

Ur, P. 1996. *A Course in Language Teaching*. New York: Cambridge University Press.

van Dijk, T. 1985. Introduction: Discourse as a new cross-discipline. In T. van Dijk (ed.), *Handbook of Discourse Analysis, Vol. 1: Disciplines of Discourse*, pp. 1–10. New York: Academic Press.

Van Ek, J. A. 1976. *The Threshold Level for Modern Language Learning in Schools*. London: Longman.

Wade, T. F. and W. C. Hillier. 1886. *A Progressive Course* (字和词), Vol. I–III. Shanghai: Kelly and Welsh, Ltd.

Walker, G. 1989. Intensive Chinese curriculum: The ESL1 model. *Journal of the Chinese Language Teachers Association* 24(2): 43–84.

Walker, G. 1996. Intensive Chinese curriculum. In S. McGinnis (ed.) *Chinese Pedagogy: An Emerging Field*, Chinese Language Teachers Association Monograph Series, No. 2, pp. 181–227. Columbus, OH: Foreign Language Publications.

Walker, G. and M. Li. 2003. *Report on the Survey of East Asian Language Programs*. The University of Ohio: National East Asian Languages Resource Center.

Walton, R. A. 1989. Chinese language instruction in the United States: Some reflections on the state of the art. *Journal of the Chinese Language Teachers Association* 24(2): 1–42.

Walton, R. 1992. *Expanding the Vision of Foreign Language Education: Enter the Less Commonly Taught Languages*, pp. 1–16. Washington, DC: The National Foreign Language Center Occasional Papers.

Walton, R. 1996. Reinventing language fields: The Chinese case. In S. McGinnis (ed.), *Chinese Pedagogy: An Emerging Field*, Chinese Language Teachers Association Monograph Series, No. 2, pp. 29–79. Columbus, OH: Foreign Language Publications.

Wang, H. (王还). 1957. 《把字句和被字句》(The *ba* construction and the *bei* construction). Shanghai: Education Press.

Wang, H. (王还). 1983. 〈英语和汉语的被动句〉(The passive construction in both English and Chinese). *Zhongguo Yuwen* Vol. 6: 409–18.

Wang, J., A. W. Inhoff and H.-C. Chen (eds.) 1999. *Reading Chinese Script: A Cognitive Analysis*. Mahwah, NJ: Erlbaum.

Wang, J. J. 1995. *Outrageous Chinese: A Guide to Chinese Street Language*. San Francisco: China Book and Periodicals.

Wang, L. (王力). 1943–44.《中国语法理论》(The theory of Chinese grammar). Shanghai: Zhonghua Shuju.

Wang, P. (王璞). 1930.《国语会话》(Guoyu Huihua [Conversational Chinese]). Shanghai: Zhonghua shuju.

Wang, S. H. 1999. Crossing the bridge: A Chinese case from mother tongue maintenance to foreign language education. In M. Chu (ed.), *Mapping the Course of the Chinese Language Field,* pp. 271–312. Kalamazoo, MI: Chinese Language Teachers Association, Inc.

Wang, Y. (王颖). 2003. 〈"书面语"和"口语"的语体差别与对外汉语教学〉(The difference between written and spoken genres and teaching Chinese as L2). *Journal of the Chinese Language Teachers Association*, 38(3): 91–102.

Ware, J. R. 1939a. *Elementary Chinese Texts Used at Harvard University*. New Haven: Yale University Press.

Ware, J. R. 1939b. *Intermediate Chinese Texts Used at Harvard University*. New Haven: Yale University Press.

Watzke, J. L. 2003. *Lasting Change in Foreign Language Education: A Historical Case for Change in National Policy*. Westport: Praeger Publishers.

Wen, X. H. 1999. Chinese language learning motivation: A comparative study of different ethnic groups. In M. Chu (ed.), *Mapping the Course of the Chinese Language Field*, pp. 121–50. Kalamazoo, MI: Chinese Language Teachers Association, Inc.

Wertsch, J. 1994. The primacy of mediated action in sociocultural studies. *Mind, Culture, and Activity* 1(4): 202–8.

White, C. M. 1981. Tonal perception errors and interference from English intonation. *Journal of the Chinese Language Teachers Association* 16(2): 27–56.

Widdowson, H. G. 1978. *Teaching Language as Communication*. Oxford: Oxford University Press.

Wierzbicka, A. 1997. *Understanding Cultures through Their Words: English, Russian, Polish, German, and Japanese*. New York: Oxford University Press.

Wong, M. 1996. Starting a secondary school Chinese program. In S. McGinnis (ed.), *Chinese Pedagogy: An Emerging Field*, pp. 159–80. Columbus, OH: Foreign Language Publications.

Xie, T. W. 1999. Using computers in Chinese language teaching. In M. Chu (ed.), *Mapping the Course of the Chinese Language Field*, pp. 103–19. Kalamazoo, MI: Chinese Language Teachers Association, Inc.

Xing, Z. 1993. *Discourse Functions of Word Order in Chinese*. University of Michigan, Ann Arbor, dissertation.

Xing, Z. 1994. Word order flexibility in Chinese: A comparative study of Mandarin, Min, and Yue dialect. *Proceedings of the Fourth International Symposium on Chinese Languages and Linguistics*, pp. 411–30. Taiwan: Academia Sinica.

Xing, Z. 1996. Discourse considerations in teaching advanced students patient-verb constructions. *Journal of the Chinese Language Teachers Association* 31(1): 1–14.

Xing, Z. 1998. Pedagogical grammar of Chinese: Perspectives on discourse and pragmatics. *Journal of the Chinese Language Teachers Association* 33(3): 63–78.

Xing, Z. 2000. Pedagogical grammar of Chinese: Spatial and temporal expressions. *Journal of Chinese Language Teachers Association* 35(2): 75–90.

Xing, Z. 2001a. The art of teaching Chinese characters. *Yuyan Yanjiu [Studies in Language]: Proceedings of the International Conference on Chinese Pedagogy*, pp. 87–89.

Xing, Z. 2001b. What Chinese and American like to hear? *Journal of the Chinese Language Teachers Association* 36(3): 61–74.

Xing, J. Z. 2003. Toward a pedagogical grammar of Chinese: Approach, content, and process. *Journal of the Chinese Language Teachers Association* 38(3): 41–67.

Xing, J. Z. 2004. Grammaticalization of *lian* in Mandarin Chinese. *Journal of Historical Pragmatic* 5(1): 81–106.

Xing, J. Z. 2005. *Discourse coherence and acquisition* [Gao nianji hanyu pianzhang lianguan jiaoxue fa]. *Proceedings of Harvard Symposium on Advanced Chinese Teaching*. Beijing: Beijing Language University Press.

Yang, J. 1993. Chinese children's stories: Teaching discourse strategies for begging Chinese. *Journal of the Chinese Language Teachers Association* 28(3): 35–48.

Yang, J. 2000. Orthographic effect on word recognition by learners of Chinese as a foreign language. *Journal of the Chinese Language Teachers Association* 35(2): 1–18.

Yang, L. C. 1991. A semantic and pragmatic analysis of tone and intonation in Mandarin Chinese. *Proceedings of the International Conference on Spoken Language Processing*. University of Alberta.

Yao, T. 1996. A review of some computer-assisted language learning software for Chinese. In S. McGinnis (ed.), *Chinese Pedagogy: An Emerging Field*, pp. 255–84. Columbus, OH: Foreign Language Publications.

Yao, T. et al. 2005 [1997]. *Integrated Chinese Level I–II*. Boston: Cheng and Tsui.

Yeh, M. 1997. Enhance the listening comprehension in mandarin: Designing active listening activities. *Journal of the Chinese Language Teachers Association* 32(3): 65–92.

Yin, B. Y. 1997. *Modern Chinese Characters*《现代汉字》. Beijing: Sinolingua.

Yin, J. H. 2002.〈汉字笔划教学〉(Teaching Chinese characters). *Journal of the Chinese Language Teachers Association* 37(2): 113–22.

Yue-Hashimoto, A. O. 1980. Word play in language acquisition: A Mandarin case. *Journal of Chinese Linguistics* 6: 181–204.

Yuyan Wenzi Guifan Shouce《语言文字规范手册》1993. Beijing: Yuwen Chuban She.

Zhang, D. Z. (张道真). 1983.《实用英语语法》(A practical English grammar). Beijing: Commercial Press.

Zhang M. Q. (张美青). 2001.〈汉语入门阶段的汉字教学〉(Character teaching and learning at the elementary level). *Journal of the Chinese Language Teachers Association* 36(2): 55–62.

Zhang, W. X. (张旺熹). 1990.〈从汉字部件到汉字结构〉(Chinese character parts and structures).《世界汉语教学》(Journal of Teaching Chinese in the World), Vol. 2.

Zhang, Z. Y. (张占一). 1984.〈汉语个别教学及其教材〉(Individualized teaching and teaching materials).《语言教学与研究》(Language Teaching and Study), Vol. 3.

Zhang, Z. Y. (张占一). 1990.〈试议交际文化和知识文化〉(On communicative culture and intellectual culture).《语言教学与研究》(Language Teaching and Study), Vol. 3.

Zhang, Z. S. 1998. CALL for Chinese: Issues and practice. *Journal of the Chinese Language Teachers Association* 33(1): 51–82.

Zimmerman, C. B. 1997. Historical trends in second language vocabulary instruction. In J. Coady and T. Huckin (eds.), *Second Language Vocabulary Acquisition*, pp. 5–19.

Zhao, J. M. (ed.) (赵金铭主编). 2004.《对外汉语教学概论》(Introduction to teaching and learning Chinese as a second language). Beijng: Shangwu Yinshu Guan.

Index

Wade-Giles 31–2
Wenlin 128, 131, 270
word game 125, 127–8
word order 42, 37–8, 53, 55, 134–5, 160–2,
    173, 192–5, 208, 234
writing class 36
writing competence 36

Xǔ Shèn 102, 108
xūcí (see function word)

Yao, Ted 41, 54, 130, 145